William Franklin

WILLIAM FRANKLIN

Son of a Patriot, Servant of a King

SHEILA L. SKEMP

New York   Oxford
Oxford University Press
1990

Oxford University Press

Oxford   New York   Toronto
Delhi   Bombay   Calcutta   Madras   Karachi
Petaling Jaya   Singapore   Hong Kong   Tokyo
Nairobi   Dar es Salaam   Cape Town
Melbourne   Auckland
and associated companies in
Berlin   Ibadan

Published by Oxford University Press, Inc.,
200 Madison Avenue, New York, New York 10016

Oxford is a registered trademark of Oxford University Press

Library of Congress Cataloging-in-Publication Data
Skemp, Sheila L.
William Franklin : son of a patriot, servant of a king / Sheila L. Skemp.
p.   cm.   Includes bibliographical references.
1. Franklin, William, 1731–1813.   2. Franklin, Benjamin, 1706–1790—Family.
3. New Jersey—Governors—Biography.
4. American loyalists—Biography.
5. Statesmen's children—United States—Biography.
6. New Jersey—Politics and government—
Revolution, 1775–1783.
I. Title.
F137.F82S54   1990   973.3′092′2—dc20   [B]
89–26627   CIP
ISBN 0–19–505745–7

2 4 6 8 9 7 5 3 1
Printed in the United States of America
on acid-free paper

To

Lucy Leet Skemp
and
Kenneth Warren Skemp

Acknowledgments

When I first began to enumerate all those individuals who contributed to the completion of this book, the list grew predictably long and cumbersome. I wanted to thank everyone from my seventh grade teacher (Esther Boeke) to the Chicago Cubs (who, even before William Franklin, taught me that adherence to a losing cause is not necessarily a badge of dishonor).

Mercifully, I have pared my original list considerably. Many individuals have read the entire manuscript in at least one of its many editions. Sydney James, Winthrop Jordan, Linda Kerber, James Kettner, and Robert Middlekauff all provided valuable comments and offered me considerable encouragement, as they unselfishly volunteered their time to read the manuscript seriously and carefully. Milton M. Klein, James Kirby Martin, and Charles Wilson read parts of the book. Their observations were invariably astute and always helpful.

The History Department at the University of Mississippi deserves special credit for making the completion of this book possible. Two summer grants enabled me to forsake the dubious pleasures of teaching summer school, and paid part of my travel expenses to the various manuscript collections. The department's typists, Rebecca Bowers, Amanda Cook, Fredonia Hairston, Beth Allen, and Virginia Williams cheerfully typed and retyped myriad versions of each chapter. I have been fortunate to have worked with a number of unusually capable graduate assistants. James Dauphine, Sheila Moore, and Suzanne Flandreau Steel contributed greatly to the final product. Marie Antoon, Laura Boughton, Susan Curry, Robert Ginn, John Herman, and Deborah Northart also lightened my load.

The staffs of the various research libraries I visited also merit praise and thanks for their efficiency and help. They include the staff at the American Philosophical Society, the Historical Society of Pennsylvania, the New-York Historical Society, the New York Public Library, the New Jersey Historical Society, the Clements Library, and the Library of Congress. I am especially greatful for the kindness of Claude-Anne Lopez and Jonathan Dull, both of the Benjamin Franklin Papers at Yale University's Sterling Library, whose interest in my work went well beyond the perfunctory.

Finally, I want to thank Barbara Ewell, Penny and Robert Haws, Gray

Manakee Johnson, Cora Jordan, Kathy and Fred Laurenzo, Ruth Ostenson, Nina Noring, Murphy Richardson, and Jerry Spier for the personal, and ultimately immeasurable, services they rendered as I researched, wrote, and re-wrote the book.

I am dedicating this volume to my parents, who, for better or for worse, developed in me my love of history and have always supported my endeavors.

S.L.S.

Contents

Introduction, xi

I. An "Indulgent" Father, a Loyal Son, 3

II. Father, Brother, and Companion, 22

III. An Easy, Agreeable Administration, 43

IV. "Times of Ferment and Confusion", 61

V. The Letter of the Law, 81

VI. Walking a Tightrope, 99

VII. Seeds of Controversy, 122

VIII. A Government Man, 141

IX. "Two Roads", 160

X. An "Appearance of Government", 173

XI. "An Enemy to the Liberties
of This Country", 192

XII. "Like a Bear Through the Country", 209

XIII. "An Unwillingness to Quit the Scene of Action", 227

XIV. "Deprived of Their All", 247

Epilogue, 267

Selected Bibliography: A Note on Sources, 277

Notes, 291

Index, 349

Introduction

On the nineteenth of June, 1776, William Franklin, royal governor of New Jersey, rode under heavy guard to provincial headquarters at Burlington, the prisoner of a government whose legitimacy he did not recognize. As he passed through the countryside of the colony he had called home for over a decade, he was eyed by curious bystanders who laughed, shouted derisively, or occasionally offered him muted glances of sympathy. It was all the same to him. He had begun his career with the blessing of his father, Benjamin Franklin, and had once entertained high hopes of earning fame, fortune and honor as he served King and country in his native land. Now, as representatives of the thirteen separate colonies met in Philadelphia to enunciate the "self evident" truths that impelled them to revolt from what Franklin regarded as the freest and most benevolent empire that history had ever known, his dreams were shattered. His father had turned against him; a "pretended government" had assumed control of New Jersey; his King could no longer protect him.

William Franklin's story is a compelling one. The illegitimate son of Benjamin Franklin, the last—and arguably the ablest—royal governor of New Jersey, he became president of the Board of Associated Loyalists after his release from a rebel prison in 1778, and, finally, lapsed into uneasy exile in the country for which he had sacrificed his property, his family, and most especially, the love and respect of his father. His story is his own, complete with all the quirks and foibles that make any individual's life unique. But at the same time, it represents the experience of many moderate, lawful, and obedient English colonists whose lives were irrevocably altered by the American Revolution. A man who disliked change and craved order, he clung steadily—some would say stubbornly—to his principles when to do otherwise would have been easier, and the material rewards incalculably greater.

Franklin was vain, ambitious and authoritarian. He could be unbending, vindictive, and a little paranoid. But he was also intelligent, industrious, and charming. His vanity and vindictiveness masked his insecurities, his almost painful need to earn the approbation of his superiors. If he was stiff and unbending, he acted out of a dedication to principle as much as for

personal aggrandizement. If he never forgave a slight, he never forgot a
kindness, and he remained fiercely loyal to anyone who offered him a
helping hand. But above all, his youthful upbringing, his circumstances,
his character allowed him, within certain broad strictures, to see both sides
of nearly every isue, to avoid conflict and to seek to reconcile the divergent
loyalties that were tearing his family and his empire apart in the fateful
days before the American Revolution.

Like his more celebrated father, William Franklin was a self-made man.
He had to carve out a place for himself in an unusually volatile and un-
stable world, using his talents, connections, and whatever good fortune
came his way to find a profession suitable to his own considerable ambitions. As he embarked upon his career as New Jersey's royal governor, he
had every reason to believe that his prospects were bright. He enjoyed an
especially close relationship with his father, who was his friend, companion,
and partner in a multitude of public and private endeavors. He honored
his King and loved his country, assuming—as did Benjamin Franklin—that
English and American interests were harmonious, that it was entirely possible to serve King and colony simultaneously. While he recognized that
occasional differences blotted the imperial landscape, he thought these
difficulties derived from ignorance and lack of communication and were
not sufficient to shatter the network of mutual rights and obligations that
bound the empire together. He assumed that he was ideally suited to bridge
the gap between the mother country and its colonial possessions.

An American who had spent considerable time in England's capital, he
understood the wheelings and dealings of British politics, and could never
subscribe to the radical notion that the mother country harbored some
grand and secret "design" to enslave the colonists. He felt confident of his
ability to explain English motives and attitudes to the members of New
Jersey's assembly. Conversely, as an American, his sympathies were less
predictable and more complex than those of most other Crown surrogates.
A thoroughgoing Whig, he understood colonial antipathy to parliamentary
taxation and to the growing intransigence of London bureaucrats. He knew
that the colonies were an integral, if clearly subordinate, part of the empire,
and he emphasized the benefits the mother country derived from its possessions as much as he did the advantages the colonies enjoyed as a result
of their ties with England. He was always a firm supporter of the rights of
colonial assemblies. Indeed it was his attempt to call a special session of
the New Jersey legislature that ultimately led to his arrest and incarceration
in a Connecticut prison. Admittedly, he was never able to consider independence as a viable solution to the ills that beset the empire. To question
imperial authority was, for him, to bring the entire matrix of social, economic, and political ideals that constituted his world, tumbling to the

ground. But he was perfectly able to consider and appreciate American quarrels with King and Parliament so long as independence was not at issue. Surely he, of all royal governors, should have been able to represent and interpret American interests to the government in London.

But William Franklin was a man with a foot in both worlds. And as those worlds moved apart, there was nothing he could do to bring them together again. His entire adult life was devoted to reconciling opposing interests. He served a colony with two rival capitals—Burlington in West Jersey and Perth Amboy in the East—which often represented two distinct constituencies. Like all colonial governors, he was the powerless pawn between the colonial assembly and the King and Parliament, as he sought to steer his "little bark" safely between two increasingly implacable foes. Quarrels over paper money, salaries, and quartering the King's troops tried his patience and reinforced his sense that he was, more often than not, the impotent victim of events beyond his control. As governor of New Jersey, William Franklin served two masters, occupying the middle ground between the claims of his assembly and the demands of the Crown.

Personally, as well as politically, he tried to accommodate competing, sometimes antithetical interests. He served as a mediator between his father, who resided in London throughout the sixties and early seventies, and his half-sister Sally and his stepmother Deborah, trying to smooth over animosities and earning the occasional anger of both sides for his trouble. William cherished his close ties to Benjamin Franklin. Both men, at one time, shared a profound admiration for the British empire and a devotion to the King. Ben, as much as William, once had believed that the Crown was the best guarantor of colonial rights. But their relationship gradually succumbed to the corrosive effect of their divergent experiences and the growing tensions between England and America. In the end, William Franklin had to choose between England and America, father and King.

Ironically, even during the War for Independence, when the time for conciliation was surely at an end, William Franklin was not totally comfortable in a world dominated exclusively by the King's men. As president of the Board of Associated Loyalists, he became aware that he remained as much an American as he was an Englishman, that his desire for autonomy, equality, and a society in which merit, not birth, was rewarded, indicated that his world-view would always be colored by his American experience. He was still a "man in the middle."

William Franklin's story reveals a great deal about America in the chaotic decades prior to the Revolution. He was an active participant in many of the major events of his day, and was intimately acquainted with many diverse facets of pre-revolutionary politics. A governor who worked with his assembly as often as he opposed it, his understanding of colonial views was somewhat more astute and less jaded—at least until the mid-seventies—than that of most royal governors. While his loyalty to the empire was never in doubt, neither was it a foregone conclusion as it was for his counterparts in other colonies. He had compelling, if not ultimately convincing, reasons to join the forces for independence. He had a choice to make, other options to follow, and he had at least to consider his father's perspective on American affairs. Thus to see imperial relationships through his eyes gives us a unique opportunity to re-examine the pre-war world. He reminds historians that the Revolution was not inevitable, that all Americans faced serious and difficult choices in the years before independence.

Moreover, to view the America of the sixties and seventies from William Franklin's perspective makes the Revolution itself seem more revolutionary than is often supposed. While the war may not have constituted a "class conflict," it produced profound political and ideological changes. Congresses, conventions, and committees replaced legitimate institutions emanating from the King-in-Parliament. Self-appointed leaders assumed and rationalized their authority by identifying with the people they served. Old notions of propriety, deference, and honor were discarded. Those who tried to bridge the gap between England and America were rudely shoved aside by selfish and short-sighted men on both sides of the Atlantic; moderates were labeled as Tories in America and as trimmers in England. Rebel governments treated loyal Americans as rebels, proclaiming their own legality in the process.

The experiences of William Franklin, and others like him, offer a fresh perspective on the American Revolution, forcing us to analyze the very meaning of terms such as "moderate" and "radical." One man's experience is surely not every man's, and Franklin's was surely unique. Nevertheless, as a man with one foot in England and another in America, his career helps us appreciate the painful and tumultuous changes that accompanied the birth of the nation.

William Franklin

1

An "Indulgent" Father, a Loyal Son

"Every one, that knows me, thinks I am too indulgent a parent, as well as master."—Benjamin Franklin to Jane Mecom, 1748.[1]

"My son waits upon you with this, whom I heartily recommend to your motherly care and advice. He is indeed a sober and discreet lad of his years, but he is young and unacquainted with the ways of your place."—Benjamin Franklin to Jane Mecom, 1751.[2]

William Franklin was the illegitimate son of a self-made man. He was raised above his father's printer's shop on lower Market Street in the heart of Philadelphia, but from the beginning his expectations rose far above those of any ordinary artisan. As he watched his restless, energetic, and consumingly ambitious father dabble in politics, science, and a potpourri of projects designed both to improve his adopted city and to enhance his own reputation, William always knew that Benjamin Franklin's aspirations for himself and his son were virtually limitless.

Benjamin Franklin was self-taught, and self-created. His success represented a triumph of character, perseverance, and common sense over inheritance, education, and class. His self-assurance grew in direct correlation to the degree he distanced himself from the circumstances of his birth.[3] Because he was always changing, growing, advancing, he was not the steady and dependable role model William may well have needed in the years when he was reaching maturity. Franklin's unpredictability, his wide-ranging interests, his unbounded ambition made him a fascinating and successful man. But these same characteristics may have contributed to his son's insecurity.

William was the illegitimate son of a man who himself had no clear niche in a society that valued birth and social position. The younger Franklin's uncertainty about his own roots was no doubt partly responsible for

3

his obsessive determination to be accepted by the "best" people. He craved approval and a well-defined identity that would provide him with the security and parameters he needed to give direction to his life. For a child with these needs, he could not have been born into a worse place, at a worse time, to a worse father.

William was raised by Benjamin, his natural father, and Deborah Read Franklin, his stepmother. Ben's relationship with his wife was hardly the stuff of which romantic dreams are made. His own account of their courtship strongly suggests that he wanted a wife—any wife—primarily for practical considerations. Marriage would provide him with the accouterments of middle-class respectability and would also free him from "that hard-to-be-govern'd Passion of Youth" that led him into "Intrigues with low Women." Deborah was a hard-working and faithful helpmeet, the ideal partner for an aspiring tradesman of uncertain prospects. Perhaps most importantly, Benjamin Franklin needed a suitable mother for his son.[4]

Ben and Deborah were married on September 1, 1730; William was born some time between September 1730 and March 1731 to a woman whose identity, despite all the speculation wasted on the subject, remains unknown.[5] Historians today lean toward the theory that William's mother was one of the "low women" whose company Franklin admitted frequenting in the period when he was casting about for a wife.[6] Neither father nor son ever denied William's illegitimacy, although they were both given ample incentive to do so. George Roberts, one of Ben's closest friends, offered what was probably the most reliable contemporary account of William's origins when he acknowledged that "Tis generally known here his Birth is illegitimate and his Mother not in good Circumstances." But he firmly denied "the Report of her begging Bread in the Streets of this City. . . . I understand," he said, "some small provision is made by him for her, but her being one of the most agreeable of Women prevents particular Notice being shown, or the Father and Son acknowledging any Connection With her."[7]

William was never allowed to forget his dishonorable beginnings. The Franklin's enemies seldom missed an opportunity to use his illegitimacy to attack the credibility and character of both father and son. And the taunts of his detractors followed William from his cradle to his grave—and beyond. He was, in the final analysis, a "base-born Brat."[8]

William's illegitimacy affected him fundamentally and immediately, for it severely strained his relationship with Deborah. His stepmother may have grudgingly allowed her husband's son to remain in the Franklin household—she really had little choice—but she did not, as Paul Ford suggests, take "the babe not only to her home, but really to her heart." Rather, there existed between Deborah and William "a coldness bordering on hostility." On occasion, Deborah's smoldering animosity gave way to vituperative attacks as she proclaimed "in the foulest terms . . . ever heard from a Gentlewoman" that William was "the greatest Villain upon Earth."[9]

The relations between the two were surely not meliorated when, in 1732 a possible rival for his parents' affection was born to Deborah and Benjamen. Francis Folger Franklin was named after Benjamin's maternal grandfather, Peter Folger, thus providing the child a palpable link with his father's past, a link that William could never claim. While "Franky" died of smallpox in December, 1736, a month after his fourth birthday, his shadowy presence continued to haunt the Franklin household, reminding everyone that there had once been a legitimate heir to the Franklin name. Deborah prominently displayed a portrait of her only son in her home, and thirty-six years after Francis's death, Ben reminisced with affectionate melancholy about the boy "whom [he had] seldom since seen equal'd in every thing, and whom to this Day I cannot think of without a Sigh."[10]

Even after Franky's death, William continued to compete for his father's attention if not for his affection. The household was always crowded, for Ben welcomed anyone with a claim to his largess into the family's cramped quarters. At one time or another, Deborah's mother lived with the family, as did Franklin's apprentice, Joseph Rose, his journeyman, Thomas Whitmarsh, and Deborah's brother and sister. After 1735, William also had in his cousin James Franklin, a male companion who was approximately his own age. And in 1743, his half-sister Sally was born, according Deborah another opportunity to lavish her affections on a child of her own.[11]

But William's most formidable rival was his father's voracious appetite for public affairs. The house and shop were always filled with visitors from home and abroad, anxious to discuss philosophy and science, politics and religion with the always entertaining Benjamin Franklin.[12] For these were the years when Ben finally had enough financial security to allow him to think of matters other than providing a comfortable living for his family. He became Clerk of the Pennsylvania assembly in 1736, was named Post Master General of the colony the following year, and was the instigator and first secretary of the American Philosophical Society in 1744. All these activities drew some of the brightest, most ambitious of Philadelphia's inhabitants to the Franklins' doorstep. No one was ever turned away.[13]

William's proximity to older men made him comfortable with his elders, and he impressed men of his father's generation with his charm and ability. Moreover, the presence of a variety of "parental figures" in the Franklin household may well have compensated for Deborah's hostility and Ben's preoccupation. Even so, there must have been times when the young boy felt lost and slightly bewildered amid all the bustle and confusion swirling around him.[14]

The world outside William's home was similarly unsettled. When he was born, Philadelphia had 11,500 inhabitants; by 1742 the city's population had increased to 13,000; and by 1760 its population of 23,750 made it by far the largest urban center in the colonies. It was noisy, dirty, and crowded, and the Franklins lived in the busiest and most congested part of the city. Merchant ships clogged the mile-long waterfront. Industrious shopkeepers began opening their businesses at five o'clock in the morning and kept them open until the sun set.[15]

William's world was an ever-growing, ever-changing city, which impressed even foreign visitors with its vitality and its ethnic and religious heterogeneity. No one who visited Philadelphia failed to notice its "very flourishing state," and the "very mixed company of different nations and religions" that rubbed elbows there on a daily basis. It was a city that had not one identity, but many, a community where Scots, English, Dutch, Germans, and Irish sat down at the same table in the same tavern and broke bread together. It was a city, as well, whose government one observer characterized as "a kind of anarchy," where clashes between proprietor and assembly, Quaker, Presbyterian and Churchman, impinged upon the consciousness of even the most apolitical inhabitant. Such an atmosphere was bracing, challenging, exciting. But it was hardly calculated to provide stability or a sense of settled identity.[16]

If Philadelphia did not provide serenity, it did offer ample opportunity for its shrewd and ambitious inhabitants. Thrifty and industrious men like Benjamin Franklin thrived in a community that almost begged them to look for the main chance. Yet as Philadelphia grew larger and more sophisticated, it became less possible for even the wealthiest of the city's newcomers to penetrate the ranks of the elite. Philadelphia was dominated by two distinct and exclusive oligarchies. The older Quaker families controlled the colonial assembly, and while they welcomed support in their chronic quarrel with Pennsylvania's proprietors, their religious heritage precluded them from accepting Benjamin Franklin as one of their own. Socially more important than the Quakers was the interrelated group of families, tied by blood, land, merchant activities, and politics, that prevailed in the city and tended to throw its support to the proprietors. Families like the Shippens, the Rosses, the Graemes, and the Swifts resided in relative seclusion, away from the din of the markets and docks in large brick mansions that compared favorably with the great London houses upon which they were modeled. The gap between these genteel palaces and the Franklins' dusty and crowded little printer's shop was much greater than the physical distance between them indicated.[17]

Inherited status—not wealth, character, and ability—was the prerequisite for real acceptance among the leaders of Philadelphia society. When Benjamin Franklin retired from his printing business in 1748, his income was "slightly higher than that of the governor." Yet he remained a "social nobody" who never penetrated the closed circles of Philadelphia's elite. Such a social structure both tantalized and frustrated the ambitions of men like William Franklin. His father could, with some hyperbole, boast of his own rise from rags to middle-class respectability, and would one day dismiss the snubs of the local gentry with reasonable equanimity. His most important roles were, after all, played on a much grander stage and for a more important audience than provincial Philadelphia could provide. Nevertheless, Philadelphia was Benjamin Franklin's chosen home, and it had served as the springboard from which all his farflung ventures emanated. But for William, Philadelphia was a dead end—even as Boston had been for his father. Born into the middle class, as anxious to improve his lot as Ben had been, handsome, intelligent, possessed of all the social graces, he could not transcend the position into which he was born. Character, ability, and ambition had served Benjamin Franklin well; but they served only to mock his son. Raised to be a gentleman and aspiring to be much more than a tradesman, William was unfit for the life of a Philadelphia printer and was never completely at home in the exclusive environs of the Philadelphia elite. If he was to find an identity, he would have to find it elsewhere.[18]

William Franklin's youth may not have been idyllic, but it was in many ways an enviable one. It is tempting to exaggerate the importance of his illegitimacy, but it is probably true that William's childhood was not fundamentally unhappy.[19] If he sometimes suffered pangs of anxiety and wished that his father was a little less distracted and his stepmother much less hostile, he nevertheless grew up sure of his father's affection. Ben had risked humiliation abroad and invited resentment in his own home when he acknowledged his bastard son, and William had reason to be more grateful than most children for the attention he received from his paternal benefactor. Moreover, whether he did so intentionally or not, Ben provided his son with the basic moral, political, and intellectual characteristics that would serve him for the rest of his life. It was the development of a strong and secure bond with his father that proved to be the single most formative influence on William's character.

Ben Franklin's approach to raising "Billy," as William was known in the family, was largely influenced by the new, increasingly "modern" attitude toward child-rearing that characterized many members of the colonial middle class by the eighteenth century.[20] Rebelling against old Puritan notions of original sin, many parents embraced the "enlightened" views of John Locke, who argued that children were malleable and potentially rational, not inherently evil. Locke maintained that experience determined character, and so he advised parents to shape their children, but not to "break" their wills. A parent's primary goal was to prepare his offspring for independence. Anyone failing to accomplish that end sacrificed his claim to legitimacy and obedience, for while power was legitimate, it had to be earned. In the end, the parent-child relationship was voluntary and contractual. William and Ben's early relationship was especially conducive to this view. The elder Fanklin had obviously made a conscious and rational decision to assume responsibility for his natural son. And, as Locke had predicted, the voluntary nature of that original bond strengthened rather than weakened Ben's influence.[21]

Benjamin Franklin heartily endorsed Locke's educational theories. Moreover, he was suited by temperament to walk the fine line between indulgence and authority that Locke advised. On the one hand, he never denied the need for judicious discipline and careful training. Too much misplaced fondness, he warned, could result in an overindulged child.[22] Still, while it is unlikely that Billy escaped his share of chores, Ben's approach seemed to err more on the side of laxity than severity. This was in part due to his preoccupation with business and politics. But it was also a consequence of his own experiences as a printer's apprentice to his elder brother James. At the very least Ben wanted to avoid the "harsh and tyrannical Treatment" he later credited with having first impressed him "with that Aversion to arbitrary Power that has stuck to me thro' my whole Life."[23] William's early experiences, unlike those of his father, taught him to view authority as beneficent. His secure position helped him develop a sense of well-being and self-respect. It was, paradoxically, because of his generally positive relationship with his father that he was eventually able to achieve his own autonomy.[24]

Ben provided William with material comforts and educational opportunities that were beyond the reach of most tradesmen's children. Like many another self-made man, he was determined that his son would not have to suffer the indignities and frustrations that had characterized his own youth. Billy would have all the advantages that his own father had never been able to afford him. He would be raised as a gentleman, have a pony of his own, and be accorded the best possible education. When his son was only four, Ben advertised for a tutor, and in 1738 he sent William and his nephew James to study privately with Theopholis Grew, an able master who later became a professor of mathematics at the Academy and received an M.A. at the College of Philadelphia. At the end of the year, both boys began their studies at Alexander Annand's classical academy, where many of Philadelphia's gentry families sent their sons to acquire a patina of culture. James left the school after a year, but William remained until 1743, obtaining a young gentleman's education and rubbing shoulders with the sons of some of Philadelphia's most distinguished leaders. His formal studies, when combined with his access to his father's growing library, satisfied any scholarly predilections that William entertained, and his early education was far superior to Ben's spotty and informal studies. There was little chance that William would be unceremoniously pulled out of school and pushed into learning a trade under the auspices of an unsympathetic master. Ben characterized himself as an "indulgent" parent, and in many ways he was.[25]

Despite his relatively pampered existence, William was not much happier in Philadelphia than his father had been in Boston. Ben may not have been as indulgent as he claimed to be. Or perhaps William's relationship with his stepmother simply grew unbearable. Moreover, after he left Annand's Academy, the lad was probably at loose ends. The College of Philadelphia was still but a gleam in his father's eye in 1743, and there was apparently no talk of sending William to Yale, Harvard, or the College of William and Mary to complete his studies. No doubt he worked in his father's print shop, running errands, trying to avoid Deborah's carping tongue, and contemplating his dead-end existence with increasing impatience and a tinge of bitterness. What good were his fine learning and his childhood contacts so long as he remained tied to a printer's apron?

Like his father before him, William was restless and ambitious, and he hankered after adventure. The sight of ships streaming daily into America's busiest seaport, heavily laden with prizes captured in King George's War only heightened his desire to escape the comfortable restraints of his routine existence, to try his mettle and make his way in the world. Ben never tired of telling the story of his own successful flight from family and security, and William may simply have wanted to imitate his father's youthful example.

At any rate, when he was about fifteen years old, William tried to run away from home, boarding a privateer resting in Philadelphia's harbor. Ben "fetched him" from the ship, and, as was his wont, disclaimed any responsibility for his son's little rebellion. "No one," he assured his beloved sister Jane Mecom, "imagined it was hard usage at home, that made him do this." Indeed Ben tried to make light of the entire incident, attributing it to the naturally buoyant spirits of all normal lads. "When boys see prizes brought in," he explained, "and quantities of money shared among the men, and their gay living, it fills their heads with notions, that half distract them, and put them quite out of conceit with trades, and the dull ways of getting money by working." But Ben was more concerned about his son's escapade than he cared to admit. His own brother had run away when he was young; and Ben himself once had a "strong Inclination for the Sea."

He knew from personal experience that "hard usage" at home could drive a rebellious child away forever. He had lost one son to smallpox and certainly did not want to lose the other.[26]

Franklin's response to the incident was of the sort that Locke would have heartily approved. He did not try to break his son's will; instead he tried to channel William's desire for adventure into more acceptable avenues, arranging for him to sign on as an ensign in one of the four companies raised in Philadelphia for a campaign against Canada. The War of Austrian Succession or, as the colonials would have it, King George's War, was being waged, and William enthusiastically enlisted as a defender of King and empire.[27]

Ben was surprised and not especially pleased with his son's enthusiasm for the rigors of military life, but he did not stand in his way. Franklin was commissioned under Captain John Diemar, one of one hundred men who left Philadelphia in September of 1746 to spend what proved to be a wretched winter in Albany. The promised expedition to Canada never materialized, and the members of his predominantly German company had no chance to win glory or recognition. Instead the troops endured the ill effects of bureaucratic bungling, arrears in pay, rusted guns, defective cutlasses, and "stinking beef." The expedition, according to one observer, was riddled with "gross mismanagement, criminal negligence, and corruption." Significantly, many if not all the difficulties suffered by the provincial troops were the result of local jealousies and colonial politics and were not the fault of Crown policy. Predictably, desertion reached near epidemic proportions as the winter wore on.[28]

But William Franklin was not among the ranks of the deserters. To the contrary, when he returned briefly to Philadelphia in May of 1747 with the rank of captain, he came to search for malingerers and to "Tacke care" of four prisoners entrusted to his supervision. He did not even contemplate remaining at home, but fulfilled his duties efficiently and quickly returned to his regiment. Moreover, he volunteered for active, even dangerous duty whenever he had the chance. He was young, brave, and anxious to succeed. And he acquitted himself well, earned a promotion, and was apparently comfortable in an environment characterized by clear-cut rank where obedience to orders promised tangible rewards.[29]

Persuaded that William's interest in things military was no passing fancy, Ben characteristically shrugged his shoulders and set out on a private campaign to pave the way for his son's success. Despite what seemed like obvious drawbacks, William was "fond of a military Life" and while Ben had hoped that his inclinations "would have been cool'd with the last Winter" they obviously continued "as warm as ever." Thus Ben arranged to have London printer William Strahan send some maps and the works of Polybius from England so that his "soldier son" could prepare more effectively for a military career. And he asked former Philadelphian Cadwallader Colden, now lieutenant governor of New York, to ease William's way should the company remain in that colony for another winter. While he hoped that his son's taste for the army would abate, he did what he could to promote William's interests. By giving him a chance to pursue his own goals, Ben made it impossible for him to rebel.[30]

In fact, it was the prospect of a temporary peace with France, not Benjamin Franklin's wishes, that forced William to abandon his dreams of a life in the King's army by cutting off any "Prospect of Advancement in that Way." In time of peace, opportunities for military promotions were rare. And for an American, it was virtually impossible to rise above the rank of captain under any circumstances. Commissions in the British army were expensive, and were nearly always reserved for Englishmen with powerful connections and hefty purses. Franklin had reached an impasse, and like it or not, he had to "apply himself to other Business."[31]

William had not yet quenched his thirst for adventure, and he wanted to postpone his return to the humdrum existence at the printer's office as long as possible. Fortunately, an attractive alternative to city life materialized in the summer of 1748 when the colonies of Virginia and Pennsylvania combined forces to finance an expedition into the Ohio territory. Hoping to take advantage of the Miami Confederacy's disenchantment with the inflated prices and inferior goods of the French, the two colonies—often rivals themselves—sent an expedition to Logtown, just a few miles from the Ohio Forks, to negotiate a treaty with the western Indians.[32]

The men chosen to conduct the Logtown negotiations were all experienced Indian traders. Conrad Weiser was an agent and interpreter of acknowledged skill. William Trent, a well-connected Philadelphian, had been involved in the fur trade prior to King George's War, an occupation he had only temporarily abandoned after receiving a captain's commission in one of the companies accompanying William Franklin's unit to Albany. George Croghan, a hard-drinking, gregarious Irishman, had been Trent's partner since 1745 and had considerable first-hand knowledge of western Pennsylvania's Indian affairs. Croghan and Trent were no strangers to intrigue and never hesitated to shade the truth whenever their own fortunes were on the line. They joined almost any trading enterprise that would have them, carelessly playing both ends against the middle with irrepressible optimism. They would eventually involve William Franklin in a confusing and entangled series of schemes designed to reap untold wealth from the American wilderness.[33]

But for the present, William was content to join Weiser's expedition to Lancaster, Pennsylvania, and to travel from there to Logtown, Croghan's headquarters on the Allegheny river.[34] The negotiators arrived at Lancaster in mid-July, accompanied by four members of the Pennsylvania council who joined fifty-five Twightwee representatives at the conference. By August 11, the Lancaster negotiations had ended successfully, and Trent, along with the Pennsylvania councilors, returned to Philadelphia. Weiser, Croghan, and Franklin forged ahead on the most arduous leg of the journey. It was the first official expedition made by the English colonists west of the Allegheny mountains.[35]

Franklin's role in the negotiations at Logtown was negligible at best, but the entire trip made a profound impression on the young man, as the careful journal he kept of the expedition attested.[36] It was not an easy journey, but the life of a soldier had conditioned William's body to hardship. He had evidently inherited his father's strength and stamina as well as his love for adventure, and he seemed to thrive on the grueling pace and the physical indignities he endured each day. Marching through western Pennsylvania, canoeing 60 miles down the Allegheny river, seeing first hand the wonders of a virtually untouched land, William was becoming convinced that the future glory of the British empire lay in westward expansion, and that abundant wealth awaited those with the intelligence, resources, and courage to exploit the promise of the American West. His father had found success in the streets of Philadelphia and, despite occasional nods to the virtues of a rural existence, would always remain a child of the city. But William saw his hopes for fame and wealth arising from the abundant resources of the Ohio River Valley. Untilled land, not cobblestone and printer's ink, would provide him his fortune.

William's dreams were not immediately realized. His father was sympathetic but not overly enthusiastic about his aspirations. He read his son's journal with care, and proudly sent it to Peter Collinson, a member of the Royal Society.[37] The elder Franklin, however, was not ready to plunge wholeheartedly into the Indian trade or to provide economic support for his son's venture. The French still had claims to the Ohio River Valley. William, himself, had neither the financial resources nor the political influence to realize his ambitions. He could, perhaps, have struck out on his own, using his newly forged ties with Croghan, Weiser, and Trent to make a paper fortune based more on hope than reality. But William Franklin preferred to build his fortunes on a more solid foundation. Speculation in the American West would have to be deferred.

And so in 1748 he returned to Philadelphia, and to a life that must have seemed especially stultifying after his military adventures. With no immediate prospects, William was at loose ends. One thing was clear. He would not follow his father into the printing business. Just as William returned from the Weiser expedition, the elder Franklin made David Hall, his employee of the last four years, his partner in the Philadelphia print shop. Hall ran the operations on a day-to-day basis and paid Franklin an annual share of the profits. For all practical purposes, Ben had retired. But he did not hand his business over to his son who had no wish to spend the rest of his life behind a printer's press. Nor is their any indication that his father wanted him to do so. If Ben was ambitious on his own account, he had equally high hopes for his talented son.[38]

Upon his return to Philadelphia, Franklin did not re-enter Ben's household, and he tried to ignore Deborah's jealous harangues whenever he visited his father "upon Business." Away from home, William led a pleasant if aimless existence. He was soon caught up in the social whirl that was the birthright of Philadelphia's elite. He was a handsome young man, well-educated and charming, who spent money freely and could lay claims to being a war hero. The doors of the city's inner circle seemed about to open to this illegitimate son of an upstart printer. He assiduously studied his copy of The True Conduct of Persons of Quality and eagerly accepted an invitation to join the exclusive Annual Assembly, a social club organized in 1749 by a group of Philadelphia gentlemen, that held balls and plays for the city's young socialites. Dominated by proprietary supporters, it was totally immune to Quaker influence.[39] William was becoming, complained his father, "much of a Beau." He had acquired a "Habit of Idleness on the Expedition" and seemed content to live indefinitely off of Ben's ample income.[40]

And for a time Ben was willing to let William meander without direction or purpose. He did not want to lose the affection of his only son by forcing him immediately into a new career and he no doubt felt that William had earned a vacation after the rigors of his short-lived military career. He may well have enjoyed watching him pursue the gentleman's pleasures that had been beyond his own youthful reach. Moreover, Benjamin Franklin, at the age of forty-two, was preoccupied with major changes in his own life, distracted by a series of disparate projects, and was in no position to direct his son toward any meaningful goal. His early retirement forced him to begin searching for other ways to test his limits and advance his own prospects.[41] How could he possibly censure William for attempting to do much the same thing? Father and son were both trying to advance beyond the status that was their birthright, and neither was clear about the best means for realizing his ambitions.

Ben found an outlet for his energies more readily than William did. He devoted some of his time to the electrical experiments that would one day bring him international renown. But he was increasingly drawn by circumstances and inclination into "public Affairs," as Franklin's supporters, considering him to be a "Man of Leisure, laid hold of [him] for their

Purposes." At first, Ben turned no one down, serving all masters with apparent satisfaction. Thus he sat on the Governor's Commission for peace; accepted posts as Councilman and Alderman for the Corporation of the City of Philadelphia; and won election as the city's representative to the Pennylvania assembly. Franklin was understandably flattered by his little successes, especially when he considered his "low Beginning." But in fact, he was simply one of many political operatives in the city and there was little to suggest that he would one day dine with kings and be venerated by his countrymen.[42] Both Ben and William were making inroads into Philadelphia society in 1748 and 1749. Both men were busy and preoccupied; each was proud of the other's small successes; each hoped to use the other's victories to unlock more doors.

In 1750, Ben Franklin encountered one of his first real failures. He "try'd a little" to fill the office of Justice of the Peace, but discovered that for once in his life, his natural charm and innate intelligence were insufficient to the task. A self-educated man could go far in provincial America, but there were some areas that even then required a modicum of special training. Franklin stepped down from his post, to "attend the higher Dutys of a Legislator in the Assembly," but the experience rankled. He was too old to begin legal training himself, but he began seriously to contemplate a career in law for his son.[43]

Consequently Ben Franklin began to take a more active and sustained interest in William's future. A legal career promised the prestige that both father and son coveted.[44] William's expertise would enable him to accomplish tasks that were beyond Ben's capabilities. And if he studied law under the "right" person, Philadelphia society might be persuaded to ignore the Franklins' humble birth. With William's law degree, Ben's native ability, and the contacts both men had developed, father and son could fashion a real partnership based on their shared interests and aspirations.

The "right" person to introduce the younger Franklin to the mysteries of law was Joseph Galloway, a young man about William's age with a sound mind and impeccable social credentials. Vain, haughty, and ambitious he may have been, but he also exhibited a steady attentiveness to his business that Ben undoubtedly hoped would rub off on his son.[45] And so Ben arranged for William to study law with young Galloway, and asked London printer William Strahan to enter his name at one of the appropriate Inns of Court. There was nothing unusual about Ben's plans. He was simply following the practice of many colonial pretenders to gentility, who educated their progeny in England sending them on a Continental tour before bringing them home to begin their careers in earnest. Future patriots as well as future loyalists put the finishing touches on their legal training at the Inns of Court.[46]

Not content merely to provide William with an entrée into the legal profession, Ben embarked upon a determined program to put his son's life in order, and in the fall of 1751, sent William to Massachusetts to stay for a short while with his sister Jane. In Boston, the boy made a "favorable impression," was welcomed into the Franklin family, and met a number of the city's notables as well. At long last he had some link with his New England roots and a sense of continuity with his past.[47]

Some time before William left for Massachusetts, Ben was elected to the Pennsylvania assembly. He swiftly handed his clerk's position to his son. It was a minor post, one that both Franklins found extremely tedious.[48] Ben occupied much of his time drawing "magic squares or circles," as he recorded the assembly procedures; William wrote hymns of praise to the "Belles of Philadelphia" to while away the hours. But even if the clerkship was not elective and gave William no opportunity to express his own views officially, it provided him with a marvelous opportunity to develop important contacts with leading politicians in the colony. It gave him a chance to utilize his newly honed legal skills, and provided him with a real education in the vagaries of factional politics in one of the most acrimonious of His Majesty's colonies. It also furnished him with his first unpleasant experience with Pennsylvania's proprietary government. In the spring of 1755, the assembly sent the young Franklin to call on Governor Robert Morris to make a routine request for a warrant to affix the great seal to the legislature's minutes. By this time, William had been at his clerk's post for four years, but Morris pretended to be unaware of the young man's status and sent him back to the assembly for official confirmation of his position. It was the kind of gratuitous snub the sensitive clerk was not likely to forget.[49]

The clerkship was not the only position the elder Franklin procured for his son. When he secured a joint appointment as Postmaster General of America, Ben named William the new Postmaster of Philadelphia, and a year later he promoted his son to controller of the North American postal system. As Ben climbed the political ladder, he brought William along with him, using his own rising fortunes to gain public employment and a measure of economic independence for his son.[50]

Historians have remarked that William was clinging to Ben's coat tails in this period, living off his father's achievements and existing uncomfortably in the shadow of the "great" Benjamin Franklin. But it is unlikely that William resented Ben's interference in his affairs, or that his acceptance of Ben's largess indicated any child-like dependence on his father. "Nepotism" was the norm in eighteenth-century Philadelphia, and William, far from balking at his father's help, was probably pleased that Ben finally had sufficient connections to secure favor for his son.[51] In fact, the two men grew steadily closer in this period. Their paths crossed frequently, and William became increasingly appreciative of Ben's talents. Father and son contributed to the same charities and joined the Masons at the same time. In 1750, William began meeting weekly with Charles Thomson and others in a society patterned after Ben's famous Junto, and while the society's progress was uneven at best, it exemplifies the admiration William had for the elder Franklin.[52]

The following year, father and son shared a spectacular experience, when they conducted the famous kite experiment, managing "to bring lightning from the heavens" by flying a kite, with a metal key attached to the kite string, during an electrical storm. William shared in an achievement that for the first time raised his father above the level of an ordinary provincial politician, earning him universal recognition from the scientific community. Because Ben had feared public ridicule if he failed, William was the only one he trusted with his plans. The two shared the secret, made the preparations together, and rejoiced in their ultimate success. William's pleasure was genuine; he basked in his father's reflected glory and continued to provide Ben with data to substantiate the results of the experiment. Occasionally his enthusiastic efforts even resulted in new insights that corrected his more celebrated father's assumptions. In their scientific endeavors the Franklins were becoming an effective team.[53]

It was the affairs of empire, however, not the taming of lightning, that solidified the bond between father and son, and gave the two men a chance to work together as partners, each using his own talents to contribute to the success of an endeavor they both supported. By 1754 the French and British were once again preparing for war, and as usual the assembly and the governor were at odds over financing Pennsylvania's defenses. At one level, the battle lines were drawn between the Quaker-dominated legislature and the Pennsylvania proprietors, Thomas and Richard Penn. At another level, the conflict entailed a struggle for control of the assembly itself. While the Franklins supported the house against the proprietors, Ben, in particular, became convinced that the non-resisting Quakers were not suited to lead the assembly when the colony's defenses were at risk.

The issues dividing the assembly and the proprietors were many, but at bottom they involved a struggle between differing conceptions of assembly rights and proprietary prerogatives. Such differences were inevitable but the quarrel was exacerbated and brought into sharp focus by the legislature's distrust of the proprietors' rigid secret instructions to the governor, the reluctance of many Quakers to support any war effort, and the Penns' stubborn refusal to allow their own vast estates to be taxed by the house.[54]

As a relative newcomer to Pennsylvania politics, Benjamin Franklin was not at first deeply committed to either the proprietary or the Quaker party;

he had his feet in both camps. He often condemned the "incredible Mean-ness" of the Penns, and generally supported the assembly's definition of its own privileges. Nevertheless, he claimed to remain on friendly personal terms with the governor and both he and William valued their many ties with important proprietary supporters.[55]

While the Franklins viewed the proprietors with increased distaste, their zeal for the British cause knew no bounds. Ben was determined to enroll Pennsylvania as an active participant in Britain's war for empire, and he quickly found opportunities to further his cause.[56] In the summer of 1754, Ben tried out his diplomatic skills in the service of colony and country when he served as Pennsylvania's delegate to the Albany conference. Wil-liam accompanied his father to New York, where he saw Ben engage in an ultimately futile effort to counter colonial provincialism and military weak-ness in the face of a growing French threat.[57]

The elder Franklin utilized another chance to advance himself, Pennsyl-vania, and the empire when General Edward Braddock arrived in the colonies with two regiments designed to defend America from anticipated French attack. By 1755, Braddock was stationed in Frederic Town, Mary-land, trying to round up wagons and provisions to supply his army. The Pennsylvania assembly, knowing that the British government viewed the colony with disfavor because of its past reluctance to support the mother country's military efforts, sent Benjamin Franklin to confer with the general.[58]

William accompanied his father to Maryland. The two men arrived to find an impatient General Braddock contemplating the demise of his pro-jected campaign because he could not obtain adequate provisions for his army. Always quick to take advantage of any opportunity, Ben "happen'd to say" that it was unfortunate that Braddock had not been stationed in Pennsylvania where nearly every farmer had a wagon. Braddock immedi-ately took Franklin's bait and the two worked out an agreement for the hire of horses and wagons from the farmers of western Pennsylvania.[59]

William made good use of his time as well, enjoying the hospitality of the Chesapeake gentry, riding through the Maryland countryside with his father, dining almost daily with General Braddock, and escaping for awhile the routine of city life. Moreover, he contributed his own expertise to the enterprise, riding to Carlisle and Lancaster to secure wagons, rounding up forage for the horses, and offering badly needed advice on the supplies that the army would need during the coming campaign. He served as much more than his father's companion, becoming Braddock's American adviser and one of the most successful procurers of provisions for His Majesty's forces.[60]

Braddock was "highly satisfied" with the Franklins' efforts, but his expedition to western Pennsylvania proved disastrous. Despite his superior numbers, the French and their Indian allies soundly defeated his forces, and the general was fatally wounded in the debacle. Braddock's defeat shook even the Philadelphia Quakers out of their lethargy. The colony's defenses were in total disarray, and the western frontier was the scene of bloody fighting. Indians from the Ohio country attacked helpless families living on isolated farms in the interior, and panic-stricken settlers began streaming into Philadelphia. Peace-loving Quakers were afraid to venture into the streets for fear of encountering the wrath of roving bands of refugees demanding protection for themselves and their property.[61]

With Pennsylvania politics at a virtual standstill, and a full-scale mutiny threatening the colony's western borders, Benjamin Franklin had a chance to gain control of a badly divided and demoralized Quaker party and to strike a blow for assembly prerogatives. His real hope lay in the creation of a new party composed of a coalition of anti-proprietary, pro-defense assemblymen. The French and Indian War, the concomitant weakening of the Quaker party and the erosion of respect for the proprietors, offered Franklin the opportunity to build a power base of his own.[62]

With the colony in real danger, Governor Morris put increasing pressure on the assembly to appropriate money for Pennsylvania's defense. His instructions forced him to veto any money bill that taxed the Penn family estates. This threatened both the legislative and tax prerogatives of the assembly, causing even sympathetic representatives to balk at the "Meanness and Injustice" of the proprietors. At the heart of the matter were the proprietary instructions. And the struggle between Morris and the assembly was nothing less than a contest for the control of the Pennsylvania government.[63]

At first neither side would back down. But with the frontier facing imminent collapse, the two feuding parties were forced to reach a compromise of sorts. The Penns freely "donated" £5000 toward colonial defense and the assembly enacted a militia bill, composed by Franklin, excluding the proprietary estates from taxation. The legislature also created a voluntary militia with elected officers, a solution that was acceptable to all but the most pacifistic Quakers. The immediate problem of defending the colony was resolved; and Franklin, as the chief architect of the compromise, had laid the fragile foundations for a new anti-proprietary faction with himself at its head.[64]

William Franklin was only too willing to advance his father's efforts. Ben's success would obviously redound to his own benefit. Moreover, he was still smarting from the personal insult he had suffered at Morris's hands in June. He did not have to wait long to get his revenge and to enter the fray in defense of his father's policies. At the end of 1755, William Smith,

once a Franklin ally, but now, as a staunch defender of proprietary interests, a declared enemy to Ben, launched an attack on Franklin and his
militia bill. The malicious diatribe, which tried to drive a wedge between
Ben and the Quaker party, could not go unanswered. Ben hesitated to
reply to his former friend's accusations, but his son was not so circumspect.
Under a pseudonym that fooled no one, William Franklin, along with his
friends Joseph Galloway and George Bryan, combined to write *Tit for Tat,
or the Score Wip'd Off* to counteract Smith's accusations. What the piece
lacked in substance, it more than compensated for in scurrility. Its tone
was mocking and vicious throughout, portraying the proprietors as French
allies and Smith as a sycophantic courtier with jesuitic ambitions. The proprietors and their allies, the tract insisted, were "guilty of Treason of the
highest species" for trying to abrogate the legislative rights of the colony,
thus destroying the balanced government that all Englishmen prized as the
bulwark of their liberties. "In short," the authors argued, "all our Disputes
terminate on this single Point, whether our G--rs shall, or shall not, have
the sole legislative Power of this Province." The pamphlet was brimming
with venom; even the Quakers disavowed it, labeling it a "virulent, seditious, and scandalous Libel." But the attention it received from friend and
foe alike was highly gratifying to its young authors, and Galloway, in particular, continued the pamphlet warfare with Smith throughout 1756.[65]

Still, there were more pressing issues than the widening gap between
the Franklins and the proprietary camp. Even after the Militia Act was
passed, it took time to prepare the troops for action. Time was the one
commodity in short supply in the fall of 1755. In late November, word
arrived that a party of Shawnee had attacked and destroyed the Moravian
mission as Gnadenhütten, a mere seventy-five miles northwest of Philadelphia. The western frontier was about to explode in a paroxysm of warfare.
Enraged by the indifference of the colony's lawmakers, the western farmers
marched to the capital city, carrying the mutilated bodies of a German
man, his wife, and his grown son and paraded the remains throughout the
town before depositing them ceremoniously at the doors of the State
House.[66]

Immediate action was essential, and once again the two Franklins were
asked to combine the diplomatic skills of the one and the military experience of the other in an effort to avert disaster. Governor Morris asked Ben,
Joseph Fox, and former governor James Hamilton to head an expedition
to the northwestern part of the colony to raise troops and erect a line of
forts.[67] They left Philadelphia in December. William rode beside his father
at the head of the parade, resplendent in his old British grenadier's uniform, ready to do battle for King and colony. As his father's aide de camp
and field secretary, his services were substantial. Traveling from one demor-

alized settlement to another, rallying the spirits of frightened inhabitants, organizing their defenses and overseeing the building of forts, the two men worked in tandem as they devoted themselves to the defense of Pennsylvania and the defense of the empire—tasks that in 1755 were not mutually exclusive.[68]

On January 3, 1756, an opportunity for William to exhibit his military expertise materialized. The Franklins were in Reading for a conference with the governor when news arrived that the newly posted garrison at Gnadenhütten had been attacked and that the centerpiece of Pennsylvania's western defense had been destroyed. Ben and William hurried to Bethlehem where they prepared for a twenty-mile march to Gnadenhütten.[69]

In less than two weeks, the band of fewer than 150 men set out on the dangerous and difficult journey. A cold winter rain pelted the men, and at night they camped in barns that provided them scant protection. The second day proved especially hazardous, as the motley crew traversed a narrow mountain pass "where the Rocks over hang the Roads on each Side and render it practicable for a small Number to destroy a Thousand." The welcome sight of Uplinger's tavern located just north of the Lehigh gap, greeted them at sunset, and they rejoiced at the safe conclusion to what they all hoped would be their most harrowing day. Perhaps to give themselves courage or to impress any potential attackers with their strength, they drew up their companies "on a Parade" and attended an "excellent Prayer and animating Exhortation" by New Light Minister Charles Beatty. William Franklin led the forces "with great Order and Regularity."[70]

The rain continued to drench the exhausted troops for the next two days, stopping only on the eighteenth, when they traveled through narrow roads lined on either side by "Hills like Alps," and across a swollen creek that boasted a single log for a bridge. As they forded the river, they were fully open to enemy attack. Anyone watching them from the rocky caves overlooking their position could easily have destroyed them all.[71]

Despite their fears, they arrived safely at Gnadenhütten. There they set up camp, threw up a breastwork, and tried not to think of the desolation around them. Charred houses and mangled bodies were everywhere, and it was their task to bury the dead and minister to the living. The men constructed a fort, finishing it in a week despite the rain that still fell intermittently. William served as his father's assistant, writing letters, issuing orders, keeping muster rolls, and handling the many tiny details that made the often disheartening expedition a success. The little fort was scarcely completed when the Franklins received word that a special session of the assembly had been called, and both men were needed in Philadelphia. It was time to return home.[72]

The adventure had been arduous for the older Franklin and difficult for

William as well. But neither complained. They had faced the frontier together and had acquitted themselves with honor. William seemed to thrive in an environment that tested his physical prowess, required the use of his organizational skills, and allowed him to display his ability as a leader of men. Despite the physical hardships and real dangers he faced in the Pennsylvania countryside, the experience had been a positive one. William Franklin was never a coward. He was often at his best when he faced palpable threats to his personal well-being. He responded well to a situation in which his goals were prescribed, the issues were clear, and his own role was sharply defined. A military life gave him his place and his purpose, demanding only that he accomplish his duties with efficiency and honor.

Indeed, William came away from the experience more enchanted than ever with the wonders of the western frontier, convinced that here, removed from the narrow and artificial strictures of Philadelphia society he might be able to earn respect and position that eluded him in the stultifying atmosphere of the city of his birth. His hankering for a fortune based on land speculation was stronger than ever. And by now his father seemed to understand his son's vision. A move west would provide Ben with the means to help the British empire expand; it would give him a fitting end with which to cap an altogether satisfactory career; and it would allow him to bequeath to William a patrimony worthy of the finest man. To organize and govern a new colony, and to hand it, at the end of his life, to his son, would give a meaning to his existence that far transcended the meager material and political successes he had achieved so far.[73]

2

Friend, Brother, and Companion

"Few are the Inducements that will tempt me to pass the Ocean again, if ever I am so happy as to return to my native Country."—William Franklin to Betsy Graeme, 1757.[1]

"Your son I really think one of the prettiest young gentlemen I ever knew from America. He seems to me [to] have a solidity of judgment, not very often to be met with in one of his years. This with the daily opportunities he has of improving himself in the company of his father, who is at the same time his friend, his brother, his intimate, and easy companion, affords an agreeable prospect, that your husband's virtues and usefulness to his country, may be prolonged beyond the date of his own life."—William Strahan to Deborah Franklin, 1757.[2]

As William and Benjamin Franklin raced back to Philadelphia, they both knew that the battle they faced there would be as vicious as the warfare that dominated western Pennsylvania. Together, father and son had succeeded in temporarily halting the frightened flight of settlers from the frontier and had begun the arduous process of setting up a line of defense on the colony's borders. Best of all, the western expedition had considerably enhanced Benjamin Franklin's reputation. But the success was a two-edged sword. Ben's popularity served only to exacerbate the tensions between him and the proprietary party. Governor Morris and his minions genuinely feared the prospect of an assembly dominated by as astute a political animal as Franklin was proving to be. And neither Ben nor William did anything to assuage proprietary misgivings.

Father and son plunged immediately into the vortex of Philadelphia politics. Ben waged a bitter but ultimately successful campaign to win recognition for the military units formed under the auspices of his militia act. When the company officers elected him colonel of the regiment, he eagerly accepted, and forced a reluctant Governor Morris to sign his commission.[3] By the end of the summer, both the proprietary supporters and

the peace-loving Quakers were watching Franklin's rise with scarcely concealed nervousness. And in October it appeared that Ben's meteoric career
had reached its zenith when he won a resounding victory in the general
election.[4]

William watched his father's rapid ascendance with approval, doing what
he could to aid Ben's cause. When the elder Franklin twice reviewed his
troops in the streets of Philadelphia in an effort to demonstrate their
prowess, William put the regiment through its paces. He was also at his
father's side in the spring of 1756 when Ben traveled to Virginia on postal
business and about fifty officers and grenadiers showed up at the Franklins'
door to escort the colonel out of town. As the party left the house, the
grenadiers "took it in their heads" to draw their swords from their sheaths,
holding them high above their heads in a gesture of respect generally reserved for "Princes of the Blood Royal." Even some of Ben's admirers were
taken aback by the display, half wondering if the Franklins were planning
a military coup. But father and son alike felt that such niggling criticisms
were a small price to pay for the discomfort the incident caused their
enemies.[5]

Yet, despite his apparent power, Ben remained boxed in by the policies
of the Pennsylvania proprietors. He did not have long to wait before he
confronted the Penns in yet another struggle over assembly rights. Renewed
troubles on the frontier, and the demands of General John Loudoun for
contributions to the empire's defense, once again brought the legislature
and governor into direct conflict. William, still the assembly clerk, watched
his father in action. He was receiving a valuable lesson in the workings of
colonial politics. He was learning, as well, that proprietary governments
were characterized by their owners' selfishness and penury. In Pennsylvania
it seemed that the assembly, not the governor, best served the public
interest.

Largely at the elder Franklin's bidding, the house agreed to donate at
least some money to Loudoun's coffers, but its members continued to insist
upon their right to tax the proprietary estates. The new governor, William
Denny, obeyed his ironclad instructions and refused to accept the bill.
Nothing had changed, nor did it appear likely that anything ever would. In
desperation, the legislators decided to send two envoys to London to plead
their cause personally. They selected Quaker Isaac Norris, the venerated
Speaker of the House, and Benjamin Franklin.[6]

The aging Norris quickly resigned his position, but Franklin did not plan
to take a solo voyage to England's capital. He wanted his son with him to
serve as his private secretary, aide, and companion. William had completed
his legal studies, and it was high time that he began his long-postponed
work at the Middle Temple. And Ben no doubt wanted to spare William

the indignities he had faced when he arrived in England penniless with no friends at his side. He looked forward to showing William his old haunts as they explored the English countryside together.[7]

William however, did not embrace the prospect with unadulterated enthusiasm. For, at the age of twenty-five, William Franklin had fallen madly—if not deeply—in love. The object of his affections was Elizabeth Graeme. And he resented anything that even briefly separated him from his "dear Tormenter." "Betsy's" attraction were obvious. She was not a mere social butterfly; even in her youth she attracted the notice of Philadelphia's literati. Well-read and public-spirited, her conversation was always stimulating. Moreover, Graeme represented all that William Franklin admired but could never quite achieve. Her family traveled in the most exclusive circles. Betsy's father, Dr. Thomas Graeme, was director of the Pennsylvania Hospital and a provincial councilor. Her mother, Ann, was the step-daughter of former governor William Keith. The Graemes wintered in Philadelphia, but their summer home, Graeme Park, was a sumptuous estate located twenty miles from the noise and heat of the city. There, surrounded by a three-hundred-acre deer park, the family resided in rural splendor. It was a far cry from the bustle and confusion of the crowded little house on Market Street.[8]

Ben's response to his son's infatuation was ambivalent. He could not help but relish the prospect of a connection by marriage with the wealthy and prominent Graemes. He remembered Betsy's mother from the days when he was a frequent visitor at the home of then governor Keith. And he was genuinely fond of Betsy herself. Charming, pretty and bright, she would in most respects make a perfect daughter-in-law.[9] Still, the Graemes were staunch supporters of the proprietary interest. Admittedly, Pennsylvania councilors seldom took an active part in the quarrels between governor and assembly. Nevertheless, they did urge both Morris and Denny to "stand firm" in the face of assembly assaults, and their attitude toward the colony's representatives was smug and casually disrepectful. Moreover, the Graemes had close personal ties with the Franklins' nemesis, William Smith, and had, as well, strong connections with other men on Ben's rapidly growing enemies list.[10]

The real obstacle to a union between William and Betsy, however, was Dr. Graeme. A proud, doting father he shuddered at the prospect of welcoming the son of one of the proprietors' greatest foes, and himself the reputed co-author of the reprehensible *Tit for Tat* into his home.[11] But he was helpless to do much to discourage the match. His wife threw her support to the couple. William and Betsy frequented the same social circles, so that it was impossible to stop them from seeing one another. Moreover, Betsy's friends seemed as taken with the handsome and intelligent young man as she was. With a sigh, but with many misgivings, Dr. Graeme reluctantly allowed the affair to proceed.[12]

William and Betsy were caught in the middle of a political quarrel that threatened their own relationship. That each of them tended toward the views of their respective fathers made matters no easier. Fearing that their affections might not survive either the vicissitudes of Pennsylvania politics or William's projected absence, they considered a secret marriage. Ultimately they decided against such an "improper" course, agreeing instead to an unofficial engagement. They would wait until William's return before making any firmer commitment. Perhaps the Franklins' discussions with the Penns would resolve the difficulties between the assembly and the proprietors, and the greatest source of their unhappiness would disappear.[13]

By the time he and his son left Philadelphia, Ben was as pleased as anyone that William and Betsy would be separated. Remembering the cooling effect London had once had on his own relationship with Deborah, he felt that a timely trip to the capital city might distract his son, saving him from possible public humiliation. If nothing else, it would provide him some badly needed perspective.[14]

Father and son headed for New York, their planned point of departure, on April 4, 1757, leaving Deborah, Sally, and the enchanting Miss Graeme behind. The further William got from home, the more concerned he became about the effect his absence would have on his romantic fancies. The first leg of the journey only deepened his gloom. At Brunswick, the foul weather and "extreme Badness" of New Jersey's roads forced the Franklins to abandon their carriage and gallop to Elizabeth on horseback. The melancholy youth could not help but compare his inauspicious circumstances to the obstacles that faced his attachment to his fiancée. "The Morning of our Love," he declared, "has likewise been and is still overcast, threat'ning a Wrecking Storm; who knows but kind Heav'n may graciously permit a chearing Sun to scatter those Clouds of Difficulties which hang over us, and afford a Noon and Evening of Life calm and serene."[15]

The Franklins' arrival in New York did not greatly improve matters. They had already been delayed once, even before leaving Philadelphia, when Ben was pressed into service at the last minute, trying to arrange a compromise between the assembly and the governor. By the time he had completed his negotiations, the Franklins' packet had sailed. General Loudoun had promised that another vessel would sail momentarily, and they arrived breathlessly in New York on the day of the ship's scheduled departure. But this vessel could not leave America until Loudoun delivered some dispatches, "which were always to be ready tomorrow" to the Captain, and so the Franklins' leave-taking was perpetually postponed. Their frantic attempt to reach New York on time had proved unnecessary.[16]

While Ben chafed irritably at the delay, William sent a stream of letters to Philadelphia. But despite his protestations that his thoughts could not be diverted from his Betsy, he was clearly having a fine time. He dipped freely into his father's coffers. There were parties to attend that often included a "mixed Company of both Sexes." And he soon met some of the other passengers who would accompany them on their voyage, becoming particularly fond of John Temple, a young Bostonian gentleman and former naval officer, and James Abercrombie, son of Major General Abercrombie, vice-commander of the British forces in America. William's own military experience no doubt made him feel comfortable with these men, and they whiled away the days pleasantly.[17]

Ben, always impatient at inactivity, was not so easily diverted. By mid-May he had found the wait so "tedious" that he organized an excursion to Woodbridge, New Jersey. Deborah and Sally traveled from Philadelphia to join them. And there, along with other "gentlemen and ladies," William explored a part of the colony he would one day claim as his own. Like most visitors to the region he was overwhelmed by the Passaic Falls, which cascaded down a seventy-foot cliff, tumbling with "Inconceivable force & Velocity" into the foaming river below. Always attracted to bucolic pleasures, William was captivated. Although he had seen more of the American countryside than most men twice his age, he was immediately taken with the "Face of the Country." Its "Variety of romantic Prospects," he rhapsodized, "afforded me far greater Pleasure than any Thing I had ever seen before. Indeed I had not the least Idea that Views so aggreeably enchanting were to be met with in America." He longed for the day when he could return to the colony, and he and Betsy could wander together through the countryside.[18]

Thoughts of Betsy caused a note of disquiet to dampen his euphoria. Betsy had not accompanied the Franklin women to Woodbridge, although she had been invited to join them. He found it unsettling that she had not jumped at the opportunity to see him once more before he sailed across the rough and forbidding seas. He had to admit that their correspondence was already beginning to wane. Betsy did not write as often as he expected her to. And he himself was so occupied with "Public Business" and the demands of his new friends that he often could not find time even to think of her, much less to write. Still, he shrugged off his uneasiness. Soon he would return from London, sharing in the triumph Ben was sure to achieve in his negotiations with the Penns. Then he would be in a position to focus his attention on his own ambitions. "The Happiness which flows from a Retirement and a Country Life" would be his. Such a prospect, he insisted, "is the main Scope of all my Wishes." Thinking, no doubt, of

Graeme Park, he was convinced that marriage to his dear Betsy was the surest and most pleasant avenue to the realization of his dreams.[19]

Finally, on the second of June, despite the delays that "By one Accident or other" had plagued the party, the Franklins boarded the *General Wall* and embarked on the second leg of their journey. Fortunately the vessel was built for speed, for it was continually harassed by enemy ships during the twenty-seven-day crossing. Even when they neared the coast of Falmouth where they planned to disembark, their safety was not assured. Enemy privateers lurked everywhere, hungry for prey. In a desperate effort to outmaneuver potential captors, the captain attempted to sail into the harbor at night. But the vessel was caught in a heavy current and barely escaped being smashed against the rocks of an island that loomed suddenly before them. Only the faint beam from a lonely lighthouse saved them from certain death. The next morning they were in sight of the port and were able to watch as "the Fog began to rise, and seem'd to be lifted up from the Water like the Curtain at a Play-house." They had arrived at their destination shaken, but in one piece. William, at least, felt that he had already earned whatever pleasures awaited him in London. "Few are the Inducements," he said fervently, "that will tempt me to pass the Ocean again, if ever I am so happy as to return to my native Country."[20]

Once on firm ground, the Franklins fairly raced to London, stopping only long enough to glance at Stonehenge, and to visit Lord Pembroke's house and gardens at Wilton. They arrived in the capital less than three weeks after setting foot on England's shores. The elder Franklin took immediate advantage of his Quaker connections and his reputation in scientific circles, contacting John Fothergill and Peter Collinson and gaining an audience with Lord Granville, president of the Privy Council.[21] But the Franklins' closest friend in these early days proved to be printer William Strahan. It was Strahan who had originally helped David Hall secure a position in Ben's print shop, and the two men used this connection to develop a trans-Atlantic business relationship, and eventually a friendship, by mail. Once in London, Franklin hurried to meet his long-time correspondent. They took to one another immediately, and William, too, was swiftly welcomed into the Strahan household.[22]

By the end of the summer, the Franklins had secured comfortable lodgings with Mrs. Margaret Stevenson and her daughter "Polly" on Craven Street. There, father and son settled into a life-style that was highly pleasing to them both. Ben, ever the joiner, was delighted by the many philosophical clubs that attracted middle-class Londoners who could boast a nodding interest in "natural philosophy." At the Royal Society Club he was most often the guest of Dr. John Pringle, whose dinner parties and

Sunday evening "conversations" introduced him to some of the best
scientific minds in London and on the Continent.[23] William also emersed
himself in the sights and sounds of London. He began his legal studies,
continued as his father's aide and confidant, and set out to explore the
capital. Everything he saw made Philadelphia look provincial, and it took
almost no time for the image of his "dear Betsy" to blur. When William
finally wrote to her, his apologies were almost subsumed by his enchant-
ment with the "great Metropolis." He marveled at London's "infinite
Variety of new Objects; the continued Noise and Bustle in the Streets,"
and he protested that "the Viewing such Things as were esteem'd most
curious, engross'd all [his] Attention." His father's connections gained him
entry into London's literary and scientific circles, and both he and Ben
were wined and dined by "Politicians, Philosophers, and Men of Business."
He never tired of the "publick Diversions and Entertainments" of the
"bewitching Country." William took it all in, visiting Windsor Castle and
Vauxhall, traveling to the sleepy country villages surrounding London, and
attending musical productions and plays with no apparent concern for
cost.[24]

His first trip to the mother country helped William shape and solidify
his political views, launched him on a promising career, and smoothed the
remaining rough edges off of his provincial personality. As he worked
closely with his father in their prolonged fight with the Pennsylvania proprietors, and as the two men traveled around England and the Continent
together, Ben and William put the final touches on a partnership that
would make them fast friends and strong political allies in the years to
come. Ironically, their work served at the same time to sow the seeds of
future discord, as it helped draw William politically and personally closer
to the England that his father would one day disavow. But all that was in
the distant future. For the moment, the differences between Ben and
William—both personal and political—were virtually non-existent.

Many historians have seen William's love affair with London as the first
evidence of his "aristocratic" tendencies and have implied that his admiration for England in 1757 foreshadowed his loyalism in 1776.[25] Admittedly,
Franklin's enemies were quick to criticize his "high and mighty" demeanor,
his "many extravagances," his "courtier-like airs" and "courtier-like propensities."[26] But William's fascination with the pleasures of one of the
world's premier centers of art and sophistication was hardly unusual. It was
no different from the response of other young colonial visitors to the
capital city, all of whom were enthralled by the myriad "Curiosities" and
amusements they encountered in London's "social wilderness."[27]

Ben, as much as William, was intent upon making a good impression in
the capital city. He had learned early that appearances were an essential

attribute of success. In London, he "had to live in a Fashion and Expence, suitable to the Publick Character I sustain'd." He ignored accusations that he was parading around London at the colony's expense, and did not hesitate to use the assembly's money, as well as his own, to sustain himself and his son in style. He immediately purchased wigs, shoes, and linen to be made up into new shirts for them both. He lived lavishly, hiring a coach, and hobnobbing with anyone who might be of use to him and his cause.[28] This new convivial life-style was no burden for the simple tradesman from Philadelphia. William was certainly not the only Franklin who gravitated toward the "aristocratic" manner befitting a gentleman of leisure.[29]

Nor was William's attachment to the mother country any more fervent than his father's. Benjamin Franklin came to London as an Englishman, a staunch defender of the empire who was conscious of his provincialism even before he set sail, and who, despite his loyalty to Pennsylvania, longed to belong to those circles where real power was exercised. He treasured Anglo-American unity, and envisioned an empire where the new world would enhance the power of the old, while the old world would graciously recognize and reward the contributions of the new. He had a deep appreciation of the ties that bound the American colonies to the mother country, and his fondest hope, well into the sixties, was to draw the two faces of the empire ever closer together. His quarrel in 1757 was with the proprietors, not with the Crown.[30]

That William was devoted to England and things English was not surprising. But even in his youthful ardor, he was not an uncritical admirer of all he observed. He had expected the "Obstinacy and Wickedness of the Proprietors." But he was a little taken back by the myopia of London bureaucrats who had "little knowledge of (or indeed Inclination to know) American Affairs" and he was dismayed by "their Prejudices against the Colonies in general, and ours in particular." When he referred to "My Country" he was thinking of Pennsylvania, not England. And he was always quick to take offense at the "Aspersions" British soldiers cast upon the colonial war effort, as he praised the "Gentlemen of America who have so nobly signaliz'd themselves" in defense of the empire. If William Franklin was not altogether comfortable in the land of his birth, neither did he truly belong in England. He never doubted that his sojourn in London was a temporary one, and that his destiny would be worked out in America.[31]

William's most important task in London, after he had enrolled in the Middle Temple, was to serve as his father's secretary and aide in the fight to preserve the Pennsylvania assembly's privileges. Both men had a taste of the up-hill battle they faced during Ben's first encounter with Lord Granville. During the interview, Granville, who was related to the Penns by marriage, pompously lectured Ben on the nature of royal instructions to the governors which, he insisted, had the full force of law and were not subject to alteration by the colonial assemblies. It went without saying, he contended, that proprietary instructions were similarly immutable. Granville was wrong, and Ben did not hesitate to tell him so. But his remonstrances were in vain, and he came away from the meeting "a little alarm'd."[32]

The first meeting between Benjamin Franklin and Thomas Penn was similarly inauspicious. They met in August at Penn's house at Spring Garden. There the two adversaries eyed each other nervously, pretended to want a "reasonable" accommodation of their differences, and came out fighting. Agreement was impossible. Franklin distrusted the Penns' solicitor, Ferdinando John Paris, who, Ben contended, had already "conceived a mortal Enmity" to him. When Franklin refused to deal with so implacable a foe, the proprietors turned the entire matter over to the Attorney and Solicitor General, where it sat gathering dust for "a Year wanting eight Days." Ben had only succeeded in further alienating the suspicious Penns.[33]

It was time for the Franklins to attempt another tactic. They instituted a propaganda campaign aimed at countering proprietary claims that Pennsylvania was dominated by stubborn Quaker pacifists who alone were responsible for the sorry state of the colony's defenses. Both men had experience with pamphlet warfare. In this kind of battle, father and son could combine to present their case to the English people.

In the fall of 1757, when the Franklins decided to confront head-on the "scandalous and malicious Falsehoods" of the Penns' minions, William submitted a letter to a London newspaper, the Citizen or General Advertiser, defending the colony and insisting that proprietary instructions, not the Quakers, were the real "Clogs or Obstructions" to Pennsylvania's defense. William's efforts were essential, for Ben, still ostensibly involved in "a friendly Negotiation" with the Penns, could not properly take note of "nameless Aspersions in a News Paper." But, as William told Betsy, "there could be no Reason why I, as an Inhabitant of Pennsylvania, now on my Travels in England, no ways concerned in conducting the Negotiation, should not vindicate the Honour and Reputation of my Country when I saw it so injuriously attacked." Nevertheless, everyone knew that while the words in the letter may have been William's, its sentiments, and no doubt its inspiration, emanated from Ben himself.[34]

William's letter put him in the spotlight almost immediately. It was reprinted in the Gentleman's Magazine, and eventually it even appeared in the Pennsylvania Gazette. Speaker Isaac Norris complimented him on his "prudent measure" in publishing "incontestable facts" under his own name instead of hiding behind a pseudonym. And while Thomas Penn disdained to reply to the "impudent" piece, he recognized its telling effect. William was understandably a little puffed up by the attention his letter received. It had, he crowed to Elizabeth Graeme, "all the good Effects I could have wish'd." The proprietors, of course, were "much incens'd," but they could do little to defend themselves. He was highly pleased with his effort, and clearly counted himself as one of the Penns' staunchest foes.[35]

William had other opportunities to use his talents in the continuing war against the Penns. By the winter of 1757 he was busily at work with Richard Jackson amassing material for a political history of Pennsylvania that would tell the assembly's side of the story. Jackson, an amateur scientist, lawyer at the Inner Temple, and a true friend of America was William's closest friend and adviser in London. While the younger Franklin probably did not write the *Historical Review of the Constitution and Government of Pennsylvania*, his work in gathering the necessary documentation for the long and often tedious treatise was invaluable.[36]

William's importance to the assembly's cause was magnified in September when Ben fell seriously ill. For eight weeks he worked almost full time in his father's service, running errands and meeting daily with Ben's friends and advisers. He also represented the colony at Court, where he often ran into Thomas Penn. At each encounter Penn pretended not to recognize William. This slight did nothing to alter his already unfavorable impression of the proprietors. Ben's illness may have taken his son away from his legal studies, but it gave William the opportunity to be evaluated strictly on his own merits without risking pejorative comparisons with his father. He easily passed inspection. While William Strahan hoped that the younger Franklin would be fortunate enough to absorb all of Ben's manifold virtues, he readily conceded that the young man was already "one of the prettiest young gentlemen I ever knew from America." He exhibited a "solidity of judgment, not very often to be met with in one of his years."[37]

Ben's illness also altered the relationship between father and son, as the elder Franklin learned to rely on William's help and advice. He was, Ben acknowledged, very "serviceable" both to himself and the assembly. Theirs became a more egalitarian relationship. And William Strahan noted that by the end of the year Ben viewed William as "his friend, his brother, his intimate, and easy companion."[38]

Despite both Franklins' best efforts, nothing they did forced the Penns to relinquish their claims. In January of 1758, Ben abandoned any hope of accommodation, when a quarrel with Thomas Penn put an end to their discussions. The attempt to win over the proprietors by sweet reason had failed, and the Franklins began to search for another way to defend assembly rights. It became increasingly apparent to Ben that the best way to solve Pennsylvania's problems was to seek revocation of the proprietary charter and to win recognition as a royal colony. William, disgusted with the Penns' "little dirty Aspersions they were continually publishing" and with their "low contemptible" attacks on the assembly, quickly agreed.[39]

The decision to seek closer ties to the Crown was based, for both Franklins, on solid Whig principles. They had come to England as defenders of the assembly. William, as much as Ben, deplored the Penns' "selfish" attacks on assembly privilege. And he fulminated against their "iniquitous System of Government" and the "villainy" of proprietary instructions. To both father and son, advocacy of a royal government appeared eminently logical. Both men were staunch supporters of the British empire and it was hardly surprising that they would advocate a move to strengthen the power of a government they cherished. They were, moreover, convinced that dissolution of the charter would help guarantee assembly liberties and assure Pennsylvanians the rights of Englishmen. Neither saw any conflict between firm loyalty to the Crown and the preservation of colonial rights. For them, the proprietors, not the King, represented the greatest threat to Pennsylvania liberties.[40]

In the short run, they seemed to be right. In April of 1759, Governor Denny caved in to the demands of the Pennsylvania assembly and accepted a defense bill that raised £100,000 by taxing the proprietary estates. The Penns immediately denounced the bill and asked the Privy Council to declare it unconstitutional. Hearings were held in May before the Board of Trade, and William attended the sessions with his father. Franklin's lawyers repeated the arguments that Ben had advanced tirelessly for so many years. Equity, practicality, and the rights of Englishmen were all on his side. But the Board of Trade was not. Franklin lost his case.[41]

Undaunted, Ben sought the help of William Pitt and turned to the Privy Council for relief. Surprisingly, Franklin managed to win both a reversal of the Board of Trade's decision and a minor concession from the Privy Councilors. The assembly was allowed to tax the proprietary estates if it promised to assess them at the lowest rate at which other Pennsylvania land was taxed. As events would prove, it was not much of a victory, but it was the best that Franklin could have expected.[42]

For all practical purposes, the Franklins' battle with the Penns was over by 1760; only Ben's need to seek reimbursements for Pennsylvania's military expenditures induced him to remain in London. Politically, his trip abroad had been a disappointment. Neither personal confrontation nor the power of the pen had worked in his favor. He was much more successful in influencing events in Philadelphia than in London. Scientists may have been impressed by his reputation, but politicians were not so easily awed by this provincial representative of a remote colonial possession.

The protracted quarrel with the proprietors served, however, to bring father and son closer together, even while it drew them both more tightly into the imperial system. But it was not only the arrogance of the Penns that strengthened William's emotional ties to his father and his King. The two men did not spend all their time in stuffy court rooms or at strategy sessions in Craven Street. Much of their London sojourn was devoted to pleasure, not duty. Beginning in the spring of 1758, they took what would be a series of delightful trips together. In May they traveled to Cambridge where they were "kindly entertain'd" by chemistry professor John Hadley, who was eager to share his own scientific interests with the renowned Mr. Franklin. Ben found the trip so soothing to his vanity and so "advantageous" to his health, that he and William returned to Cambridge in July for the commencement exercises. From there the two continued their travels, making a sentimental journey that was to have a profound effect on William Franklin.[43] They journeyed to Willingborough in Northamptonshire, Ben's ancestral home, where they talked with Mary Fisher, the only child of Ben's uncle, Thomas Franklin. Mary, although she was "weak with age," remembered Josiah and his first wife, and talked readily about their departure for America. The old world had treated Franklin's relatives well, for Mary and her grazier husband were "wealthy," living "comfortably" in the community that Ben's father had long ago rejected.[44]

From Willingborough, William and Ben traced their roots to Ecton, a few miles away, where Benjamin's father had been born. There the two prowled around the old house and grounds and found the ancient church register "in which were the births, marriages, and burials of our ancestors for 200 years." They went with the rector's wife to view the moss-covered grave stones, and while Ben's slave Peter washed the markers, and William copied down the inscriptions on the slabs, the "goodnatured chatty old lady" regaled them with stories from their collective past. She talked especially of Ben's uncle Thomas "a very leading man in all county affairs, and much employed in public business," whose practical advice, like that of his nephew, was "sought for on all occasions."[45]

William was overwhelmed. The similarity between Thomas and Ben was obvious. But even more uncanny, his gravestone revealed that Thomas had died a mere four years before Ben was born, on the same month and the same day. In an awed tone, William remarked on the "extraordinary" coincidence, for had Thomas "died on the same Day . . . one might have suppos'd a Transmigration." William was encountering his own and his father's heritage. He was given a link with the past, a sense of his own connections, a framework within which he could begin to define his own existence. It was a moment that obviously moved Ben almost as much as it did William, and it brought the two closer together than ever. It gave them both, as well, a visceral sense of belonging to the England they had already grown to love.[46]

The leisurely trip continued as father and son traveled through North-hampton, on to Coventry, and then to Birmingham where they met some of Deborah's relatives. All of Deborah's clan turned out to welcome their American cousins, one of them traveling twenty miles on foot from Birmingham in order to pay his respects. The two men moved on to Tunbridge Wells, located about thirty-six miles south of London, where they joined Richard Jackson who frequented the fashionable resort. Ben remained there for about two weeks before returning to London in August, leaving his son in Jackson's care. The two lawyers enjoyed their meanderings in the countryside, and William was the proud bearer of the news that Frederick the Great of Prussia had defeated the Russians at Zorndorf, using information Ben had forwarded to him from London to his own best advantage. He was able to contribute "Particulars which no one else had" on the affair. So pleased were Jackson and Franklin with one another's company, that they began at once to plan another trip to Norfolk, where Jackson had some estates.[47]

But William's happiness was not unspoiled. Thinking of his father, embroiled in continual controversies with the proprietors, breathing the smoke-filled air of London as another fruitless summer wound to a close, he felt uneasy about the carefree existence he enjoyed at his father's expense. In a fit of remorse, he told Ben, "I am extremely oblig'd to you for your Care in supplying me with Money, and shall ever have a grateful Sense of that with the other numberless Indulgences I have received from your paternal Affection." And, he promised, "I shall be ready to return to America, or to any other Part of the World, whenever you think it necessary." Such a promise was easy to make, for Ben would never demand such an unreasonable test of loyalty from the son whose companionship he obviously enjoyed.[48]

Their travels revived the Franklins' spirits and were a particular joy for Ben. No matter where he went, he was fêted and honored for his scientific achievements, and both men took every opportunity to explore the world outside London. Their trips were many, but none pleased them so much as their journey to the walled city of Edinburgh in the fall of 1759. The venture took two difficult, even dangerous, weeks by stagecoach, but it was well worth the effort. Their reception in Scotland was assured in advance. Both John Pringle and William Strahan hailed from Edinburgh and they gladly provided the Franklins with introductions to the city's intelligentsia. They dined with Adam Smith, Alexander Carlyle, Sir Alexander Dick, and David Hume, and the conversation flowed freely, as these leaders of the "Scottish Renaissance" exchanged thoughts on science, politics, and the law with their American visitors.[49]

William who had been called to the bar in the fall of 1758, took full advantage of the esteem with which the legal profession was held in Scotland, and was his usual charming self on these occasions. Adam Smith was particularly taken with him, and Carlyle later pronounced him more "Open and communicative" than his father. But both Franklins felt truly at ease in this part of the empire, where, unlike London, self-improvement was valued and profession mattered more than birth. Its inhabitants shared the love-hate relationship with the empire so characteristic of colonials. Here they could relax, forgetting for a moment the sense of inferiority that haunted them in London, enjoying the company of men whose outlook was similar to their own.[50]

But there was more than good conversation with like-minded men to give them pleasure. They explored the ruins of the old city that lay beneath Edinburgh Castle before making a brief trip to Glasgow, where William presented a gift to the University. And on the first of October they traveled north to the University of St. Andrews, where Ben received the degree of doctor of laws. St. Andrews was housed in a "plain, mean and unadorned building," and the institution itself had seen better days. Still, as Ben knelt before the President of Senatus, and felt the robe of crimson silk and white satin being draped carefully over his shoulders, the unschooled American was moved by the signal honor, and both he and his son were immensely proud of the gesture.[51]

The return trip through Berwickshire included a visit with Lord and Lady Kames, whose lavish hospitality and beautiful country estate near the river Tween thoroughly charmed both father and son. Riding back to London, Ben remarked that he had just spent "Six Weeks of the *densest* Happiness I have met with in any Part of my Life." Were it not for his "strong Connections" elsewhere, he thought he could live happily in Scotland forever. For Ben, as well as for William, the image of Philadelphia's little charms was growing dim.[52]

As long as they stayed in London, the Franklins grabbed every opportunity to escape the city's summer heat. In 1760 they traveled to Coventry, Wales, and Bristol and then on to fashionable Bath before returning to London in mid-November. And the following summer they enjoyed a five-week excursion on the Continent with Richard Jackson. Their journey to "Flanders and Holland" was their first time on European soil. William meticulously kept a journal of the tour. Wherever they went they were received by dignitaries and men of letters all of whom were anxious to meet the man who had brought lightning from the skies. Only the wretched crossing of the English Channel on the return marred what was otherwise a perfect trip.[53]

In the spring of 1762 the Franklins journeyed to Oxford, where Ben was made a Doctor of Civil Laws and William, more or less as a courteous gesture, was awarded a Master of Arts degree. Ben cherished his honor, referring to himself as "Doctor Franklin" from that time on. And William once more received recognition as a result of his father's eminence.[54]

Despite the personal pleasures Ben enjoyed in Britain and the esteem with which he was held by his many admirers, by 1762 he was ready to leave for home.[55] His battle with the proprietors had reached its equivocal conclusion. Vacations and honors were well and good, but they were no substitute for the challenges that awaited him on the other side of the Atlantic.[56]

For Ben, the London sojourn was over. For William there were a few loose ends to tie up before he returned to his native land. His plans for his future had been considerably altered since his arrival in London. One change in William's status Ben no doubt endorsed. By the fall of 1758, his love affair with Elizabeth Graeme was over. Significantly it was Graeme, not William, who ended the relationship, though William may well have been the first to realize that their plans were doomed. Problems emerged almost immediately upon his arrival in England. After his first letter to Betsy in July, William waited five months before writing again. He was much too busy with his law studies, his official duties, and his travels to take a moment to write to the woman who had so occupied his thoughts on the other side of the water. To be fair, William was "ever a bad Correspondent." But absence does not always make the heart grow fonder, and while William insisted that his feelings for Graeme had not altered, the "Intimacy" he enjoyed with "several Ladies of distinguished'd Rank and Merit" undoubtedly made it easy for him to postpone his excellent intentions to write home.[57]

Elizabeth Graeme was hurt by William's ability to ignore her. The final insult came when he finally did write at the beginning of December. Full of enthusiasm for London and replete with fulminations against the proprietors, his letter seemed a direct attack on her and her family. William was so proud of the piece he had written for the *Citizen* in September that he seemed to forget—or perhaps not to care—that his sentiments would be met in the Graeme household with icy anger. He, who was usually so diplomatic, totally disregarded the tender feelings of the woman he professed to love. The "Muffs and Tippets" he sent, assuring her that they were "worn by the gayest Ladies of Quality at this End of the Town," served only as a reminder of Philadelphia's provinciality when compared with the "Elysium" he so obviously enjoyed.[58]

Elizabeth's angry response was one she would soon regret. Convinced that William no longer loved her, assuming that his December letter had been his cowardly way of terminating their relationship, she savagely attacked his involvement in his father's schemes. Ben, she said, was nothing but "a Collection of Party Malice." And William was totally lacking in morals and judgment. It would be utter "*Folly, nay Madness*" to risk an attachment to such a man.[59]

Betsy's letter was waiting when William returned from his vacation in Norwalk. There is no indication that he ever responded directly to her nearly hysterical harangue. A letter to Mrs. Abercrombie was his closest approximation of a reply. And while the good lady assumed that it was written with a "Design to be Communicated," for his part, the relationship was over. If Graeme's attack had been made in an attempt to revive his former passions, it had the opposite effect. "She could not," said Franklin, "have fallen upon a more effectual Method of bringing me to [a] State of Indifference." Although he professed heartbreak over the loss of his love, he spent most of his letter defending himself, saving face, and throwing the blame for the quarrel elsewhere. The proprietors, and even Betsy herself, were at fault. He was a mere helpless bystander. William Franklin never accepted criticism easily, nor did he like to quarrel. Whenever he became involved in a conflict, he made every effort to prove that he had neither instigated the conflagration nor fanned its flames.[60]

He began by proclaiming his own good intentions. The Penns, he argued, had fomented and prolonged the quarrel that continued to divide Pennsylvania, destroying his personal dreams for happiness in the process. He and his father had done everything possible to ameliorate their differences. Knowing that hostile relations between the assembly and the proprietors would mean the end of his romance with Betsy, he had written his letter to the *Citizen* not to stir up trouble but to reach an accommodation between the Franklins and the Penns. If the proprietors refused all attempts at compromise, he was surely not to blame for their recalcitrance. With the chasm between the Penns and the Franklins too wide to overcome, William had realized that marriage was now out of the question. His own sentiments had not altered, he insisted, but he now knew that he would never be able to contribute to Betsy's happiness. He had planned to free her from any obligations she may have felt toward him. Now, of course, that was no longer necessary.

William pictured himself as an injured innocent. Betsy had changed; he had not. She was young, flighty, temperamental, while he was mature and steadfastly loyal. William was convinced that his behavior was totally blameless, that Betsy's conduct was unforgivable, and that somehow he had to pick up the pieces of his shattered life. "I, only I," he sighed, "have to learn Forgetfulness."[61]

For William, forgetfulness came easily. His conscience was clear. Betsy had rejected him; he had not forsaken her. And England's brilliant society beckoned. His trips were a magnificent diversion. In London he was so busy working for Ben and making the rounds of the social scene that even William Strahan had a hard time pinning him down. Money was readily available, if not from his father, then from his father's friends. And when Ben could not leave his duties, William found his own companions and amusements in and away from the capital city. In the fall of 1761 he even managed to secure a coveted ticket to George III's coronation. There, he walked with William Strahan in the procession to Westminster Abby, and got a close-up view of the "splendid show" which "surely nothing earthly" could ever exceed.[62]

At least some of William's diversions were not so innocent. Following a bit too closely in Ben's footsteps, he became the father of an illegitimate son, William Temple, some time after 1759. Temple's existence remained a secret from all but their closest friends, and the boy was placed in a foster home where he was raised and educated primarily at Ben's expense. William did not abandon his son; he was even willing to give the boy his own name. But neither did he openly assume responsibility for him as his father had done for him.[63] It would take the younger Franklin many years before he welcomed Temple into his household without fearing the social opprobrium that would surely follow an acknowledgment of his indiscretion. It took more confidence than William had at the age of thirty to take such a step. Moreover, he may have thought he was doing his son a favor when he did not raise him in his own home. He had suffered the verbal slings and arrows of a jealous stepmother when he was a boy, and he may have wanted to spare Temple a similar fate.[64]

William had another more pleasant reason to forget Elizabeth Graeme. Some time after 1758 he met, courted, and in 1762 finally married Elizabeth Downes, the well-connected daughter of a wealthy Barbadian planter. Quiet, dignified, and well-educated, she won the approval of all William's friends. But Ben was not so enthusiastic. He had grown very fond of Polly Stevenson, his landlady's daughter, and fervently hoped that his son would share his sentiments. He had done all he could to encourage the match, and his disappointment was obvious. But he bowed to his son's wishes. Young people were beginning to choose their own marriage partners by the middle of the eighteenth century, and Ben could do little to dissuade William from the match even had he wanted to do so. He was not averse to guiding William in the proper direction, but he was not one to command or forbid. A direct confrontation with his son was to be avoided at all costs, and so he gave his "Consent & approbation" to the marriage and sailed for home before the wedding took place. There he nursed his grievance in private for a while, avoiding all discussion of the match.[65]

William's marriage has been the occasion of much wasted analysis. Historians have suggested that his choice of the demure Miss Downes was dictated by William's need to "have a lady to act as hostess in the governor's mansion," and that it was little more than an astute career move. But William had wooed his future bride long before the possibility of a colonial governorship had opened up and he was, like many young men of his class, a true romantic who would not be likely to marry for convenience alone.[66] Others have seen William's decision as a "declaration of independence," a means of carving out an identity that helped him escape the shadow of his overpowering father. He had married late, even by colonial standards, but he was, according to this view, at last ready to stand on his own merits and become his own man. Granted, William waited a long time before marrying, but the delay need not be attributed either to his reluctance to "grow up" or to his abject dependence on his father. He was ready to wed in 1757 and only the trip to London prevented him from following his inclinations.[67] Nor can his choice of a marriage partner be attributed to a willful attempt to fly in the face of his father's authority. Ben's indulgent treatment of his son made any full-scale rebellion a virtual impossibility in any case. How could anyone launch a revolt against a father like Benjamin Franklin?[68]

In fact, William's motives for marrying Elizabeth Downes were probably quite straightforward. She had an "amiable character," was a "very agreeable, sensible, and good-natured Lady," and promised to make him a "Suitable and Agreeable wife." Franklin's friends were not at all surprised at the match. Elizabeth was a "Favorite" with all who knew her, and "they love[d] one another extremely." William's decision was as simple—or as complex— as that.[69]

Young Franklin gained a child and a wife in London. He was also able to use his time there as the springboard from which to launch his career. His government connections were surely the result of his father's influence. But he took advantage of every opportunity to impress those he met with his charm and ability. Once the Franklins' business with the proprietors was at an end, it became apparent to them both that their days in the mother country were numbered. William may have delighted in his life away from the provinces, but, like his father, he could not afford to remain in London forever with nothing to do but traverse the English countryside and hobnob with friends. Neither Ben nor William really *belonged* in London society; it was time for both to get on with their lives.

William hoped to use his own and his father's influence to secure some minor post in the colonial bureaucracy. He thought in terms of a place in the customs service or the Admiralty Court. Just a month before he was named governor of New Jersey, he applied for a position as Deputy Secretary of Carolina. But then a combination of good luck and the right connections catapulted him into a position that a young, inexperienced colonial could scarcely have dared contemplate. Josiah Hardy, the popular governor of New Jersey, was precipitously removed from office. Thomas Pownall refused the offer of the job. And furtive negotiations were begun to secure the position for William Franklin.[70]

No one knows the exact train of events that led to the rather surprising appointment. Because the Penns would surely oppose William's efforts, all of the arrangements were "transacted in so private a manner that not a tittle of it escaped until it was seen in the public papers." Certainly, the Franklins' connections with Lord Bute, young George III's tutor, confidant, and closest adviser from 1760 to 1763, and Dr. John Pringle were essential.[71]

It is impossible to ascertain what role Benjamin Franklin had in the negotiations. He left for home before the appointment was announced, and was extremely tight-lipped about the entire affair. "My Son stays a little longer in England," he cryptically told his friends when they expressed curiosity over William's prospects. Ben's silence did not stop the paranoid speculations of the Penns, who saw in the appointment a conspiratorial plot to increase the Franklins' influence. Some historians have argued that William was given the appointment to secure Ben's allegiance to the ministry. But Franklin was already a strong Crown defender and he surely did not need this position for his son to tie him to George III's regime. Others insist that it was the elder Franklin's influence alone that made the governorship a reality, that he handed William the position in virtually the same way he had given him the clerkship of the Pennsylvania assembly. Still others have stated that William got the job on his own, "without any solicitation on the part of his father." Some even insist that Ben opposed the appointment, and that the seeds of dissension between the two men were sown when William took his oath of office.[72]

It is doubtful that William won his position without the aid of at least a word or two being dropped in the right places by his father. And there is no question but what Ben was pleased with his son's success. William's governorship was a tribute to him, another indication of the distance he had traveled from his lowly beginnings. Still, William did not receive his appointment without at least some consideration of his qualifications. Admittedly, the governorship of New Jersey was hardly a choice position.[73] But it was too important to offer to a mere figurehead, and William Franklin had some obstacles to overcome if he was to secure it.

He was, first of all, a colonial, and while the government did not always shrink from hiring Americans to represent its interests, it could be forgiven for preferring to select one of its own for such a potentially delicate task. Moreover, William was young and inexperienced. Surely it would have been wiser to give him a period of probation in a minor post or two before promoting him to the position of colonial governor. And then there was the question of his illegitimacy. Such matters were less important in cosmopolitan London than they may have been elsewhere. Nevertheless rumor had it that "there was some difficulty in his being Confirmed in his place," for "many Scruples were raised on account of his *being illegitimate.*" It was only after a "severe personal examination" conducted by Lord Halifax that William Franklin convinced his judges that he was equipped for the job. On August 20, word of Franklin's appointment was sent to the Privy Council. His position secure, William embarked to "the land of matrimony" taking his marriage vows at St. George's Church on Hanover Square.[74]

The next few months were hectic for Franklin and his new bride. Remembering the dangers of his last Atlantic voyage, he took out an £800 insurance policy. He ordered 100 prints of Mason Chamberlain's painting of his father. Magazines and books had to be forwarded to New Jersey. Learning that it was customary for the government to supply a new governor with a portrait of the King and some furnishings for a chapel, he asked Strahan to obtain a copy of Ramsay's painting of George III. He also arranged for the printer to secure some furniture and silver plate, and hold them for him in London until he could persuade the New Jersey government to "erect a Chapple to the House they are now building for the Residence of their Governor." William was determined to overlook no detail, for he wanted to give his enemies no opportunity to criticize him as he assumed his new responsibilities.[75]

By November, William and his new wife were ready to depart. They visited briefly with Elizabeth's relations near Fareham, where they resided in a large old family seat formerly belonging to the late Lord Angon. They met with a "good reception" and whiled away the time, anxiously waiting for their ship to sail. By mid-November they were on their way. The beginning of the journey was hardly auspicious; the stormy weather beat against the vessels in their convoy, driving the ships back to Plymouth for repair. While Elizabeth recovered from fright and sea sickness, and marshalled her resources for another assault on the violent waters, William chafed at the delay. Despite the lateness of the season, he was determined to leave for America before the end of the year.[76]

Neither he nor Elizabeth admitted to being "disheartn'd." They were young and resilient. A new life awaited them on the other side of the forbidding ocean. Britain was even now negotiating a treaty with France that promised to bring "lasting Peace" to America. And with France removed from the continent, the untouched forests of the Ohio Valley were open to American settlers who had long gazed at them with a mixture of desire and trepidation. Despite the wintery storms that lay between England and America, William was anxious to begin his promising career. "We must now take our Chance," he said, "which I do with the more Confidence, as I know I am in the way of my duty, & have reason to expect the Prayers of many good Friends whom I leave behind." His duty to England and to the colonies would sustain him on the passage home. He had no doubt of his ability to satisfy the demands of Crown and assembly as head of the royal colony of New Jersey.[77]

3

An Easy, Agreeable
Administration

"I have no doubt but that he will make as good a
Governor as Husband: for he has good Principles and
good Dispositions, and I think is not deficient in good
Understanding."—Benjamin Franklin to Jane Mecom,
1762.[1]

"I believe no governor was ever more affectionately
received by all ranks of people. Even with those for
whom I might have expected opposition I am on very
good terms."—William Franklin to William Strahan,
1763.[2]

The vessel that carried William Franklin and his bride to America's shores
tossed and turned on the icy Atlantic seas. A storm off the Bay of Biscay
produced such violent waves that the water crashed through the windows
of their cabin, ruining much of their baggage and stores. William would
not have wished this "disagreeable" trip on anyone. Not the devil. Not
even his old enemy Parson Smith, provost of the College of Pennsylvania.
The ship could not land in Philadelphia because the river there was clogged
with ice and they had to disembark a full 150 miles from their destination.
Even with land in sight, their bad luck continued, and they had to wait another six days until the "contrary" winds abated and they were finally able
to struggle ashore on the twelfth of February.[3]

The ordeal was not over, for it would be a week before they arrived safely
at their destination. They could find nothing but an open carriage to convey them to Philadelphia and so, despite the "severe" weather they rode
over 100 miles with no protection from the wind and cold. Elizabeth must
have been devastated by her first view of the wild and inhospitable country
that was to be her new home. Cut off from family and friends, weak from
a miserable ocean voyage, she now had to endure a seemingly unending trip
through a forbidding land of snow and ice. William "had much ado to keep

43

up poor Mrs. Franklin's spirits" as they made their way across the wind-swept countryside. Perhaps he entertained her with descriptions of the New Jersey he remembered from the summer of 1757, as he tried to kindle her interest in the "Variety of romantic Prospects" that had once seemed so "enchanting" to him. If he did, he may have had a twinge of remorse as he remembered another Elizabeth who he had planned to take on a leisurely visit through the rural paradise he had so admired. How different this was from his youthful vision of the return to his native land.[4]

But such thoughts, if they occurred, were fleeting. Elizabeth made the best of the situation. "She behaved," said Franklin proudly, "much beyond my expectations." And eventually their luck changed. About fifty miles from Philadelphia they "met with a chariot" that had been awaiting their arrival, and they traveled the rest of the way in relative comfort. As they approached the city, Sally and Ben, accompanied by a "considerable number of gentlemen," rode out to escort them into town.[5]

William did not linger in Philadelphia. He needed only a few days to recuperate and visit old friends before he set out for his new home. He was no doubt anxious about this, his first real position, and he wanted to get started as soon as possible. Not since his days as a soldier had he fulfilled his duties without the day-to-day guidance of father or friends. His ability to do the job well would in large measure determine his chances for future promotion. In New Jersey he had a real opportunity to make use of his talents. But he had at least an equal chance of falling flat on his face. William Franklin was determined to succeed.

Ben predicted that William would be an excellent governor, for, he said, "he has good Principles and good Dispositions and I think is not deficient in good Understanding."[6] It would take all his good "Dispositions" and "Understanding" to govern New Jersey successfully. No colonial governor had an easy task in the years following the French and Indian War. The powers of provincial chief executives had atrophied over the years. Governors had little to offer in the way of patronage, and received only feeble backing from a home government crippled by factionalism and ministerial instability. Most importantly, with the French government removed from the continent, the colonists no longer felt much need to compromise with the mother country. The mutuality of interest between England and America that was provided by the imminent danger of foreign invasion had disappeared.[7]

In New Jersey the governor's problems were in some ways magnified. The colony's very existence was an historical accident. Once a part of New Amsterdam and then ceded to the Duke of York, it became a separate proprietary colony in 1664. By 1676 it had been divided into two governments—East and West Jersey—and while the colony was reunited in 1702, the early division continued to have some effect. East Jersey, which looked to New York for its trade, information, and culture, was dominated by English-speaking yeoman farmers; its salient feature, however, was its ethnic and religious diversity. Many of its settlers had migrated there from Puritan New England and they brought with them their religion as well as their dedication to the town meeting form of government. West Jersey had once been a Quaker stronghold, and Quaker influence still thrived there. For geographical, historical, and religious reasons, its center of influence was Pennsylvania. Western New Jersey, like its eastern counterpart, had an economy dominated by farming, but landholdings there tended to be slightly larger and it was generally more rural. As a result, the county, not the town, was the local unit of government.[8]

The government reflected the divisions that made New Jersey two colonies in one. There were two capitals, one at Burlington, in West Jersey, and the other at Perth Amboy, in the East. The assembly alternated its meetings between the two cities. The governor's council was composed of twelve members, who were to be equally divided between East and West Jersey; some effort was also made to maintain a sectional balance in the assembly.[9] Each section retained its own Council of Proprietors who distributed land and collected quit-rents in the area. Each had its own treasurer. While the leaders of the sections had learned to govern in relative harmony by the time Franklin came to New Jersey, it was nevertheless true that he would need considerable tact to govern effectively in this bipolar colony.[10]

His task was made more difficult because New Jersey was so often at the mercy of its two larger and more powerful neighbors. So much that happened in the colony was beyond the control of even the most able governor. Its trade was dominated by New York in the East and Pennsylvania in the West. New Jersey enjoyed its reputation as the "garden of North America," but its inability to secure any appreciable foreign trade, meant that it was "deprived of those riches and advantages, which it would otherwise soon acquire."[11]

New Jersey's paucity of foreign trade affected its character. It could claim no real urban center, so that if its inhabitants yearned for any but bucolic pleasures, they had to travel to New York or Philadelphia. The colony could not even sustain its own newspaper. All its news came from Philadelphia or New York, and the governor always had to contend with the effect of political views that penetrated his colony's borders from outside. It was difficult to control a province whose inhabitants received their cue from their neighbors, not from the governor who vainly attempted to unify and lead them.

These were problems that confronted any New Jersey governor. For Franklin, the special difficulties he faced appeared particularly ominous.

He arrived at a time of unusual chaos, coming at the tail-end of a twenty-year furor created by the Great Awakening. The heady doctrines of George Whitefield, Gilbert Tennant, and Theodore Frelinghuysen had periodically washed over New Jersey during the preceding two decades, leaving deep divisions in their wake. Politically, the colony was also unsettled. The London agent, Richard Partridge, had died in 1760, leaving New Jersey virtually without a voice in the capital city. Since 1757 the province had endured four different governors; Franklin's immediate predecessor, Josiah Hardy, had lasted a mere six months. Most troubling, however, Franklin could not have been unaware that many in New Jersey, especially the powerful East Jersey proprietors, viewed him with suspicion. Josiah Hardy had curried the favor of these men, and they were sorry to see him go. Moreover, they had close ties to William's Pennsylvania enemies through their own connections with the Penns and with former Governor Robert Hunter Morris, himself an East Jersey proprietor. Ironically, Morris had been responsible for Hardy's precipitous departure from the colony. He had persuaded the governor to grant him a "good behavior" commission as chief justice of New Jersey instead of the "for pleasure" commission required by the Board of Trade. It was Hardy's violation of his instructions that had paved the way for Franklin's appointment.[12]

The East Jersey proprietors' negative reaction to William's governorship was predictable. The Franklins were known for their hostility to Morris. Moreover, William was a Pennsylvania native, and they assumed his sympathies would lie with the West Jersey Quakers. They had endured unpleasant experiences with unfriendly governors in the past, and saw no reason to welcome this new executive who they regarded as potentially dangerous. "The news," said one of the governor's enemies, "came upon us like a Thunder Clap." Franklin's governorship was a "Burlesque on all Government," and his appointment was an "insult" to the colony. Pennsylvania's Governor James Hamilton gloomily predicted that Franklin "would certainly make wild work without his Father's experience and good Understanding to check and moderate his Passion." Even William's friends, doubted his ability to deal with the "unruly Spirits" of some of the leading council members. William Franklin had his work cut out for him.[13]

The new governor's prospects were not, however, as dark as they appeared. For in some ways, New Jersey's weaknesses could be counted as advantages. It may have lacked wealth, culture, and cohesion, but as a rural colony characterized by ethnic and religious diversity, it had few artisans or mechanics, and no well-organized political factions. Moreover, its dearth of trade may have cost the colony, but it also meant that New Jersey was not directly affected by many of the new regulations emanating from Parliament in the 1760s. Nor did it have to deal with the volatile presence of seamen whose disruptive influence caused other governors untold grief.[14]

Moreover, while the East Jersey proprietors initially opposed Franklin's appointment, others did not. The West Jersey proprietors, many members of the assembly, and a sizable number of East Jersey residents, particularly those living near Elizabeth and Monmouth, welcomed anyone who might clip the wings of the powerful East Jersey establishment.[15] If Franklin could win their favor without alienating the East Jersey proprietors, he might be an effective leader. It was a task that required delicacy, skill, and a dose of good fortune. Franklin, no stranger to factional politics, had learned the art of compromise at the feet of a master. It remained to be seen whether good fortune would be his.

William and Elizabeth traveled to New Jersey on February 23, 1763. Ben accompanied them, wanting to attend his son's inauguration and to lend his support on William's initial introduction to the members of his new government. The elder Franklin had friends as well as enemies in New Jersey, and his presence may have helped smooth the way for the governor. The reception William received during his first halcyon days in the colony no doubt assuaged many of his fears. He spent his first night in New Brunswick before heading for Perth Amboy, the bastion of the East Jersey proprietors' influence, the following day. The snow and cold continued, but despite the "great Inclemency of the Weather," a small group of townsmen rode out in sleighs to greet the governor and his wife, and the Middlesex troop of horse escorted them into town. There, "admidst a numerous Concourse of People," William proudly took his oath of office in a ceremony attended with "as much decency and good decorum as the severity of the season could possibly admit of."[16]

Even in the midst of the celebration, William had to display a little fancy footwork, as he picked his way carefully through the difficulties that threatened to entrap him during his first days as governor. Josiah Hardy greeted him upon his arrival and attended the inauguration. It would not do to make any blunder in front of the man he had replaced. His enemies were watching his every move, and would gleefully seize upon even the tiniest error. Addresses by Perth Amboy dignitaries wished him an "easy and agreeable" administration, but they also referred pointedly to the "loss we sustain" at the removal of his "mild, benign and just" predecessor. They hoped Franklin would take up residence in their town, for the governor had the option of residing either in Perth Amboy or Burlington. Because his choice would be viewed as an indication of his future sympathies, it was of major symbolic and practical importance. At the dinner held in his honor that evening, his hosts described the new governor's mansion that the proprietors had built for chief executives who elected to live in the eastern capital. The offer was tempting, but William prudently promised nothing. He was "as yet uncertain," he murmured, about his plans.[17]

The party traveled next to Burlington, where William took a second oath of office. On the way they passed through Prince Town where they visited the College of New Jersey, and William was received "with great Respect" by president Samuel Finley and the tutors of the college, who were impressed by the new governor's "Education under the Influence and Direction of the very eminent DOCTOR FRANKLIN." William did not resent the praise heaped upon his father. He was confident of his own abilities, and his speech to a mixed assembly of students and townspeople won the approval of those who had gathered to get their first look at the young governor. Members of the audience nodded as he told them that "the careful Instruction of Youth in the Principles of Religion, Loyalty and Sound Learning is of the greatest Utility to Society."[18]

On the evening of March 3, Franklin reached Burlington, where he was treated to a reception that easily rivaled the one accorded him in Perth Amboy. He was met outside town not just by the Corporation of Burlington, but by the "principal Inhabitants" of Trenton and Borden Town as well. His arrival occasioned the "greatest Demonstrations of Joy, and the evening was concluded with Bonfires, Ringing of Bells, Firing of Guns, &c." Like their counterparts at Perth Amboy, the officials at Burlington pressured William to take up his residence with them. Although they could not offer him a mansion, they were sure he could find suitable private accommodations in their town. Once again, William thanked his hosts, but postponed any decision.[19]

The Franklins returned to Philadelphia a few days later to savor William's reception and make serious plans for the future. Ben was elated by his son's welcome, writing William Strahan of the pleasure he had taken in seeing him "receiv'd with the utmost Respect and even Affection by all Ranks of People." It seemed that the gloomy predictions of their enemies had been wrong, and William could expect clear sailing. Still, it was important to exercise caution. William's most important immediate decision was his choice of residence. He leaned first toward Perth Amboy. The governor's mansion had its appeal, and in Burlington he could not even find a suitable place to rent. Staying at Amboy would also alleviate some of the fears of the East Jersey proprietors that he would be a pawn in the hands of the West Jersey Quakers. But there were equally good reasons to opt for a Burlington home.[20]

Neither town was impressive. Perth Amboy was the chief seaport of New Jersey. Built on a neck of land between the Raritan River and the sound dividing it from Staten Island, it had a "fine" harbor that begged to be exploited by enterprising merchants. But, said its visitors, with New York so near, trade was swallowed up by the larger entrepôt. Perth Amboy was nothing but a little country village. Its pine board houses, topped with unpainted cedar shingles, were scattered haphazardly about the town. It was pleasant enough, but it was "thin Built and the houses and Gardens &c So interspersed that it's hard for a Stranger to form a Notion how the Streets ought to run." It had fewer than one hundred residences, one good tavern, a courthouse and jail, and a "pretty market house." The rolling beauty of the Raritan Hills surrounding the town was attractive, but Perth Amboy itself was unimpressive compared with London, or even Philadelphia.[21]

New Jersey's "chief town" of Burlington was not much of an improvement. Located on the Delaware River, it was as dominated by Philadelphia as Perth Amboy was by New York. Burlington was twice as big as its rival; its brick and stone houses were "regularly built" along "one Spacious Street" running down to the river, and the surrounding countryside displayed a "variety of agreeable prospects and rural scenes." Its two Quaker meeting houses drew some visitors to the town, for Quarterly meetings were occasionally held there, and the Friends often entertained English and American visitors. Perhaps most importantly, Burlington was less than twenty miles from Philadelphia where the Franklins could go for recreation and companionship. There, too, William and his father could exchange political confidences and hold the strategy sessions they had so enjoyed in London.[22]

William carefully weighed the relative merits of the competing capitals. His reluctance to come down firmly on one side or another was an indication of the importance he attached to his decision. It revealed as well a touch of insecurity. By the first week in April he had found temporary lodgings in Burlington but still had not made up his mind. In the end, politics tipped the scales in favor of the western location. The governor's house at Perth Amboy had been financed by the East Jersey proprietors, not by the colony. Under the circumstances, he told William Strahan, "I have reason to think that my living in their house will not be a little unpopular as it is suspected by some to be intended as a means of byassing the Governor to their interest." He decided to make it clear from the beginning that he would not become the tool of the East Jersey proprietors, no doubt confirming the fears those powerful gentlemen had of their new governor.[23]

Once he and Elizabeth had settled into their temporary home, Franklin waited anxiously for instructions from London. His sense of vulnerability was augmented in the spring when he learned that Lord Bute had been forced to leave the King's government. With his most important supporter out of office, he could easily lose his governorship through no fault of his own. Exasperated, he fulminated to Strahan, "I can't think what the Devil the people of England would be at. If one may form a judgement of them from the Publick prints they are certainly out of their senses." Five months later, Franklin's London friends were keeping a watchful eye on political affairs, promising to report "any Thing material to his Conduct," and hoping that his "Prudence" would keep him out of the "Party Bypasses" that were throwing the home government into so much turmoil.[24]

Franklin could do nothing to control English politics. His task was to govern New Jersey and serve the King. Fortunately, his political instincts were sure and he moved quickly to establish contacts with the men whose support he would need in the days to come. Perhaps his most important conquest was William Alexander, or, as he preferred to call himself, Lord Stirling. Alexander was an East Jersey proprietor, a Surveyor General of East Jersey, and by June of 1762 a member of the Governor's council. He was far wealthier than William. His Georgian-style residence at Basking Ridge was a "notable landmark." Replete with stables, gardens, and the obligatory deer park, it was, says his biographer, "as close to a British peer's house as any American could be expected to come." Indeed, Alexander had some pretensions to nobility, although his claims to an earldom were never recognized by the House of Lords. Still, he continued to call himself "Lord Stirling" in America where his colonial friends were not so punctilious about such details.[25]

Alexander was a man worth cultivating, but he was not predisposed in Franklin's favor. The two men had been in London at the same time, often frequenting the same circles. But Alexander had grown close to the Penn brothers, and the Pennsylvania proprietors had poisoned their American friend's mind against the Franklins. Alexander saw no reason to question the judgment of men who treated him with unfailing generosity. Moreover, he had led the effort to build the governor's mansion at Perth Amboy, and could not have been pleased when Franklin took up residence in Burlington.[26]

But Alexander was shrewd as well as affable, and Franklin was a charming companion and a superb politician. The governor soon managed to dispel his misgivings, and the two men became friends and allies. They had a great deal in common. They loved to talk of their London days, sharing fond memories of their experiences in England's capital. They were both successful sons of even more successful fathers, and they may have shared an occasional sense of irritation when they were compared unfavorably with their more illustrious parents. Most importantly, they needed each other. Franklin valued Alexander's support and learned to rely on his often excellent advice. Alexander quickly realized that William was not the monster the Penns had described, and knew that it was better to have a governor as a friend than an enemy. Within a year the Franklins were vacationing at Basking Ridge, and the two families remained close until the coming of the Revolution.[27]

William would later realize that his first years in New Jersey were in many ways his happiest. He was not successful in every project he essayed, and many of the issues he tackled represented ominous portents of the limits of his power. But he enjoyed a few minor successes, won the good will of his assembly and council, and had every reason to look to the future with confidence. In his personal affairs as well as in his public role, he trod carefully over unfamiliar ground paying meticulous attention to even the tiniest details.

By the end of June, William anticipated the pleasure of moving into permanent quarters at Burlington and he and Elizabeth were busily planning the decor for their new home.[28] They wanted the best the governor's salary could afford. William in particular insisted that his furnishings reflect favorably upon his office. It was not for pride alone that he agonized over the selection of the silk curtains "to be hung festoon fashion" in his home or that he demanded that the curtains exactly match the damask chairs in the dining room. Nor did he plan to do without intellectual refinements merely because his surroundings smacked of rustic provinciality. He embarked immediately upon a project to build what would become one of the finest libraries in the province. He would be, William vowed, the cultural as well as the political leader of New Jersey.[29]

Franklin settled easily into the routine of daily life. At first he had plenty of time to devote to ceremonial duties. He informed his fellow governors that he had arrived in New Jersey. He appointed a day of prayer and thanksgiving to celebrate the proclamation of peace between Great Britain and its European enemies. He entertained a deputation of Presbyterian ministers and attended a convention of Anglican clergymen in Perth Amboy. The colony was quiet; not much was going on there at all, he assured Strahan. While he, like all Americans, had a strong appetite for politics, "that kind of food" had to emanate from London.[30]

William performed his first duties as governor with such natural grace and political acumen, it was difficult to believe that he had never before held a significant administrative post. While he was a little nervous, and anxiously awaited specific direction from England, he handled himself with sensitivity and intelligence. But he got his first real taste of his political prospects when the assembly convened in May at Perth Amboy. As he rode toward the eastern capital, he looked forward to the session with nervous anticipation. Entering the tavern where the council sat in readiness, he could not help but compare these makeshift rooms to the elegant Philadelphia statehouse. He resolved to push vigorously for "proper Rooms for the Uses of the Council & Assembly." But for now he would have to deliver his maiden speech before the New Jersey assembly in a setting that symbolized the indifference with which the colony's government was viewed.[31]

He had obviously done his homework, for his speech was brimming with specific proposals. His would be an active government. He knew that "it is not what is promised but what is done, in any Administration, that must finally settle its Character." Displaying a knowledge of the colony's economic problems, he argued that New Jersey needed to encourage agriculture and commerce and improve its roads and navigable waterways. He also appealed to the legislators to suggest other ways the colony's interests might be served. He hoped they would be partners, not adversaries, and he promised to support any improvements, so long as they were consistent with his duty to the Crown, which, he said, "I can never depart from." From the perspective of hindsight, his caveat had an ominous ring, but it was scarcely noticed in the peaceful spring of 1763, when Britons were celebrating the birth of an heir to the throne and the future was filled with promise. Franklin was convinced that the best way to serve the empire was by fulfilling New Jersey's needs. Conversely, New Jersey's "Prosperity and Happiness" could be assured by a "truly dutiful Behaviour" to a sovereign "from whom they derive Protection in the Enjoyment of their Liberties, Properties, Religion, and every Thing that is valuable." Loyalty to the Crown would secure the King's favor, serving the interest of both empire and colony.[32]

The assembly's response was gratifying. While its members deferred action on his proposals for internal improvements, they agreed to pay for the New Jersey regiment's expenses for the past November. By a slim margin, they also provided for one of Franklin's most pressing needs, raising his salary by £200 and increasing the compensation of the chief justice by £50 and that of each Associate Judge by £25. This was a victory, he could not refrain from noting, that had "been fruitlessly attempted by other Governors." With such an auspicious beginning to his credit, he was convinced that by the "Seizing of proper Opportunities" more increments would soon follow.[33]

Franklin took particular pleasure in the assembly's kind treatment because his old nemesis, Parson Smith, had publicly proclaimed that his appointment had been "disagreeable to the people" and had predicted that his governorship would be an unhappy one. To counteract Smith's claims, Franklin asked William Strahan to publish the laudatory addresses he had already received. Claiming that "no governor was ever more affectionately received by all ranks of the people," he noted that he was on "good terms" even with those men who he had most expected to oppose him.[34]

Franklin's horizon was not unclouded. Despite his early successes, he had to face, even at the beginning of his administration, several interrelated problems that would plague him throughout his long term as governor. He was chronically preoccupied with the need to augment his and his chief officers' salaries. He had to find some acceptable currency that New Jersey could use as a medium of exchange. And he had to persuade a notoriously penurious assembly to pay the expenses incurred by the King's troops stationed periodically in the colony.

Although Franklin managed to convince the assembly to raise the salaries of the governor and the chief and associate justices in 1763, the new salaries still bore "no Proportion to the encreased Expense of Living in America." His own stipend was "barely sufficient to support him suitable to his Rank," and New Jersey offered its governors few chances to augment their meager income through fees or patronage. He wished the assembly would grant him a permanent stipend, but recognized that this was highly unlikely. It was a "principal riveted in the Minds of all the Assemblies on this Continent," he explained, "that none of the publick Officers ought to have any settled Salaries, but depend upon such Allowances as may from time to time be agreed upon by the Legislature." And so he always hoped that the colony's chief officials would be put on the Civil List. This had been done elsewhere, and Franklin longed for the time when New Jersey would be similarly blessed. But that was a decision that was virtually out of his hands. Consequently he badgered the assembly constantly, pleading for more money and a permanent stipend. Franklin found this distasteful. It reduced him to beg for what he assumed was rightfully his and damaged his relationship with the lower house. In the end, William's attempt to augment his salary became a near obsession as he was rebuffed time and again by the legislature as well as by the ministry in London.[35]

New Jersey was known for its penny-pinching ways.[36] Indeed the colony had little alternative. It had an underdeveloped economy and was perennially embarrassed by a specie shortage, a lack of British credit, and an unfavorable trade balance. Because it was little more than an economic tributary to New York and Pennsylvania, it shared in some of the financial distress those colonies suffered at the end of the French and Indian War. While New Jersey was marginally better off than its neighbors when Franklin took office, astute observers knew that it was just a matter of time before ready cash would dry up, affecting prices and land values everywhere.[37]

Like many colonies, New Jersey was highly sympathetic to paper money. During the French and Indian War, currency emissions to cover military expenses and parliamentary grants to compensate for those expenses had created unprecedented, if artificial, prosperity. At war's end New Jersey had nearly £200,000 sterling in outstanding bills, and while its currency remained remarkably stable, it became apparent that the assembly would soon have to resort either to taxation or to the emission of still more paper money to meet its expenses. The latter alternative was obviously preferable.[38]

Franklin knew that if New Jersey was to support a growing economy, avoid undue taxation, and contribute its share to the empire's defense, the colony needed a responsible currency emission. The governor's perspective was not altogether disinterested. He saw no way of securing either an official residence or a respectable salary without bills of credit. Moreover, he must have known that Lewis Morris, the only New Jersey governor who seriously opposed paper money, had been locked in bitter conflict with the assembly and had even been deprived of his salary.[39]

In 1763 the Board of Trade's response to Franklin's request for a currency emission was ominous, when its members insisted that all future emissions should conform to the terms of the Currency Act of 1751. This act limited the life of all bills emitted in peacetime to two years. This, Franklin assured the Board, was "too short a Term to induce a sufficient Number to become Borrowers."[40] Even more worrisome was the Board's broad hint that it hoped to extend the Currency Act's provisions to all the American colonies. In April of 1764, Parliament did just that, when it banned paper money serving as legal tender, and mandated the prompt retirement of all outstanding bills. As William Franklin was to discover, the act signaled the end of New Jersey's popular currency policy.[41]

It would be a long time before Franklin would become discouraged by the mother country's strictures. In the early years of his administration he remained confident that he could negotiate some accommodation between the Board of Trade's orders and New Jersey's needs. As an American, he felt that he was in an excellent position to explain the colonial situation to the Crown's advisers. As a loyal Englishman who had spent some time in the nation's capital, he felt competent to convey the Board of Trade's perspective to the members of the New Jersey assembly. Better communication and a mutual attempt at understanding were all that was needed to reconcile the minor differences between America and England, for their interests were, he was convinced, fundamentally identical. Moreover, William Franklin was no ideologue. He always sought practical solutions to his problems and he was confident that the needs of both mother country and colonies could be met if only the right formula could be devised. The man who devised such a formula would earn the admiration of all parties, making the conflict he so abhorred disappear.

A third problem facing Franklin during his first year as colonial governor was in some ways the most troublesome of all. The rebellion of Chief Pontiac's forces in the summer of 1763 made England call upon its American dominions for help in controlling its newly won western possessions.

At a time when New Jersey had imagined that peace with France had rendered further military obligations obsolete, it was once again called upon to contribute to the empire's defense. Throughout the summer of 1763, and on into the fall of 1764, New Jersey received repeated requisitions for troops to put down an uprising that did not even threaten the safety of its own borders. Even with Pontiac's defeat, the mother country's demands for military assistance did not cease.[42]

The Crown's request for troops was critical to William Franklin's personal and political image. A former military man, he prided himself on his martial prowess and was anxious to display his expertise. In Pennsylvania he had witnessed at first hand the weakness of colonial defenses when the army was at the mercy of a selfish governor and a recalcitrant assembly. It was incumbent upon him to prove that royal colonies, unlike their proprietary counterparts, were loyal servants of the Crown. It would not do for New Jersey to drag its feet at a time when Benjamin Franklin and his allies were trying to win Crown favor and secure a royal charter for Pennsylvania. Finally, the home government's request for troops represented the first important test of Franklin's ability to work with his assembly. To fail such a test might mean a very quick end to what promised to be an illustrious career.

Franklin tried desperately to support the Crown's military efforts, but often as not he found himself caught between the conflicting interests of colony and empire. As early as 1761, New Jersey had begun to ignore its military obligations. Now, with the war over and its finances shaky, the province had little stomach for further expenditures. In October, Sir Jeffrey Amherst, commander of the King's North American forces, asked the governor for six hundred men to help him pacify the western frontier. Because the "savages" had recently murdered some New Jersey inhabitants, the governor was confident that the assembly would supply the necessary troops.[43]

But, by the middle of November, Franklin was beginning to have doubts. Difficulties quickly arose over the mode of financing the troops. The assembly wanted to raise the money through a new paper currency emission, for the treasury had almost no unappropriated specie at its disposal. While Franklin did not quarrel with the legislators' logic, he had to insist that any paper money bill include a suspending clause, rendering the bill useless in the short run. If the governor ignored his instructions and authorized the emission without a suspending clause, he risked his own commission. He must have recalled with a twinge of irony his fulminations against the "villainy" of proprietary instructions just a few years earlier. Royal instructions, he was discovering, could be just as rigid as proprietary ones had been.[44]

Governor Franklin was swiftly discovering the limits on the powers of a colonial governor. His was a "Dilemma," he said, in an obvious understatement, "in which we Plantation Governors are in several Instances involv'd." He had, he explained, risked his life for King and country in the past, and did not object to risking his commission now. Still, it seemed unfair to ask him to choose between following his instructions—which would mean that he would not be able to supply Amherst the troops he obviously needed—or disobeying those instructions, furthering the interests of the empire but losing his job in the process. By the end of November, Amherst had been recalled, to be replaced by General Thomas Gage. Gage sympathized with Franklin's predicament and offered him some carefully crafted advice. As he saw it, royal instructions were meant to serve as "a General Tenor of Conduct." Governors could "Exceed" or "Deviate" from them only when the circumstances made it "Absolutely Necessary." Franklin alone would be answerable for any deviations from the rule, but Gage thought that in this instance he was on firm ground.[45]

By the time Franklin received the general's letter, however, the question of currency emissions was not his only obstacle. In fact, despite its earlier protestations, the assembly managed to grant £10,000 without relying on new emissions. But the legislators had other objections to supplying Gage's troops. Although Franklin "practiced every Piece of Management" in his power, he was only able to secure a promise for one-third of the soldiers Gage requested. The legislature stubbornly refused to raise any more troops until it knew how the other colonies would respond to the King's request. The matter was, for all practical purposes, out of Franklin's hands. The people of New Jersey would not act independently.[46]

By December, the governor and assembly had reached an impasse. Franklin was somewhat reassured by private promises that the legislators would honor Gage's complete request if New York complied as well. But New York continued to delay its own requisitions until it learned what the New England colonies would contribute. Franklin felt ill-used by all concerned. The Board of Trade ignored his repeated requests for guidance. Despite his private maneuvering and public pleas, the assembly refused to be moved. Meanwhile he was convinced that unless the colonies mounted a major offensive against the Indians, their "Barbarities" would escalate. Caught between an oblivious Board and a stubborn assembly, forced into inactivity until other colonies made their own decisions, he feared that he would receive all the blame for his colony's recalcitrance. In his anger, he lashed out at the Board of Trade. If, he said, Amherst had asked the New England colonies for help in the first place, none of this would have happened. It was as much in their interest, as it was in New Jersey's, to put down the frontier uprising, and it was only fair that New England contribute its share to America's defense.[47]

Franklin called the assembly to Perth Amboy in February to ask it to reconsider its position. By that time, Pennsylvania had "Chearfully" met the terms of its requisition, but the New England colonies continued to procrastinate. Still, Franklin begged the house to act. Only its forthright compliance would "Confirm the favourable Sentiments his Majesty already entertains of the people of this province." And, Franklin might well have added, only an obedient colony would earn its governor the King's approbation.[48]

The assembly was only partially persuaded by Franklin's eloquence. In the end, after considerable maneuvering, the legislators finally agreed to raise six hundred troops in proportion to what New York would raise. As New York had filled half its levies, New Jersey would do the same. It was not a perfect solution, but even this had been secured only by a "good deal of Management." Moreover, this was the best deal he could secure and the council unanimously advised the governor to sign it.[49]

Franklin's first conflict with the New Jersey assembly had been resolved. But the obstinacy he had encountered both from the colonists and the home government foreshadowed the difficulties he would have so long as he remained a colonial governor. He tried desperately to obey the letter as well as the spirit of England's commands, and his "Zeal and Diligence" were even commended by Halifax and Gage. Still, it was apparent that there were limits to the governor's ability to reconcile the competing interests of King and colony.[50]

Franklin had to deal with an assembly that was naturally tight-fisted, and extremely jealous of its rights. To a certain extent, he could sympathize with this jealousy. It was a sentiment he had shared with his father when they had fought together against the claims of the Pennsylvania proprietors. Nevertheless, he quickly became convinced that many colonial objections to raising troops were not the result of principled protest but were a consequence of selfish particularism, which threatened to destroy British military effectiveness in America. "The Want of Union among the Colonies must ever occasion Delay in their military Operations," he told the members of the Board of Trade. Each colony waited for the others to act; none would contribute more than its most niggardly neighbor. "This procrastinating Conduct," he continued, "owing to the Jealousies and Apprehensions each Colony has lest it should happen to contribute somewhat more than its Share, is the Reason why the American levies are sometimes delay'd till the Season for Action is nearly elapsed." Benjamin Franklin had recognized the need for imperial reorganization at the Albany Conference in

1754, as he, too, had tried to persuade the colonies to abandon their private interests for the public good. As the governor of a small and dependent colony, his son perceived a heartfelt necessity for the same kind of reform.[51]

Even as he decried the consequences of American disunity, Franklin recognized that the blame did not lie entirely on his side of the Atlantic. London was sending signals that it intended to be much more demanding of its colonial appendages than it had been in the past. Such a shift could augur nothing but trouble for a governor caught between loyalty to Crown and assembly. Franklin learned how awkward his position could be in 1764 when the New Jersey legislature insisted upon passing its troop bill "in the accustomed Form," voting pay to its own designated officers, in effect establishing "in the Assembly a Negative in the nomination of those Officers." This meant that at least in principle, the lower house had encroached upon the governor's—and hence the King's—prerogative. When Franklin signed the troop bill despite its irregularities, he earned a stiff reprimand from the president of the Board of Trade, Lord Hillsborough. The Board gave him small praise for attempting to "check the Assembly in their unconstitutional Method of providing those Services," but it expressed real displeasure that the colony had not exhibited a "due dependence" upon the Crown.[52]

Franklin's careful response to the Board of Trade's reprimand revealed an awareness of how difficult his job would be if the ministry persisted in demanding "due dependence" from its colonies. He promised only that he would strive to make the New Jersey assembly's proceedings "correspond as nearly to the Principles of the British Constitution as the Circumstances of a Colony will admit." He could do no more than that. There would always be times when full compliance was neither possible nor even desirable, and Franklin hoped that the Board would allow him to judge those situations for himself.[53]

On balance, by the middle of 1764, William could give himself good marks as governor. He was pleased with his reception in the colony, and satisfied with his performance. His record was not unblemished. He did not foresee any real possibility that the legislature would grant him a permanent salary. He had not persuaded the assembly to raise its required number of troops during Pontiac's Rebellion. Even worse, he had incurred the wrath of Lord Hillsborough for consenting to a bill that, on the face of it, threatened Crown prerogative. Nevertheless, he had secured a raise for himself and his justices. And he had won the respect of many of the most important political leaders in New Jersey.

He was not out of line when he assured his friends that his term as governor promised to be an unqualified success. He enjoyed a "perfect harmony with everybody in the province," and there seemed to be little reason that a man of his "Prudence" would not be able to avoid all "Party By-passes." Careful management, flexibility, and charm, plus an occasional drop of oil on the troubled waters of imperial politics, would guarantee his continued good fortune. He was happy "in his Government as well as in his Marriage." And he was aware that his successes were not his to savor alone but would work to the benefit of his father as well. A tranquil and loyal New Jersey served as a pointed contrast to the turbulence characterizing the proprietary colonies, where, William claimed, "Anarchy" prevailed. Such a contrast could be used in the Franklins' campaign to make Pennsylvania a royal colony. By preserving the peace in New Jersey, William Franklin was doing his part to promote his father's plans for a change of government in Pennsylvania. In his role as royal governor, he continued to act as Ben's aide and partner.[54]

It had not taken William Franklin long to establish himself satisfactorily in his new home. The "principal people" of the colony honored and entertained him, and he returned the favors granted to him with dignity and grace. His lifestyle was reflected in his figure, which, he said complacently, had "increased considerably in flesh" since he left London. Admittedly he chafed a bit at New Jersey's provinciality. The colony's rural landscape may have resembled the English countryside, but he often felt isolated from the rest of the world. Post riders bypassed both Burlington and Perth Amboy. If Franklin wanted to enjoy an afternoon of horseracing, he had to travel to Philadelphia or New York. And, fresh from the glitter of London, he was painfully aware of American parochialism. Colonial politics was dull and offered "nothing of any consequence." Even the best colonists were culturally backward. "We Americans," he laughingly told William Strahan, "when we go to England have as much curiosity to see a live author as Englishmen have to see a live ostrich, or Cherokee Sachem."[55]

Elizabeth must have been a little more disquieted by her new home. She was not as prepared as her husband for New Jersey's wilderness, which even sympathetic observers described as "a world half emerged out of Chaos." Her first view of Princeton, with its scraggly saplings that provided no shade for the fifty or so houses on either side of the campus, hardly invited favorable comparison to English universities. And she was undoubtedly shocked when she observed women sitting around their homes, hatless and barefooted, cheerfully munching chocolate and sipping tea. While New Jersey, like all the colonies, had a social structure skewed in favor of the wealthy, it was nevertheless true that the lower orders there exhibited an easy air of equality with their superiors that a person of her experience could find unsettling. Elizabeth longed for a sight of the land she had left behind. And she frequently reminded her husband of William Strahan's admonition that they should always look upon England as their home.[56]

But Franklin, although he sometimes wished that he could "put Great Britain under sail, bring it over to this country and anchor it near us," was not anxious to return to the frivolous amusements he had enjoyed in London. He loved "the pleasure which that delightful spot affords," but his place, at least for the present, was in New Jersey. It was from there that he could best serve his King and his country, and, not incidentally, his father's needs as well.[57]

4

"Times of Ferment and Confusion"

"The utmost Harmony subsists between the several Branches of the Legislature. There are no Parties existing in the Province. All is Peace and Quietness, & likely to remain so."—William Franklin to Lords of Trade, 1765.[1]

"I have had a difficult Part to manage so as to steer clear of giving any Umbrage to the People here, and of embarrassing myself with the Ministry in England."—William Franklin to Benjamin Franklin, 1767.[2]

William Franklin was complacent on the eve of his first real crisis as New Jersey's royal governor. Everything, he told the Lords of Trade, was "Peace and Quietness, & likely to remain so." His initial introduction to New Jersey politics had been relatively painless, although he had encountered a bit more colonial resistance to imperial dictate than he had expected, and he had been unnerved by the paucity of instructions from London. Eager to please, Franklin was almost pathetically grateful for any sign of approval from the home government. It was, he said, his "highest Ambition" to "merit a Continuance of the Approbation of His Majesty & his Ministers."[3]

But his best intentions and greatest efforts could not assure his success. Franklin's problems were, at bottom, not of his own making. Predictably, they were caused partly by the demands placed upon him by his father and partly by the tensions produced as a result of the different, even conflicting needs of provincial leaders and the King's ministers. Pushed and pulled by various interest groups, the governor found it difficult to impose order upon the myriad problems confronting him. As a result, he tended to react to events rather than to provide strong leadership and a coherent program of his own. Only considerable luck, the essential conservatism of his assembly, and London's ultimate willingess to compromise helped him weather the storm precipitated by the Stamp Act as successfully as he did.

The Stamp Act crisis did not pose as severe a threat to Franklin as it did to some colonial governors. But in one way, his situation was worse. He assumed his governorship at the very time that his father was stepping up his assault on Pennsylvania's proprietary charter. As governor of New Jersey, William was expected to provide a shining example of the virtues of royal government to England and America alike. If New Jersey's inhabitants failed to remain quiet, obedient, and cheerful in the face of unpopular parliamentary decisions, then Franklin was neither an effective partner in his father's endeavors, nor was he earning the esteem of his superiors in London. Anxious to please, William saw the Stamp Act controversy as a time of personal as well as political crisis.

The Franklins' desire to abrogate the proprietary charter had begun in London. Their determination solidified with Ben's return to Philadelphia. And by the spring of 1764, Benjamin Franklin and his cohorts had launched an all-out onslaught on the proprietors. Ben's influence was everywhere. He spent a week with his son in Burlington, where the two men put their heads together to plan the best possible offense against the Penns. He also initiated a propaganda campaign whose centerpiece, *Cool Thoughts on the Present Situation of our Public Affairs*, used New Jersey as a prominent example of the virtues of royal government. Ben scoffed at the fears of opposition leader John Dickinson who predicted that royal control over Pennsylvania would result in less local autonomy, the loss of religious liberty and parliamentary taxation. Apparently he relied on his close connections with Lord Bute to protect Pennsylvania from Crown meddling, and his friends were persuaded by the influence he claimed to wield. He had transformed his own son, the bastard child of an unknown Philadelphia woman, a young and inexperienced provincial, into a royal governor. If he could accomplish this amazing feat then his other assurances were surely to be relied upon.[4]

William was an active partner in Ben's campaign. He wrote letters decrying the deplorable state of affairs in Pennsylvania, and during the fall of 1764, he left the governor's mansion to lobby for his father's cause in Germantown. There he kept "open house" and could be found nearly every day "Canvassing among the Germans & endeavoring to get votes by propagating the most infamous lies he could invent. He is," complained John Penn, "as bad as his father." Because William worked so assiduously for Ben's cause, his father's opponents did everything they could to undermine his influence and destroy his character. William's illegitimate birth provided an especially tempting target. His honor was besmirched and his name dragged through the mud by the proprietors' men. Involvement in his father's affairs almost inevitably brought some pain and humiliation.[5]

Despite the Franklins' combined efforts, the colony-wide elections in October resulted in a dismal defeat. Neither Franklin nor Galloway was returned to office and their party managed only the slimmest of victories. But Benjamin Franklin was stubbornly—perhaps blindly—committed to his position and would not be deterred. He immediately demanded and narrowly won assembly permission to return to London to lobby for a royal charter.[6]

Franklin's mission was never an easy one. He had to combat bureaucratic inertia and convince English officials that a Crown take-over would be greeted with enthusiasm by most Pennsylvanians. Unfortunately, he undertook his quest at the very time when the quarrel over the Sugar and Stamp acts was driving England and America further apart than they had been for over three-quarters of a century. It was the awkward task of Franklin and his supporters to stifle the Stamp Act protests in Pennsylvania in an effort to curry Crown favor.[7]

In this effort, Franklin was joined by his son. It was obviously in William's interest to secure New Jersey's obedience to the commands of King and Parliament. And, because he was often involved at least tangentially in Pennsylvania affairs and because that colony's politics so often impinged upon New Jersey, he was not a little interested in upholding the government position in his native colony as well as in his adopted one. Conversely, New Jersey's stance was important to Benjamin Franklin, for it promised to give credibility to his claims that royal colonies could be effectively governed. Consequently, both father and son, future patriot and future loyalist, lent at least their qualified support to the Crown during the Stamp Act crisis.

Ominous straws were in the wind by 1764, when Lord Grenville announced the Sugar or Revenue Act, designed to tighten existing customs regulations in America and to garner a much-needed revenue from the colonies. During his first year in office, William Franklin had himself advocated a policy similar to Grenville's initial proposal. While agreeing that a prohibition on foreign sugar would be disastrous in New England, he thought that a lower duty designed to raise revenue "would be regularly paid." He was convinced that profit, not principle, was the essential concern of most Americans. Moreover, he knew that such a duty would affect New Jersey only minimally.[8]

It was true that the Sugar Act did not directly threaten New Jersey's economy. Still, by the summer of 1765 the colony was experiencing a specie shortage resulting in falling real estate values and a rash of business failures.

The Sugar Act strained an already weak economy. Even intercolonial trade, not the object of Parliament's attention, was altered by overzealous customs collectors. Flats and small boats traveling between West Jersey and Philadelphia often had to travel thirty or forty miles out of their way in order to give bond before continuing to their destination. "The Burthen," said one future Crown supporter, was "intolerable." Nevertheless, New Jersey's reaction to the Sugar Act was mild, and William Franklin rested easy. There were a few efforts to organize austerity campaigns, but they were not likely to reach the ears of King or Parliament and would do little if anything to damage the governor's reputation.[9]

This would not be the case, however, after the enactment of the Stamp Act, which was slated to take effect on November 1, 1765. Franklin received formal notice that the legislation was being considered in the fall of 1764, in a circular letter from the Earl of Halifax asking each governor to forward a list of public documents that might be the object of a possible stamp tax. The governor complied without hesitation, even instructing Attorney General Cortlandt Skinner to point out those items that would "bear the highest Stamp Duty."[10]

Rumors of the proposed Stamp Act soon swept the provinces, and the Massachusetts assembly began to organize support for a united protest against the "Threatening blow of Imposing Taxes." New Jersey's Speaker of the House, Robert Ogden, received the Massachusetts call for action in August, but was not sure how to respond. Perhaps, he wrote Cortlandt Skinner, they should press the governor for a special meeting of the New Jersey assembly. Still, Ogden did not indicate the need for any great haste, and indeed nothing was done.[11]

Throughout the winter, New Jersey remained calm, and William was blissfully unaware that he and his assembly were about to lock horns over English policy. But while he dabbled in abortive schemes to raise his own salary without offending the legislature, opposition to the Stamp Act steadily mounted. And, in the spring of 1765, when word leaked out that stamp distributors had been chosen for each of the colonies, protestors finally had a focal point upon which to vent their anger. William Coxe was reputed to be New Jersey's stamp distributor, and the Franklins' old crony, John Hughes, had secured the position in Pennsylvania. Hughes's appointment came through the good offices of Benjamin Franklin, a fact that surprised even his ever-loyal sister, Jane Mecom.[12]

Franklin's recommendation of Hughes revealed how much the usually astute defender of assembly rights was caught off-guard by the colonial reaction to the Stamp Act. His monolithic obsession with the effort to obtain a royal charter gave him an uncharacteristically blinkered vision, as he virtually brushed aside any issue that threatened Pennsylvania's good standing with the Crown. His objections to Grenville's proposed tax were perfunctory at best.[13] And he accepted his failure to change the Secretary's mind with a philosophical shrug. "We might as well have hinder'd the Sun's setting," he said. "That we could not do." Once the act was passed, he hoped that in Pennsylvania, at least, it would be received with good grace, providing evidence of the colony's loyalty to the Crown. "Let us make as good a Night of it as we can," he told his friend Charles Thomson. Urging frugality rather than protests upon the colonists, he argued somewhat cavalierly, "Idleness and Pride Tax with a heavier Hand than Kings and Parliaments; If we can get rid of the former we may easily bear the Latter."[14]

At first, William Franklin was no more concerned about the Stamp Act than his father. In June of 1765, he and Elizabeth hosted a magnificent celebration in honor of the King's birthday. The celebrants marched to the governor's house where they toasted the King's health, and cheered the firing of the brass cannon that had been planted on the lawn for the occasion. The evening's highlight was the unveiling of the full-length portraits of the King and Queen, just arrived from England, that would grace the governor's home. As the Franklins moved through the crowd, greeting their guests and engaging in the polite social banter at which William, in particular, was so adept, they could be excused for assuming that no threat to the governor's position would emanate from so respectable a gathering.[15]

Franklin's meeting with the New Jersey legislature at the end of May accorded him his first real opportunity to test the extent of the colony's opposition to the Stamp Act. His opening remarks gave no indication that he anticipated any difficulties. Only his plea for continued harmony provided even an oblique clue that he was worried about assembly reaction to the Stamp Act. At first the governor's complacency appeared justified. The legislators complied with his request for bounties. They even promised to renew the Militia Act. It was, by all accounts, an amicable session.[16]

Most importantly, the assembly fashioned no formal protest against parliamentary taxation. Indeed, no one even broached the issue until the last full day of the session. Many members had already left for home when Robert Ogden announced that Massachusetts had issued New Jersey an invitation to send delegates to a Stamp Act congress to be held in New York that fall. According to Ogden, the house gave the request "deliberate Consideration" before unanimously rejecting it. The colony's trade, Ogden explained, was "insignificant in comparison of others" and the assembly wanted to avoid any precipitous action. Franklin was pleased, assuming that he had every reason to hope that New Jersey's demeanor would continue to be low-key.[17]

Throughout the early summer of 1765, the American scene remained untroubled by violence. Some of the colonies circulated anti-tax resolutions, but both William and Benjamin Franklin saw this as a mistake. The elder Franklin deplored the "Rashness" of the Virginia resolves as he pursued what one historian has called the "politics of ingratiation" in London.[18] "A firm Loyalty to the Crown" was essential, and he decried the "Madness of the Populace" and "their blind Leaders," who could "only bring themselves and Country into Trouble." With these sentiments, his son fervently agreed.[19]

By the end of August, however, it became apparent that even peaceful New Jersey would be infected by the growing opposition to the English tax. Beginning with the riots in Boston on the night of August 14, public protest spread quickly, and there was little that William Franklin could do to hold off the impending crisis. New Jersey opponents of the Stamp Act were delighted with an item in the New York Gazette on August 22, announcing that when William Coxe had recently tried to rent a house, his application was refused "unless he would insure the House from being pulled down, or damaged."[20] The incident was probably apocryphal, but Coxe intended to take no chances. He left New Jersey for the relative safety of Philadelphia, and sent word to governor Franklin that he had decided to resign his post.[21]

Franklin's reaction to Coxe's abrupt resignation was a combination of surprise, anger, and embarrassment. He hated being caught off guard, and felt personally betrayed by Coxe's "Surrender." Coxe had not been "threaten'd or insulted," and the governor was convinced that while "the Inhabitants here have their Objections to the Stamp Act," there was no reason to assume that the distributor was in any danger. The people of New Jersey, Franklin insisted, thought that "as good Subjects, they ought not to make any Opposition to the Act, now it is pass'd, till they have first try'd all dutiful Means of obtaining Redress." At bottom, Franklin simply could not understand the type of man who so readily abdicated his responsibilities. It smacked of cowardice and lack of honor to break and run at the merest hint of trouble. "I cannot help thinking," he lectured Coxe, "as you made Application for the Office, that you are bound in Honour to endeavour, at least, to carry it into Execution." To fail was one thing. To refuse even to try was another matter.[22]

If Franklin was angered by Coxe's resignation, he was also embarrassed. It drew unfavorable attention to himself and the colony, and would convince people that New Jersey "was as culpable as the New England Governments." He hoped that Coxe would be held responsible for the "ill consequences" arising from his resignation, and that he himself would be perceived as blameless. Franklin was placed in a potentially awkward position. He did not know if he had the authority to appoint an interim stamp distributor, and with no distributor it would be impossible to enforce the new law. Still, at this juncture he envisioned no difficulties in finding someone to replace Coxe. The obstacle, as he saw it, was not physical danger but the hefty security that any distributor would have to post. Were it not for this requirement, he would have nominated his cousin, Josiah Davenport, for the position.[23]

Nevertheless, Franklin was operating in a vacuum. He received no instructions from the home government, and he was understandably reluctant to act on his own. He turned to his council, asking its members to travel to Burlington to discuss the situation with him. And he asked General Gage to be prepared to send sixty men into the province should they be needed to enforce the Stamp Act.[24] While some observers saw New Jersey as a model of moderation and sobriety, Franklin preferred to take no chances. His career was on the line; one false move would mean certain disaster for himself, New Jersey, and the Crown.[25]

By the end of September the governor had every reason to be concerned. On the twentieth, a group of lawyers met at Perth Amboy with Chief Justice Frederick Smyth to discuss the legal ramifications of the Stamp Act. While they condemned "all indecent and riotous behavior," they resolved to take whatever "quiet methods" they could to secure the act's repeal. They promised that if the stamps actually arrived in New Jersey they would neither purchase nor use them. They also offered their opinion that the governor had no authority to appoint an interim stamp distributor. Five days later, the students at the College of New Jersey gathered for their annual commencement ceremonies. Three candidates for the bachelor's degree delivered a "polite dialogue on liberty," before a student body whose members were all clad in "American manufactures" to protest British policy. Everywhere he looked, the governor saw evidence of growing antipathy to the Stamp Act.[26]

Franklin's difficulties were not confined to New Jersey. In Pennsylvania, his father's enemies were using popular distaste for parliamentary taxation as a weapon against Benjamin Franklin and his governor-son. William Smith, William Allen, and "two or three other prostitute writers" accused Ben of supporting the Stamp Act while he worked to secure a government that would one day enslave the colony. David Hall, Franklin's partner on the *Pennsylvania Gazette*, was also under fire. As a supporter of the plan for royal government, he refused to print anything that could be construed as an attack on British policy. Ben's enemies used his noticeable silence as proof that Franklin "had a Hand" in framing the Stamp Act. Subscriptions were down; the "Clamours of the People" were growing louder; friends and enemies alike warned Hall that unless he altered his policy he would be forced to "stand to the Consequences."[27]

Nor was Hall the only recipient of threats from the Franklins' enemies. Word spread throughout Philadelphia in mid-September that a mob was ready to march on the Franklin home. Sally fled the house to stay with friends, and William came to town to persuade both his mother and sister to return with him to Burlington until the trouble blew over. Deborah stubbornly refused his offer and prepared to defend herself and her possessions against all comers. In the end, the Franklin house was spared, when upwards of eight hundred of Ben's supporters promised to come to the rescue of anyone who was the object of mob violence. But the experience was unnerving. Deborah nearly quit going into town after this, isolating herself completely from Philadelphia society.[28]

As the October elections drew near, the proprietary faction stepped up its attacks, focusing its attention directly on William Franklin. At a public meeting designed to whip up support for the government slate, James Biddle, a Philadelphia attorney, accused the governor of intercepting the Massachusetts assembly's invitation to the Stamp Act congress. Biddle also claimed that Franklin had made "strong efforts to subdue the spirit of liberty in his government." Not only had he refused to call a special session of his own legislature, but he had meddled in Pennsylvania politics. Governor Penn attended the meeting, and reportedly led the cheering crowd with loud "huzzas" at each attack on New Jersey's chief executive. The irony of the situation was not lost on William's friend, merchant Samuel Wharton. It was, he noted, the proprietary government that was inflaming the passions of the "low drunken Dutch" and encouraging resistance to the Stamp Act, while Benjamin Franklin's assembly party was doing its best to keep Pennsylvania from following the lead of its more rebellious neighbors.[29]

It seemed to William Franklin that he was being unfairly attacked from all sides. He was in no way responsible for the Stamp Act, nor could he lift the burden of parliamentary taxation from the colonies. Yet everywhere he was the object of opprobrium and slander. He was especially concerned about the situation in Pennsylvania, where attacks on him could be a liability to his father, and where riots might endanger Deborah and Sally. Moreover, the people of New Jersey would soon hear the vicious partisan attacks on their governor. If this happened, the violence threatening Pennsylvania might spill over into his own backyard.[30]

It was with these concerns in mind that Franklin fired off a reply to Biddle's scurillous accusations. He firmly denied that he had ever attempted to influence the New Jersey assembly's attitude toward the Stamp Act congress. He further insisted that he had never refused to call a special legislative session so that house members could reconsider their earlier decision not to send delegates to New York. Indeed he reaffirmed his promise to recall the assembly at the request of the Speaker and nine or ten other representatives. Finally, somewhat disingenuously, Franklin claimed that he had not interfered in Pennsylvania's internal affairs and had not even discussed the Stamp Act with Galloway and his compatriots. Nor did he neglect his father's interests. He used the letter to refute persistent rumors that Ben had helped write the Stamp Act.[31]

Franklin experienced a measure of relief in responding to his Pennsylvania critics. He found less satisfaction inside New Jersey where he felt nearly paralyzed without any firm instructions from London. He took the occasion of congratulating Henry Conway on his appointment as the new Secretary for the Southern Department to clarify his position. Trying to strike just the right note, he assured Conway that "notwithstanding the Phrensy which prevailed in other Colonies" in New Jersey the inhabitants were "sober, dutiful, and loyal subjects." He insisted that Coxe's resignation had been unwarranted, and promised to take every step to protect both the next stamp distributor and the stamps from possible violence. He was sure that General Gage's guarantee of military aid would be unnecessary, but he was ready for all eventualities. Most of all, he wanted approbation of his conduct and clear instructions from British authorities.[32]

But such aid and assurances never arrived and Franklin's subsequent letters to London reflected his growing anxiety.[33] In fact, he performed a delicate balancing act. On the one hand, he continued to claim that his province was an island of "Peace and good Order." At the same time, he gently reminded his superiors that he needed their help in dealing with a situation that threatened the very "Peace and good Order" of which he was so proud. The governor was able to explain his two seemingly antithetical positions by pointing the finger of blame elsewhere. "Inflammatory Publications" had been sent to New Jersey "from the neighbouring Governments," he said, "with a View of exciting in the Inhabitants of New Jersey the same Spirit of Riot & Violence which has appeared in the other Colonies." Outside agitators had stirred up the New Jersey populace, and only Franklin's "prudent Management" was keeping the situation from blowing up in his face.[34]

Franklin did his best to secure his position. He obtained the reluctant promise of Captain James Hawker to put the stamps aboard his ship the *Sardoine* whenever they arrived in America. And he continued to remind the Board that the office of stamp distributor lay vacant. While he indicated a willingness to appoint an interim distributor, he did not relish the thought. By now he knew that it would be virtually impossible to find a candidate, for the job had become "obnoxious to the People." At any rate, the governor would not make his own appointment without London's express authorization. Meanwhile he played a waiting game, hoping somehow to hold the colony together until help arrived.[35]

But as Franklin watched the agitation against the Stamp Act whirl and eddy around him, growing more powerful and attracting a larger mass of support with each passing day, his ability to control events rapidly dwindled. Rumors mingled with fact in a web of intrigue that was almost impossible for any one person to untangle. On October 3, Speaker Robert Ogden succumbed to popular pressure and called "of his own Authority," a rump session of the New Jersey assembly to gather at Robert Sproul's tavern in Perth Amboy. The extra-legal meeting designated Ogden, Hendrick Fisher, and Joseph Borden, Jr., as New Jersey's delegates to the Stamp Act congress, and the three hurried to New York for the opening ceremonies four days later. Governor Franklin watched the proceedings from Burlington, helpless to prevent either the meeting or its outcome.[36]

Six days after the Stamp Act was slated to go into effect, Franklin met with his council. He wanted to know if he should appoint an interim stamp distributor. He also needed help in guaranteeing the safety of New Jersey's stamps, which were then sitting in the harbor at New Castle on the Delaware under the protection of a man-of-war. Most importantly, he was searching for a compromise that would be acceptable to London without stirring up the populace at home. He wondered whether he might allow government officials, particularly officers of the court, to continue with their usual business so that there would not be even a temporary halt in the administration of justice. He also wanted to know if he, as a governor under oath to enforce the Stamp Act, might continue to issue customary writs and papers without affixing the stamps to any official documents. In essence, he was asking for permission to violate the Stamp Act.[37]

Six of Franklin's ten councilors traveled to Burlington to discuss New Jersey's situation. All were firm friends of the government.[38] Still, they proceeded with caution. William Alexander, whose illness prevented him from attending the session, set the tone for the meeting in a letter to Franklin. "Avoid every step," he admonished, "that can irritate or that can discover a Distrust of the good Behaviour of the People." The other members of the council agreed. They told the governor that in their opinion he was powerless either to accept William Coxe's resignation or to appoint his replacement. They also advised him against bringing the stamps ashore. And, in a thinly veiled rebuke, they criticized Franklin for turning to the military as a bulwark against potential mob action. Were Gage's troops to be called into the colony at this juncture, they were convinced that "the

Peace of the Province would be immediately broken, and nothing less than a Civil War would ensue."[39]

Not knowing what else to do, Franklin followed his council's advice to the letter. He did not even admonish his advisers for their failure to address the thorny issue of carrying on business as usual without using the stamps. He himself was convinced that the colony "might legally go on with Business in the usual Way," but he knew that the members of the council were afraid to incur the wrath of either the ministry or the people. Without the council's support, Franklin, too, was afraid to act. And so affairs continued to drift.[40]

The governor made only one decision as a result of the meeting, and this reluctantly. He agreed to a session of the assembly upon the request of the speaker and nine other representatives, even though he "had no particular Commands of the Crown, or other Business" to discuss. He clearly wanted to avoid addressing the legislature on the subject of the Stamp Act. He could not bring himself to question Parliament's authority to pass the act, but it would "answer no good End whatever to attempt to reason with the People in their present Temper." He could hardly refuse to call the assembly, but he could at least place the burden for the special session on someone else's shoulders. This would obviate the need for him to make an opening speech to the legislature. As he smugly explained to his father, "I have Nothing to do when they let me know they are met, but to tell them that I am ready to receive anything they may have to Communicate."[41]

Franklin was floundering. His main concern was to avoid any action that would incur the wrath of his colony or the ministry. As a result, he did almost nothing at all. He watched with horror as other governors became the objects of mob violence, and he was determined that he would not be treated similarly. He vainly continued to seek advice from London. And he even complained to his father, who remained strangely silent in this period, of the lack of direction he received.[42]

He could scarcely conceal his anxiety as he plied Whitehall with his letters. On the thirteenth, and again on the thirtieth of November he informed the ministry of the gradual distintegration of the government's position and begged the authorities to replace William Coxe. He continued to maintain that New Jersey was the victim of "seditious Inflammatory Writings" as he indicated that the "Infection" afflicting the neighboring colonies had at last spread to the once healthy province of New Jersey. Even the most prudent management had not immunized the province from the disease of lawlessness and rebellion, although he was proud to say that his efforts had minimized the damage.[43]

Franklin seemed to have abandoned any attempt to control New Jersey's political affairs, directing what little energy he had to protecting his own reputation. "I have had," he told his father, "a difficult Part to manage so as to steer clear of giving any Umbrage to the People here, and of embarrassing myself with the Ministry in England." He felt that his letters to the Pennsylvania papers had effectively quieted his detractors from that quarter. And when Robert Ogden became the object of popular wrath for refusing to sign the petition drawn up by the New York congress, the governor was unabashedly delighted. So long as Ogden was being burned in effigy in nearly every town in East Jersey, Franklin felt reasonably assured that he himself was not in any immediate danger. Still, his day of reckoning was coming. At the end of November he finally faced a hostile assembly. He had postponed the session as long as he could, but delay was no longer possible.[44]

When the governor described the meeting to his superiors, he portrayed himself as a resolute defender of royal prerogative. He claimed that his first instinct had been to dissolve the session immediately. He restrained himself, he said, only because to do so would have thrown New Jersey into the "utmost Confusion."[45] In fact, Franklin did not risk a direct confrontation with the assembly. He worked behind the scenes, garnering information about the rump session and trying to persuade sympathetic legislators to censure those who had attended the extralegal meeting. But he refused to make any official statement that would antagonize the assembly, and he turned the initiative over to the representatives. They had wanted the meeting and he had called it. He would have nothing more to do with the proceedings. As he had told his father earlier, governors Bernard and Colden had ignored political reality in Massachusetts and New York and, "by an unnecessary Officiousness" had only made matters worse. Franklin did not intend to make the same mistake. He may have been willing to risk his neck for a cause that had some chance of succeeding. But, he argued, "for any Man to set himself up as an Advocate for the S＿＿P Act in the Colonies is a meer Piece of Quixotism, and can answer no good Purpose whatever." William Franklin did not relish tilting at windmills. His devotion to principle was always tempered by a realistic assessment of his position. And so, he sat back and let the leaders of the Stamp Act opposition take charge.[46]

On the second day of the session, Robert Ogden tried to explain his refusal to sign the petition composed by the Stamp Act congress, arguing that "separate Addresses" from the colonial legislatures would be more useful than a petition from an extra-legal congress. The New Jersey representatives were singularly unimpressed by Ogden's logic, and so the Speaker submitted his resignation. After an hour's desultory discussion, the house unanimously accepted Ogden's offer, replacing him with East Jersey proprietor Cortlandt Skinner. Its first objective easily accomplished, the assembly then voted approval of the Stamp Act congress petition, and went on to enact a separate petition of its own.[47]

Only at the session's end did Franklin publicly shake himself from his lethargy, delivering a stern but disingenuous lecture before dissolving the legislature. While he found it "painful" to fault the assembly, he thought it would be "unjustifiable both to his Majesty and the People" to avoid signifying his disapproval of its conduct. He berated the members for their "late unprecedented, irregular, and unconstitutional Meeting" at Perth Amboy, and pretended surprise that the legislature had not rebuked its members for calling the "unnecessary" session.[48] While he castigated the assembly in "pretty strong Terms," his speech was clearly designed to put his opinions on record so as to avoid a "Precedent for such kind of Meetings." He had to show London that he was upholding the King's prerogative. Moreover, he was personally damaged by the rump session because it seemed to give "a Sanction to the villainous Reports" lodged against him by the Pennsylvania proprietors.[49]

Having defended himself, and in the process offended his detractors in the house, the governor attempted to find some common ground with New Jersey's representatives. He seized upon the one assembly resolution that he could endorse without equivocation, using the legislators' own words in appealing to them to "calm and heal all Animosities and Divisions, to support the Authority of Government, and to preserve the Peace and good Order of the Province." And he reminded them that he, more than they, was concerned with defending the British constitution. As a servant of both Crown and colony, his was a more disinterested perspective. He knew that "every Breach of the Constitution, whether it proceeds from the Crown or the People, is, in its Effects, equally destructive to the Rights of both," And he promised to "be equally careful in guarding against Encroachments from the one as the other." As Franklin saw it, it was his duty to mediate the differences between London and the colonies, between rulers and subjects, and to defend the constitution from attacks on either side. But his brave words had a hollow ring. Everyone knew that the governor was utterly incapable of forcing either the Crown or the assembly to uphold the constitution.[50]

There was little that Franklin could have done to alter the course of events. By at least attempting to find some *modus vivendi* between himself and the house, and by refusing either to defend or attack the Stamp Act, he no doubt felt he had managed affairs as prudently as anyone could expect. Nevertheless, parliamentary taxation had cost him at least the temporary support of the legislature, and unless one side or the other altered its course, his duty was destined to become increasingly difficult to perform. For really the first time in his life, William Franklin was on his own.

He had been ignored by the ministry and directly opposed by his assembly. Even his father, upon whom he had always been able to rely in times of crisis, appears to have given him little advice or comfort.

By the beginning of January 1766 the governor had to admit that the Stamp Act was unenforceable.[51] But he blamed Parliament and even the ministry, more than his own countrymen, for the failure of government policy. Parliament had erred, he thought, in delaying the Stamp Act until November 1, giving opponents time to mobilize public opinion against taxation. Had the Act gone into effect immediately, he believed that at least in New Jersey it would have been obeyed. He reminded Grey Cooper, the Treasury Secretary, that the principal people in the colony had been initially "disposed to acquiesce" to Parliament, even though they found aspects of the Stamp Act "grievous." No one, said Franklin thought taxation was constitutional. Americans were divided only by the means they chose to combat the obnoxious legislation. One side, egged on by the "seditious and inflammatory Pieces published in the neighboring Governments," advocated violence and lawlessness to secure its ends. The other preferred to make "proper application for redress." Franklin condemned the excesses of some of the Stamp Act's opponents, but he did not dismiss their grievances. At the same time, he took some credit for the relative quiet of New Jersey. He pointed out that his severest critics had accused him of giving his assembly a "Dose of Poppies and Laudanum" in order to lull its members into inactivity. While dismissing such insinuations, Franklin was obviously proud of them. Still, he was convinced that even with the best management, he could not contain the situation much longer. It was clearly up to England's legislators to find some honorable means to defuse the crisis.[52]

Franklin created the impression that opposition to the Stamp Act was nearly universal. He presented the colony in a positive light, placing the blame for violence and lawlessness on the shoulders of Parliament, notorious malcontents, and the excesses of the neighboring colonies. There was blame enough for everyone—everyone, that is, but William Franklin. While he could do little to control the actual tide of events that threatened to overwhelm him, he could still put the best face possible on affairs.

But, appearances were not everything, and the governor knew it. By February, he faced the distinct possibility that New Jersey would begin to transact its business without using the hated stamps. The courts were virtually at a standstill; debtors were refusing to pay their creditors, and there was "almost a total Stagnation of Business at the Publick Offices." If the government did not act quickly, Franklin would not even hazard a guess as to what calamities might next befall himself or his colony.[53]

In fact, Parliament did repeal the Stamp Act on February 22, and the King approved the decision the next month. Unofficial word of the repeal began to trickle into the colonies in April. Franklin was elated when he learned that his father had spoken out publicly against parliamentary taxation in a four-hour audience before the House of Commons. The news also delighted Ben's American friends, for it helped combat the chronic rumors that he had supported, even authored, a piece of legislation that was repugnant to nearly everyone in the colonies. No one was prouder of Ben's effort than William Franklin.[54]

Only the knowledge that he had earned his father's disapproval spoiled William's happiness. For in April, just as it became apparent that he had survived the Stamp Act crisis with his property and reputation intact, William received a stinging rebuke from his father for his public attempt to defend himself from his critics in Philadelphia nearly a year earlier. Ben could not understand why his son had let himself be drawn into a quarrel with his proprietary opponents. He feared that William's meddling would weaken his own case for royal government. Moreover, he thought his son had lowered himself by quarreling with members of the proprietary party. In trying to save face, he told William, he had ended in losing it.[55]

William had already felt the pain of dealing with his first crisis as governor without much guidance from his father. Ben's disapproval was especially hurtful to a man whose tender ego had been bruised by the events of the past year, and whose confidence had already sunk to a low level. He reacted angrily, telling Ben that it was impossible to judge American affairs "at so great a Distance" or "to be acquainted with every Circumstance necessary to form a right Judgment of the Expediency or Inexpedience of particular Transactions." He was convinced that it was always best to "nip in the Bud every Report which may tend to hurt a man's Character or Interest." Moreover, his actions had been necessary for his very survival. "Had it not been for the Paper I publish'd in Answer to the Lodge-Paper," he assured his father, "I should have had my House pull'd down about my Ears and all my effects destroy'd." He was not, he insisted, meddling in the affairs of Pennsylvania. Rather, he was attempting to "fix a Brand of Infamy" on men who had tried to destroy his good name. This he would have done "had the Officers of New York, or any other Colony, given the like Occasion." Besides, he said almost plaintively, "All my Friends in every Part of the Province have approv'd my Conduct." Why, he seemed to be asking his father, can you not do the same?[56]

William was particularly stung by his father's insinuation that he had sullied his own reputation by engaging in mud-slinging with his opponents. No man, he protested, should consider the kind of slanders put forth by the Pennsylvania proprietors below his notice. "On the whole," he argued, "I am of Opinion that it is best at all Times, but more especially in Times of Ferment and Confusion, for a Man to *lower himself* a little, rather than let *others lower* him." He reminded his father of Thomas Hutchinson, who "thought it beneath him" even to acknowledge the "Intrigues" of his enemies. His house was destroyed and his life endangered, all as the result of false pride. Surely his father, himself the master of expedience, would not wish such painful consequences upon his son. Especially when it was so easy to avoid them![57]

Despite the argument with his father, the spring of 1766 proved to be comparatively pleasant. By May, official word reached the colony that the Stamp Act had been repealed, and William and his wife basked in the glow of patriotic feeling that washed over New Jersey in the wake of Parliament's decision. Once again Franklin could convincingly argue that no difference existed between the needs of the empire and the interests of America. It was with profound joy that he hosted an "elegant entertainment" at Burlington in honor of the repeal. Bonfires blazed; nineteen toasts—including one to Benjamin Franklin—were drunk; and the city was "handsomely illuminated," as everyone gathered to celebrate the colonial victory. Like his father, William sanguinely believed that the Stamp Act had been an unfortunate aberration which, once disposed of, would never recur. Indeed the relatively quick response to colonial objections proved to both men that King and Parliament had the best interests of the colonies at heart.[58]

Franklin remained optimistic until June, when the assembly met at Perth Amboy under much more congenial conditions than it had faced six months earlier. This time the governor was not reluctant to face the legislators, as he offered them his heartiest "Congratulations on the happy Termination of this most Important Affair." Characterizing the Stamp Act repeal as "kind & indulgent," he implied that London had earned the loyalty of its recalcitrant children. He also complimented the lower house on the relative peace that had been maintained in the colony during the protracted struggle over parliamentary taxation. "No Act of Outrage or Violence, no Hurt to Person or Property, has been committed by the Inhabitants of this Province," he said. And he assured the legislators that he would make their "prudent Behaviour" known in England.[59]

"Happily," he proclaimed, "the Storm which for some Time past raged so violently as to threaten the future Welfare of Great Britain and her Colonies, is at length subsided." He continued stronger than ever in his belief that England and America were united in spirit, interest, and goals. And he welcomed a future that promised an "indissoluable Union of the

Hearts of all the King's Subjects in the Bonds of mutual Affection, so that there may remain no other Contention among them, but who shall exceed the other in contributing to advance the general Interest, Happiness, and Glory of the British Empire."[60]

These were noble sentiments, but the assembly's response was not at all what the governor expected. The legislators had waited a long time to answer Franklin's dressing down at the close of the November session, when he had prorogued the assembly without allowing it to speak in its own defense. They had not forgotten his "unmerited Censure of their Conduct," and they intended to have their say. They were especially determined to defend the rump session at Perth Amboy. The unusual temper of the times, they insisted, had made the extraordinary meeting necessary to preserve the "Peace, Quiet, and good Order of the Government" for which Franklin had just praised them. "The Members thought so then, they think so yet, and" they added defiantly, "had the Legislature been called, this Meeting had not happened." Clearly this was not going to be the amicable session Franklin had envisioned.[61]

Stung by the assembly's rebuke, the governor was too proud to let the matter drop. Eight days later, he responded to the attack. Ignoring the legislators' expression of gratitude to the King for the repeal of the Stamp Act, he continued his argument with the lower house. Using all the debating tricks he had learned at the Middle Temple, he seemed to relish the chance to score points. Once again he emphasized the unconstitutionality of the rump session, pointing out that its participants had in fact overturned the unanimous decision of a duly elected assembly when they had voted to send representatives to the New York congress. This kind of precedent, he insisted, had to be condemned. Otherwise the assembly's power would be worthless. "This is the Door you are opening," he proclaimed, "to let in sure Destruction to the Constitution."[62]

The debate quickly disintegrated. The lower house accused the governor of meddling in its affairs, and showing off his "Abilities in Controversy" at its own expense. Resentful of the "ill Treatment" he had received, and clearly shaken by the assembly's hostility, Franklin abruptly dismissed the legislature a little over two weeks after the unhappy session began.[63]

By the end of June, New Jersey had returned to its former quiescent state, and Franklin could be excused for assuming that the short-lived turmoil surrounding the Stamp Act crisis had been a mere ripple on an otherwise calm sea. While he recognized that America's "pretended Patriots" had seized upon the Declaratory Act as a pretext to launch further protests, he assumed these agitators were unprincipled demagogues, actuated by a "mere Propensity to Mischief." All-in-all, Franklin was sanguine. His friends were convinced that he had done nothing to lose the affection of New Jersey's inhabitants; indeed they thought him to be the "darling of the World." The governor was inclined to agree.[64]

Franklin settled easily into his old routine, purchasing silver, china, and the "best Green Tea" to help him in his duties as New Jersey's official host. He even began to inquire after the welfare of his son Temple, an indication that he was considering putting his personal as well as his political affairs in order. He was relieved that the unpleasantness of the past was over. He thought he had handled the Stamp Act crisis with just the right balance between undue harshness and inappropriate leniency. "I have," he boasted to his father, "come off with Flying Colours in the Brush I had with my Assembly." But while Franklin was more secure in his position than many other royal governors, his memory of recent events was highly selective. While he survived his first government crisis without serious damage, he could scarcely give credence to his inflated claims. Indeed he owed thanks both to Parliament for repealing the Stamp Act, and to New Jersey's essential conservatism for his comparative good fortune. And while the Stamp Act crisis had concluded satisfactorily, it had laid the groundwork for future conflict. William Franklin's reaction to the controversy foreshadowed his responses to the protracted series of disagreements that would eventually destroy the empire.[65]

The Stamp Act crisis illustrated the inherent weakness of even the most able and sympathetic royal governor. Lord Shelburne had warned Franklin that "the ease and honor of His Majestys Government in America will greatly depend on the Temper and Wisdom of those who are entrusted with the Administration" of the colonies. It was a good administrator's task to regulate his colony "by Just and liberal Principals suffering no Encroachment on the one hand on His Majestys just and lawfull Prerogative, on the other hand beholding with Pleasure the prudent & decent Exercise of that Freedom which belongs to the People." But the argument over parliamentary taxation indicated that Shelburne's view was myopic at best. Franklin had not been able to prevent London from embarking upon unwise and dangerous policy. Nor had he been able to stop the colonists from countenancing extra-legal activity to protest that policy. As Crown representative, he was responsible for enforcing unpopular government dictates, and consequently he drew the opprobrium of the assembly for doing the job he had been appointed to perform. Yet he received no backing from England, no instructions, nothing to enable him to carry out an increasingly difficult task. Franklin was left alone, abandoned, it seemed, from above as well as from below, a mere victim of events.[66]

William Franklin did not relish his helplessness. He was a man who enjoyed order and predictability. Above all, he craved harmony. Raised by a father who constantly exhorted him to seek diplomatic solutions to every problem, he was personally inclined to seek the good-will of colleagues and friends. Moreover, as royal governor it was essential that he maintain the peace. Any indication that he was losing control of the colony, that riots and lawlessness were the norm there, would be interpreted as a sign of weakness. Failure in his first job could easily mean the end of a promising career. Thus for personal as well as for political reasons the Stamp Act crisis caused Franklin to become obsessed with maintaining order in New Jersey. He was willing to take nearly any step, try almost any plan, to achieve that all-important goal.

In this effort, Franklin could boast of his good fortune while simultaneously cursing his bad luck. As one of a handful of royal governors who was also an American, he was able to view the conflict between England and America with an eye to understanding the position of both sides. A man who appreciated London's virtues and who did not have the provincial's automatic distrust of the British ruling class, he knew that Parliament's motives were not insidious or mercenary. On the other hand, as an American who had actively defended assembly rights, he was not as quick to condemn colonial protests as were many of his English-born counterparts. He was familiar with the American insistence upon the rights of Englishmen, and sympathized with colonial objections to the Stamp Act. His ability to understand colonial views and his willingness to explain them to his superiors helped blunt some of the criticism leveled at him by his American detractors. Still, his American roots proved to be a mixed blessing, making him vulnerable to criticism from political foes in both Pennsylvania and New Jersey. His involvement in Pennsylvania politics had earned him more enmity than accrued to the average colonial governor. And because his record was so well-known in America, attacks on him and his character were probably more personal, pointed, and vicious.[67]

Franklin's desire for harmony led to one of his greatest shortcomings. His habit of searching for scapegoats was firmly established in this period, and he never abandoned it. Thus he alternately blamed English policy, William Coxe's betrayal, and outside agitators for demonstrations against the Stamp Act. He was simply unwilling to recognize the indigenous strength of the colonial protest movement. He could not believe that the anti-British sentiments that surfaced in America after 1763 had any deep or legitimate roots, or that the belief in parliamentary "tyranny" was genuine and widespread. By underestimating the force of anti-British feeling unleashed by the Stamp Act crisis, William Franklin put himself in a position where he would become increasingly unable to comprehend the colonial view. At the same time, his ability to understand the dilemma facing King and Parliament, and to reject the notion that England was purposefully conspiring to destroy American liberty, never diminished. Indeed it grew stronger with each passing year.

Finally, despite Franklin's penchant for harmony, the Stamp Act crisis revealed his willingness to lash out at anyone who questioned his motives or impugned his reputation. He could not ignore criticism, and when his back was against the wall, he became stubbornly determined to vindicate himself, his conduct, and his views. It was not an attractive side to his character, and it was one that would cause him a great deal of grief.

But in 1766, William Franklin was still malleable, and could fairly pride himself on his ability to stand squarely in the center, seeing most issues from all vantage points. For the immediate future, it was clear that he had learned a few lessons. He resolved never again to be caught in such a vulnerable position. He was determined not to let the assembly get the upper hand and assume the initiative. He would work to establish lines of communication with London and to seek the advice of his father. He had been left dangling with no one to help him, and he had found the experience unnerving. And if he was determined to win the favor of his superiors, he was also just a little more leery of those in the assembly who had made life so difficult for him during the height of the Stamp Act protest. Never again would he take the assembly's loyalty for granted. Never again would he allow himself to be taken by surprise, ignored, and even humiliated, as he had been during his first major crisis as colonial governor.

5

The Letter of the Law

". . . No Governor ever stood better with the People in general than I do at present."—William Franklin to Benjamin Franklin, October 23, 1767.[1]

"Mens Minds are sour'd, a Sullen Discontent prevails, and, in my Opinion, no Force on Earth is sufficient to make the Assemblies acknowledge by any Act of theirs, that the Parliament has a Right to impose Taxes on America."—William Franklin to Lord Hillsborough, November 23, 1768.[2]

In the years immediately following the repeal of the Stamp Act, William Franklin was as much an American as he would ever be. He enjoyed the respect of most New Jersey inhabitants and the friendship of a select few. He was more secure in his position and more optimistic about his future than he had been in either Philadelphia or London. Most of his quarrels were not with American lawmakers, but with an increasingly unbending bureaucracy in England. If William Franklin possessed a "loyalist personality" in these years, he kept it very well hidden.[3]

After 1766, Franklin began to put down roots in his adopted colony. He started to build a magnificent three-story house facing the Delaware River, and accumulated choice parcels of land outside Burlington. There he "entered far into the Spirit of Farming," realizing at last the dream he had once shared with Elizabeth Graeme. He hired an English overseer, read the latest books on agriculture, and experimented with new methods for uprooting trees and developing a more useful screw. He must have felt like a true gentleman when he acquired a park suitable for grazing one hundred deer. It was a sign that he had arrived.[4]

Franklin had his complaints. He chafed at unimaginative Americans who refused to imitate the modern farming techniques he assumed were the vogue in England. He had to send to London for a new drain plow, because the stubbornly traditional craftsmen of New Jersey would not make one according to his specifications. And he never ceased complaining that his salary was not commensurate with his needs. But although he continued to rely on his father to supplement his income, from a material perspective Franklin had few legitimate complaints.[5]

While he read with obvious pride Ben's accounts of the social whirl and political wheelings and dealings of cosmopolitan London, William did not appear to envy his father's position. He no longer dreamed of putting Great Britain "under sail" and anchoring it on American shores. He was much too busy to indulge such whimsical fancies. A colonial governor's duties were extensive, and William Franklin was a conscientious chief executive. Moreover, the penny-pinching assembly refused to provide him with a clerk, and he could not afford one of his own. Consequently he had to make copies of all his letters and assume responsibility for the most routine correspondence. It was tedious work, but he had no alternative.[6]

One of William's duties as Crown representative was to tend to the interests of the Church of England. As his father's child he had never paid undue attention to religious matters. But now he played the role of defender of the faith with quiet dignity and even some enthusiasm. When the Franklins arrived in Burlington, St. Mary's was old and in need of repairs, and the Reverend Colin Campbell was retiring after serving the parish for over a quarter of a century. Both William and Elizabeth attended services regularly and made handsome donations to the fund for remodeling the old building. Ben and William worked in tandem to bring Jonathan Odell to Burlington as Campbell's replacement, and William presided at Odell's induction ceremonies in 1767.[7]

Franklin was a solid but circumspect supporter of the Establishment. His experience in heterodox Philadelphia and the example of his latitudinarian father, prepared him to respect the religious opinions of any denomination. Even so, William ruffled a few feathers on occasion. Some New Side Presbyterians thought he used the death of Samuel Finley, president of the College of New Jersey, to attempt an anglicization of Nassau Hall. Others suspected that his grant of a charter to Queens College masked a dark design to destroy "the Interests of Presbyterians."[8] But in fact, the governor was deliberately low-key. He made no effort to stop Scotsman John Witherspoon's appointment as the new Presbyterian president of the College of New Jersey. And he assiduously ignored the controversy over the establishment of an American bishop then raging throughout the northern colonies. He no doubt agreed with his father that the "Squabbles about a Bishop" had been blown out of proportion by everyone, and he saw no advantage in entering the fray.[9]

William was most comfortable when he could eschew controversy and concentrate on practical means of serving the church. One of his pet projects was his plan for an Anglican "Corporation for the Relief of Widows and Children of Clergymen," chartered in 1769.[10] Clerics from New York, Pennsylvania, and, of course, New Jersey traveled to Burlington for the corporation's first meeting, where they heaped praises upon its founder. It thrived throughout the pre-war years, giving the Franklins ample opportunity to mingle with America's leading churchmen.[11]

Franklin's responsibilities were never confined to official functions. Both he and his wife relished their social duties, and they indulged in a constant round of visiting and entertaining during this peaceful interlude. They enjoyed the company of William Alexander and his wife; they hobnobbed with Crown officials in New York and Pennsylvania; and they spent considerable time in Philadelphia, where they visited family and friends, attended the horse races, and frequented the still-popular Dancing Assembly. Indeed whenever the Franklins traveled to William's home town, they embarked upon such "a Course of Eating and Drinking" that they had time for little else.[12]

William had personal responsibilities as well, as he assumed the role of family patriarch that Ben virtually abandoned during these years. He opened his home to his half-sister, and even to Deborah who necessarily relied upon him during the long silences between letters from her absentee husband.[13] He spread his largess widely. A barrel of flour or a few pounds here, and the promise of a job there were all gratefully accepted by members of Franklin's extended family.[14]

William also began to take a sustained, if somewhat hesitant interest in his son. Perhaps he realized that his often sickly wife would never bear children of her own. Or he may have felt secure enough at least to consider assuming full responsibility for the child he had virtually abandoned to his father's care.[15] Whether he was motivated by guilt, maturity, or a simple desire to establish a connection with the son he did not know, William inquired about Temple's progress and tentatively planned to bring him to America. He gave the possibility considerable thought, even devising a way to introduce Temple to Burlington society without embarrassment. He intended to present him "as the Son of a poor Relative for whom I stood God Father and intended to bring up as my own." He did not want Temple to suffer the ridicule he had endured because of his illegitimate birth. Nor was he willing to be known as the bastard father of a bastard son. In the end, as Ben continually postponed his own return to Philadelphia, William abandoned the effort. The pleasure he anticipated from having his son near him was in no way equal to the difficulties he would inevitably encounter if he acted on his plan.[16]

William delighted in playing the kindly benefactor to his relatives and enjoyed at least contemplating the joys of raising Temple as his own. Still, his ability to assume the patriarchal role was limited. His embarrassed financial position made him the supplicant as often as the bestower of favors, and he was always reminded of his own dependence on his father's largess. Moreover, while Benjamin Franklin may have been a negligent husband and a casual parent, he remained, after all, the head of the Franklin household, and it was his good opinion that everyone in the family desired. Even from the other side of the ocean, fear of his disapproval could make Deborah tremble. William's status was awkward and poorly defined. He was both dutiful son and surrogate father. He had to make decisions that affected the rest of the family; yet he had no power to enforce those decisions. The consequences of his anomalous position were extremely distasteful to a man who liked to know exactly where he stood in the chain of command and who wanted to control the events that touched his life.[17]

William's dual role as subject and ruler was especially painful when he faced the prospect of his sister's marriage to Richard Bache, a Philadelphia merchant of uncertain means. At first Deborah hesitated to approve the relationship, but she was soon won over to her daughter's side. William was not so easily persuaded. His own investigation of Bache's background indicated that Sally's suitor was "a mere Fortune Hunter, who wants to better his Circumstances [by] marrying into a Family that will support him."[18]

Ben had once harbored great hopes for his daughter's prospects and had even contemplated arranging her marriage to William Strahan's oldest son. Still, he was content at first to leave the matter entirely in the hands of Deborah and William. But when he learned of Bache's financial history, he tried to discourage the couple from proceeding with their plans. So far, William was at one with his father. But eventually, Benjamin Franklin decided to bow gracefully to the inevitable. His failure to dictate his son's choice of a marriage partner had not ended so badly. Perhaps this would not be a disaster, either. And so he granted Deborah full responsibility for Sally's marriage. William pretended to be "well pleased" with his father's decision, as he stiffly told Deborah that he hoped she would consider Sally's lasting happiness before she made up her mind. But he was clearly hurt by Ben's withdrawal of his authority. He quit writing to Philadelphia, did not attend his sister's wedding that October, and refused to discuss the match any further.[19]

It scarcely mattered that his father shared his disapprobation of his sister's marriage.[20] William had lost out in a power struggle with his stepmother and had endured the indignity of having his authority questioned and his advice disregarded. Worse, the controversy had provided the occasion for a brief but painful quarrel with his father. Ben had grown weary of the gossip and innuendo surrounding Richard Bache, and with the marriage an accomplished fact, he wanted an end to the discussion. He admonished William to quit listening to the idle gossip of "Whisperers and

Makebates" and he chided his son for being drawn into family alterca-
tions, an accusation William hotly denied. "On the contrary," he insisted,
"I can safely say, it has been the constant Endeavor of my Life to avoid all
such Quarrels, and I have not only pass'd over quietly what I have been
told by others, but Things of the most provoking Nature which I have seen
and heard in Person." Only regard for his father's "Peace and Happiness"
had kept him from airing his grievances earlier.[21]

Both William and Deborah always tried to present themselves to the patriarch of the Franklin family as peacemakers. Ben would not tolerate family disputes, and was likely to condemn any one who instigated conflict.
For this, if for no other reason, their quarrel soon subsided, and William
grudgingly accepted Richard Bache into the family and served as godfather
to his sister's first child. Even then he could not resist pointing out that his
nephew was "not so fat and lusty as some Children at his Time are." The
best that William would say was that he "improves in his Looks every
Day."[22]

Franklin had political as well as personal duties to perform on his father's behalf. By the end of 1766, he became convinced that David Hall
had joined the proprietary camp, and he combined with Joseph Galloway
and the Wharton family to set up William Goddard as printer of a rival
newspaper. Typically, William insisted, that he had not initiated the quarrel with Hall, claiming he had done everything possible to maintain a civil
relationship with Ben's erstwhile partner. But in the end, the printer's conduct had made a breach inevitable. "I am now quite satisfied," he explained
to his father, "that he has no Friendship for you, and is as great an Enemy
to your Side of the Question as ever Smith was." The only difference, he
said, was one of style. Parson Smith openly opposed the Franklins, while
Hall was a "mere Snake in the Grass." Having declared his enmity to Hall,
William refused all efforts to ameliorate their differences. Once he was
sure that he or his father had been misused, it became impossible for him
to forgive or forget.[23]

Despite his preoccupation with family affairs and social pleasures, William Franklin focused most of his attention on his duties as governor. In
the years following the Stamp Act crisis, his relations with the assembly ran
a relatively smooth course. He was quicker to take the initiative, more aware
of colonial needs, more willing to seek compromises and less determined to
pick quarrels with the lower house. What grievances he had were directed
most often, not at the colony's lawmakers, but at the ministry in London.
Three issues in particular disturbed his relationship with his superiors. The
Currency Act, the Mutiny Act, and the Townshend Acts were all perceived
in America as a threat to colonial automony. And any royal governor who
tried to enforce them was in for rough sledding.

Franklin's job was made especially difficult because of the growing perception in England that the colonies were deliberately challenging parliamentary authority and moving dangerously close to independence.[24] Even sympathetic ministers like Shelburne and Pitt were occasionally annoyed by the ungrateful attitude of Americans and were determined to exercise control over colonial affairs.[25] After January 1768, royal governors were under increasing pressure when Wills Hills, Earl of Hillsborough, became Secretary of a newly created American Department. An experienced and active administrator, Hillsborough was personally likeable. But he was above all a staunch and unbending defender of Crown prerogative. The new Secretary intended to observe the letter of the law, and he expected his subordinates to do the same.[26] Hillsborough's appointment was not a happy one for American interests, and it was nearly disastrous for William Franklin, whose relations with England deteriorated under his tenure.[27]

Because money was at the heart of so many of Franklin's quarrels with the New Jersey assembly, his failure to secure ministerial approval for the emission of paper currency was especially critical. His approach to the quarrel over the Currency Bill reflected his views of the relationship between his own interests, the requirements of the Crown, and the needs of the colony of New Jersey. As he saw it, a flexible currency policy would satisfy everyone. It was obviously in the governor's own interest to secure ministerial approval for the emission of paper currency. Indeed this issue more than any other gave Franklin and his legislature a common bond in the years following the Stamp Act crisis.[28]

Franklin's devotion to paper currency was due, in large part, to his obsessive desire for a permanent salary. Ever the realist, he appreciated the assembly's reluctance to relinquish its control of the purse strings. Accordingly, he offered his legislators a compromise. Convinced that penury, not constitutional principle, was his main obstacle, he hoped to induce the assembly to grant him a permanent salary appropriated from part of the interest earned by an issue of paper currency. In return, he planned to offer the house complete control of the rest of the money. Sensitive to the colonial fear that a financially independent governor would also be politically independent, he suggested that the governor be required to convene the assembly upon the request of the Speaker and a designated number of legislators. But Franklin's plan depended upon Crown consent to a currency emission.[29]

If the governor knew that his own material happiness depended on a paper money bill, he was also able to argue convincingly that such legislation served the interests of Crown and colony alike. By the spring of 1768, New Jersey's economic situation had deteriorated, and petitions from the colony's debtors flooded the assembly begging for relief. Only a healthy infusion of paper money into the economy could solve the colony's financial problems. And only a sounder economy would allow New Jersey to pay its Crown officers and support the King's troops that were stationed in its borders in the years following the Stamp Act crisis. Ministerial approval of a currency emission would serve both the colony and the mother country, proving that the interests of the Crown and the provinces were identical. But the ministry seemed unable to comprehend Franklin's logic, and in this, as in so many other areas, his efforts were wasted.

Franklin began lobbying for a currency emission in August of 1768, and at first Lord Hillsborough appeared sympathetic to his arguments. When the governor forwarded a draft of a paper money act to London, the government encouraged him to proceed, cautioning him that no assembly bill could treat colonial currency as legal tender, and reminding him that the proposed legislation had to include a suspending clause. It was with a sense of personal satisfaction that the governor stood before the house in the fall of 1769. Recounting his assiduous efforts on their behalf, he glossed over the obstacles still facing the legislators, assuring them that there was the "greatest Probability" that a properly framed act would win Crown approval. While the lawmakers thought Whitehall's terms remained "very hard," they vowed to attempt an acceptable law.[30]

The legislators were confident. The governor himself had virtually promised them victory. Moreover, Benjamin Franklin had just become New Jersey's London agent. They knew that Ben was sympathetic to the colonial desire for paper money. And because he understood "so well" the nature of the tacit agreement with Whitehall, they were even surer of success. Unfortunately, although their bill seemed to anticipate all possible governmental objections, both Franklin and his assembly were disappointed by a nitpicking Board of Trade.[31] The Board rejected the New Jersey Currency Act, insisting that because it allowed the Loan Office to accept currency for purposes of liquidation, the assembly had in effect made the money legal tender. The Governor was as furious as he was embarrassed. The Board's reasoning he exploded, was the "Height of Absurdity." And because he had assured the legislators that they would be successful if they submitted a bill according to his specifications, the ministry's decision gravely damaged Franklin's relations with the lower house. The legislators realized that his influence in London was not as great as they had imagined, and they categorically rejected his suggestion that they make another attempt to pass a money bill. So far as the assembly was concerned, the issue was dead.[32]

The home government's stubborn and legalistic approach to the Currency Act was not an aberration. The same attitude was reflected in London's attempts to secure military appropriations from New Jersey. After the Peace of Paris, England decided to maintain a force of some 7500 men in the colonies to secure order, protect the frontiers, and stop British-Americans from settling in the territory west of the Proclamation Line. While most of the soldiers were garrisoned in the West, a few remained in the East, especially in New York, Pennsylvania, and New Jersey, where they developed supply lines to the Great Lakes or the Ohio Valley. Many Americans were uneasy about the presence of the troops, imbued as they were with the Commonwealth fear of standing armies in peacetime. They suspected English motives for keeping troops in their midst, and resented paying for the army's maintenance. After the Stamp Act riots, when General Gage began stationing more of his men in the East, tensions between the King's soldiers and the civilian populace increased.[33]

With the enactment of the Mutiny Act in the spring of 1765, the colonists became even more distrustful of Crown policy. The Act demanded that each colony furnish suitable quarters for the troops, insisting that the King's men be supplied with specific items, including bedding and cooking utensils, firewood and candles, and beer, cider, or rum. It also required that all commissions for purchasing supplies be granted by the governor, not the assembly. These provisions were a constant bone of contention between the assembly and the ministry, and Franklin was in the middle of the quarrel.

Franklin was caught between two implacable foes, appreciating the views of each, but finding it impossible to persuade either to budge an inch in the direction of the other. A former army man, he prided himself on his ability to provide for the soldiers entrusted to the colony's care. As governor, he had to answer for the assembly's disobedience, and he was irritated on more than one occasion by legislative parsimony. Moreover, his own father had a small hand in drafting the Mutiny Act. Ben had anticipated no colonial opposition to the Act, and at first neither did his son.[34]

Still, William understood colonial complaints that the quartering policy fell more heavily on some colonies than on others. He hated any quarrel with his assembly, and dreaded instructions that threatened to precipitate acrimony. Moreover, he himself chafed at London's growing rigidity. He always preferred personal governance to bureaucratic dictate. But now he faced miserly selfishness and obstinacy from one quarter, and an overbearing bureaucracy from the other.

Before the passage of the Mutiny Act, New Jersey was one of the least troublesome of His Majesty's colonies. But as early as the spring of 1766, the picture began to change. In and of themselves, the presence of troops in the province made Franklin's task more difficult. Battalions often appeared at "short notice" demanding to be fed and quartered. Irate citizens took the law into their own hands, assaulting the King's officers when they dared to search out deserters or recruit American "volunteers" to fill their

ranks. Franklin himself grew more than a little irritated by the unreasonable demands of some officers, especially when they made light of his own
military experience and treated him, a royal governor, as a "mere" American. And there were even instances when the troops fulfilled the gloomy
predictions of the Commonwealth men, turning on the citizenry they were
ostensibly paid to protect.[35]

Such was the case on the night of July 27, 1767, when the men of the
28th regiment, whose troops had a deservedly bad reputation in the American colonies, turned their weapons on the sleepy little town of Elizabeth.
Just as the regiment prepared to quit the colony for good, its members
went on a midnight rampage. They marched through the village, breaking
windows, attacking the courthouse and jail, and hammering down the doors
of some of the public buildings. A wholesale brawl ensued. Amazingly, although the soldiers were armed with fixed bayonets, no one was killed. And
by four o'clock the troops were aboard ships headed for Amboy. Eventually
the ring leaders apologized to the civil authorities, paying £25 each to compensate the town. But many New Jersey inhabitants muttered darkly that
the punishment was grossly inadequate.[36]

Franklin's biggest problem, the one that put him squarely in the middle
of a seemingly unending quarrel between Crown and assembly, was precipitated by the ministry's insistence on strict colonial compliance with the
Mutiny Act. The first sign of serious trouble occurred in 1766, when the
New Jersey assembly enacted, and the governor reluctantly approved, a bill
for furnishing "Firewood, Bedding, Blankets & such other Necessaries as
have been heretofore usually furnished to the several Barracks within this
Colony." Franklin claimed that he did his best to convince the legislators
"to insert the very Words of the Act of Parliament" in their bill, "But it
was to no Purpose." For once the assembly seemed less concerned with saving money than it was with constitutional principle. Following the lead of
the New York legislature, the representatives characterized the Mutiny Act
as "virtually as much an Act for laying Taxes on the Inhabitants as the
Stamp Act." The lower house decided to avoid compliance by refusing to
follow the letter of the King's regulations, thus appearing to provide supplies as a free gift.[37]

Despite Franklin's efforts, he continued to be caught between an unbending bureaucracy and a stubborn assembly. Neither side would budge.
In the spring of 1767, the lower house again refused to abide by the specific terms of the Mutiny Act, even when the governor offered the legislators a compromise that would have given them all real power over military
appropriations if they only consented to obey parliamentary dictate. That
fall, the governor received a stern letter from Lord Shelburne, Secretary of
State for the Southern Department, disallowing the previous year's supply

bill and rebuking the assembly for failing to render "exact and complete obedience to the Mutiny Act." Shelburne instructed Franklin to force the assembly to observe the letter of the law. The governor was not convinced that the legislature would accede to his pressure. Nor was he persuaded that New Jersey was in the wrong. Franklin tried to make Shelburne understand the colony's perspective. He insisted, with a little dissimulation, that the troops stationed in New Jersey had never complained about their provisions.[38] Indeed, "many of them acknowledg'd they were better accommodated here than they had ever been at Barracks in Europe." Surely, he argued, a satisfactory end was more important to His Majesty than the means used to achieve it. Moreover, Franklin thought the colonists' position had merit. It was, he argued, "the Inequality of the Expense, more than the Expense itself" that was so troublesome.[39]

Typically, the governor offered a solution. He suggested that the Crown apply some of the money collected from quitrents and duties on trade to the expense of quartering the troops. This would equalize the burden, removing it from the Middle Colonies. If everyone benefited from the protection of the King's troops, then everyone should contribute to their maintenance. It is hard to know how seriously Franklin took his own proposal. It had many drawbacks. The revenue from quitrents was relatively insignificant, and money collected by customs officials was paltry. Moreover, the governor did not even allude to the issues of taxation or Crown prerogative. Franklin was interested in avoiding conflict, not in stirring it up. Significantly, his "solution" removed the burden of providing for the King's troops almost completely from New Jersey's shoulders. For Franklin, this, more than the issue of equality was no doubt at the heart of his proposal. But whatever the governor's intentions may have been, his suggestion fell on deaf ears.[40]

Meanwhile, something had to be done to meliorate the situation, for if the 1766 bill had been disallowed, the 1767 bill would certainly meet a similar fate. Unfortunately, the news from Whitehall promised nothing but continued trouble. This was especially true after January of 1768, when Lord Hillsborough, became Secretary of State for colonial affairs.

The new Secretary lost little time in informing Franklin that he expected New Jersey to comply with every detail of the Mutiny Act. And in April, when the assembly met at Perth Amboy, the governor urged its members to adhere to the wishes of the King-in-Parliament. But while the legislators enacted a Quartering Bill, they once more ignored the Mutiny Act, refusing even to consider any of the council's proposed amendments to the legislation. Money bills, they explained, could not be amended. If the King was jealous of his prerogatives, the assembly was equally insistent on preserving its rights. As usual, Governor Franklin was caught in the middle.[41]

Strangely, William did not appear overly concerned. While he knew that the supply bill was not "exactly conformable" to the law, and he anticipated that the ministry would reject it, he continued to defend the legislation, insisting that "the only Difference indeed is about the Mode, not the Essentials." He clearly thought Whitehall would be well-advised to abandon its legalistic quibbling and he was confident that he had handled the matter conformable to his duty. He anticipated no serious reprimands from Hillsborough or anyone else.[42]

In November he was shocked when he received not only the expected news that the 1767 supply bill had been disallowed, but a stinging personal attack on his conduct from Lord Hillsborough. Franklin was dismayed that the ministry had seen fit to "Adominish" him, and he was devastated by the King's "Disapprobation." While he insisted that he never intended to disobey Parliament, he pleaded for a modicum of flexibility. Franklin was bewildered by a condemnation that seemed fundamentally unfair. He had consented to the act of 1767 before he learned of the disallowance of the 1766 bill. He had taken great pains to compare the New Jersey legislation with a similar supply bill passed in New York and approved by the Board of Trade, and he had found the New Jersey bill superior in every way. He had used public pressure and private diplomacy in an admittedly futile attempt to induce the assembly to conform to the Mutiny Act. By signing the bill, he had at least guaranteed provisions for the royal troops for another season. What more, he wondered, could he have done?[43]

He had almost no patronage power. He was at the mercy of the house for his pitifully small salary. Dissolving the assembly would only anger the voters, encouraging them to return an even more recalcitrant set of representatives at the next election. His options, as he saw them, were nonexistent. Frustrated, he delivered a word of warning, indeed almost an ultimatum. "Let the Event be what it may," he told Hillsborough, "I shall never Venture again to give my Assent to any Act of the like Nature, without positive Orders for the Purpose." He would no longer be the whipping boy for administrators who would second-guess him in London. If he had felt ill-used by the assembly during the Stamp Act crisis, he now felt abused by his superiors at home.[44]

Fortunately for Franklin, the quartering issue proved less intractable after 1769. Parliament altered the Mutiny Act, rendering it somewhat easier for the assembly to obey. And in 1769, and again in the following year, the assembly was relatively compliant, appropriating the funds Franklin requested, even while it continued to deny the King's army the items specified in the Mutiny Act. In the fall of 1770, the governor even won a major concession from the legislators. Because their own barracks masters had squandered the colony's resources in the past, the assembly finally authorized Franklin to commission his own suppliers. William was elated, and was determined to prove that the legislature's confidence in him was not misplaced. The incident convinced him that the public interest was best guarded by granting the governor more power. It also rekindled his suspicion that money rather than principle was the top priority for most New Jersey legislators. For the moment, the issue had abated, and Franklin could correctly feel that he had preserved a solid working relationship with the lower house. Unfortunately, to please the assembly in these troubled times was almost invariably to displease London. It was a dilemma that plagued all colonial governors in pre-revolutionary America, and it was one that particularly troubled a peace-loving man like William Franklin.[45]

The issues of paper currency and military support were fought out alone between New Jersey and the home government. But there was another difficulty facing Franklin in these years, one that he shared with other governors, and that in turn drew New Jersey more tightly into the web that would eventually bind all the colonies together. The Townshend Acts, intended to raise revenue in America by levying duties on designated imports, also envisioned a reorganization of the customs service and the expansion of the vice admiralty courts. From the colonial perspective, the Acts were yet another instance of taxation without representation. Because New Jersey's level of imports was relatively low, it felt the effects of the new legislation less acutely than its neighbors. Still, it was clear from the beginning that an imperial crisis was brewing, and William would not be able to ignore it completely.

There is no evidence that any of the colonial agents opposed Townshend's proposals when they were discussed in Parliament. Ben was so little alarmed that he did not even mention them in his correspondence. At first, American reaction was similarly low-key. There were some efforts to boycott British manufactures. And John Dickinson of Pennsylvania began turning out his "Letters from an American Farmer," arguing that Parliament could regulate but not tax the colonies. Typically, it was Massachusetts that provided the spark igniting American protests and precipitating the events that put William Franklin on a collision course with Lord Hillsborough.

At the beginning of 1768, the Massachusetts legislature wrote to the other provinces attempting to organize American resistance to the Townshend Acts. Unfortunately for Franklin, the New Jersey assembly was sitting in Perth Amboy when the Massachusetts letter arrived, and Speaker Cortlandt Skinner laid it before the legislators on April 15. The next day a committee was appointed to draft a reply, after which the representatives went on to other, presumably more important business.[46]

Skinner did not show the Massachusetts letter to the governor, but when Franklin found out about it on his own, he immediately made inquiries about the assembly's plans. His sources assured him that New Jersey's response, if any, would take the form of a humble—and legal—petition to the King asking for repeal of the Townshend duties. Satisfied that the legislature would not embarrass him, he let the matter rest. He was incapacitated by illness throughout most of the session, recovering in time to prorogue the assembly on the tenth of May. Only when he perused the minutes of the spring meeting, did he discover that the legislators had approved a petition to the King and had sent it directly to the colony's London agent.[47]

Even while the assembly was preparing its petition, Lord Hillsborough was dashing off instructions to the colonial governors commanding them to exert their "utmost influence to defeat this flagitious attempt to disturb the Public Peace." But the instructions arrived in June, too late to be of any use. Franklin was unnerved by Hillsborough's directive and did his best to shore up his defenses. He wrote immediately to the Secretary, admitting that his assembly had already sent a petition to the King. But he insisted that the legislators had not answered the Massachusetts letter, and that there was no "Disposition in the People of this Colony to enter into any unwarrantable Combination" with the Bay Colony.[48]

Franklin was nearly overwhelmed by panic in July when he discovered that Cortlandt Skinner had indeed sent a letter to Massachusetts, expressing New Jersey's approval of the Bay Colony's initiative. The governor was furious. He was particularly hurt by Skinner's duplicity, for Franklin had not been given the "least Intimation" that a response to the Massachusetts effort was even being considered. The best that he could do now was lamely to assure Lord Hillsborough that he thought New Jersey had no intention of "uniting farther" with the other colonies. But the damage had already been done.[49]

Franklin may have been angered by the assembly's underhanded methods, but he was confident that New Jersey's intentions were not subversive. The ministry was not convinced. Lord Hillsborough lost no time informing the governor of the King's "concern." In the same letter that contained the King's disallowance of the 1767 Quartering Act and the King's personal condemnation of Franklin for assenting to the bill, the Secretary berated the governor and his assembly for what appeared to him as a blatant assault on parliamentary supremacy. He argued that the legislators' petition sought "to draw in Question, the Power and Authority of Parliament to enact Laws binding upon the Colonies in all Cases whatever." And, he pointed out, Franklin could not use his usual alibi and blame New Jersey's neighbors for leading the colony astray. For this time, New Jersey had been at the forefront of the "rebellion."[50]

The Secretary reserved the worst of his pointed barbs for governor Franklin himself. Hillsborough harshly condemned him for his "entire Ignorance of what was passing in the Assembly." The Massachusetts initiative had been, he lectured, "the constant Object of their Deliberations almost from Day to Day for a Course of more than three Weeks" and to be unaware of this was to be "very blameable" indeed. More outrageous was Franklin's myopic observation that the assembly did not intend to enter into any "unwarrantable Combinations" with the other colonies. This, said Hillsborough sternly, "indicates a Disposition that does not correspond with those Principles which ought to be the Rule of your Conduct."[51]

Nothing that Franklin had done seemed to please the prickly Secretary. While he was perusing the assembly's minutes, Hillsborough had noticed that Franklin had laid some of his own "Letters and Papers" before the house. He professed to find nothing in his correspondence that was "either necessary or proper to be laid entire before the Assembly." It seemed clear that the governor had violated the Secretary's confidence and had weakened and demeaned his own office. It was the first time that Franklin had been censured by the home government, and it was a painful experience, particularly when it came at the end of a letter fairly reeking of the ministry's displeasure.[52]

William Franklin struck back. In a rambling, sometimes incoherent and always furious letter to Lord Hillsborough, he defended himself against each of the Secretary's accusations. He later claimed that he expected to be removed from office as soon as his reply reached Hillsborough's desk, but he was willing to take the risk. Anything was better than suffering in silence, allowing "unmerited" accusations to go unanswered. William was determined to place his side of the story on the record so that "every impartial Person" could see that "there was not even a shadow of pretence" for the Secretary's accusations.[53]

Franklin addressed each of Hillsborough's "Animadversions and Censures" separately. He was determined that his superiors should not see New Jersey's conduct as "singular." While he did not defend the assembly's attitude toward parliamentary taxation, neither did he condemn it. It was his "firm Opinion, that there is scarce an Assembly man in America, but what either believes that the Parliament has not a Right to impose Taxes for the Purposes of a Revenue in America, or thinks that it is contrary to Justice, Equity and Sound Policy to exercise that Right." If the other legislatures had not responded to the Massachusetts circular letter by the time Hillsborough had delivered his stinging denunciation, it was only because they had not yet convened. By the end of 1768 they had drafted petitions that were at least as disrespectful as New Jersey's had been.[54]

William proceeded to lecture the ministry on its handling of a dispute which he correctly diagnosed as "of the utmost Importance to the British

Interest." Convinced that Parliament's repeated attempts to tax the colonies were ill-advised, he blamed England more than America for the hard feelings that plagued the once united empire. He pointed out that while the colonists had been unhappy with the Declaratory Act, they had nevertheless "quietly acquiesc'd in it." But the Townshend Acts had "rekindled the Flame" and had "occasioned as general Dissatisfaction and Uneasiness as ever prevailed among any People."[55]

Having passed on this "Information," the governor began an agonized defense of his honor. First he wished to point out the Secretary's "Mistakes." Franklin declared that he had not been "entirely ignorant" of the assembly's activities during the spring session. Nor had the Massachusetts letter been the "constant Object" of the legislators' deliberations. Indeed, "not the least Notice was taken" of the issue between the sixteenth of April, when it was handed over to a committee, and the tenth of May when the session ended.[56]

Franklin blamed everyone but himself for the assembly's actions. The Speaker should have informed him of the legislature's intentions. The assembly itself had acted in a duplicitous fashion. And Lord Hillsborough's instructions had arrived nearly a month after the lawmakers had packed their bags and headed for home. How, he wondered, could he have obeyed an order he had not received? And why should he have gone forward on his own, picking a fight and increasing tensions between himself and the colony's representatives? This would only have resulted in accusations from America and England alike that he had engaged in "an unwarrantable Stretch of Power."[57]

Franklin also insisted that he had never violated the Secretary's confidentiality. He had always been careful to summarize, rather than to repeat verbatim, any private messages from his superiors. But his most heated defense came in response to Lord Hillsborough's reprimand for his handling of the Mutiny Act. Franklin was deeply hurt by accusations that he had failed to fulfill one of his most important obligations to the King. He pretended to give his superiors the benefit of the doubt, hoping that their censure was the result of misinformation. At any rate, he felt compelled to repeat in tiresome detail his own view of the circumstances.[58]

By the time Franklin had finished his exhaustive diatribe, the words literally poured from his pen. His style became more convoluted. His usual conservative prose was clotted with words that were underlined and capitalized with reckless abandon, as all the frustration he had suffered because of the home government he tried so hard to serve gushed forth. Franklin's letter reveals a great deal about both his personal and professional position in the years following the Stamp Act crisis. It provides insight into his understanding of the relationship between England and America, assembly and governor. It depicts a practical man who, within certain broad strictures, was flexible and always sought the common ground between two opposing points of view. And it hints at the fears he was beginning to have that he was being singled out for punishment, perhaps because he was the son of the increasingly troublesome Benjamin Franklin.

The governor's self-defense involved, as well, a defense of the New Jersey assembly. He saw nothing inherently wrong with the decision to go directly to the King with a "humble and diffident" explanation of grievances. "Petitioning the King," he lectured his superior, "is generally deem'd an inherent Right of the Subject, provided the Language be decent." And while Franklin was eager to defend Crown prerogative, he refused to encroach upon the rights of the assembly. He recognized that the legislators had a legitimate role to play, and from a practical perspective, he had no wish to create ill will between himself and the "democratical" part of the government. He was always as careful to praise the meritorious behavior of his assembly as he was to point out its failures. It was, he argued, because he had acted upon these principles that New Jersey had "been kept so quiet during the late & present Disturbances in America." Mutual recognition and respect, not nitpicking attention to legalistic niceties, was the way to imperial tranquility.[59]

Franklin retained a belief in the basic good will of the New Jersey legislature. He did not agree with the assembly on every point, but he thought most of his quarrels with the lower house resulted from honest differences of opinion with people who were as loyal to the monarch as he himself was. He was not, he said, "one of those Governors . . . who because they happen to differ in Sentiments, or fail in carrying a Point, with an Assembly, think themselves justifiable in misrepresenting all their Actions, catching at every Trifle, & magnifying it to that Degree that it may appear a Matter of the utmost Consequence." He would not make a mountain out of the proverbial mole hill. He had made this mistake during the waning days of the Stamp Act crisis and he had learned how counter-productive such a course could be. He only hoped that the stiff-necked Lord Hillsborough would profit from the lesson he himself had so painfully learned.[60]

The governor came precariously close to sympathizing with the colonists' substantive grievances. He knew that in this case at least, miserliness alone did not explain American attitudes. For it was "not so much the Quantum of the Tax impos'd upon them, as its being imposed by a Body of Men among whom they had no Representatives" that was at the heart of the problem. And he was convinced that compromise, not force, was the only means to resolve the issue. Now that troops had been sent to Boston to enforce the Townshend Acts, William was even more disturbed. The troops might, he conceded, prevent "scandalous Riots, and Attacks on the Officers of Government." But Franklin was a good enough student of human nature in general and the American situation in particular to doubt that this was anything but a means of temporarily papering over the real problem. "Men's Minds are sour'd," he insisted, and "a sullen Discontent prevails." There was "no Force on Earth," he added prophetically, "to make the Assemblies acknowledge, by any Act of theirs, that the Parliament has a Right to impose Taxes on America." While the government might be able to control the colonists, it could not capture their hearts and minds.[61]

Franklin's letter provides a perfect picture of a man who values ends over means, results over method. What good did it do to insist on collecting the Townshend duties if this stubborn determination to uphold parliamentary authority resulted in a colonial boycott of British goods, and less money for the King's coffers? Why should he veto the assembly's supply bill when it represented an "absolute Compliance with the spirit of the Act of Parliament?" Why should the government refuse to grant the already weak colonial governors a modicum of flexibility so that they could bargain with the legislators and secure the best deal for the King? "I do not mean," he hastily added, "that Governors have, or ought to have a Power of Dispensing with Acts of Parliament." But at the same time they should be able to "consent to some small Deviation from the *Mode*, provided the *principal End* of that Act is obtain'd." Without that discretion, the governor was a mere cipher, caught between an unmovable ministry and a recalcitrant assembly.[62]

Underneath Franklin's protestations ran a thread of genuine bewilderment. He could not understand why this was happening to him. His whole record had been one of service to the Crown. He had risked his life in the royal army, served General Braddock, and helped defend western Pennsylvania "at a Time when the Indians were Spreading Desolation and Terror throughout the Province." Never before had he been faulted by King or ministry. Now he was being reprimanded for doing what had heretofore been found perfectly acceptable. Even worse he was castigated for pursuing a policy virtually identical to that followed by other royal governors. It was difficult not to regard Hillsborough's treatment as evidence of personal malice.[63]

The governor refused to suggest a reason for such animosity. But he hinted that he feared that his ties to Benjamin Franklin might be contributing to his difficulties. Thus he assured the Secretary that he had no "particular Attachment" to the assembly. His defense of its actions was merely an attempt to be impartial and to serve the empire. Although he did not say so directly, the implication was clear. His attitude had nothing whatsoever to do with any undue loyalty he may have had either to the land of his birth or to his own father. His need to defend himself, even implicitly, against possible charges that he had divided loyalties was unsettling. If he was truly afraid that he was to be judged by a different and higher standard than other royal governors, he might well try to compensate by leaning ever more strongly in the direction of defending the King's prerogative.[64]

Franklin's letter covered all the bases. From a painstaking defense of his conduct to an embarrassing plea for more money he expressed his dissatisfaction and almost invited direct reprisal from London. Had such reprisal been forthcoming, he may well have joined his father in the move toward independence. Instead, Hillsborough took no official notice of his diatribe, and Franklin continued to perform his duties as governor of New Jersey.[65]

In a way, the letter was an echo of William's angry response to Elizabeth Graeme's epistle a decade earlier. Both were products of his anger and frustration. Both had a defensive tone and were dedicated to proving that he was the highly principled target of unmerited accusations. And both stopped short of unequivocally severing the ties that bound him to an increasingly unsatisfactory relationship. If conditions demanded that ties be broken and relationships ended, he always sought to shift the responsibility elsewhere, to force someone else to make the first move. No matter how unhappy he was, William Franklin was incapable of initiating any action that would result in the destruction of the bonds that gave form and meaning to his life. And so he continued to serve the King.

6

Walking a Tightrope

"The Governor has had a very critical Part to act during all these Turmoils; and what is very extraordinary, and very much to his Honour, I never heard his Conduct arraigned in any one Instance."—William Strahan to David Hall, 1770.[1]

"My sentiments are really in many respects different from those which have yet been published on either side of the question; but as I could not expect the voice of an individual be attended to in the temper both parties were in, I for the most part kept my sentiments to myself, and only endeavored to steer my little bark quietly through all the storms of political contest with which I was everywhere surrounded."—William Franklin to William Strahan, 1771.[2]

As the turbulent sixties drew to a close, William Franklin could congratulate himself. He had been governor for over half a decade, and had survived both the Stamp Act controversy and the furor over the Townshend Acts. He had not neglected his duty to the Crown; he had tried to preserve the liberties of the assembly; and he had tended to his own interests. He was still young. He had lost none of the charm that had helped him advance so far in such a short period of time. He had grown genuinely fond of his adopted home, feeling more comfortable there than he had in either Philadelphia or London. "I may with Propriety enough, call myself a Farmer of *New Jersey*," he told the assembly. "It is here, if I return to a private station, that I propose to spend the Remainder of my Days."[3]

Indeed, his long tenure in New Jersey had made him, if anything, more likely to defend American interests and to balk at the ill-advised and often heavy-handed policy of the British government. If he was prudent enough to avoid questioning Parliament's authority, he did argue against the "impropriety" of imposing taxes in America. Even when he read that his father had publicly denied Parliament's *right* to tax the colonies, he did not seem unduly alarmed, nor did he quarrel with Ben's perspective. And William

99

continued to correspond with opposition leaders like his old friend John Temple, who objected strongly to British taxation of American imports. He even attended Princeton commencement exercises in the fall of 1770, where he knew he would have to sit through a one-sided debate on the merits of America's non-importation agreement.[4]

William Franklin longed for a renewal of America's sense of common purpose with England. He agreed with Strahan's sentiments that the "Prosperity and Security" of England and America "depend upon our Union, our firm and lasting Union." Consequently, he supported his father's attempts at constitutional reform. Ben feared that even mildly coercive measures in London would result in violence on a scale heretofore unimagined. And he assumed that the best way to avoid coercion was to move toward a more united empire. He knew that England would "never be satisfied without some Revenue from America," and he was equally certain that the colonists would not submit to parliamentary taxation. The solution seemed obvious. England and America should be consolidated, and the colonists represented in Parliament. Without such a practical adjustment of the empire's machinery, the future looked bleak.[5]

William clearly sympathized with his father's plan to secure American representation in the House of Commons, even while he saw its weaknesses. He knew, as Ben apparently did not, that American radicals would have led the opposition to such a proposal. Still, it was the kind of approach the governor preferred. It was essential that right-minded men on both sides of the Atlantic continue to search for acceptable compromises to the issues that divided the empire.[6]

Both Franklins had sound practical reasons for their desire for Anglo-American amity. By the end of the decade, father and son had become entangled in another shared venture, whose success hinged upon ministerial whims. They had become deeply involved in a series of efforts to amass huge blocks of land west of the Proclamation Line. Their motives ranged from a simple desire for profit and social position, to a hankering after political power in a newly created colony.[7] The Franklins' machinations, most of which they conducted in secret, necessitated ministerial approval, making it essential that they remain in Whitehall's good graces. At the same time, the ministry's failure to approve their plans alienated both men from a government that blocked their most cherished dreams.

William was especially frustrated. His low stipend, his chronic indebtedness, and his early attachment to the ideal of a western empire all made him yearn for success in his speculative endeavors. But the long, complicated, and ultimately fruitless effort was also instrumental in making him more conscious of the multiple, and sometimes conflicting loyalties that he had somehow to control and mold into a coherent whole. The western land projects helped him retain close ties with his father as both men worked tirelessly to secure the ministry's blessings. But while William's schemes made him more anxious than ever to do nothing that would anger his superiors, they also forced him once again to confront a wall of ministerial intransigence, making him admit that the interests of the empire—at least as they were perceived by men like Lord Hillsborough—were not always compatible with the concerns of even its most loyal American subjects. As his frustration grew, and his impatience mounted, it became apparent that William Franklin was not a rubber stamp for the administration. Indeed, whenever land speculation was involved, he was quite willing to engage in activities that directly challenged English authority.

William Franklin's interest in western land speculation was as old as his trip across the Alleghenies with Conrad Weiser in 1748. As he had forded creeks and steered his canoe through the headwaters of the Ohio River he had drunk in the sights and sounds of a totally new world, a world that represented wealth and position to any one with ability, foresight, and courage. William Franklin counted himself as one of these. Even in England, as he had prepared to return to his native America, the soon-to-become governor had mused over ways to turn his vague dreams of western empire into concrete reality. England was at peace; the French had been driven from Canada. The "extensive & more permanent Advantages" to be derived from the American West lay begging to be exploited. With his father's help and the proper cultivation of the many connections both men had in the innermost circles of the English government, nothing seemed impossible. Even the temporary ban on settlement beyond the Proclamation Line did not dampen Franklin's ardor; he saw the policy as a setback, not an insurmountable obstacle.[8]

As governor of New Jersey, he soon had a chance to practice a little of the Indian diplomacy he had witnessed as a youth in the Pennsylvania wilderness. When raiding parties crossed into New Jersey in the fall of 1763, Franklin quickly organized the militia in the western counties, stemming the tide of frightened settlers who might otherwise have abandoned their homes. He even contemplated an all-out offensive against the "Skulking Savages." To do otherwise, he argued, would only prolong hostilities.[9]

But by the end of 1765 the governor was becoming involved in a series of projects that would make him do everything possible to preserve at least the semblance of peace in the American West. His partners in these ventures included the Philadelphia merchant company of Baynton, Wharton and Morgan, old Quaker allies of his father. George Croghan, whom Franklin had met on the Weiser expedition, was also a central figure in the group. Croghan was now Deputy Indian Agent for the Northern District. The most important member of what became known as the Illinois Company was Croghan's superior, Sir William Johnson, a colorful character who resided in feudal splendor on a vast tract of land in New York's Mohawk Valley. Johnson, superintendent of all Indian policy in northern America, was a man of excellent reputation and a friend of the Six Nations. Securing his support was a major coup.[10]

William was involved in two, sometimes separate, speculative projects. One was the plan to seek compensation for Pennsylvania merchants who had endured substantial losses during Pontiac's Rebellion.[11] In 1765 the "Suffering Traders" secured the promise of a land grant west of Fort Pitt from the Six Nations in recompense for their damages. But if the group was to assume possession of the territory, the Proclamation Line had to be removed or altered. William Franklin, an underwriter for the traders, asked his father to plead their case in London.[12]

Of greater importance to both Franklins was the Illinois Company. In November of 1765, Samuel Wharton and George Croghan stopped by the governor's mansion in Burlington. They were interested in acquiring tracts of land in the Illinois country, over a million acres of sparsely populated land stretching west from the forks of the Ohio River. The governor was taken by the project, but insisted on adding his own touches to the plan. Instead of merely obtaining land, he asked, why not form a colony in the territory? Wharton and Croghan were easily convinced, and they traveled to New York to broach the idea to Sir William Johnson.[13]

By spring of 1766, the project was under way. Croghan used William Franklin's name to secure Johnson's support. And Franklin used his lawyer's skills to draw up an agreement to create the land company. He also prepared—but prudently did not sign—a masterful piece of propaganda, the "Reasons for Establishing a British Colony at the Illinois," to persuade the ministry to approve the Illinois Company's proposal.[14] Franklin extolled the virtues of this "*Terrestrial Paradise.*" It would serve as a supply base for British troops, and provide England with hemp, silk and flax, copper and iron as well as the best furs in North America. The colony could, of course, only be secured under the guidance of a governor who was "experienced in the management of Indian affairs, and who has given proofs of his influence with the savages." Did he mean George Croghan? Or Sir William Johnson? Or was he slyly preparing the way for his own appointment?[15] He wisely said no more, letting each shareholder dream of being the first governor in this western Eden.[16]

By the end of April, William was ready to ask his father to join his little group. Ben could hardly have been surprised when his son broached the subject, for he already knew that Croghan had some speculative enterprise afloat involving land deals in the Illinois country. Only the specific details remained hazy. Now William was ready to flesh out the plan, taking care to let his father know that it was he who had turned Croghan's modest proposal into a full-scale project to form a colony. And he suggested that Ben, along with a few "Gentlemen of Character and Fortune in England," should add their names to the undertaking.[17]

The elder Franklin was as enthusiastic about the project as his son, and by fall he was hard at work lobbying for the plan. He was cautiously optimistic. Lord Shelburne, Secretary of State of the Southern Department, was a friend of American expansion. And with the help of Richard Jackson, Franklin swiftly won the Secretary's lukewarm approval of the Illinois Company's proposal. The biggest obstacle was Lord Hillsborough, whose interests in Ireland made him suspicious of any plan that threatened to depopulate his own country. But William was convinced that the value of the colony to Great Britain was so obvious that even the likes of Hillsborough would eventually recognize it.[18]

While Ben was doing his part to secure ministerial approval, William did what he could for the project from his position in America. To him fell the task of keeping peace between the Indians and the white settlers of New Jersey. He wanted no news reaching London indicating that it might be wise to keep Englishmen and Indians apart. Moreover, if he harbored any hopes of being appointed the first governor of Illinois, he had to present himself as a man competent to deal with Indian affairs. Thus he listened with genuine concern when both General Gage and Lord Shelburne warned him about unsettling rumors that the colonists regularly murdered Indians without fear of legal retribution. Franklin responded with alacrity. With little help from the assembly, and even less support from western settlers, he supervised a policy resulting in the arrest, conviction, and execution of the men responsible for the murder of one Oneida and two other Indians on New Jersey's western border. By the winter of 1767, Franklin assured Lord Shelburne that "whatever may be the Case in other Colonies," in New Jersey, no crime against the natives had "been suffered to pass with Impunity." The governor had eased tensions with the Indians. This was good for New Jersey and good for the empire. It was also good for William and Benjamin Franklin.[19]

Throughout 1767, despite occasional setbacks, the partners in the Illinois Company remained confident. Ben made a pitch for the proposal at every opportunity, and he thought he had convinced everyone but the obstinate Lord Hillsborough of the value of the Illinois project. The affair proceeded at a pace that frustrated the impatient shareholders, but it proceeded nevertheless. By October, Ben thought that success was in his grasp, when he learned that the Cabinet Council had approved his plan, and only awaited the imprimatur of the Board of Trade.[20]

On October 27, Franklin, along with Richard Jackson and a group of

London merchants, appeared before the Board of Trade posing as disinterested experts willing to offer their opinions on the merits of the Illinois land scheme. They unanimously recommended the plan. At last, on December 23, the Board recommended that a new boundary line be established on America's western frontier. The scheme had worked. The machinery of the British empire had operated in its usual slow and cumbersome manner. But as always, the authorities had ultimately provided for the best interests of their subjects, in this case paving the way for making some of their American countrymen fabulously rich.[21]

But within weeks, the Illinois project received a blow from which it would never recover. Even as Samuel Wharton prepared to sail for England to help Franklin lobby for the speculators' cause, Lord Hillsborough became Secretary of State for a newly created American Department. Also president of the Board of Trade, he was now the most powerful man in England dealing directly with the American scene. In March, Ben told his son that the Illinois project had been temporarily abandoned. Both men were devastated. Once again, blind English policy had disregarded the best interests of the empire, destroying Franklin's dreams in the bargain.[22]

By April, both Lord Hillsborough and the shareholders in the Illinois Company had modified their respective positions. The Secretary agreed to move the Proclamation Line westward, and instructed William Johnson to negotiate a treaty for that purpose. The Franklins and their cohorts, discouraged by their failures, dropped the Illinois project in favor of their earlier undertaking on behalf of the Suffering Traders. Calling themselves the Indiana Company, they began to look for land in the Pittsburgh region, which they thought would fall within colonial jurisdiction after the boundary line had been redrawn.[23]

William Johnson met at Fort Stanwix, New York, with more than three thousand Indians in November of 1768 in order to verify the westward movement of the proposed boundary. Governor William Franklin was also there. Ostensibly he came as a representative of the colony of New Jersey.[24] In fact the formal treaty negotiations were a front for a full-scale land grab. Governor Franklin and some of his Burlington neighbors bought 30,000 acres of land in Albany County, New York. And the Indians sold 1.8 million acres of wilderness land to the Suffering Traders. The Six Nations ceded yet another 104,000 acres to Franklin, Croghan, and their partners.[25]

The speculators were jubilant. For the Indians had linked the formal treaty to Crown acceptance of their land cessions. If the government refused to countenance their private deals, the entire agreement would be nullified. Franklin gained personally from his three months' stay. His newly acquired land promised to make him rich. And the tribes gathered at Stanwix awarded him the title "Dispenser of Justice" in recognition of the execution of the Oneida murderers in New Jersey. This singular recognition would sit well with the assembly and would quiet the suspicions of anyone who had the temerity to wonder why the governor had spent so much time away from home.[26] So confident was William that the land sales would go forward without a hitch that he lent George Croghan a hefty sum of money based on the value of the Indian trader's newly granted lands. He was becoming so involved with the project that its failure would spell not only disappointment but financial ruin.[27]

In January, Samuel Wharton crossed the Atlantic to press for sanction of the Indiana Company's claims. Franklin hoped that Wharton's stay would be short, for he was partly responsible for the merchant's London expenses. But nothing happened quickly in London. Hillsborough remained stubbornly opposed to western expansion and was furious with William Johnson, whose treaty at Fort Stanwix had vastly exceeded his modest instructions. Moreover, ministerial infighting and the fear that any false move might result in Indian warfare caused all parties to drag their feet.[28]

As desultory discussions continued, some of the partners grew impatient. And by the summer of 1769 they decided to embark upon yet another venture, calling themselves the Walpole Company. At the end of July, its members petitioned the Privy Council for permission to purchase 2,400,000 acres of the Fort Stanwix grant from the Crown. The Board of Trade considered the petition in December, with Benjamin Franklin in attendance. Ben was astonished at Lord Hillsborough's contribution to the discussion. Why not, the Secretary asked, enlarge the request to upwards of twenty million acres? And why not include plans to turn the grant into a separate colony?[29]

The Franklins were understandably suspicious. Was the Secretary merely employing a delaying tactic? Was he toying with them and their dreams? Still, the suggestion had been made. They had already expended too much money and effort on the project to back off now. George Croghan was in serious financial trouble, and the rest of the potential investors were not far behind.[30] Besides, they knew what Hillsborough did not. They enjoyed considerable influence in the Treasury Department, and the Department's approval was essential to their plans. They decided to call the Secretary's bluff. A week after the Board of Trade met, Franklin presided over a meeting of some of the partners at London's Crown and Anchor tavern. There they formed the Grand Ohio Company (also known as Vandalia) and began to devise a request based on Hillsborough's suggestion. Once again, their fate was in his hands.[31]

In fact, the Secretary's opposition to the Grand Ohio Company was sufficient to destroy its chances for success. While Hillsborough could not kill the project outright, he simply delayed its implementation, insisting upon investigating all competing claims to the Vandalia territory.[32] The Company's supporters tried to fend off the other claimants, or, failing that, to buy them off with shares in their own venture. But this took time, and meanwhile many of them were watching their fortunes dwindle and their debts mount. Franklin, himself, was caught up in an entanglement of confusing and at times mutually contradictory land deals. His Otsego, New York, tracts—obtained at Fort Stanwix—brought him nothing but an "infinite deal of Difficulty & Trouble." And his loans to George Croghan brought him to the verge of bankruptcy, as he even considered selling his own farm in Burlington County to extricate himself from massive financial obligations. Wharton and Trent were also short of cash, and the governor would not, or could not, advance them more money. As the affair dragged on, tempers grew shorter and the Company's London lobbyists fell to blaming each other for their misfortunes. They were growing tired of the delays, tired of the project, and tired of each other.[33]

The impasse over the disposition of the Vandalia grant reflected William Franklin's prickly relationship with London officialdom, especially with Lord Hillsborough, in the late sixties. He received constant petty reminders that he was "at present out of Favour" with the ministry. When the governor suggested that Richard Stockton be seated on the New Jersey council, Hillsborough agreed, but refused to credit Franklin with the recommendation. Twisting the knife, he began signing his official letters without the pro forma expression of his "regard" for New Jersey's chief executive. This kind of behavior devastated an already insecure William Franklin, and while he pretended that it was "hardly worth mentioning," he was clearly uneasy. "There is a Meanness in this Kind of Conduct," he complained, "extremely unbecoming one in his Station." In the spring of 1769 he became convinced that his letters were being intercepted and jumped to the conclusion that Lord Hillsborough was to blame. If he had ever harbored notions of using the New Jersey governorship to launch a successful career as a Crown servant, he was watching his dreams disintegrate.[34]

In small ways and large, Franklin had a difficult time dealing effectively with the British bureaucracy. His struggle with John Hatton, customs collector for the counties of Salem, Cumberland and Cape May, is a case in point. The two men were both royal employees and by 1776 they would be loyalist allies. But in 1768 and again in 1770 they were virtual enemies. The thin-skinned governor badly needed to ease tensions between New Jersey and the empire. The activities of the ill-tempered and corrupt customs collector were calculated to undermine Franklin's position.

In the spring of 1768, John Hatton filed complaints with the governor and the Board of Customs Commissioners, claiming that Salem officials refused to help him perform his duties and had brutally attacked him when he tried to force them to come to his aid. Franklin viewed the allegations with skepticism. Hatton, he explained, was "of such an unhappy Temper" that it was almost inconceivable that he could "live long in any Place without involving himself in Squabbles with his Neighbors." Nevertheless, following the instructions of the customs commissioners, he and three of his councilors investigated—and summarily dismissed—Hatton's allegations. The governor even recommended that the collector be dismissed.[35]

Hatton refused to accept the council's decision, and appealed to the Board of Customs Commissioners, claiming that the New Jersey government had ignored his allegations out of sympathy with the colony's smugglers. Such an accusation was embarrassing to Franklin, who was sworn to secure the colony's obedience to King and Parliament. While the Board's own investigation into the matter ultimately exonerated the governor, the collector kept his job and Franklin was furious. He found it "extraordinary" that the Board had paid any attention at all to a notorious malcontent. Why had they even stooped to listen to Hatton's spurious slanders? Why would they not accept his own word that the whole matter was but a "trifling Affair scarce worth Attention"?[36]

Unfortunately, Franklin had not seen the last of John Hatton. In November of 1770 the collector, along with his son and his slave Ned, boarded a pilot boat that they claimed was laden with contraband goods. A fracas ensued; Hatton and his two assistants were "most cruelly beat, and dangerously wounded"; and when Hatton's son made his way to Philadelphia to seek help, he was assaulted once again by seven or eight sailors.[37] Hatton appealed for assistance, and Franklin issued a proclamation calling for the capture and arrest of the perpetrators. But the collector was impatient. He returned to the area around Cape May, making threats and complaining that local magistrates were interfering with his attempts to bring the smugglers to justice. In retaliation, Cape May officials issued warrants for the arrest of Hatton, his son, and Ned. Franklin was caught in the middle of a squabble that had imperial as well as provincial overtones. To support either side was to invite trouble.[38]

At first it appeared that the governor might be able to side-step the controversy altogether. Attorney General Skinner ruled that the original incident had occurred on the "high seas," and thus belonged under the jurisdiction of the admiralty court. Similarly, restitution for the assault on Hatton's son had to be sought in Pennsylvania. When the New Jersey privy council reviewed the collector's appeal, it agreed. But Hatton refused to let the matter drop, pressing for help from the customs commissioners, who prudently left the matter to local authorities. The commissioners' restraint should have pleased Franklin. But when he discovered that the Board had forwarded Hatton's complaints to the Treasury without informing him of their intentions, he exploded. The collector's criticisms, in the hands of the wrong people, could destroy whatever remained of the governor's prospects for advancement.[39]

In defending his council against the interference of British bureaucrats he attacked Hatton's character. The collector was "a Man of very unhappy, violent Temper, sometimes bordering on Madness." With more than a little hyperbole, he claimed that "I have had more Trouble with him than with all the other People in New Jersey." Typically, Franklin's defense went well beyond the bounds of necessity. He simply could not resist dredging up old grievances, going over the well-worn ground of his first run-in with Hatton, berating the commissioners for questioning his judgment and ignoring his advice at that time. William Franklin never allowed a slight to pass unnoticed, or a grudge to fade away. He was a true compromiser when it came to discussing impersonal issues or abstract positions. But he was unable to countenance an attack on his character or ability.[40]

In the end, Franklin and the council prevailed, although Hatton remained in his post until the Revolution. But the quarrels with the customs collector had drawn both William Franklin and the colony of New Jersey into an imperial controversy that both would have preferred to avoid. And the governor had firmly defended the colony's merchants against the claims of the royally appointed customs collector. Both Franklin's distaste for Hatton and his reading of the political situation made it impossible for him blindly and automatically to defend the King's officers from all aspersions. His desire to avoid the unfavorable judgment of imperial authorities made him ache simply to be left alone to deal with the colony's internal affairs. He did not want total autonomy, but a little more discretion, a bit more independence, would certainly be a welcome relief from the second-guessing to which he was constantly subjected.[41]

If Governor Franklin was finding it difficult to work with the home government in the years after the Townshend Acts crisis, he remained on relatively good terms with the people of New Jersey. This was in large measure due to the colony's moderation, but it had a great deal to do with the governor's own determination to avoid controversy. Franklin kept a low profile. He ignored the American boycott of British goods and did not risk a confrontation with the colony's representatives. He waited a full eighteen months before convening the assembly in October of 1769, for he hesitated to face the new crop of legislators that had been elected the previous year. He also wanted to avoid discussion of the Townshend Acts when he knew that Parliament was working to repeal the legislation. Only when he was certain that the Acts would soon be rescinded did he call the New Jersey legislators to Burlington.[42]

The session was amicable. Because the assembly had not met for so long, its members spent most of their time attending to a backlog of routine business. They also responded favorably to Franklin's opening remarks, taking comfort from his assurance that there were "strong Reasons" for assuming that the Townshend duties would soon be revoked. Franklin begged for a return to "that mutual Confidence and Affection" that was "so essential to the Glory and Safety of the whole British Empire." This was the rock upon which his political philosophy was based. Anything that threatened the mutuality of interest that bound the "two countries" together, also threatened his role as colonial governor.[43]

It was with considerable relief that Franklin heard the assembly accede to his plea for understanding. To be sure, the lower house insisted upon drafting a resolution thanking New Jersey's merchants for supporting the colonial boycott of British goods. But at least as important, the legislators promised that they would do nothing to separate America from England. The governor was pleased by the tone of the session. How different it had been in the waning days of the Stamp Act crisis! His success was a measure of the lessons he had learned as a result of that near debacle. It seemed to be a solid indication that his relations with the assembly were improving. And, so long as Parliament refrained from taxing the colonies, there was no reason to assume that they would not continue to improve with each passing year.[44]

The assembly session of 1770 only deepened Franklin's conviction that he was at one with the legislators, as the house met to confront an internal challenge to the establishment, when riots aimed at reducing fees and correcting alleged abuses in the legal system brought a virtual halt to the system of justice in the eastern counties of Monmouth and Essex. Talk of colonial rights, a depressed economy, and an almost instinctive distaste for avaricious lawyers all combined to stir many inhabitants of Monmouth county to protest their legal system. Voting with their feet, when elected representatives ignored their cries for reform, a sullen crowd had gathered at the court house in Freehold in July of 1769. When their ringleaders were arrested, the protestors melted away. But their complaints did not dissolve, and they had awaited the fall session of the assembly with more than their usual interest. While the legislators received a flood of petitions begging for economic relief and judicial reform, the lawmakers had done virtually nothing to satisfy their constituents.[45]

The provincial government's cavalier response prompted many frustrated East Jersey residents to return to the streets. In January 1770, Monmouth crowds were on the move. Club-wielding protestors marched into Freehold, temporarily shutting down the courts. The riots quickly spread to Newark in Essex County. There, long-smoldering conflicts between the East Jersey

Proprietors and farmers who claimed land titles based on Indian purchases inflamed the countryside.[46] When Newark authorities arrested some of the leading troublemakers, a band of nearly 150 men invaded the town and a full-scale riot was barely averted. A few days later, protestors sporting signs calling for "Liberty and Property" almost closed down the courts. While the city escaped damage, the property of East Jersey proprietor, Judge David Ogden, did not. A band of demonstrators marched on his farm in the dead of night, setting fire to two of his barns.[47]

William Franklin, New Jersey's chief defender of law and order, acted quickly. While there may have been no direct causal connection between the Monmouth and Essex disturbances, there was an understandable tendency to see them as part of a pattern of assaults on authority. Franklin summoned his council to Perth Amboy and issued commissions for a court of oyer and terminer to be held in both counties. The snow was still on the ground when New Jersey's Supreme Court justices traveled east to begin restoring order. Meanwhile, some protestors threatened to repeat their disturbances when the county courts convened in March.[48]

Determined to prevent further mob action, the governor called an early session of the assembly in mid-March 1770. The legislators gathered at Burlington in a somber mood, and the governor devoted his entire opening speech to the court riots. William Franklin's pride in his military expertise was rivaled only by the importance he attached to his education at London's Middle Temple. He had never been reluctant to display either his knowledge of the law or his ability to craft a finely honed argument. Both his oath to the King and his regard for legitimate authority inevitably led him to view the Essex and Monmouth rioters with distaste.

Governor Franklin's opening speech was short and to the point. He pretended to give the rioters the benefit of the doubt. But, he said sternly, all legitimate complaints could be resolved legally. The governor, the council, and the people's own representatives stood ready to hear their grievances. The assembly, he insisted, conveniently forgetting the lower house's recent failure to reform judicial abuses, would always "pay Attention to the Complaints of the meanest" inhabitants.[49]

The governor had serious doubts about the protestors' complaints. Always willing to attribute base motives to those who opposed him, he felt that the cries against the lawyers were simply ruses devised by those who were unable or unwilling to pay their justly contracted debts. Nor did he believe grievances were widespread. The riots were instigated by a few "factious designing Persons" whose emotional appeals had persuaded a "deluded" populace to countenance their "outrageous Behavior." Encouraged by the "Licentiousness of the Times," they were sacrificing New Jersey's reputation for their own temporary gain.[50]

Franklin's speech was a composite of some of his most firmly held beliefs. He abhorred extremism and emotionalism, and felt that all rioters were invariably "deluded," pulled hither and yon by a small group of "artful and designing" men. He always felt compelled to uphold the law, "the best Cement of Societies." If properly constituted authority was weakened, the colony's future would be dominated by "the most despotic and worst of all Tyrannies—the Tyranny of the Mob." And so he appealed to the legally constituted representatives of the people to quash an incipient rebellion of the people themselves. His quarrel was not with the legislature, whose right to exist he did not question, and to whom he looked to provide a proper balance in America's skewed version of a mixed government. His dispute was with those who, perhaps without realizing it, were proceeding along a path that would destroy that delicate balance, moving America inexorably toward anarchy.[51]

In the case of the Essex and Monmouth rioters, Franklin encountered little disagreement from the members of the assembly, many of whom were themselves lawyers, landowners, and creditors. Thus they "loudly" thanked the governor, promising that they would "ever discountenance such riotous Proceedings." With little dissent, they adopted bills encompassing nearly all the governor's recommendations. But they did little to respond to the rioters' complaints.[52]

The assembly of 1770 proved to be the last tranquil meeting with his legislators that Franklin would enjoy. Even so an ominous note was sounded at the tail-end of the session, when the lower house tried to expand its own power, proposing that the governor relinquish his practice of appointing the colony's coroners. Franklin was clearly taken aback by the suggestion. He felt particularly ill-used because he had always gone out of his way to solicit assembly recommendations whenever he had named a new coroner. The proposal threatened his already minuscule patronage. It was, moreover, an attack on Crown prerogative. But the legislators quickly receded from their request, almost chastened by the governor's strong defense of his position, and the session ended amicably. William had successfully defended both New Jersey law and the King's prerogative. The rioters were "entirely quell'd and humbled." And when the county court met in Monmouth County in April, it conducted its business uninterrupted. Even news of the Boston "Massacre" could not undo the sense of well-being that Franklin had at the close of the March meeting.[53]

Governor Franklin's position began to unravel in the spring of 1771. His duties had always demanded that he perform a delicate balancing act. Caught between King and assembly, America and England, it became increasingly difficult for him to serve two masters. He was sworn by oath to uphold the Crown's prerogative, and despite his sympathetic understanding of the assembly's place in the imperial scheme of things, he took his obligations seriously. Yet, while he sometimes remarked that the colonial legislatures were assuming "more Powers . . . than a British H. of C. would presume to do," he resented London's rigidity. Significantly, after 1771, it was more often the ministry, not the New Jersey assembly, that gave him the breathing room he needed.[54]

Most of Franklin's difficulties were rooted, as always, in New Jersey's unhealthy economic position. With money scarce in the colony and likely to remain so, tempers were short, and especially after the disallowance of the Currency Act, the colony's lawmakers were in no mood to compromise with a governor who appeared to have less influence in London than they had imagined. They came to Burlington in 1771 determined to force a show-down with the governor. David Ogden had filed for bankruptcy and resigned his assembly seat in the fall of 1770. He had never recovered from the destruction of his property during the Essex riots, and he had suffered other financial reverses as well. Consequently, he was no longer qualified to serve in the lower house. The assembly had accepted his resignation, asking the clerk for a writ calling for a new election. But by April of 1771, the governor had failed to affix the Crown's seal to the writ, and Ogden's seat remained vacant.

The issues dividing governor and legislature were fairly simple. The assembly claimed the sole right to judge its members' credentials. Ogden's declaration of bankruptcy disqualified him from the house. Hence the assembly demanded a new election. But Franklin, with the support of his council, hesitated to comply with the legislators' wishes. If, he argued, the assembly had the "uncontroulable right" to let its members resign at will, it would be "nearly the same Thing as allowing them the Power to dissolve themselves." By resigning en masse they could force the governor to issue writs for a new assembly at their command. Even the House of Commons did not have the power now casually claimed by the New Jersey assembly.[55]

It appeared to Franklin that the lower house was beginning a calculated attack on his, and hence on the King's, prerogative, and he refused to sit quietly as the legislators chipped away at the very foundations of his power. William Franklin always preferred to compromise with his adversaries. But when he was backed into a corner, he had the energy and fortitude to wage a tough and unyielding defense. He had exhibited such resolve in his quarrel with Lord Hillsborough in 1768. He would do so again in his almost continuous battles with the New Jersey lawmakers after 1771.

The governor had to act quickly, for rumor had it that the house planned to use his refusal to grant a writ as an excuse to withhold money for future supply bills. But Franklin was shrewd, and his success was at least as much a tribute to his political dexterity as it was to the still generally noncombative nature of the New Jersey assembly. He simply made Ogden a justice of the peace, rendering him ineligible for a legislative seat. He then prorogued the house, and issued a writ for a newly elected representative. There was little the lawmakers could do. Many were displeased, but they had been outmaneuvered, and they knew it.[56]

The disagreement over Ogden's seat was child's play compared with the major battle dominating the assembly during the spring of 1771. The renewed quarrel over military expenditures was joined almost from the first day of the lengthy session, when Franklin asked for additional money to supply the King's troops for another season. He argued that the support of the empire redounded to New Jersey's benefit, reminding the legislators that the last war had been fought with colonial interests in mind. You should not, he lectured, bask in the peace provided by the King's troops without doing your part to ensure that peace. Only royal troops were equipped to defend the colonies. The militia was simply too weak, widely scattered, and undisciplined to protect America's borders. As always, William Franklin remained confident that English and American interests were identical.[57]

But the assembly was not persuaded. The next day, the legislators resolved, with only three dissenting votes, that the colony was unable to provide more supplies without raising taxes. And this they resolutely refused to do. The lawmakers insisted that their decision was not intended as a personal affront to William Franklin. But with no paper currency, a precipitous decline in land values, and the financial losses the colony had suffered as a result of the recent robbery of the East Jersey treasury, they had little choice.[58]

The usually cool and flexible governor flew into a rage. This was the most blatant slap-in-the-face he had endured since the Stamp Act crisis. Moreover, he was just returning to Lord Hillsborough's good graces, and he had no wish to endure a repeat performance of the nasty quarrel the two men had joined in 1768. That quarrel still weighed heavily on his mind, and while he was thankful that Hillsborough had written him some "tolerably complaisant" letters of late, he remained convinced that his superior thought he had an "improper Bias to American Politics." In self-defense, if nothing else, he had to prove his loyalty to the Crown. Finally, he was angry because he questioned the assembly's motives. In the mid-sixties, objections to military expenditures had been based at least partly on principle. But now, stinginess, not a concern for colonial rights, motivated the lower house.[59]

As always, when he felt boxed in and his authority in doubt, he dusted off his old debating techniques and began to score points. Underneath all his specific charges, ran one common thread. The colony was not in "distressed Circumstances." Indeed it had recently been enjoying a "gradual Course of Improvement." The assembly's refusal was short-sighted, selfish, and wrong-headed. By questioning the honesty and patriotism of the lower house, Franklin destroyed any chance for a face-saving compromise. And he had temporarily lost touch with political and economic reality as well. The legislators may have exaggerated New Jersey's problems but their claims were well-grounded, and the governor knew it.[60]

The argument swiftly degenerated into a series of mutual recriminations and outraged denials, as both parties played fast-and-loose with the truth. By the end of the month, there was no point in continuing the debate, and Franklin prorogued the assembly. But when the legislators returned to Burlington at the end of May, the month's recess had changed nothing.[61]

Once again the governor prorogued the assembly. In desperation he turned to the ministry for help. Perhaps because of his complete frustration, Franklin was more critical of New Jersey lawmakers than he had ever been. He told Hillsborough that the assembly's behavior was "entirely inexcusable." The colony had never been more "flourishing," and the legislators were simply playing a political game. They were expecting new elections momentarily, and their posturing was done with an eye to catering to potential voters. The entire problem would disappear, Franklin told Hillsborough, if only the ministry would approve the Loan Office Bill. "But," he said almost wistfully, I suppose "This cannot be done." He was right of course. Ironically, the usually astute governor had made ministerial capitulation less likely. By assuring the home government that New Jersey was thriving, he had reinforced Hillsborough's prejudices and made compromise seem unnecessary. New York had directly tied its promise of military aid to ministerial approval of paper money. When Franklin refused to allow his own assembly to do the same, he lost his most effective bargaining tool.[62]

The governor did not communicate formally with the legislature during the summer of 1771. What comfort he received came, not from the lower house, but from the King's men. General Gage sent a letter to Lord Hillsborough praising Franklin's efforts. Even the Secretary expressed his approval of the governor's conduct. He accepted Franklin's assessment of the assembly's motives, viewing its obduracy as "willful Contempt" of parliamentary authority. Significantly, William Franklin did nothing to correct this view. Indeed, it was the heretofore uncompromising Lord Hillsborough who found an honorable way to end the confrontation. By mid-July, the Secretary began exploring the possibility of withdrawing all troops from New Jersey, and by October, he had agreed to move the remaining soldiers to St. Augustine. This time it was London that gave Franklin a graceful way out of a potentially explosive situation. And it was the assembly that refused to alter its course.[63]

Franklin viewed the decision with mixed emotions. On the one hand, it removed the major source of controversy dividing him from his assembly. Nevertheless, the troop withdrawal was tantamount to admitting defeat, and he was troubled by the inability of the royal government to force compliance with its legitimate requests. At a time when his father was almost daily losing favor with the ministry in general and Lord Hillsborough in particular, and when the Secretary still suspected him of being unduly influenced by his American connections, William's failure to influence the assembly was particularly embarrassing. Moreover, in this instance, he did not have to compromise his principles to defend the Crown prerogative. He had always been eager to support military requests. Just as important, he refused to believe that any constitutional issue was at stake. The King's request for military supplies did not deviate from traditional practice, and it did not violate the rights claimed by American assemblies. The issue was money, not principle.[64]

Thanks to the ministry's flexibility, Franklin emerged from the stormy session relatively intact. He even managed, though not without difficulty, to persuade the assembly to pay for the expenses incurred by the 29th regiment as it withdrew from New Jersey. The legislature was reasonably happy now that the troops were leaving the colony for good. And even Franklin could reflect upon the results of his prolonged controversy with some satisfaction. He had used the disagreement with his assembly to improve his position with the ministry. Yet, despite the harsh words that had flown back and forth between governor and legislature, he thought that he had not irretrievably lost the good will of most of the colony's lawmakers. While he did not under-estimate the animosity that had engulfed the lower house, he could, with some justice, be assured that most of the anger directed toward him was political, not personal, and did not necessarily bode ill for his future relations with the colony.[65]

Throughout the early seventies, Franklin managed, as he put it, to "steer my little bark quietly through all the storms of political contest with which I was everywhere surrounded." He tried valiantly to occupy the middle ground between the claims of the assembly and the demands of the Crown. That he managed to serve both masters reasonably well was partly to his credit. And while he was becoming frustrated with what he perceived as the growing aggressiveness of the lower house, few would have predicted that just a few years later he would help lead the forces aiming to destroy colonial "liberties" and American independence. For despite his quarrels with the lower house, he remained willing to defend the colony from outside interference. Within certain carefully defined limits, he was as much a servant of New Jersey as he was a representative of the Crown. It was his ability to see both sides of most issues that enabled him to be a relatively successful governor for so many years. Stephen Crane's assertion that Franklin himself was always viewed with "general Satisfaction" was clearly not idle chatter. Perhaps nowhere was the mutual good will between Franklin and the house more evident than when both parties faced a potential impasse over the appointment of the colonial agent. It was an issue that threatened his relationship with his father, the assembly, and Lord Hillsborough. The governor handled the problem masterfully, managing, at least for the moment, to satisfy everyone.[66]

Typically, troubles arose from policies initiated by Lord Hillsborough. As part of his attempt to exert control over the colonies and to regularize the often haphazard procedures of the ministry, the Secretary refused to approve the credentials of any colonial agent who received his appointment solely from the lower house.[67] In the fall of 1769, when Ben first became the New Jersey Assembly's agent, his credentials had been accepted without a murmur of protest. But in January of 1771 he became the employee of the far more controversial colony of Massachusetts. And in a stormy confrontation with Lord Hillsborough, for which Franklin was at least partly to blame, the Secretary refused to approve Ben's appointment. Six months later, the Board of Trade instructed William Franklin to persuade his assembly to share its appointment power with the governor and council. Father and son, governor and assembly, were on a collision course.[68]

William was reluctant to broach the subject with the lower house. It was calculated, he sighed, "to lead me into another Squabble with the Assembly for it is a point they will never give up." But he could not ignore a direct order from London. Much to Franklin's evident surprise, the New Jersey legislators granted the governor and council a voice in appointing the colonial agent. Using "a good deal of Pesrsuasion, and many Arguments" he managed in "a private way" to win them over to his side. One can only imagine the "many arguments" Franklin employed. The fact that the colony's current agent was his own father could hardly have hurt his cause. And he may well have promised to accept any nominee the legislators proposed. No doubt New Jersey's representatives were more amenable to compromise than were their Massachusetts counterparts. They were most likely to dig in their heels when their pocketbooks were at stake, but in matters of principle, they tended to be less determined to have their own way.[69]

Franklin's pleasure in his victory was not unadulterated. He dreaded sending the news to his father, who had already claimed that an agent chosen jointly by the governor, council, and assembly would be little more than a Whitehall cipher. Thus it was with a mixture of pride and trepidation that he informed Ben of the assembly's decision. He could not help but boast a little of his personal triumph, which he had achieved "contrary to the Expectation of every Body. . . . This last," he acknowledged, "I suppose you [will] not be altogether pleas'd with. However," he rushed on, "it really (*inter nos*) makes no kind of Difference." It merely gave the Board the feeling of a "Point gained" without altering the balance of power. It changed the means, not the end. And he hoped that his father, a man of moderation and good sense, would see the matter in this light.[70]

William would not have been comforted by the message that crossed the Atlantic toward New Jersey, even as his own missive was headed in the other direction. For in a letter written at the end of January, Ben had bluntly proclaimed that he would refuse to serve as agent for any colony on Hillsborough's terms. But William need not have worried. Ben continued as New Jersey's agent until the eve of the Revolution.[71]

Their disagreement over the appointment of the colonial agent might have made the Franklins a little uneasy. For, whether they realized it or not, father and son were serving very different masters, whose goals were increasingly in conflict. The one was dedicated to upholding the interests of "the people," owing his identity as well as his livelihood to those Americans who were growing more and more willing to set themselves against the Crown. The other was accountable to London, and had sworn an oath to preserve the King's powers in his American dominions. But in fact, the personal relationship between the two men continued as strong as ever. William eagerly awaited his father's letters, worried when none arrived, and unfailingly made excuses for gaps in Ben's correspondence. He scanned the pages of the *London Chronicle* for fresh examples of Ben's propaganda efforts and relished the points his father scored against his political foes.[72]

But William was more than his father's greatest admirer. He kept abreast of the latest developments in electrical research, reading, performing his own experiments, and forwarding the results to Craven Street. He continued to perform all sorts of duties, great and small, to further his father's political aims. He wrote pamphlets designed to lay to rest any lingering charges of Ben's disloyalty to American interests. And he made sure that his father's tracts were printed in the colonies. He also served as a vital source of information on colonial affairs.[73]

William's continued willingness to serve as surrogate patriarch to Deborah and Sally was a godsend. He visited them regularly and invited them both to Burlington for extended stays. He had grown concerned about his stepmother. Deborah had become withdrawn in the years after the Stamp Act crisis, and as her husband's absence stretched on year after year, her condition deteriorated. Some time during the winter of 1769, she suffered a stroke and thereafter William worried that she was unfit to be left alone. Without his son's willingness to assume responsibility for the family, Ben may not have found it so easy to remain in London.[74]

In return, Benjamin Franklin made an effort to further his son's interests. He helped him secure the most modern equipment for his farm. He used his influence on behalf of William's friends. He offered careful advice on how to win favor with the King's ministers. And after the governor's blowup with Lord Hillsborough, he agreed to review all of his son's correspondence with the American Secretary, altering, and rewriting some letters before sending them on. Ben sent sound political advice to his son, worried about his health, and even devised an exercise program for the increasingly corpulent governor. In 1771, he began his famous "Autobiography," whose first pages were dedicated to William Franklin.[75] And if William tended to the needs of Deborah and Sally in America, there was a trade-off. For Ben handled Temple's affairs in London. He insisted that William pay for all his son's expenses. Indeed these constituted the bulk of his outstanding debts. But Ben himself acted as Temple's guardian, growing increasingly fond of his grandson as the lad matured.[76]

Some historians have remarked that William's reliance on his father's advice and largess indicated an unnatural or "pathetic" dependence. But Ben was never the governor's only London contact. And the relationship between father and son was not a one-way street. Ben relied on William's judgment, always sharing his plans and political views with him. And William was never reluctant to disagree with the elder Franklin when the occasion warranted it.[77]

But most importantly, William was confident that he and his father shared the same basic political philosophy. He knew that Ben had been jubilant when the Stamp Act had been repealed, seeing Parliament's willingness to accede to colonial demands as a sign of good will toward America. And Ben was just as likely as William to condemn the "violent Heats" of the New York and Boston assemblies, which did nothing but embarrass English supporters of the colonies. To be sure, Ben was always a Whiggish supporter of assembly rights. And after 1767 he became increasingly chary of Parliament's motives. As the elder Franklin's influence in London diminished, and as his hopes for a royal charter faded, his disaffection with parliamentary incompetence and corruption grew and his attacks became more frequent and strident.[78]

But William, too, had his quarrels with Parliament and the ministry. He, too, wished that England's lawmakers would stop trying to tax the colonies. Like his father, he was disturbed by the increasingly hard line that the King's ministers, especially Lord Hillsborough, were taking in American affairs. Most importantly, it was neither to Parliament alone, nor to the ministry, that William had taken his oath of office. So long as Ben refrained from attacking King and empire there was no danger of a serious rupture between father and son. And throughout the 1760s there seemed to be little cause for alarm on that score. Ben's doubts did not lead him to call for the destruction of the empire. Rather they caused him to step up his pleas for a transatlantic union.[79]

Even after Benjamin Franklin began to question Parliament, his allegiance to King and empire continued. It was not the King he blamed for the disagreements between England and America. What rankled, he wrote, was a "new kind of loyalty" that seemed to be required of the colonists, a "loyalty to P[arliamen]t." William gave his father's pamphlet high marks, claiming that its sentiments echoed his own. He obviously did not imagine that Ben's virulent attack on colonial governors, which portrayed them as parasitical interlopers with no "natural connection, or relation" in America was aimed at him. And his father continued to hope that "nothing that has happened or may happen will diminish in the least our Loyalty to our Sovereign, or Affection for this Nation in general." William Franklin agreed.[80]

Despite their shared interests, goals, and vision of a united empire, the relationship between father and son was not always untroubled. This was particularly true after 1768, when Ben's last hopes for a royal charter were dashed and he grew increasingly alienated from an administration that ignored and at times even spurned him. Indeed, Ben's stock had sunk so low in government circles by July of 1768 that there was a real, although aborted effort to remove him from his Post Office position. While the elder Franklin's reaction to the attempt was unusually low-key, William's was not. Without Ben to uphold his end of their partnership, he would have no one in London who would attend to his interests with so much alacrity and unfeigned devotion, no one upon whose judgment and good will he could rely so completely. And, of course, the Vandalia project would have lost one of its most effective lobbyists.[81]

Benjamin Franklin did not lose his Post Office job. And despite his chronic threats and promises, he did not leave England. He remained his son's and Vandalia's strong advocate. Even so his position was not quite what it once had been. As William borrowed more and more heavily from his father, tensions inevitably developed. He usually viewed Ben as a magnanimous creditor, knowing that an occasional promise of eventual payment in full was apparently all that Ben required. But William grew irritated when Ben occasionally pressed for evidence that he intended to pay his debts. At times his replies to his father were testy, almost churlish. He corrected Ben's bookkeeping with some asperity, pointing out that Ben occasionally charged him twice for the same items. In an obvious slap at his father's ledger-book mentality, he tersely remarked, "I have wrote you

6 letters by this Opportunity to make up for past Deficiencies." If Ben wanted to judge their relationship in terms of accounts received and accounts due, he could play that game as well as anyone.[82]

There were other signs that father and son did not always see eye to eye. As the elder Franklin allied himself more openly with America and distanced himself from the powerful Lord Hillsborough, his relationship with William was sometimes strained. Neither man wanted to discuss their differences directly. Ben no doubt resented insinuations of more radical colonials that because he had a "son in a high post at pleasure" he was "not the dupe but the instrument of Lord Hillsborough's treachery." But he contented himself with sly digs at men whose patronage positions kept them at the mercy of a ministry he neither admired nor trusted. I "rather wish," he pontificated, "to see all I am connected with in an Independent Station, supported by their own Industry."[83]

William steadfastly refused to be drawn into an argument. He was sometimes pained by Lord Hillsborough's hostility toward his father, and felt that the Secretary singled him out unfairly as a result. But his rare complaints were seldom addressed to Ben. He reserved his most anguished comments for their mutual friend, William Strahan. When Strahan told him that in London everyone branded him with the same opinions as his father, the governor was quick to react. There is, he insisted, "no reason (other than the natural connexion between us) to imagine that I entertain the same political opinion with my father with regard to the disputes between Britain and America." He refused to clarify his views, claiming only that they were "really in many respects different from those which have yet been published on either side of the question." He desperately wanted to steer a middle course between his father and Lord Hillsborough, rejecting neither completely, but not veering too close toward one or the other. It remained to be seen how long he would be able to remain in the middle.[84]

William's devotion to his father was unshaken, even when it became apparent that Ben's run-in with Lord Hillsborough over his credentials as Massachusetts agent had done the Ohio Company no good, and indeed had occasioned a serious falling out between his father and the other lobbyists. The situation had grown so tense that Ben had even offered—one wonders how seriously!—to resign from the company. Strahan claimed that Ben had become so moody that he was doing virtually nothing on behalf of the project. It was Samuel Wharton alone, he said, who continued to make contacts and lobby for the grant.[85]

William assured his friend that he was maintaining a safe distance from his father these days, but he was not as willing to write off Ben's efforts as Strahan apparently was. While William was becoming convinced that nothing would save the Ohio Company unless Lord Hillsborough left the Board of Trade, he refused to blame his father for Hillsborough's antipathy to the project. He knew from personal experience how spiteful, unreasonable, and unbending the Secretary could be. It would not have been surprising if he occasionally wondered if he had been wise to make his father so central to his schemes. But if he harbored such thoughts he kept them to himself. Just the opposite, in the first draft of a letter he wrote to Strahan, he disparaged Wharton's effectiveness as a lobbyist. Franklin did not doubt that Wharton was a hard worker, but he was convinced that Wharton could not have connected himself "with the greatest Names in Britain" without help from Benjamin Franklin. He deleted this caustic comment from his final draft only because he thought Strahan would "look upon it as a Sneer"—which it was—and because he feared that his comments would find their way to Wharton. Whatever his private misgivings, William remained unflinchingly loyal to his father.[86]

By the end of 1771, William Franklin was still both an American and an Englishman. Despite his quarrels with the assembly over troop supplies, he had reason to believe that most inhabitants of New Jersey bore him no personal animosity. And despite his continued difficulties with Lord Hillsborough, he had managed to earn some grudging compliments from the Secretary, and to prove his willingness to discipline the assembly. He had served both King and colony honorably. "I have," he said, "on no occasion given up a single point of the Crown's Prerogatives, nor have I ever attempted the least infringement of the People's Privileges." He was deeply involved in his efforts to make his farm in Burlington County a showplace for modern agricultural techniques. At the same time he harbored dreams of leaving New Jersey to govern his own empire in the West, dreams, ironically, that only reminded him of his dependence on the whims of the ministry. He was walking a tightrope, balancing the desires of the assembly against the needs of the empire, his loyalty to his father against the aspersions cast upon him by Hillsborough, the Whartons, and even William Strahan. But in 1771 there was no reason to assume that the astute and able governor would not continue to "steer his little bark" between his various interests and loyalties with good grace. If worse came to worst, he could always spend the rest of his days on his New Jersey estate, a possibility that was scarcely equal to his ambitions, but was not an altogether unpleasing prospect.[87]

7

Seeds of Controversy

"Controversy is, however, really disagreeable to me; and tho' I never seek it, yet I never avoid it where it is necessary to my Character, let the Consequences be what they may. And I now think it proper to tell you, Gentlemen, once for all, that you will ever find me ready to oblige you and serve the Province, as far as it may be in my Power; but that as I never have, so I never will suffer any Man, or Body of Men, in Stations so respectable as yours, to pass an unmerited Censure on my Publick Conduct, without endeavouring to do myself Justice."—William Franklin to the New Jersey Assembly, 1772.[1]

"I can safely call God to Witness, that I have not, as I told you before, any Attachments which can come in Competition with my Duty; nor do I know any thing that I should have in greater Abhorrence than for a Man in my Station to suffer himself to be influenced in his publick Conduct by either private Affection or Resentment. My publick Conduct may at Times be wrong through Mistake, but never through Design. I pretend not to Infallibility, but I do to Principle, from which not all the Entreaties of Friends nor Threats of Enemies shall ever make me deviate."—William Franklin to the New Jersey Assembly, 1773.[2]

Many residents of Perth Amboy did not sleep soundly on the night of July 21, 1768. Perhaps it was the rising moon shining brightly in their windows that made them so restless. Or it may have been the "uncommon barking and howling of Dogs" or the uneasy lowing of Richard Steven's cow that woke so many of the villagers. Maybe it was the soft slapping of oars on the Raritan River as a boat slipped toward the shore. In one house, however, no one was disturbed by the sounds of the summer night. Stephen Skinner, the treasurer of East Jersey, was not awakened by his neighbors' dogs. Elizabeth Ingliss, asleep with the children at the rear of the house, was similarly oblivious, as were six other servants who slept there that evening.[3]

Their serenity was abruptly ended about six o'clock in the morning when William Campbell, the treasurer's carpenter, and a young black servant clambored up the stairs to Skinner's bedroom with the news that someone had broken into the house. The treasurer and a bevy of curious neighbors quickly gathered to assess the damage. And it was with a sinking feeling that Skinner realized that someone had stumbled upon the colony funds, all safely locked away in a metal chest resting in his first floor office. Well over £6000 of New Jersey's money was gone.[4]

Stephen Skinner was a member of a prominent Perth Amboy family. His brother William was married to the sister-in-law of the Duke of Grafton, then first minister in England. Another brother, Cortlandt, was attorney general, speaker of the house, and one of Franklin's closest political allies. It would have been audacious to blame the treasurer for the robbery. And in the summer of 1768, this thought apparently entered no one's mind.[5]

Indeed Skinner's reaction to the unfortunate incident was above reproach. He immediately sent out a party to apprehend the thieves, offered a £100 reward to anyone assisting in their capture, and forwarded all details of the tragic event to governor Franklin. Franklin was as quick to act as the treasurer had been, for the loss of so much money when New Jersey was already groaning under a heavy burden of debt was a matter of grave concern. He ordered the chief justice to conduct a thorough investigation.[6] He also sent word of the robbery to Pennsylvania and New York, offering £50 to anyone who helped identify the thieves or recover the money. Despite all his efforts, he faced the assembly in the fall of 1769 with a treasury still bereft of the stolen funds. Franklin's inclination was to accept the colony's loss and to focus on finding ways to assure that such a calamity was not repeated.[7]

The assembly did not question the governor's approach.[8] The legislators conducted their own investigation of the robbery, but while they reserved final judgment until they questioned William Campbell, a principal witness, they saw no reason "to impeach the Conduct or Character of the said Treasurer." There was not the slightest indication that the robbery would do more than any other single incident to poison the minds of governor and assembly alike, leading to a mutual distrust from which neither would fully recover.[9]

The first hints of trouble occurred in the fall of 1770. There had already been grumbling when Skinner joined the New Jersey council in December of 1769. Some assemblymen saw this as evidence that he and the governor were uncommonly close, even though the treasurer was not Franklin's first choice for the job. At a time when the assembly was flexing its muscles, and many members complained that in New York and Pennsylvania, the house, not the governor, appointed the treasurer, such apparent collusion seemed unhealthy at best.[10]

More ominously, the legislators used the fall session to conduct their own extensive investigation, calling a parade of witnesses before coming to a resolution that was in marked contrast to the one issued immediately following the robbery. The money was stolen, they now declared, "for want of that Security and Care that was necessary to keep it in Safety." Stephen Skinner's negligence was responsible for the robbery. Consequently, the lawmakers demanded that he reimburse the colony for its loss.[11]

It was not until the fall of 1772 that the governor was drawn into a direct confrontation with the assembly over the issue of the treasury robbery. While the legislature still indicated its general approbation of his conduct, Franklin's position was almost imperceptibly deteriorating. His inability to secure ministerial approval of the Currency Bill and his uncompromising attitude during the quarrel over supplying the King's troops had not helped him. New Jersey's still desperate need for liquid capital encouraged the assembly to press Skinner to reimburse the colony. Perhaps most important, a new assembly met in Perth Amboy in the fall of 1772. General elections had been held to include representatives from the counties of Morris, Sussex, and Cumberland. Not only did this increase the number of legislators, but it altered the composition of the house as well. Just over half of the thirty men attending the fall session were newcomers, and many of Franklin's closest allies were not returned. Moreover, the assembly included more West Jersey representatives than in previous sessions. And it was from West Jersey that the leaders of the anti-Skinner faction came. This legislature was not predestined to oppose the governor, but it would not be as easily controlled as its predecessors had been.[12]

The issue was joined by Stephen Skinner himself, who submitted a "Memorial" to the assembly protesting the demand for reimbursement. Despite his emotional plea, the legislators were unmoved. Instead they unanimously voted to tell Governor Franklin to initiate proceedings ordering reimbursement from Skinner. The assembly's instructions were drafted by James Kinsey, a freshman legislator from the West Jersey capital. Kinsey would become one of Franklin's most vocal detractors in the years before the Revolution.[13] His first message to the chief executive was not politic. Criticizing Skinner for his irresponsibility, it came close to censuring the governor as well. Kinsey's motives were clear from the beginning, as he implied that the affair would have been better handled if the assembly had possessed the power to remove the treasurer. Skinner, he thought, would have lost his job in 1770 had the assembly been in charge.[14]

Franklin's response was predictably hostile. Instead of ignoring Kinsey's injudicious remarks, he escalated the controversy. Two things in particular rankled the govenor. First, he resented the implication that he should already have removed Skinner from office. The assembly had never so much as hinted that it wanted the treasurer fired, and had even voted to continue his salary. Second, he took umbrage at Kinsey's thinly veiled attack on the governor's control of the treasury. Was this, he wondered, another attack on Crown prerogative? If so, it was surely unjust, for the New Jersey assembly, not the governor, had all practical control over the treasury. Franklin threw down the gauntlet. He told the legislators to stop hiding behind sly insinuations and to tell him "in plain Terms" if they wanted Skinner's removal. He also warned that the treasurer might not be legally obliged to reimburse the colony, and he doubted that Skinner could be tried in New Jersey, where every freeholder was an interested party in the suit. Franklin could never resist flaunting his knowledge of the law.[15]

By insisting that the legislators go on record instead of engaging in endless carping complaints, the governor hoped the assembly would back down in the face of his firm resolve. Unfortunately, his strategy backfired. The legislators rose to his challenge. On September 18, they formally requested Stephen Skinner's removal from his post. With evident sarcasm, they hoped "that this Answer will be as plain as his Excellency seems to desire." They argued, with little concern for honesty, that their desire for his dismissal in 1770 should have been obvious. In language that seemed calculated to be disrespectful, the lawmakers hinted, for the first time, that the money entrusted to the treasurer may never have actually been stolen. And they insisted that Skinner be replaced and that the new treasurer be instructed to institute a suit to reimburse the colony.[16] Between them, the assembly and the governor had made compromise virtually impossible. The legislators had hurled insults at Franklin which he could not be expected to tolerate and from which they would not recede. By 1772, four years after the robbery, the issue had gone from penury to principle. The assembly was intent on forcing the governor to remove the treasurer from office. And while he made a few conciliatory gestures, Franklin acted as he usually did when he was backed into a corner, becoming increasingly intransigent. He had publicly declared his loyalty to Stephen Skinner, and from that loyalty he would not budge.[17]

After 1772 the controversy simply degenerated. When Chief Justice Smyth returned from England at the beginning of October he was appalled at the "violent contest." He was especially unhappy with the usually politic governor, whose antagonistic approach left the government "much degraded." He also condemned Franklin's "extraordinary attachment" to Skinner, predicting that the governor's loyalty to the treasurer would be his undoing.[18]

Franklin defended his position with every conceivable argument. He took exception to the house's selective recollection of events following the robbery, claiming that it had purposefully omitted "every Circumstance which any ways tended to set my Conduct, or the Conduct of the Treasurer, in a favourable Light." Most importantly, he saw the assembly's accusations as an attack on Crown prerogative and as an attempt to destroy the balanced government upon which New Jersey's stability rested. If, he argued, the assembly's "mere Opinion" was "*satisfactory Proof*" of an officer's guilt, then it "would be in the Power of an Assembly to turn out any Officer in the Government." Even if Franklin wanted to comply with the assembly's demands he could not do so, for no governor could remove any provincial officer without clearing his decision with the home government. This procedure, said Franklin, guarded "against that arbitrary despotic Temper which sometimes actuates Governors, as well as that levelling democratic Disposition which too often prevails in popular Assemblies."[19]

Franklin's defense was a *tour de force*, even if it failed to convince an aroused legislature. He had couched the controversy in terms that made an attack on the governor appear as an attack on the King. He had, furthermore, managed to turn his own uncompromising stance into a defense of moderation. He alone could maintain the ever precarious balance between executive tyranny and leveling democracy that was the object of any government.

Still, one unalterable fact remained. Despite his attempt to take the high ground, despite his painstaking, lawyerly and often tedious refutation of every accusation, Franklin refused even to consider removing Skinner from office until he had been proved guilty of negligence. Convinced that the law was on his side, he would not back down. Political considerations, the obvious need for compromise, meant little to him when he was sure that he was right. "Controversy," he told the members of the House in words that were eerily prophetic is "really disagreeable to me; and Tho' I never seek it, yet I never avoid it where it is necessary to my Character, let the Consequences be what they may." And so the quarrel continued.[20]

Stephen Skinner tried to meliorate matters, promising to testify in any suit that the New Jersey government brought against him, but the assembly ignored Skinner's offer.[21] A five-man committee, headed by James Kinsey, continued to take potshots at the governor, and its members raised the stakes of the debate when they suggested that the assembly, not the governor, should nominate all future treasurers.[22]

If Franklin had harbored any doubts about the ulterior motives of some legislators, they were now dispelled. As he had suspected all along, the quarrel was not about money or Skinner's negligence. These were mere ruses to mask the desire of Kinsey and his cohorts to augment the strength of the assembly at the expense of the royal governor. The session ended on a sour note. Each side accused the other of bad faith. Each questioned the other's honesty, motives, and judgment. In one session, the argument had escalated from a concern over lost revenue to a quarrel over the power to appoint the colonial treasurer.[23]

The controversy remained unresolved for over a year. Skinner continued in his post; the assembly continued to pay him for his services; and the treasury was still bereft of the stolen funds. At last, in the summer of 1773, Franklin hoped that the stalemate might be broken. In July, law enforcement officials apprehended a ring of counterfeiters headed by one Samuel Ford, and some members of Ford's gang implicated their leader in the East Jersey treasury robbery. The governor's council eagerly questioned the accusers in mid-September, promising most of them pardons for evidence bringing Ford to justice. But while his confederates were falling all over themselves putting the finger of blame on their leader, Ford, along with some of his accomplices, escaped fom his jail cell and headed toward New Orleans.[24]

Still, when Franklin went before the assembly in November he thought he had every reason to be pleased. "Striking circumstances" indicated that the mystery "which had remained so long enveloped in Darkness" had been "brought to light." All he needed now was money from the assembly to be used in apprehending Samuel Ford. Ominously the lawmakers offered rewards for the capture of three of the convicts, but they did not think it "expedient" to send a posse after the escapees. Even worse, the assembly asked the governor to substantiate his claim that "striking circumstances" linked the counterfeiters to the treasury robbery. As usual, James Kinsey was on the committee commissioned to draft the request.[25]

Franklin took ten days to respond to the assembly's message. Once more on the defensive, he wanted to make the best case possible. Professing surprise at the legislators' doubts, he offered to share all of the evidence with them. Acting like a prosecuting attorney, he carefully built an impressive case. He was convinced that his account was sufficient "to satisfy every Man of Candour—every Man capable of devesting himself of ill conceived Prejudices—and in Short, every Man who will not shut his Eyes to the Light of Truth and Conviction."[26]

Despite Franklin's contention that his view was the only logical and legitimate one, the assembly appointed a committee to examine the evidence for itself. By now some observers were convinced that at least a few legislators were determined to have the treasurer's head no matter what the evidence indicated. "I believe," said Cortlandt Skinner, "that some would rather that the robbery was never discovered than the favorite scheme disappointed." For, he went on, "the nomination of the Treasurer by the

House and removal only by them is the darling object to which every other Consideration would be sacrificed." The Speaker's assessment, while obviously biased, was not totally inaccurate. The house committee did little to investigate Franklin's "striking circumstances," even refusing as "improper" the governor's magnanimous offer to let them question Ford's accusers. And they handed the job of drafting a report to James Kinsey, who had been heard to proclaim that even if lightning had destroyed the East Jersey money he would hold Skinner responsible for the loss. Throughout the early days of December, Kinsey buried himself in his office, scribbling feverishly away at his response. No one knew what he would say; all other business was at a virtual standstill.[27]

Finally, on December 18, Kinsey laid his "tremendous" seventy-five-page report before the house. The opus discounted all the evidence against Ford, and after some debate, the assembly overwhelmingly accepted Kinsey's reading of the case. Three days later the house reaffirmed its determination not to grant Skinner a trial until he had vacated his office. William Franklin was no closer to resolving his differences with the legislature than he had been over a year earlier. If anything, the division was sharper than ever.[28]

By February, when the house returned from its Christmas recess, the representatives had lost all patience. Circumstances were stacked in their favor. Using their control of the purse strings as a weapon, they informed Franklin that the disposition of the annual support bill hinged on the immediate removal of the treasurer. Only seven lawmakers voted against the ultimatum.[29] Meanwhile, petitions—mostly from West Jersey—asking for the treasurer's removal flooded the assembly.[30]

Franklin waited nearly a week before unleashing a diatribe against the members of the lower house. By now, he knew he was waging a losing battle, but he had not lost his will to fight. He accused the house of finding Skinner guilty before proving him so—a neat trick, for Kinsey's report had censured Franklin for doing the same thing to Samuel Ford. He also maintained that the assembly, not Skinner, was guilty of negligence, for the legislators had not given the treasurer adequate instructions when it entrusted the colony's money to his care. And he deplored the way certain ambitious men had manipulated the minds of the public to serve their own selfish ends. "A Flame has been kindled," he said, "which some Persons think it in their Interest to keep up." He, on the other hand, was dedicated to serving the people, not to pleasing them, and he refused to bow to the wishes of a misinformed populace.[31]

Having completed his offense, Franklin began to defend his own conduct. He grabbed the high ground, portraying himself not as a rigid, uncompromising adversary but as a voice of moderation and reason, as he insisted that his entire tenure as governor had been dedicated to avoiding disputes. Only when his duty to the Crown, the people or his own honor demanded it did he permit himself to be drawn into a quarrel with New Jersey's representatives. Indeed, he claimed to be the only one in the colony willing to work out an amicable solution to the problem. Everyone, he insisted, wanted to recover the stolen funds. The argument, he said, in language reminiscent of his old quarrel with Lord Hillsborough, was over the best means to achieve a desirable end. If the assembly really cared about the public interest it would avail itself of Skinner's offer to appear before a court of law where a resolution of their differences might be achieved. The legislators' demand of all or nothing was helpful to no one. "There never existed a more unnecessary Dispute between a Governor and an Assembly," he opined. The lawmakers were disregarding the public interest in a frivolous "Dispute about Modes." The governor neglected to mention that he was as adamant in insisting upon his own "mode" of handling the case as was the assembly.[32]

Franklin claimed that his determination to support Skinner had nothing to do with his personal ties to the treasurer. His motives were pure, his "Attachments" irrelevant. "Nor," he said, "do I know any thing that I should have in greater Abhorrence than for a Man in my Station to suffer himself to be influenced in his publick Conduct by either private Affection or Resentment." While he did not claim to be correct in every instance, his mistakes were honest ones. "I pretend not to Infallibility," he said, "but I do to Principle." These were words that should have caused Benjamin Franklin a little uneasiness. For they revealed an attitude from which the governor never receded in the difficult months that faced father, son, and the American colonies. If William Franklin had to choose between his attachment to anyone—even his father—and his duty as he defined it, there was little doubt what decision he would make.[33]

Finally, on February 19, the assembly voted overwhelmingly to deny Skinner control over the colony funds. It also made an end-run around the governor, drafting a petition to the King asking him to remove Skinner from office. The prospect of involving London in what had been a local problem made Franklin shudder. It would be the Hatton affair all over again. But this time the very real possibility existed that his superiors would disapprove of his own conduct. Something had to be done. Government had ground to a halt; Stephen Skinner was treasurer in name only.[34]

It was Skinner, not the assembly or the governor, who finally resolved the conflict, when on February 24, he submitted his resignation. The council unanimously urged Franklin to accept it. With considerable bad grace, William bowed to the inevitable.[35] As the session drew to a close, the assembly prepared to bring Skinner to trial. Franklin, dragging his feet, authorized John Smyth, the new treasurer, to bring suit against his predecessor. Meanwhile, he made a few last-ditch efforts to prove Samuel Ford's guilt. The self-proclaimed apostle of moderation could not concede defeat gracefully.[36]

To assign responsibility for the controversy is as difficult as it is pointless. No one acted with diplomacy, wisdom, or grace. House leaders seemed determined to achieve their objectives at any cost and appeared more interested in unseating Skinner than in finding the treasury robbers.[37] Franklin's high-handed approach, his refusal to concede that honest men could disagree with him also escalated tensions. The case against Ford, while compelling, rested on the testimony of convicted felons and a heavy dose of circumstantial evidence. His refusal to listen to legitimate differences of opinion cost Franklin the support of moderate legislators, diminishing his own influence and tarnishing the reputation of the governor's office.[38]

Whoever was at fault, the East Jersey treasury robbery clearly would have been a less significant episode in New Jersey's history had it not occurred when the relationship between England and America was rapidly deteriorating. New Jersey may not have been especially radical, but it could not remain isolated from the issues that pervaded the colonies after 1772. When leaders from South Carolina and Virginia to Massachusetts and Rhode Island professed to see tyranny everywhere, when diatribes against the despotic attempts of royal governors to destroy colonial liberties were becoming almost routine, it was not surprising that New Jersey lawmakers seized upon the robbery of the East Jersey treasury, a calamity in itself, to flex its muscles. Indeed, when compared with the behavior of some colonies, New Jersey's stance was mild. Perhaps in another, calmer time, Franklin would have used the relative moderation of the legislators to defuse an unnecessary crisis. He would have done what he had been able to do so well in the past, finding some common ground between himself and his potential allies, working out a compromise that was acceptable, if not totally pleasing.

But this was not a time for reasoned discourse. Governors in many Crown colonies were increasingly on the defensive, caught between the conflicting interest of the ministry and the assembly. Franklin himself had just survived the controversy engendered by the Mutiny Act. He was uneasy over the generally unsettled atmosphere that threatened to spread from neighboring colonies into his own. And he had never been able to accept personal criticism gracefully. Thus the issue had been joined, and once joined it proved exceedingly difficult for either side to disengage itself from a quarrel that neither had wanted in the beginning. Even worse, both the assembly and the governor hurled accusations that were never completely forgotten. An aura of distrust had poisoned the air. Franklin never again

assumed that New Jersey's lawmakers were acting with honorable intentions. Always a little prone to paranoia, he became more likely than ever
to see ulterior motives and secret designs emanating from his opponents.
Clearly, in this instance as in no other that Franklin had faced during his
long tenure as governor, the threat to his security, and power, came not
from a rigid policy contrived by some officious London bureaucrat but
solely from his own legislature.

One apparent consequence of Franklin's struggle with his assembly was
his decision to leave his home in Burlington for the more hospitable East
Jersey capital. The sumptuous Proprietary House looked increasingly inviting to a governor buffeted about by the controversy over the treasury
robbery. The move to Perth Amboy had deep symbolic importance. It
would put more distance between William and Philadelphia, curtailing his
visits to friends and family in his boyhood home. It was, moreover, a public
acknowledgment of what had long been a reality. Franklin had gradually
become more socially and politically comfortable with the East Jersey
proprietors. The treasury robbery moved him closer to this group, and by
the end of 1773 he found it neither possible nor especially desirable to conceal his sentiments. Why not, after all, move to a magnificent governor's
mansion in a place where he and his wife could live happily among their
real friends? It would take a year to sell the Burlington residence and prepare Proprietary House for occupation. Franklin took his time; he was not
fleeing Burlington in a desperate search for safer ground. Still, the move
promised to provide a comfortable haven from the storm of controversy
and criticism that threatened to overwhelm him. And his decision would
drive a small wedge that would help separate him from his past.[39]

Even the deepest wounds can heal, given time and the proper care. And
in the right circumstances, William would have been ideally suited to apply
the balm that would smooth away the lingering irritations that troubled
governor and assembly. There was still reason to believe that Franklin and
the legislators might reach a rapprochement in the years immediately preceding the Boston Tea Party. The problem of supplying the King's troops
had virtually vanished by 1772.[40] To be sure, a few minor disagreements
over the colony's obligations to the royal army dotted the political landscape from time to time. But debate over supplying an occasional batallion
or two was always low-key and hardly acrimonious. Not all the issues affecting Franklin's relations with the assembly dissipated quite as readily as
the controversy over military supplies. But no disagreement between governor and assembly appeared serious enough to turn executive and legislature into enemies.[41]

One persistent problem faced by Franklin was the issue of compensation
for New Jersey's civil officers. Since his first successful attempt to secure an

increase in the governor's stipend, Franklin had won no further increments. As his personal debts grew, as he became more deeply enmeshed in an extensive network of real estate ventures, and as he looked with envy at the position of other royal governors, nearly all of whom were on the Civil List, he could not help but feel neglected and abused. But the question of official salaries, while it soured his relations with the New Jersey assembly, could be partly blamed on London. And Franklin spent as much time begging for Crown favor as he did berating the legislators for their "ill-judged Parsimony." In this instance he blamed everyone, even his father, for his difficulties.[42]

The governor stepped up his campaign for adequate compensation in the late summer of 1772, appealing first to the assembly and then to London for help. The legislature's response to his pleas was predictable. The treasury robbery had depleted the colony's coffers, and the house was about to be locked in a protracted struggle with the governor over the fate of Stephen Skinner. It was hardly the time to expect a raise. The lawmakers refused even to admit that a problem existed, curtly explaining that some of the salaries "we imagine equal to the Dignity of the Station, and others proportionate to the Interest we have in them." Franklin was dissatisfied but not especially surprised. And despite his dogged efforts to persuade the legislators to reverse their position, they continued their penurious policy until the coming of the Revolution.[43]

But Franklin's quarrel was not with the assembly alone, and he knew it. A sympathetic ministry could easily lift this burden from his shoulders. It had done so for other, less deserving governors. Why not for him? Part of the problem was Lord Hillsborough. The Secretary's quarrel with Ben, and his consequent distrust of William, made it unlikely that the governor could expect much help from that quarter. But even after the more tractable Lord Dartmouth became the head of the Board of Trade in the fall of 1772, Franklin's situation remained unchanged.[44]

The new Secretary had scarcely assumed office when he received the governor's first desperate appeal to be placed on the civil list. Franklin ticked off every argument supporting his case. His salary was lower and his expenses higher than those of most colonial governors. Most importantly, he believed that his long and loyal service to the Crown merited some reward. He had been the head of New Jersey's government for a decade, and had an older commission than any royal governor. Yet, he pointed out, "whilst others in my Station have made handsome Fortunes, been promoted, or received considerable Honours and Rewards, my own private Fortune has been really lessening, and I have as yet only the Satisfaction of having Served His Majesty faithfully & to the best of my Ability." The satisfaction of a job well-done was not a sufficient recompense. "Goodness and Justice" demanded that his rewards take on a more tangible form. It was not a question of money, he implied, but a question of honor that made him present such a forceful petition on his own behalf.[45]

But Dartmouth ignored Franklin's plea, and when the governor repeated his request in the spring of 1773, the Secretary responded in a terse negative. Franklin fared no better in a material way under Dartmouth than he had under Hillsborough. And his longing for financial reward was rebuffed by Crown and colony alike. Neither the issue of military supplies nor his longing for an independent salary was designed to make William Franklin wash his hands of the New Jersey legislature. The one was no longer a significant issue; the other was a chronic complaint that owed as much to the failures of the ministry as it did to the parsimony of the colony's lawmakers.[46]

If Franklin found no issue that would irrevocably cut him off from the New Jersey assembly in the years before the Boston Tea Party, there were still some reasons compelling him to hold the King's ministers at arm's length. This was particularly true so long as Lord Hillsborough remained a powerful force. Admittedly, the two men had reached something approaching a *modus vivendi* by 1772. The Secretary now and again granted the governor a grudging compliment. Franklin eagerly grasped at the most perfunctory nod of approval, and he shared any sign of Hillsborough's approbation with his father. But William continued to have his run-ins with the Secretary. No matter how hard he tried, he could never meet the exacting standards set by the King's minister.[47]

Their most important quarrel continued to involve the Secretary's determination to block the progress of the Grand Ohio Company. But thanks in part to the company's machinations, it appeared by the fall of 1772 that the Franklins' nemesis would no longer be in a position to block their plans. Hillsborough's problems began in April, when the Board of Trade finally issued its report on the Ohio Company's claims. With the Secretary pulling all the right strings, the Board rejected the grant request. Ordinarily such a rejection would have put an end to the company's aspirations, but in this instance Hillsborough's exercise of power backfired.

The Privy Council's committee for plantation affairs was stacked with Vandalia stockholders, who used their influence to call for public hearings on the proposal. Five shareholders, including Benjamin Franklin and Samuel Wharton, appeared before the committee to defend their grant application. But insiders knew that the decision was a foregone conclusion. On July 1, the committee recommended approval of the grant. Lord Hillsborough, furious at being rebuked and out-maneuvered, offered the King his resignation. To his surprise, the King, accepted it. By August 11 the grant had sailed through the Board of Trade. Vandalia was about to become a reality.[48]

William Franklin was overjoyed when he heard the news. He was convinced that with Hillsborough out of the way, his future relations with the Board of Trade would be smooth, and that his dream of a colony in the West would soon be realized.[49] Despite his own jubilation, Benjamin Franklin warned his son to avoid undue optimism, "lest we render ourselves ridiculous in case of disappointment." He knew that neither he nor the Ohio Company could take credit for Hillsborough's fall from grace, no matter what the rumor-mongers said to the contrary. The Secretary had grown increasingly unpopular with his fellow ministers, and even with the King. The land grant served as an excuse, not a reason, for ousting the powerful head of the Board of Trade.[50] Thus Ben feared that with their real object—the removal of Hillsborough from office—attained, the Board might not be so enthusiastic about going forward with the Ohio grant.[51]

Benjamin Franklin's cautionary words were more prophetic than even he imagined. For in the months following Hillsborough's ouster, Vandalia's prospects vanished like smoke whenever the unlucky schemers thought they had success in their grasp. Three problems destroyed their dreams. The company itself was riddled with internal discord and confusion. The project continued to be blind-sided by counter claims from rival speculators. And the wheels of the bureaucracy ground forward so slowly that Vandalia's prospects were interminably delayed and ultimately forgotten.

Mutual suspicion and hostility had simmered beneath the surface since the Grand Ohio Company's inception. But by 1772, animosity broke into the open. The American partners, with some reason, suspected that their European counterparts were cheating them out of their shares. Even worse, the always fragile connection between the Franklins and the Whartons finally reached the breaking point. The two factions disagreed about everything. Ben had a nasty quarrel with Wharton and Trent over the validity of Virginia's claims to parts of the Ohio grant. Relying on documents and the legal analysis provided by William, he all but accused Wharton of calculated deception in his dealings with the other members of the company as well as with the ministry. Meanwhile, Wharton was secretly positioning himself for appointment as Vandalia's first governor, instructing George Croghan to begin building an executive mansion on the banks of the Monongahela, and to buy presents for the Indians there.[52] He promised to reimburse the impoverished land speculator for his expenses. But when Croghan asked for his money, Joseph Galloway and William Franklin refused, with Ben's blessing, to contribute anything toward the project. Thomas Wharton thought their behavior was "as mean and despicable,

As my Brother's Behavior, was generous and laudable." But William refused to throw good money after bad.[53]

Ill will grew when the Whartons tried to deprive William of his shares in the Suffering Traders, and Joseph Wharton Senior attempted to trick him into selling his shares in Vandalia. While their poorly plotted ruses failed miserably, they did nothing to assuage William's feelings, and he again blasted Samuel for trying to take credit for the project's success when he knew how many tedious hours his own father had devoted to the company.[54]

If internal quarrels troubled the Vandalia investors, so did the counterclaims to the Ohio land by speculators from Virginia, Maryland, and Pennsylvania. William Franklin was more concerned by these claims than Wharton and Trent, who dismissed them contemptuously if not honestly. The governor knew, as the English lobbyists apparently did not, that the Ohio Company faced strong opposition at home. Even Frederick Smyth, his own Chief Justice, had expressed outrage at the "falsehoods" perpetrated by Vandalia's lobbyists.[55]

But neither the rift between the Whartons and the Franklins, nor the threats posed by rival speculators was the real problem confronting the project. Indeed these would not have been at issue had it not been for the government's lethargy. Promises were cheap in the capital city, and a little forward movement was followed as often as not by excruciating delay. A full six months after the grant had been approved, the company was not "one Step further" in realizing its aims. And in April the formerly sympathetic Lord Dartmouth began to entertain doubts about the Vandalia grant. Ben promised to visit the Secretary to "learn where it sticks," but still there was no progress. In fact, the ministry never gave its final approval to the Vandalia plan. For issues of a more serious nature soon captured the attention of leaders on both sides of the water, rendering the entire subject practically irrelevant.[56]

These were trying times for William Franklin. The East Jersey treasury robbery had forced him into a bitter quarrel with the assembly. London bureaucrats continued to delay his quest for a fortune based on land speculation. Neither America nor England offered him much hope for a comfortable or secure future. The strains of these trials and disappointments took its toll on Franklin's private life. While he continued to rely on his solid bond with his father, tiny fissures began to appear in their relationship. Their personal ties remained close, and politically no unbreachable gap separated them. Still tension surfaced with growing regularity in the years preceding the Boston Tea Party.

The two men had not seen each other in nearly a decade. The one had been snubbed and ignored by London officials; the other had suffered the sometimes vicious barbs of the New Jersey assembly. One saw himself as the spokesman for a growing number of colonial legislatures, while the other relied on the King's good graces for his position. Father and son had gradually come to view their world from different perspectives, and even under less chaotic conditions those differences were bound to have their effect.

William reluctantly acknowledged that his father's position could be harmful to his own prospects after Ben's run-in with Lord Hillsborough over the Massachusetts agency. The quarrel had effectively ended any chance of accommodation between the proud American and the stubborn Englishman. But William refused to believe that the differences between the two men were unreconcilable. He himself had gone a long way toward mending fences with his superior, and he expected his father to do the same.

The governor seized upon every hint that rapprochement was possible. He was hopeful when, in the autumn of 1772, Ben met Hillsborough by chance during a visit to Ireland, and the Secretary did his best to ingratiate himself with the Doctor and his companion, Richard Jackson. He was upset when he realized that Ben remained suspicious of Hillsborough's motives.[57] And when he heard that Ben had only visited Hillsborough once after the two men returned from Ireland, and that "that was at a Time when you must have been morally sure of not seeing him," he could not mask his irritation. He admitted that the Secretary disagreed with his father on "some particular Points," but William was convinced that the minister saw Franklin as a "man of great Abilities, and of uncommon Knowledge in Amreican Matters." He could not understand why Ben did not make every effort at reconciliation.[58]

The elder Franklin hurt his son's prospects in other ways as well. When, in the middle of the treasury controversy, William learned that the governorship of Barbados had fallen vacant, he sent signals that he was available for the position even though he fully expected to be passed over. "I stand no Chance for any Promotion," he told his father, "while Lord H. is at the Head of the American Department, and is so much displeased with your Conduct."[59]

And then there was the question of his salary. After Lord Dartmouth replaced Hillsborough, William assumed his father would lobby for his request to be placed on the Civil List. He seemed not at all struck by the anomalous nature of his expectations. He was asking the New Jersey agent to support his efforts for financial independence. There can be no better indication of his complete trust in his father's good will. But it was a serious miscalculation as well. Ben was cool to the idea. The increasingly

Whiggish agent thought it was dangerous to free colonial governors from dependency on their legislatures. He refrained from pointing this out to his governor-son, explaining his reluctance to advance William's cause by claiming solicitude for his interests. "I fear," he said tersely, "it will embroil you with your People." But his refusal, however kindly expressed, was disappointing.[60]

There were other signs of an undercurrent of awkwardness between William and Benjamin Franklin. Open disagreements were rare, but at times their uneasiness was noticeable because of the subjects they failed to discuss. William did not, for instance, seek his father's help with the controversy precipitated by the East Jersey treasury robbery. Nor is there evidence that Ben offered him any advice. The governor handled this problem by himself.[61]

Ben's worries about his son, and his growing frustration in London, sometimes resulted in prickly comments that could not help but cause William momentary pain. Always competitive, Ben became if anything more enamored with the petty game of oneupmanship in these years. He was not above making a slap at the pretensions of common-law lawyers. He bragged about the adulation he received in literary circles, acknowledging with false humility that such praise flattered "a little" his vanity. And when he learned that his son had been made a member of the Society for the Propagation of the Gospel, the prestigious Anglican missionary society, he waited nearly two years before according him a lukewarm nod of approbation. Even then he used William's achievement to flaunt his own. "There," he said, "you match indeed my Dutch honour. But you are again behind, for last night I received a letter from Paris . . . acquainting me that I am chosen Associé étranger of the Royal Academy there." It was, he boasted, a singular achievement reserved for the "most distinguished names for science."[62]

Ben also refused to help his ne'er-do-well nephew, Josiah Davenport, in his quest for a government sinecure, and he looked askance at William's efforts to come to the aid of his unfortunate cousin. He claimed that he was on such bad terms with Lord North, the King's first minister, that any solicitation he made would surely be refused. If William had harbored hopes that the fall of Lord Hillsborough augured well for his father's relationship with the ministry, those illusions were dispelled. But the worst was yet to come. Even if he was on excellent footing with the government, Ben lectured his son, he would not lift a finger to help anyone secure a job in the customs service. He detested the "whole System of American Customs," and he wanted no one near him involved in the dirty business. William no doubt read his father's angry response with real sadness and a touch of fear.

It revealed an anger and frustration that was new to the usually affable colonial agent, and indicated a more profound alienation from the royal government than William had suspected.[63]

That same letter gave other signs that Ben was moving toward a more radical stance in the summer of 1773. In a detailed letter to William, analyzing his view of settlers' rights to Indian land, he implicitly challenged all royal authority in America and explicitly reaffirmed his belief in the right of revolution. He also shared his doubts about Lord Dartmouth. "He is truly a good Man," Ben acknowledged, "and wishes sincerely a good Understanding with the Colonies, but does not seem to have Strength equal to his Wishes." Most ominously, he confided that he was beginning to blame the King himself for colonial grievances. He still hoped the King's attitude resulted from false information fed to him by his advisers. But his private willingness to point the finger of blame at the English monarch was a significant step in the making of an American patriot.[64]

It is probably easy to make too much of the effect these remarks had on William Franklin. Reading them with the advantage of hindsight, they have an obvious impact. We can imagine William groaning over his father's pointed attack on Lord North and the King he represented. We can see the basis of the deep split between the older and the younger Franklin, and it is hard to believe that the governor did not shudder when he read his father's words. But such an interpretation would be an exaggeration. Few men on either side of the Atlantic—least of all Ben or William Franklin—saw the quarrel between England and America as leading to an irrevocable breach in the summer of 1773. While William was undoubtedly unhappy with his father's letter, he may as easily have been gratified by the trust it implied. To criticize the King was, after all, dangerous business for a colonial agent, and Ben did not confide in just anyone when he made such inflammatory remarks. The letter may be taken as a mark of the continued intimacy between father and son rather than as an unmistakable sign of the disintegration of their relationship. And if William Franklin resented his father's increasing belligerence, he kept his unhappiness to himself.

In so many ways, their partnership, their shared attitudes and mutual interests, remained firm. If Ben was *persona non grata* in Lord North's circles, he was singled out for "particular Respect" by Lord Dartmouth. And he continued to use his position to advance his son's interests. Ben was as pleased as William when the new Secretary proclaimed that the New Jersey governor had "kept his Province in good Order during Times of Difficulty." As the two men drifted apart politically, Ben expended ever more energy in nurturing the private side of their connection. No aspect of William's life was above his notice. He appeared genuinely happy with William's success and proud of his ability to mingle with members of the imperial elite.[65] He shopped for his son and his wife, paying strict attention to William's careful instructions for mahogany chairs or a tea urn, "a plated One, or a Copper One with Silver Spout and Handles."[66] And Ben's letters were replete with confidential gossip and his often irreverent opinions about government officials and imperial policy. His missives were dotted with reminders that these passages were meant for William's eyes alone, and they indicated a complete confidence in his son's good will.[67]

The two men, after all, shared a great deal. They had been partners for so long that they knew exactly how to work with each other. Their ongoing concern in western land speculation continued to bind them together. And of course, there was always William's son. As Temple matured, Ben grew increasingly fond of the "pleasing, sensible, manly" lad, even while he took some pains to involve William in major decisions about the boy's future. He made plans for his grandson's education with William's pocketbook in mind. He considered sending him to Eton and then to Oxford, giving the boy the classical education that his father and grandfather had never enjoyed. But by 1773 he was having second thoughts. Temple was doing very well at his boarding school in Kent, an institution kept by William Strahan's brother-in-law, James Elphinston. Elphinston's school had a mixed reputation, and he himself was an eccentric and unexceptional man of letters. Still, the school was inexpensive. And Ben had heard unsettling stories about the relaxed discipline and the "viciousness" of the pupils attending more elite institutions. Like so much in England, surface attractions, upon closer examination, were riddled with corruption and smacked of decay. And he worried that William would not be able to afford such a grand education, as he talked of bringing Temple home with him whenever he returned to the colonies so that William could decide for himself what option would be most suitable. Their mutual interest in young William Temple was another reason for the bond that tied father and son together.[68]

Strangely enough, the two men remained united by a similar political philosophy as well. While their differences were no doubt greater than either cared to admit, it is nevertheless true that Ben, as much as William, retained a deep and abiding love for King and empire. He, too, still longed to find a way to reconcile the differences between England and the colonies. Ben was always a defender of the rights of the assemblies, but it was with the pro-empire side of his political personality that William identified. He took comfort in his father's reluctance to abandon colonial subordination to the Crown, while he ignored Ben's increasing pessimism over the chances of securing an accommodation between England and America. He sympathized completely with Ben's love of England, and though he missed his father, he understood—or thought he did—his occasional desire to remain in the capital city forever.[69]

William was grateful for any sign that British attitudes toward America were "Softening" even when Ben cautioned him that such indications were often deceptive. Most of all he relied on his father's desire and ability to effect a rapproachement between two sections of the empire that did not seem very far apart. His reading of his father's sentiments was not merely the product of wishful thinking. Right before the Boston Tea Party, Ben was seaching for "a means of restoring Harmony between the two Countries." And he insisted to both his son and his sister Jane that the occasional pieces he wrote defending colonial rights were meant only to draw attention to the problems facing the empire so that those problems might be resolved.[70]

In the years preceding the Boston Tea Party, William Franklin's world was surely less secure, more troubling than he would have liked. But he saw no ominous clouds on the horizon, and he did not imagine that he would ever be forced to choose between England and America, father and King. The controversy over the East Jersey treasury robbery may have pushed him one step away from his support for colonial interests, but alone it could not have made him abandon his devotion to New Jersey. Two events, both originating in the city of Boston, would soon force the governor to acknowledge the extent of the chasm separating father from son, England from America.

8

A Government Man

"You are a thorough government man, which I do not wonder at, nor do I aim at converting you. I only wish you to act uprightly and steadily, avoiding that duplicity, which in Hutchinson, adds contempt to indignation. If you can promote the prosperity of your people, and leave them happier than you found them, whatever your political principles are, your memory will be honored."—Benjamin Franklin to William Franklin, 1773.[1]

"His Majesty may be assured that I shall omit nothing in my Power to keep this Province quiet, and that, let the Event be what it may, no Attachments or Connexions shall ever make me swerve from the Duty of my Station."—William Franklin to the Earl of Dartmouth, 1774.[2]

In the winter of 1772, Boston radicals were riding high. Governor Thomas Hutchinson had just been put on the Civil List, and Bay Colony leaders used this latest threat to legislative autonomy to their best advantage. William Franklin might have been moved to genuine envy by Hutchinson's fortune, but it was a red flag to many colonists, who saw in it the loss of their financial control over the chief executive. As Massachusetts protestors mounted a campaign against gubernatorial independence, their efforts were boosted from an unexpected quarter. In December, Benjamin Franklin forwarded some documents to Thomas Cushing which, once their contents became known, would cause both Hutchinson and Andrew Oliver considerable anguish. The packet contained original letters from Oliver and the governor to Thomas Whately, one of Lord Grenville's keenest supporters. Written between 1767 and 1769, they viciously attacked the opponents of the Townshend Acts who, said the authors, had to be forcefully subdued if England expected to retain control of its American possessions. Franklin asked Cushing not to publish the letters, but to show them discreetly to a few colonial leaders. He also steadfastly refused to tell anyone how he had obtained the explosive documents.[3]

By the time the Massachusetts General Assembly met in the spring of 1773, rumors about the letters had already begun to circulate. Under the circumstances, it seemed best to read them before a closed session of the legislature. After that it was impossible to keep them out of the public eye, and their contents became the talk of the colonies.[4]

William Franklin naturally sympathized with his fellow governor. Hutchinson, he told his father, was "gloomy and low spirited," and he was preparing to flee to England where he could avoid further humiliation. While William had criticized Hutchinson's handling of the Stamp Act crisis, he nevertheless was bound to commiserate with a royal official whose private correspondence had been laid before the world, inviting ridicule and hatred. He himself had experienced a similar sense of violation when anonymous interlopers had pawed through his personal letters. He, too, knew what it was like to be reviled and misinterpreted by self-interested and ambitious colonists. Moreover, he did not think the Hutchinson letters merited the outrage that they elicited. Like the Massachusetts governor, William Franklin despised the excesses that invariably accompanied mob action.[5]

He assumed that his father would share his feelings. He did not dream that Ben, who had often complained vigorously when his own letters had been intercepted, could possibly have had anything to do with so dishonorable a business. When rumors began floating through the colonies that either Franklin or John Temple[6] was behind the scandal, William naturally imagined that the allegations were as false as all the other wild stories invented by Ben's enemies over the years. He expected his father to deny his complicity immediately. But this time there was no denial.[7]

Instead, on the first of September, the elder Franklin told his son what he was still trying to conceal from interested parties on both sides of the Atlantic. The "famous Boston letters" he admitted, had fallen into his hands. Ben's explanation for his decision to send the letters to Boston gave William little comfort. He claimed that he had used them to bring America and England closer together. By showing the colonists that the ministry had been acting on bad advice emanating from America itself, the true enemy would be discovered and misunderstandings would be resolved. It seems, from hindsight, a strange sort of logic. And if Franklin meant what he said, he completely miscalculated the effect that the documents would have. It was not the first time that he failed to gauge colonial sentiments correctly.[8]

Regardless of Benjamin Franklin's original intentions, the letters had increased tensions between America and England, and even Ben's old ploy of taking his son into his confidence was hardly sufficient to mollify him. William was even more unhappy when he saw how unsympathetic Ben was to the Massachusetts governor's plight. "I don't wonder that Hutchinson should be dejected," Ben said. "It must be an uncomfortable thing to live among people who he is conscious universally detest him." And the governor was moved to real uneasiness when he realized that the government could not defend its own representative from colonial harassment or even provide Hutchinson a safe haven in London.[9]

William did not intend to violate his father's confidence. Indeed, he fervently hoped that no one would ever know who was responsible for Hutchinson's troubles.[10] By the summer of 1773, Franklin was forced to acknowledge at some level that he and his father were drifting apart. He had heard unsettling stories that Ben was advising "*Independency*" to the radicals in Boston. And Ben had rebuked his own son for failing to recognize the "heinous" nature of Hutchinson's letters. To be sure, he had groped to excuse his inability to appreciate their significance. "Perhaps," he said, "you had not read them all, nor perhaps the council's remarks on them." It was a desperate effort to ignore their growing differences. William took what comfort he could in his father's words. After all, Ben still trusted him with his secrets, though there had been a time when they would have planned such a caper together. The letters had been divulged with an eye to reconciling imperial differences. Surely Ben's motives had been unimpeachable, even laudable, although their consequences had been disastrous. Neither father nor son was willing, at this point, to disavow the other. The royal governor and the partiotic defender of assembly rights remained fast, if troubled friends.[11]

But another, and in the end a more decisive imperial controversy was brewing in the summer of 1773, though neither William nor Benjamin Franklin initially recognized its significance. The problem had its roots in the imminent collapse of the East India Tea Company, whose difficulties Ben had described dispassionately at the beginning of the year. In April, the House of Commons began discussing inexpensive ways to come to the company's rescue. To encourage the sale of English tea in the mainland colonies, Parliament virtually eliminated the duty on tea exported from England, thus making the popular beverage more competitive with rival Dutch tea. While some members of Parliament suggested that the Townshend duty also be eliminated, the proposal was rejected with little discussion. The need for some profits for the customs commission, and, to a lesser extent, the principle of Parliament's right to tax England's American possessions, induced the House to retain the import tax. Virtually no one had any idea of the ramifications this seemingly innocuous decision would have.[12]

Benjamin Franklin hoped the colonists would greet the Tea Act with firm but peaceful protests, for he remained convinced that mob action would result in military repression. Nevertheless, his rhetoric grew increasingly radical. By July he was urging Americans to exert financial pressure on the mother country in an effort to force Parliament to back down. To make their boycott effective, the colonies had to act in concert. Thus Franklin proposed "a general Congress now in Peace to be assembled," so that there would be no weak spots in colonial resolve. While the venerable agent professed a genuine love for the empire, he clearly sought unity with England on America's terms.[13]

Ben outlined his thoughts to his son in the fall of 1773. He held a view of empire that differed markedly from the governor's. William saw Britain as an organic whole, whose integrity could not be violated without certain disaster for Englishmen everywhere. But after a "long and thorough consideration of the subject," Ben had concluded that Parliament had no right to make any law binding the colonies, that the King alone, not the King-in-Parliament, was sovereign in America. Knowing full well how his views would be received, Franklin held out the olive branch to his son, the royal governor. "I know," he said, "your sentiments differ from mine on these subjects. You are a thorough government man, which I do not wonder at, nor do I aim at converting you." He only hoped that William would perform his job with honor and decency. "If you can promote the prosperity of your people," he said "and leave them happier than you found them, whatever your political principles are, your memory will be honored."[14]

While Ben urged America to stand firm and expressed his support of his son's person, if not his politics, events in America were moving much faster than either Franklin could have predicted. Ben busily scribbled essays on the American position for the London papers. William was embroiled in the controversy over the treasury robbery, and appeared not to appreciate the ramifications the Tea Act would have in New Jersey. And at first, the colony seemed likely to ignore the turmoil that characterized politics elsewhere. The assembly was meeting in Burlington when the Speaker received letters from Virginia, Massachusetts, Connecticut, and Rhode Island calling upon the legislators to form permanent committees of correspondence to coordinate colonial protests against the Tea Act. The letters were read in the house on November 21, and were promptly forgotten.[15]

But despite the wishes of either Franklin or of the New Jersey house, their own fate and that of the British empire were about to be decisively altered by a handful of Boston patriots. On December 16, approximately fifty men, partially disguised with blankets and warpaint, boarded three British ships resting in Boston's harbor and dumped their cargo, 342 crates of East India tea, into the harbor. As the crates sank to the ocean floor, the hopes of Benjamin and William Franklin for an amicable solution to the differences dividing England from its colonial possessions, sank with them.[16]

News of the Boston Tea Party did not have an immediate effect in New

Jersey. There were a few isolated protests in support of the rioters, but on the whole reaction to the incident was low-key. Nor did any one in the assembly seem anxious to broach the subject. Franklin briefly imagined that the legislators would not even form a committee of correspondence. He "took some Pains with several of the principal Members for the purpose," and for a while he was confident that his private efforts would be effective. Indeed, it was not until February 8, when the lawmakers learned that New York had formed a committee, that the New Jersey house decided to create one of its own. The legislators, explained Franklin, did not "choose to appear singular." Still, the assembly almost ignored the Tea Party and the issues surrounding it. The treasury robbery, not the affairs of empire, dominated the session. And until that issue was resolved, no one wanted to think or talk of anything else.[17]

Benjamin Franklin's personal and political crisis came more quickly than it did to his son. On January 29, 1774, a little over a month after the Boston Tea Party, the elder Franklin became the subject of a public and ritual humiliation designed to appease Englishmen who were outraged by this latest evidence of colonial treachery. Their momentary satisfaction was costly, for it ended in permanently alienating one of England's most influential American friends. Ostensibly, Franklin was called before the Privy Council to defend a Massachusetts petition for the removal of Thomas Hutchinson and Andrew Oliver. But this was a mere pretext. The ministers were still smarting from the embarrassment occasioned by the release of the Hutchinson-Oliver letters.[18] Even worse, Ben's July report to the Massachusetts house, urging resolute resistance to Parliament, had fallen into the hands of Lord Dartmouth. It had proved to many ministers what some already suspected: Franklin was an ungrateful and disloyal colonial upstart, who answered their favors with childish tantrums and outright disobedience. News of the Boston Tea Party only fueled the frustrations of English leaders. They felt increasingly ill-used and bewildered. They needed a scapegoat. And Benjamin Franklin, who, ironically was even then a supporter of imperial unity, became the convenient target for their collective wrath.[19] Franklin was harangued and browbeaten in a section of Whitehall aptly named the "Cockpit," for almost an hour. As Alexander Wedderburn, Lord North's unprincipled solicitor general, subjected him to sarcasm and invective, to the delight of a raucous, overflow crowd, Franklin stood silent, uttering not a word in his own defense. But he would never forget the humiliation he suffered that day.[20]

Within twenty-four hours, Franklin was stripped of his job as Deputy Postmaster General. Until this moment, he had seen himself as the epitome of moderation. His dual role as royal placeholder and colonial agent symbolized his disinterested perspective, his freedom to maneuver and express his own opinions with ease. Unlike his son, he owed his livelihood to no single source, and so he enjoyed the luxury of always being his own person. While he had always operated on the fringes of London society, and had lately been even more estranged from official circles, Franklin had never abandoned his government connections. He did not quit his post office position; he was fired.[21]

Ben's reaction to the loss of his royal sinecure was predictable. Before long he managed to turn his dismissal into a badge of "honour." The loss, he assured Jane Mecom, was actually a "Testimony of my being uncorrupted." In fact, his humiliation caused him considerable anguish. He grew notably silent and withdrawn in the days after the Cockpit interrogation, licking his wounds in private and contemplating revenge. In a letter written to his son just two days after his sinecure had been snatched from him, Franklin revealed his pain. It was a terse message, informing William of nothing but the barest facts. "You will hear from others the Treatment I have receiv'd," he said, and "I leave you to your own Reflections and Determinations upon it." But he clearly expected his son to share his resentment, and assumed that William would rush to resign his governorship to protest his father's treatment. There was now no prospect that he would ever be promoted. His position, Ben unkindly reminded his son, had never equaled his expenses. "I wish you were well settled in your Farm," he said. " 'Tis an honester and a more honourable because a more independent Employment."[22]

But for William, resignation was out of the question. His sole source of income, identity and purpose derived from his role as royal governor. Unlike Ben, he had no other constituents to serve. Moreover, he was too much the product of his father's training, too much a prisoner of his own personality, ever to quit anything that he started. His father was the man who, at the beginning of his political career, had proclaimed as his personal credo, "I shall never *ask*, never *refuse*, nor ever *resign* an Office." William had learned this lesson well. Once committed to any person or policy, he could not be budged. He remained loyal to his stepmother when he had every reason to avoid her. He forced Elizabeth Graeme to break off their engagement rather than do the distasteful deed himself. While he almost invited Lord Hillsborough to dismiss him in 1768, he refused to volunteer his resignation. And most recently he had stubbornly supported Stephen Skinner's claim to his treasurer's position long after common sense, or even loyalty, demanded it. This was not a man who would easily change his course of action or who would lightly abandon his responsibilities.[23]

His father's news, coupled with the peremptory advice to quit his post, must have come as a shock. Ben had obviously lost favor in London. Not only was his political usefulness at an end, he would now be a real detriment. But William's loyalty to his father was deep, and he could not denounce him. Still, he had no desire to lose everything he had worked for because of Ben's disgrace. He did not wish to force a confrontation by forthrightly refusing to quit his job. Neither did he want to abandon his post.

It was Ben himself who saved his son from an impossible dilemma, helping him to postpone the inevitable. After the elder Franklin had calmed down, he sent another message to Burlington with instructions calculated to let William pursue his own course. A little over two weeks had passed since his first letter. The rumor mill had been grinding away, and everywhere Ben heard the same story. William was about to be dismissed. Under the cricumstances, Ben advised his son to sit tight. Do not, he said, "save them the shame of depriving you whom they ought to promote." He did not want William to make anything easy for the administration. "One may make something of an Injury," he explained, but "nothing of a Resignation."[24]

For the present, William was off the hook. He could hold on to his job without risking his father's approbation. It is tempting to wonder what would have happened if the reports that he would be replaced had proven correct. If he had been thrown out of office and publicly humiliated as his father had been, would he not have offered his services to the new and illegitimate government about to be born in the American colonies? Some historians have argued that Ben's move toward independence was merely the product of a desire to seek revenge for the wrongs he had suffered at the hands of the Crown's supporters. While it would be exaggerating to say that Ben was actuated solely by self-interest, the loss of his job helped convince him that his prospects were better served "as a patriot in America than a turncoat in England." Had William Franklin been similarly convinced, his story may have been different.[25]

But Franklin did hold on to his position. And he did his best to maintain his ties to his father, as well. Observers noted that the governor wore a studious "Air of Indifference" throughout the spring. While many advised him to hold all plans in abeyance until he knew whether he would "longer continue in the Saddle," William quietly prepared for his move to Perth Amboy. Everyone was buzzing about the effect that imperial discord might have on William's relationship with Ben. But at first gossip-mongers could find no juicy tidbits to satisfy their curiosity.[26]

William waited until May before answering either of Ben's letters, and even then, his message was brief. It was, however, carefully crafted. The governor wrote from Philadelphia, where he insisted Ben's popularity was greater than ever. And he urged his father to return home as quickly as possible. The elder Franklin had obviously lost all influence in England's capital. It was time for him to come home, see his ailing wife, and meet the grandchildren he had never seen.[27]

William hoped for more from his father's return than the renewal of family ties. He wanted Ben to see the colonies for himself so that he could more accurately assess American motives. Ben had been so removed from provincial reality, and so caught up in criticizing ministerial venality that he viewed events on his native soil from an all too roseate perspective. He needed to see that error and excess, bribery and corruption, existed on this side of the Atlantic as well as in London. William had a perfect example of just the sort of thing Ben would discover upon his return. At the very time that his father had been fulminating over his disgrace at the Cockpit, his "Friends in Boston" had been plotting to seize his Post Office position and award it to printer William Goddard. Thus, argued William, had Ben not lost his post from one source, he would have been deprived of it from another. Venality and double-dealing did not adhere solely to London politicians.[28]

It hardly seemed fair, then, to blame the ministry for all of Ben's current setbacks. And William saw no point in gratuitously abandoning his own position at a time when he was held in higher esteem in London than he had been for years. Indeed, he had just received indirect word from Lord Dartmouth indicating that his governorship was safe. And Franklin intended to hold on to his job if at all possible. "I am determined," he said, "not to give any just Cause of Complaint, so that if after all I should receive any Injury from that Quarter, I shall be at no loss what to do." Without referring directly to either of Ben's letters, he had staked out his position. He had not quarreled with his father, nor his father with him. Each had acted as though he assumed the other would agree with his perspective.[29]

Even as William was pleading with his father to return home, Ben was entertaining further thoughts about his son's governorship. He did not directly instruct him to resign, but he gave every indication that he thought this would be the best course. He reminded William again that his position was not very lucrative. "With all your Prudence," he said, "you cannot avoid running behind hand, if you live suitably to your Station." He understood that so long as his son continued as governor he would remain loyal to the King, "but," he argued, "I think Independence more honourable than any Service." While his father vacillated, William ignored Ben's mixed signals, and followed a steady and unaltered course.[30]

It was the Coercive Acts, not the Boston Tea Party or Ben's humiliation at the Cockpit that irrevocably set father and son, England and America, on divergent paths. Before Parliament decided to isolate and punish the Bay Colony, the imperial debate had centered on the issue of taxation.

William Franklin (Frick Art Reference Library)

Benjamin Franklin (Yale University Library)

Deborah Franklin (The American Philosophical Society)

Philadelphia State House, 1778 (The American Philosophical Society)

Richard Penn, by Joseph Highmore (The Historical Society of Pennsylvania)

Thomas Penn, 1896, by M. J. Naylor (The Historical Society of Pennsylvania)

Benjamin Franklin's Residence in London in 1760, Anonymous engraving (Emmet Collection, The New York Public Library)

William Strahan, 1783, by Sir J. Reynolds (National Portrait Gallery, London)

William Temple Franklin, by John Trumbull
(Yale University Art Gallery)

GEN. LORD STIRLING.

Stirling

Lord William Stirling, ca. 1726–1783, engraved by G. E. Hall, published by
Putnam & Co., New York (The New York Historical Society)

Lord North (Clements Library)

Portrait of Sir Henry Clinton, ca. 1783–1795, engraved by A. H. Ritchie (The New-York Historical Society)

Now the stakes were higher, as colonial leaders openly questioned Parliament's authority and began to define the limits of its power. As soon as word of the Boston Port Act reached America, the governor hastened to assure Lord Dartmouth of his firm intention to maintain order in New Jersey. He felt compelled to remind the Secretary that "no Attachments or Connexions" would ever impel him to "swerve from [his] Duty." Franklin also wanted to provide Dartmouth his own assessment of the mood of the colonies. He recognized that "the Times [were] likely to become more and more difficult." Still, he was cautiously optimistic, and even strangely myopic. He assumed that the Port Act would have little direct effect on his own colony, for the inhabitants there did not trade much with Massachusetts anyway. In Philadelphia and New York, merchants were talking of coming to Boston's aid, but most of them wanted to avoid a boycott. While talk of a Congress had been bandied about in some circles, the governor was not convinced that a meeting was inevitable. In all, his account was judicious, and suggested no sense of panic.[31]

But the letter revealed that Franklin had lost touch with reality and failed to appreciate the serious turn that relations beween America and England had taken. So committed was he to the rule of law that he could not visualize a society based on extralegal foundations. Thus he dismissed the Committees of Correspondence as "absurd" and "unconstitutional." They cannot, he laughingly informed Dartmouth, "even answer their Purpose." For every assembly depended upon the pleasure of its governor, and each governor would prorogue or dissolve any legislature attempting to do anything "improper." Consequently, he said with a triumphant flourish, "whenever an Assembly is dissolved, the power of its Committee is of course annihilated." Legally, Franklin may have stood on firm ground; practically his gloss was irrelevant.[32]

Even without assembly support, local leaders were already taking matters into their own hands. In June, Essex County protestors gathered at the Newark court house to declare their allegiance to the Crown, condemn the Coercive Acts, and call for an inter-colonial congress. And they urged the inhabitants of Monmouth County to imitate their own example as quickly as possible.[33] Franklin was helpless before this sudden outburst of activity. "Meetings of this Nature," he sadly observed, "there are no Means of preventing, where the chief Part of the Inhabitants incline to attend them."[34]

The governor tried to remain calm, going about his business as if nothing untoward was happening. He wrote to Lord Dartmouth, telling him in some detail about the assembly's latest attempt to write a currency bill. He continued to express doubts that a non-importation agreement would ever get off the ground. And when he began receiving petitions begging for a special legislative session, he cooly ignored them. There was, he said, "no public Business of the Province which can make such a meeting necessary."[35]

Interestingly, both Ben and William were, in their own very different ways, groping for some means to effect a reconciliation between England and America. When he had first received news of the Tea Party, the elder Franklin had been taken aback at the "extremity" of the protest. He had constantly urged his American friends to be cautious and non-violent in their protests against the Tea Act, and now that private property had been destroyed and Parliament was enraged, he insisted that at the very least Boston ought to offer to pay for the ruined tea. But with the passage of the Coercive Acts, and the talk in America of a general congress and a non-importation agreement, his attitude hardened. Stiff resistance, not meek compliance, was the key to reconciliation. If the colonies organized an effective embargo on English goods, then he thought that the government would fall, the obnoxious legislation would be repealed, and the differences separating the colonists from the mother country would vanish. Such an approach had worked during the Stamp Act crisis; why would it not work now?[36]

William Franklin did not look for accommodation through resistance. There was, he told both his father and Lord Dartmouth, "no foreseeing the Consequences" of a congress that would meet when tempers on both sides of the Atlantic were so volatile. While Ben advocated defiance, the governor pushed for concessions on both sides. He found it "very extraordinary" that Boston had not offered to reimburse the East India Company for its losses. Not only would this gesture be consistent with "strict Justice," but it would serve colonial ends. Unlike his father, William was convinced that England would not back down in the face of colonial intransigence. Thus if Boston delayed paying for the tea, its already deteriorating position would be weakened; its trade would be ruined; its merchants and artisans would relocate; and Boston would be a veritable ghost town. But if the city followed his advice, delegates could attend the proposed congress after a settlement had been made, and the "grand Question" of parliamentary taxation could be taken up at a more leisurely pace. And having done justice themselves, the Americans would be in a much stronger position to wring concessions from Parliament.[37]

If Franklin asked for accommodation from the colonies, he made a similar request to Lord Dartmouth. Above all, he hoped to turn the congress from an extralegal liability into a legal asset. He believed, as many Englishmen did not, that most delegates to such a congress would be, like his good friend Joseph Galloway, sincerely searching for an honorable rapprochement with the mother country. Thus, it seemed relatively easy to devise a formula that would satisfy all but the most rancorous extremists on both sides. The thing to do, he told the American Secretary, was to co-opt the congress by legalizing it, sending Crown representatives to the meeting. The colonial governors, a few delegates from each provincial council and assembly, and a commission from England could discuss their respective needs, and devise mutually satisfactory solutions. It would be a thoughtful and balanced gathering. The "democratical" part of government would have its say, as would the Crown. Franklin's proposal was statesman-like and judicious. But the time was fast approaching when no one on either side was prepared for a moderate accommodation of differences.[38]

While the governor feverishly wrote letters and searched for some way to regain control of a rapidly deteriorating situation, politics in the colony assumed a life of its own. Delegates from the various local committees of correspondence met in New Brunswick at the end of July to choose representatives to the Continental Congress. And they assumed some governmental powers when they organized county committees to collect money and supplies for the relief of Boston. While they declared their "firm and unshaken" loyalty to the King, these delegates were more radical than their counterparts during the Stamp Act crisis had been. Then there at least had been some effort to follow legal channels, by convening a rump session of the assembly to choose representatives to the New York Congress. This time, however, the assembly was simply ignored.[39]

As William watched his position erode, he saw his personal hopes and dreams fading as well. Word was out that the Boston Tea Party had dealt a near death blow to the Vandalia grant. Just as it had been within his grasp, the actions of a few thoughtless colonists had virtually destroyed a project that had occupied Franklin's time and taken his resources during much of his governorship. This time, the blame lay completely with the American protestors. Stubborn ministers and stodgy bureaucrats were no longer responsible for the frustrations of the land company.[40]

The controversy that was destroying his chances for reaping a fortune from western lands, also caused the thin-skinned governor a little political embarrassment. While the details are not altogether clear, Franklin's moderation, his desire to see and defend both sides of every issue were partly to blame. On May 21, 1774, he wrote a confidential letter to William Strahan, which evidently contained views that could cause Franklin considerable grief in both England and America. Its contents are easy to imagine, for on many occasions the governor had indicated that he was not particularly pleased with the behavior of extremists on either side of the Atlantic. But by now, no one was in the mood to tolerate criticism, and Franklin's letter had attacked both the colonial and the ministerial positions.[41]

News of the letter, and extracts of its contents, somehow reached Philadelphia.[42] Many thought Thomas Walpole and the Whartons were responsible,[43] but the news became the talk of the town, and spread to other colonies and even to London without their help.[44] Everyone indulged in gossip about William's letter. Thomas Wharton thought that the governor's comments indicated that he was "lost to every principle, which his Aged & Honored Father had been for years supporting." And he obviously enjoyed the "great freedom" with which Franklin's name and reputation were being bandied about.[45]

But there was more at issue than simple embarrassment. Everyone knew that Thomas Hutchinson had lost both his credibility and his job over just this kind of publicity. The parallel was certainly not lost on William Franklin, who furiously tried to control the potential damage. He dashed off two letters, one to Joseph Galloway, the other to Richard Bache, trying to separate rumor from fact.[46] He also placed an advertisement in the Philadelphia papers, asserting that the stories circulating about him were "without foundation." Repeatedly Franklin proclaimed his outrage that the "entirely confidential" letter had been allowed to reach public eyes.[47]

The results of the tempest were anticlimactic. When Franklin finally galloped to Philadelphia to confront Thomas Wharton who he was convinced was behind a plot to smear his good name, he discovered that the extracts of his letter to Strahan were not as damaging to his reputation as the rumor mongers had claimed. They contained his claim that he wished to "make peace with the Administration" and his criticisms of ministerial policy had been omitted. Franklin was not, after all, in danger of losing face with London officials.[48]

Still, serious damage had been done. The extracts may have cleared his reputation with Whitehall, but they had not endeared him to many people in America. Franklin was now viewed as a defender of the ministry rather than as a man who had serious reservations about English policy. Significantly, he did little to counter that impression. He did not relish a choice between England and America. But his response to the furor over the Strahan letter, plainly showed where his ultimate loyalties lay.

William's personal life was also in turmoil. His relationship with his father, in particular, blew hot and cold. While the elder Franklin stopped sending political news to his son after July, he still made an effort to reach out and nudge him gently away from his dependence on the Crown. At times Ben tried to shame him into submission. Just as often, he attempted to coax William into a decision that he was sincerely convinced would bring him happiness and honor. And sometimes he did a little of both.

In August, Ben broached the subject of settling on a career for Temple. This seemed a safe topic and surely was one with which both men were concerned. Temple had become something of a dilettante. He painted a little, and exhibited a passing interest in medicine, but was unable to stick to any single option. Ben thought his abilities lay in the law. It was, he told

William with just a touch of flattery, "a Profession reputable in itself." But more than that, it promised independence. Lawyers could use their talents in a variety of ways and were beholden to no one. Ben seemed to be hinting that William's well-honed skills allowed him to abandon his position as a government servant, and to seek new avenues of employment. If William was clinging to his job for mere security, then he need do so no longer. Ben himself, with much less training than his son, had retired at 43 to begin an entirely new life. William, with his superior qualifications and undoubted ability, could easily do the same.[49]

Even as he tried to open his son's mind to the myriad opportunities before him, Ben could not resist the occasional snide attack, as he revealed his own disappointment at the direction William's life was taking. Thus when he discussed Temple's career options he did not refrain from twisting the knife. No matter what else befell his grandson, he said, he wanted to make sure that the boy could "at any time procure a Subsistence." Anything else would be "well and good," but Ben hoped that Temple would never embark on the precarious and degrading business of seeking government dependencies. Above all, he thundered, "I would have him a Free Man."[50]

Usually Ben's comments were subtle and indirect. The frontal assault was not his style. But occasionally he lost his temper entirely. In September he read William's letter begging him to return home, proposing his officially sanctioned American congress, and fulminating over Boston's refusal to reimburse the East India Tea Company. While William was solicitous of his father's feelings, his comments came from an alien perspective. His son did not seem to share Ben's outrage over the Cockpit humiliation, nor was he disturbed by Parliament's violation of colonial rights. He seemed more irritated by Boston's protestors than by the Coercive Acts.

Ben responded angrily, as he tried to show his son how out of touch with reality he was. He was pained by William's political views. He was also hurt by the implication that he had outlived his usefulness in London. Moreover, the governor's formula for solving the present crisis was, bluntly, all wrong. Ben dismissed the suggestion for a Crown-authorized congress with an airy wave of his hand. "I hear nothing of the Proposal," he said. England was so intransigent that no hope for reconciliation could be expected from that quarter. Rapproachement would have to come as the result of American resolve. Toughness, not compromise, was the key to success. "This," he patronized his son, "is the Opinion of all wise Men here."[51]

Franklin reserved his most vicious—and most unfair—weapons for last. "I do not, so much as you do, wonder," he said sarcastically, "that the Massachusetts have not offered Payment for the Tea." Conveniently forgetting that he himself had once advocated reimbursement, he explained how wrong-headed such a proposal was. America owed England nothing. Rather,

Parliament owed money to the colonies, for the "many Thousand Pounds" it had "extorted" from America over the years. Franklin did not expect to convince his son of the logic of his analysis. "You," he said in words that revealed the extent of his rage, "who are a thorough Courtier, see every thing with Government Eyes." Had Karl Marx accused his children of being "petite bourgeois" the effect could not have been more devastating.[52]

Had Benjamin Franklin known what his son was doing in the summer and fall of 1774, he would not have regretted his harsh language. As early as June, William began to forward information about New Jersey protests to the home government. As governor, it was only appropriate that he keep the ministry abreast of significant developments in his own colony. But by September, Franklin had systematically begun to amass information about colonial disorders everywhere. He was fully aware of the seriousness of his activity. All his messages to Dartmouth were labeled "secret and confidential" and he begged the Secretary to guard their contents. William had learned how to outwit possible spies in the days when he and his father had suspected that their correspondence was being intercepted. He put those same skills to use now, when the stakes were much higher.[53]

Some historians have suggested that Franklin's clandestine activity was evidence of his "descision" to support England against America. But Franklin was no more committed to defending the empire in 1774 than he had been a decade earlier. He did not "become" loyal to the empire in 1774 or even in 1776. He had sworn his allegiance to the King in 1762, and from that oath he never deviated. It was patriots like Benjamin Franklin, not loyalists like his son, who altered their course in the years preceding the American Revolution. William Franklin simply continued doing what he had always thought a good governor should do. He was representing Crown interests in the colonies, while he searched for a way to bring the recalcitrant elements there back into the fold. And he remained sincerely convinced that colonial interests could best be served within an imperial framework.[54]

Throughout the fall of 1774, the governor gathered information on the proeceedings of the Continental Congress, which met in Philadelphia for the first time on September 5. As Ben had predicted, the home government made no effort to attend the meeting. From William's perspective, England had lost a golden opportunity. But he did what he could to compensate for the lack of ministerial initiative. He was in a perfect position to report on congress's activities. He still lived in Burlington, where news filtered easily from one seat of government to the other. More important, Joseph Galloway led the Pennsylvania delegation, and he gladly furnished Franklin with a confidential account of congressional activities.[55]

Moreover, Franklin was aware of, and probably helped Galloway formulate, a plan of action that both men thought might take the wind out of the sails of colonial rabble rousers. Galloway hoped to persuade congress to send commissioners to London to begin personal negotiations with the ministry. And he planned to publish his pamphlet, *Arguments on Both Sides etc.* to lay the groundwork for the "Plan of Union" he would unveil during the session. The centerpiece of Galloway's plan was an interprovincial council, elected by the individual assemblies with control over colonial affairs and power equal to Parliament's on all questions affecting the empire. This, he thought, would "prove a lasting and beneficial Cement to all the Parts of the British Empire." Based on Whig notions of parliamentary supremacy, it sought to maintain American subordination, while providing the colonies with representation. It was a tricky business, but he thought his plan equal to the task.[56]

Franklin, too, pinned most of his hopes on congressional approval of some formula designed to bring the empire closer together. He knew that moderate proposals had a way of being rejected by hardliners on both ends of the political spectrum; he recognized that men caught in the middle of a protracted political struggle were often shoved aside or destroyed. Still, he thought any proposal, even if it was not "deemed perfect," was worth the effort. In fact Franklin had serious reservations of his own about Galloway's blueprint. Most importantly, he disapproved of having the Continental Congress ratify the "Plan of Union" and forward it to the King. He was convinced that the right to form a new government lay, not with an illegal congress, but with each individual assembly. He would not easily abandon his belief in legal propriety or his determination to uphold the integrity of elected legislatures.[57]

The governor had other quarrels with Galloway's proposal. He thought that the "Plan of Union" lacked balance and stability. In particular, it needed a "Middle branch or Upper House" to mediate between the "Regal and popular Part of the Legislature." This branch would be composed of a few council members and some of the "principal Gentlemen of Fortune" from each colony, who could hold their positions during good behavior or even for life. Franklin also hoped to establish some sort of privy council, composed of all royal governors as well as a number of Crown appointees. These proposals reflected the philosophical distance that separated William from his father. Ben's Albany Plan of Union, rejected so many years ago by the jealous American legislatures, had not envisioned any such "Middle Branch" as the governor now advocated. But William was trying to create what amounted to a political aristocracy, a council for life, in America. It was hard to believe that these proposals emanated from the son and close confident of a man who hated aristocracy more than monarchy.[58]

Unfortunately for men like Franklin and Galloway, no plan of union found favor with the Continental Congress. Most delegates traveled to Philadelphia fully expecting to find a way to reconcile their differences with the mother country. But a plan that gave the British Parliament as much authority as Galloway's did was simply not acceptable to the vast majority of the men sitting in Philadelphia. Galloway's agenda was his own. He had grown increasingly ineffective in his own colony, and was out of step with most members of congress. He saw radical machinations behind every move the delegates took, claiming that the real decisions were being made "by an Interest made out of Doors." But in fact he should not have been surprised at the failure of his proposal. He briefly succeeded in having it read into the minutes, but he was quickly out-maneuvered and the plan was expunged from the record.[59]

Galloway's failure symbolized the problem that he and William Franklin repeatedly refused to face in the months following the Coercive Acts. While there were few men on either side of the Atlantic who did not want to resolve the differences dividing England and America, the chances for a workable compromise were receding almost daily. No one was in the mood to concede any ground. Consequently, Galloway's plan was given short shrift by the colonial congress, and Franklin's advice to the ministry was similarly ignored without even an acknowledgement. The governor's confidence that the ministry could work out some sort of sweeping parliamentary reform whereby American, Irish and English subjects would all be equitably represented in the House of Commons, totally ignored political reality. William's vision of a responsible, intelligent, and malleable government in London, was as myopic as the romantic view of American virtue that his father harbored from his position in England.[60]

Still, if Franklin's advice was ignored, his information was valued. Gone were the days when the governor dreaded the latest message from London, never knowing what kind of insult it might contain. While his father was telling him that he was a "thorough Courtier," Lord Dartmouth praised his attempts to contain New Jersey's "democratical" impulses and did not berate him when his endeavors failed. The Secretary's confidence in his integrity could only soothe the feelings of a man who was increasingly alienated from his own society, buffeted about by forces beyond his control, and reviled by the countrymen he had once counted as his supporters, if not his friends.[61]

With Lord Hillsborough's departure from the ministry, William Franklin's relations with the home government steadily improved. Moreover, Dartmouth's rise to power reinforced Franklin's faith in the basic justice and good intentions of King and empire. It had taken a long time for the ministry to recognize its error in granting authority to a man like Hillsborough. But at last William's patience had been rewarded and he could look forward to working happily under benevolent and intelligent leaders.

And so Franklin continued to gather and transmit every morsel of intelligence he could find to his superiors. He sent a copy of Galloway's "Plan of Union," hoping that the ministry would use it as a basis for dialogue with the recalcitrant colonies. He acknowledged that the American boycott of British trade was likely to become a reality, and that a mechanism for implementing the boycott, known as the Association, was also in the works. By assuming the power of enforcing its own policies, Congress was acting as an illegal government. Franklin was clearly disturbed by this turn of events, but insisted that most Americans disapproved of congressional policy. "Few have the Courage," he explained, "to declare their Disapprobation publickly, as they well know, if they do not conform, they are in Danger of becoming Objects of popular Resentment." Paradoxically, Franklin was forced to admit that no colonial government had the power to protect those who wished to disobey congressional dictate. The radical minority was running roughshod over the moderate majority, and no one could stem the tide of events.[62]

While the delegates met, argued and resolved in Philadelphia, William and Elizabeth Franklin shored up their own position, preparing themselves for the worst that American politics could deliver. One way to remove themselves from the line of fire while at the same time signaling their resolve to remain in New Jersey was to begin the long awaited move to Perth Amboy. "Amboy Air" had been looking more inviting for some time, and by the fall of 1773, preparations for the move had begun in earnest. The Franklins put the farm on Rancocas Creek and the house in Burlington up for sale. And the Board of Proprietors in East Jersey began making repairs and improvements on Proprietary House. Franklin prepared meticulous instructions for refurbishing the governor's mansion. He insisted that every detail reflect the honor of his office. But his plans also served as his tribute to the natural beauty of a colony he had always admired and had grown to love. The pictures of Passaic falls that graced the wallpaper in the main hall were one of William's last public attempts to express his devotion to his adopted colony.[63]

By the fall of 1774, he and his wife had left their home of ten years for the hospitality of Perth Amboy. They departed with some regret. Their Burlington friends gave the Franklins "an entertainment" before they took their leave, assuring them both that they would always be welcome in the little city. But while William assured his well-wishers that he would "ever reflect" on his "many happy days" in the western capital, he clearly intended his departure to be permanent.[64]

The sadness with which the Franklins abandoned their only real home together was accentuated by William's sense that he was abandoning his stepmother. His last visit with Deborah had been painful. She had never been well since her stroke, and the most casual observer could see that her health was deteriorating. She could no longer lift her hand to write her husband, and seemed to have lost all capacity to hope or strength to endure. As Deborah clung to her departing stepson, she predicted that she would not live to see the spring, and mourned that unless Ben arrived in America before then, she would never see her "Dear Child" again.[65]

Deborah's prophecy proved accurate. Scarcely had William and Elizabeth settled into their new home, when a courier informed them that she had suffered a "paralytic Stroke" on the fourteenth of December, and had died five days later. Leaving his frail wife in Perth Amboy, William set out for Philadelphia, battling snow and cold as he struggled to make his way to his native home in time for Deborah's funeral. The experience was an emotional one, and it brought to the surface all the pent-up feelings of resentment that had lain quietly beneath William's calm exterior for so long. As he watched his "poor old mother's" coffin disappear into the icy ground, he could not deny his bitterness. He came close to accusing his father of hastening Deborah's death. And he almost hated Ben for not being there, in America where he was wanted, needed and loved.[66]

William's ardent desire to have his father back in America was based on more than simple pity for Deborah. Ben, too, was growing old, and his son wanted him to return home before the arduous ocean voyage became too much for him, and he decided, with his wife dead and the colonies in turmoil, to remain in England forever. He wanted both Ben and Temple in America. Temple, he said, could begin studying law in New York, where, he diplomatically forbore pointing out, he would live away from the rebellious atmosphere that polluted the air in Philadelphia. And Ben could move to Perth Amboy, where there would always be an apartment for him in the commodious governor's mansion.[67]

William hoped for a political as well as a personal rapprochement with his father. He had only written to Ben once since receiving the letter chastising him for his "courtier"-like propensities.[68] But though he now avoided any direct reference to Ben's angry words, the memory rankled. He tried to convince his father that the two of them could still make an effective team. There was, he pointed out, no reason for Ben to remain in London. He had no chance to influence the King's ministers. Nor was there a possibility that the ministry would fall. There are, he said, "pretty strong Proofs that neither can be reasonably expected and that you are look'd upon with an evil Eye in that Country."[69]

Thus it was better that Ben return "to a Country where the People revere you, and are inclined to pay a Deference to your Opinions." William had "heard from all Quarters" how "ardently" Ben's presence at the Continental Congress had been desired. People imagined, he said, that had the elder Franklin attended the meeting, he would have found a way to reconcile the differences between England and America. Where Joseph Galloway had failed, his old political crony would surely have succeeded. William did not seem to be aware that he and his father were now talking to different factions. Ben represented the Massachusetts assembly, feeling itself under siege and hoping for a clear victory, not another muddled compromise. William's contacts were generally limited to men like Galloway, long-time friends of both Franklins, men whose advice his father had valued in the past, but whose views were now out of step with his own.[70]

William Franklin never doubted for a moment that Ben could find a magic solution to the ills that had temporarily befallen the empire. Nor did he doubt that this was what his father would want to do once he observed the American scene first-hand. If Ben came home, he could not help but notice the "deep Designs" of the men who had controlled the Continental Congress. "However mad you may think the Measures of the Ministry are," he assured Ben, "yet I trust you have Candor enough to acknowledge that we are no ways behind hand with them in In[stances] of Madness on this Side the Water." But then, as if fearing that even this mild observation would provoke another torrent of abuse, he pulled himself up short. It was, he said, "a disagreeable Subject, and I'll drop it." Better to let Ben observe for himself the changes in the colonies since he had left America's shores. In the meantime, he would simply wait, doing what he could to provide a voice of moderation in a world of growing insanity, until his father came home to help him, and people like him, find a workable solution to America's ills.[71]

9

"Two Roads"

"You have now pointed out to you, Gentlemen, two Roads—one evidently leading to Peace, Happiness and a Restoration of the publick Tranquility—the other inevitably conducting you to Anarchy, Misery, and all the Horrors of a Civil War."—William Franklin to the New Jersey Assembly, January, 1775.[1]

"My Sentiments respecting the present publick Transactions I have no Scruple to declare do not entirely coincide with those of either Party. But I trust that those who know me best will do me the Justice to allow, that no Office or Honour in the Power of the Crown to bestow will ever influence me to forget or neglect the Duty I owe my Country, nor the most furious Rage of the most intemperate Zealots induce me to swerve from the Duty I owe His Majesty."—William Franklin to the New Jersey Assembly, May, 1775.[2]

William Franklin was not one to relinquish the reins of government without a fight. So long as he remained the duly appointed governor of New Jersey, he would continue to act the part. No matter that authority was rapidly passing into the hands of local committees, whose leaders were ignoring more than they were defying established chains of command. No matter that everywhere counties were forming Associations and preparing to enforce the congressionally mandated boycott. Franklin disregarded all signs that his position was eroding almost daily, and convened the assembly at Perth Amboy in January of 1775.[3]

He had little choice. The support bill had long since run out, and if he and his officers wanted their salaries, the legislature had to be convened. The lower house had not met in over nine months. It was the first session since its members had forced the governor to accept Stephen Skinner's resignation. It was the first session, as well, since the Franklins had moved to the eastern capital. Most importantly, it was the first session since the Continental Congress had created the Association and prepared a slate of demands to be presented directly to the King.⁴ It was with the congressional proceedings in mind, that Franklin prepared his opening address to the assembly. Hoping, somehow, to retain control of the colony, he harbored "some Hopes" that the house would not give its stamp of approval to congress's petition. Above all, he wanted to keep the lawmakers from committing themselves to the illegitimate proceedings of an extra-legal government. To succeed, it was imperative that he tread carefully, avoiding a frontal attack on ministerial policy without belittling colonial grievances. Once more he was on a tightrope. To lean too far in either direction would invite disaster.⁵

Franklin stood before the legislature on January 13, 1775. His speech was a model of conciliation. Briefly he requested continued support of the colonial government. Then he moved on to the topic that was on everyone's mind. It would, he began, be a dereliction of his duty to both the King and the "good People of this Province" were he to "pass over in Silence the late alarming Transactions in this and the neighboring Colonies." And he relied upon New Jersey's lawmakers to prevent any "Mischiefs" in the colony. But he adroitly side-stepped the substantive issues dividing England and America. "It is not," he said, "for me to decide on the particular Merits of the Dispute." He had no desire to censure those who felt aggrieved by parliamentary policy, nor would he blame those who sought to redress their grievances.⁶

So far the governor's audience was with him. Men nodded their heads, and soft murmurs of assent could be heard from various corners of the room. Franklin took a deep breath and plunged ahead. He wanted to speak to them about means, not ends, as he warned the legislators to avoid any "destructive Mode" of protest. A few enthusiasts, he said, perhaps without realizing the consequences of their actions, had struck at the heart of the constitution itself. And, he said sternly, if you give these misguided malcontents your approbation, "you will do as much as lies in your Power to destroy that Form of Government of which you are an important Part." Appealing to the lawmakers' pride, and sounding suspiciously like a Whiggish defender of assembly rights, he reminded his audience that the various congresses and committees even then meeting throughout the province were assuming the duties of the people's own representatives. You cannot, he asserted, "without a manifest breach of your Trust, suffer any Body of Men, in this or any of the other Provinces, to usurp and exercise any of the Powers vested in you by the Constitution." You, he said, are the legal representatives of the people, and it is up to you, not a self-constituted group of zealots, to defend the rights of those who have placed their fortunes in your hands.⁷

Franklin reminded the legislators that if the colony was suffering any

"Inconveniences," the time-honored method of a legislative petition lay open to them. This procedure not only had the virtue of legality, but it would "have greater Weight" coming from each individual colony. You have, Franklin told the legislators, "Two Roads—one evidently leading to Peace, Happiness and a Restoration of the public Tranquility—the other inevitably conducting you to Anarchy, Misery and the Horrors of a Civil War." Wisdom and prudence would naturally impel them toward the former alternative. Only a desire for temporary popularity would lead them to heed the wishes of a rash minority, whose violent clamors gave an appearance of strength it did not possess. It was, he thought, one of the dangers of a free society that the "*chief Men of a Country*" might sometimes "*shew a greater Regard to Popularity than to their own Judgment.*" He hoped that the men before him were leaders, not followers, that they would not abdicate their duties to an illegal congress or a faceless mob. A balanced constitution could be destroyed from below, as easily as from above, and he hoped that they would defend that vulnerable structure from encroachments on either side.[8]

It was a masterful address. At heart, it represented some of Franklin's most cherished beliefs: his veneration of the law, his admiration of balanced government, his belief that the assembly was an essential, if subordinate, component of that government, so necessary, indeed, that no one—not the King, not the people, not the assembly itself—could violate its rights. His view was not unlike that of the patriots whose vision of an independent America he would soon oppose. It was, moreover, a view that was compatible, at least in its broad outline, with that of his own father. Differences there were, to be sure. One thought that the balance was in danger of being destroyed by power-hungry despots; the other saw it being tipped by "democratical" excesses. But neither patriot nor loyalist, father nor son, wanted to see the balance destroyed.

While Franklin was unhappy with many of the results of the assembly's work during the winter of 1775, he should have evaluated the session as more-or-less a standoff. He won a few significant victories, securing the promise of continued support for the government, and retaining the allegience of his council. At his urging, the legislature prepared a separate, legal, and "humble" petition to the King protesting parliamentary treatment of the colonies in general and Boston in particular. The petition, passed with two dissenting votes, expressed the assembly's "unfeigned Attachment" to the Crown and rejected all notions of "Independency." Admittedly, Franklin preferred a version proposed by Quaker leader James Kinsey, which called for a meeting between delegates chosen by the various colonial legislatures and a royally appointed body of commissioners. But the assembly version, composed by William Livingston, John De Hart, "and the

Junto at Elizabethtown," was moderate, even if it did sound too much like congress's petition. Its authors scarcely deserved the governor's bitter cries that they were "Demagogues of Faction" who opposed anything that would have "even the remotest Tendency to conciliate Matters in an amicable Way."⁹

Franklin suffered a few crucial defeats. Most importantly, despite the hesitancy of some—especially the Quakers—the assembly joined with the other colonies in presenting a united front to the Crown. They agreed to give their approval to the congressional resolution against the "Intolerable Acts," for they knew that the "one grand End" that was so necessary to "the preserving of an Appearance of Unanimity throughout the Colonies" was on the line. Should New Jersey follow an independent course, American unity would be fragmented. And once that process began, it would be impossible to keep the protest movement from disintegrating. The legislators also asked the original congressional delegates to attend a second Continental Congress slated for the following May.¹⁰

Franklin's failure to have his way on specific pieces of legislation was probably not as important as the atmosphere of distrust and the differences of opinion on fundamental issues that pervaded the entire session. In small ways and in large, it became readily apparent that Franklin could no longer claim to be at one with his own assembly. Especially troubling was the legislator's analysis of the relationship between themselves and the people they represented. Franklin's own view of government was unabashedly paternalistic. He assumed that representatives were molders of public opinion rather than carbon copies of their constituencies. And he argued that it was each legislator's duty to rise above popular passion, to exercise judgment freed from emotion, to seek long-term solutions to difficult problems instead of immediate gratification of base and fickle desires. But the New Jersey lawmakers explicitly rejected that view. While they jealousy guarded their rights, they posited a belief in the identity of interests between themselves and the electorate. "Their Interests and our own," they said, "we look upon as inseparable." The assembly had already moved a considerable distance from the old notion of virtual representation. It was now blurring the line that separated the people's representatives from the people themselves.¹¹

This interpretation of colonial politics was ominous. But for the time being, Franklin ignored it, refusing to be drawn into a fight with the lower house. At the end of the session, he reaffirmed his devotion to America as well as his duty to the Crown. He acted, he said, with "an Heart sincerely devoted to my native Country." He was an American as well as an Englishman, and he thought his efforts merited approbation from both the ministry and the assembly.¹²

But throughout the winter and spring of 1775, Franklin's position disintegrated. Lord Dartmouth remained politely supportive, but the Secretary's orders to all of the royal governors revealed how totally out of touch
the ministry was. When he instructed the chief executives to prevent their
respective colonies from sending delegates to the second Continental Congress, Franklin patiently explained that this was a totally impossible request
to honor. Dartmouth's instructions had arrived in New Jersey after the
assembly had elected delegates to the next intercolonial meeting. But that
was not really the point. "Had it been otherwise there would have been no
possibility of preventing Delegates being appointed from this Colony," he
said, "as the popular Leaders were determined, in case the Assembly had
not done it, to have called a provincial Convention of Deputies from the
several Counties for that Purpose." If the people of New Jersey were willing to recognize illegal delegations to the Philadelphia meeting, there was
little even the most conscientious governor could do to stop them. Thus
he had not tried to prevent the assembly from appointing delegates, even
though his tacit compliance had no doubt given a tincture of legitimacy to
the second congress. Franklin did promise to make an effort to stop the
importation of arms and ammunition into the colony. But here again, it
was easier to proclaim a willingness to follow royal instructions than it was
to carry them out. The local committees appointed to enforce the Articles
of Association were more successful than William Franklin in fulfilling
their responsibilities.[13]

All Franklin could do to perform his "indispensible Duty" was to continue sending his superiors as much news concerning American affairs as
he could. For all practical purposes, he was serving as Dartmouth's self-
appointed spy. Much of the news he garnered came from sources who
trusted the governor's discretion, men who had no idea that their conversations ended up in Dartmouth's hands. It was just as well they did not know,
Franklin explained, "lest they might be deterred from giving me Information." There were obviously those who did not realize how committed to
serving the ministry the New Jersey governor really was, and Franklin
wanted to keep it that way.[14] Ironically, the governor's efforts were of little
practical importance. The ministry was already firmly committed to a position from which it would not recede. Much of his information was common knowledge. And as William knew, he was not the only royal governor
forwarding sensitive news to London.[15]

Significantly, neither Franklin nor any of the other governors shared
information or planned strategy with their American counterparts. Franklin
himself was on good terms with the governors in the region. Yet he made
no attempt to coordinate his efforts with them. He relied, as they all did,
on England to formulate an effective response to colonial protests. His

contacts were with the King and his ministers, not with Crown officials in America. Consequently, there was no united front in the colonies to counteract the growing strength and cohesiveness of American activists.[16]

Franklin had one opportunity to further the cause of reconciliation in early April 1775, when he received a copy of a resolution formulated by the North ministry and accepted by the House of Commons.[17] North's plan appeared very conciliatory to the governor. Most importantly, the minister seemed to have retreated from insisting on Parliament's right to tax the colonies. When he saw the proposal, Franklin was elated. It gave him "Strong Hopes" for a "thorough Reconciliation between the two Countries."[18]

His optimism all but vanished with the "battles" of Lexington and Concord. News of the fighting reached New Jersey on April 24. And with it, pleas for moderation were drowned in a sea of clamorous voices raised in righteous indignation. Ironically, when he first heard that General Gage had been sent to Massachusetts, William Franklin had been pleased. He hoped that a little show of military muscle and ministerial resolve might be exactly what was needed to subdue the radicals in the Bay Colony and elsewhere. But when he heard of the clash between Gage's troops and the American minutemen he was devastated. The shots fired in Massachusetts had virtually killed any chance he had to persuade the New Jersey assembly to approve the ministry's latest, and to date its finest, attempt at reconciliation. As Franklin woodenly went through the motions of preparing for his meeting with the legislature, he was already convinced that his efforts were futile. He knew that his words would go unheeded, his pleas for moderation would be ignored. And all because of the bloody clash between a motley group of Massachusetts farmers and seven hundred dust-covered redcoats.[19]

Unaware that Dartmouth himself was partly to blame for the disaster, Franklin did not hesitate to criticize Gage's judgment. While he knew that the commander "must have had very strong Reasons" for sending his troops to Concord, he was dismayed that the timing of the engagement had been so poor. At the very moment when every royal governor was "taking Measures to promote an amicable Settlement of the present unhappy Difference," English soldiers and American civilians had fought, bled, and died on the rolling hills of the Massachusetts countryside. It was unthinkable that Gage had resorted to military tactics when all peaceful avenues had not been exhausted. At the very least, the Massachusetts legislature should have had a chance to discuss the North plan, and been warned of the consequences of rejecting London's offer. The governor was convinced that the clash between American and English soldiers was "one of the most unlucky Incidents that could have occurred in the present Situation of Affairs."[20]

After the battles of Lexington and Concord, it seemed to men like William Franklin that an already lawless society was rushing ever faster toward total anarchy. Even moderates were climbing off the fence.[21] And as news of the fighting spread, there was "such an Alarm" among the people that there was "Danger of their committing some outrageous Violences before the present Heats" subsided. Everywhere coolnists were arming themselves. The turmoil had "a Tendency to keep the Minds of the People in a continual Ferment, make them suspicious, and prevent their paying any attention to the Dictates of sober Reason and common Sense." Thus, when the inhabitants of Freehold, in Monmouth County, heard that one of the King's men-of-war was lying off Sandy Hook with a plan to capture the East Jersey treasury and all of the colonial records at Amboy, thirty armed militiamen set out to defend the colony. They were finally persuaded to desist from their fool's errand, but they returned home as heroes. They marched through Perth Amboy with their colors flying high, to the beat of the drum and the tune of the fife, obviously relishing the spectacle they made as they strutted noisily past Proprietary House. It might have been worse, for had the little band of men attacked the governor himself, Franklin could have done nothing to stop them.[22]

Franklin was losing control of the colony. "All legal Authority and Government seems to be drawing to an End here," he mourned. "Congresses, Conventions and Committees" had replaced all legitimate authority. Those who tried to moderate the present high passions were branded as "Tories." Local Associations routinely complied with the directives of the Continental Congress. The governor still professed to believe that the numbers of New Jersey inhabitants supporting the Association were bloated with those who had joined out of fear or for simple expediency. Many wanted to use their influence to preserve "Peace & good Order and the Security of private Property." Once the King's government had re-established its hegemony and could guarantee their safety, he thought most Associators would gladly return their loyalty to legitimate government.[23]

Unfortunately, this did not seem likely to happen any time soon. The governor himself had felt a nervous tingle when the Freehold militia had swaggered past his house. "The Lives & properties of every Officer of Government in the King's Colonies" were now in danger. Protestors were threatening to take the officers and friends of the Crown hostage. And Franklin had little doubt that they would make good on their threats. The danger was especially strong in New Jersey, where there were no troops, forts, or ships to protect the King's men.[24]

Despite his growing despair, the governor doggedly followed Dartmouth's instructions. If he was ordered to convene his assembly to persuade its members to consider Lord North's conciliatory offer, then he would stop at nothing to honor his trust. True, the situation was totally different from what it had been on February 20 when North's proposal had been unveiled. True, New Jersey's once peaceful countryside was dotted with marching bands of volunteers preparing to defend themselves from English "aggression." William Franklin had taken an oath to obey the King, and obey the King he would. Fewer than ten days after Lexington and Concord, the governor met with his council and laid North's plan before its members. They advised him to call a special session of the assembly as soon as possible, and the date was set for the fifteenth of May, 1775.[25]

As Franklin began work on his opening address he was not optimistic. The time was simply not right; emotions were running high, and no one wanted to listen to reason. He remained sincerely convinced that eventually, if Lord North's proposal was "rightly understood," there would be a disposition to come around to England's point of view. But for now, he realized that no assembly would act without hearing the reaction of the Continental Congress. No one wanted to respond individually for fear of destroying a still fragile colonial unity. It was Franklin's job to convince the New Jersey legislators that their best interest lay in unity with the mother country, not with the illegitimate congress in Philadelphia.[26]

As the governor stood before the assembly on May 16, he gave little indication that he was aware of just how formidable a task he had before him. He was the first colonial governor to discuss the North plan with his legislators. If he succeeded, he might reverse the current trend toward illegal government and start the colonies along the path to reconciliation. He had the advantage of being governor of one of America's most conservative colonies, and he intended to use that moderation for all it was worth. Speaking as always, with the calm assurance that his analysis alone was logical and correct, he argued that the colony's self-interest demanded that the legislators act independently. He knew that the colonial newspapers had already published North's offer, and that it had received much negative publicity. But he insisted that provincial commentators had all been blinded by their own emotions and biases; no one had seen the proposal "in its proper Light." Thus he intended to help the assembly understand the nature of the British offer.[27]

Franklin had decided to "insert the Substance" of Dartmouth's letter explaining the proposal into his speech, while adding further arguments that he thought likely to win support. He was careful not to quote the Secretary directly. Remembering the way Lord Hillsborough had once dressed him down for sharing part of his private correspondence with the assembly, he was not about to repeat the same mistake! Moreover, his address clearly reflected his own thoughts and was not a perfunctory recapitulation of official dogma.[28]

The governor began by proclaiming the King's "happy Disposition, to comply with every just and reasonable Wish" of his American subjects. But he indicated that there were limits beyond which no one in England could be expected to go. The Crown, he explained, would compromise on every issue but parliamentary sovereignty. That principle alone, he said, was inviolable.[29]

North's proposal, as the governor presented it, was both simple and equitable. Parliament no longer insisted upon its right to tax the colonies. Instead, each assembly would be asked to contribute its quota to a military establishment whose expenses had skyrocketed with Britain's commitment to protect American interests. Each colony could devise its own means of raising the money. Any province feeling that it was being asked to pay more than its share of military expenses, would be given "*every possible* INDULGENCE." England had, after all, "no Design" to destroy American liberties. To be sure, Parliament's judgment would be final, but this, thought Franklin, was only reasonable. Ultimate power had to reside somewhere; sovereignty was not divisible. "Some such Supreme Judge is evident from the very Nature of the Case." Moreover, many colonies, including New Jersey itself, had occasionally complained that their neighbors were not paying their share of the empire's expenses. With Parliament acting as the arbiter of competing colonial claims, equity would finally be achieved. Perhaps as important, England would always pay a larger proportion of the empire's expenses than the colonies. Any fears that the mother country would use North's system to enslave Americans while freeing itself from economic burdens, were chimerical.[30]

The beauty of the plan, Franklin argued, was that it avoided all the pitfalls that had inhibited past attempts at reconciliation. In effect, the House of Commons would come to the colonies in "the old accustomed Manner, by Way of Requisition." Such a system had worked before; its constitutionality had never been questioned. Indeed, and he quoted freely from the colonists themselves to prove his point, Parliament required "nothing of *America* but what the Colonies have repeatedly professed themselves ready and willing to perform." Taxation, Franklin argued, was "the principal Source of the present Disorders, when that important Point is once settled, every other Subject of Complaint which has grown out of it will, no Doubt, of Course be removed." But if the various Assemblies refused to use this plan even as a basis for negotiation, then it was apparent that America's enemies had been right all along, that colonial leaders had harbored "deeper Views" from the beginning. If New Jersey rejected North's plan out of hand, he warned darkly, then it was in effect declaring its desire to be independent.[31]

Independence, he insisted, was not in America's interests. It was the "Parent State" that supported and protected the colonies "at the Expense of her Blood and Treasure." It was England that had "raised them to their present state of Opulence and Importance." Thus it seemed that "nothing can be more reasonable than that they should bear their Share of the common Burden." Justice required that Americans return England's kindness by contributing a small portion of their wealth to the good of the whole. Self-interest indicated that independence would shackle the colonists with more, not less, military expenses as they struggled to do alone what they had always done with the liberal help of the mother country.[32]

Franklin never naïvely assumed that the assembly would accept North's plan as the panacea for all the problems troubling the empire. He himself found it lacking in some respects. The minister did not even discuss his own pet project for uniting the colonies politically with Great Britain. Still, it was a beginning. It deserved serious consideration so that this whole "unnatural Contest" would be put to rest. Only human nature itself, ever disposed to consider "present Interest" instead of justice, always likely to embrace "sinister Views or improper Resentments" instead of reasonableness and equity, could prevent the lower house from recognizing the worth of the proposal.[33]

Franklin held out both a carrot and a stick to the legislators. They could, as the Crown itself was willing to do, forget past injustices, admitting that "Many Things will ever happen, in the Course of a long continued Dispute, which good Men of both Parties must reflect on with Pain, and wish to have buried in Oblivion." Or, failing this, they could expect to feel the wrath of an England that would "resist with Firmness every Attempt to violate the Rights of Parliament." They had two choices: They could seize upon North's offer as a basis for reconciliation, or they could be accused of harboring a desire for independence.[34]

Franklin's address was designed to force the legislators to examine the colony's recent history and to ask themselves just where their conventions, congresses, and militias were leading. In effect he wanted to know if they really had "designs" for independence, and if their pious protestations of a desire for rapprochement were legitimate. Unfortunately for him, events were moving forward at such a pace that the answers to those questions were changing almost as quickly as they were being asked.

Moreover, Franklin had more than his share of bad luck. The timing of the assembly had already been made unfortunate by the events at Lexington and Concord. Now, to add to his woes, as soon as he had finished speaking to a subdued, if still suspicious assembly, Samuel Tucker of Hunterdon County rose to his feet, demanding to be heard. He had in his hands a pamphlet, *The Parliamentary Register No. Five*, which he had just received from some persons in Britain friendly to the American cause. The document contained an extract of the letter the governor had sent to Lord Dartmouth on Feburary 1, condemning the assembly's endorsement of the Continental Congress. This was exactly the sort of embarrassment that Franklin had always feared whenever he had written to the ministry in confidence.[35] Thanks to Dartmouth's laxity, he now had to confront a committee of angry legislators who demanded to know if the *Register* extract was authentic.[36]

And the lower house was indeed angry. Having read the governor's comments, its members were convinced of his ill will and more than ever determined to maintain a united front. Under the circumstances, the legislators summarily refused even to consider the North plan. They intended to take their cue from the Continental Congress, and they refused to break ranks and "desert the Common Cause." As they saw it, the plan contained nothing new. It was the issue of taxation dressed up in a new costume, for it was the "Freedom of Granting, as well as the Mode of raising Monies" that was at stake. What difference did it make if each assembly could decide on the means of enslaving itself? The bondage was as cruel as ever.[37]

Franklin's disappointment was obvious. "I have done my Duty," he said tersely. He had asked only that the assembly consider North's plan as a basis for further negotiations. But, he commented sarcastically, "I could have no Suspicion that you did not think yourselves competent to the Business." He had always tried to promote harmony between America and England. The King did not want bloodshed. If war came, the blame would fall on men like themselves who refused to bargain in good faith.[38]

Before he ended the short session, the governor responded to Samuel Tucker's allegations. It was not his finest hour. Tired and frustrated, he also feared for his own safety as all his attempts to defend himself and his country were ripped apart and casually tossed aside by the raging storm of colonial dissent. Deciding that the best defense was an offense, he vented his anger on the wicked minority, who, he claimed, had always aimed at destroying his position and good name with whatever means came to hand. "It has been my unhappiness almost every Session during the Existence of the present Assembly," he cried, "that a Majority of the Members of the House have suffered themselves to be persuaded to seize on every Opportunity of arraigning my Conduct, or formenting some Dispute, let the Occasion be ever so trifling or let me be ever so careful to avoid giving any Cause of Offence." His detractors savaged him with such "Eagerness" either because they had some personal axe to grind, or, more likely, because cheap attacks on any royal governor provided the surest route to political popularity. While their scurrilous behavior no doubt reaped short-term benefits, it hurt the colony as a whole, causing nothing but delays and added expense to the body politic.[39]

With more cowardice than candor, Franklin denied that he had written the "nonsensical" missive to Dartmouth. He dismissed the entire letter, saying it was published in a "common Magazine," which customarily invented news out of whole cloth in order to sate its readers' appetite for sensationalism. He thought, he said, that the assembly would respect his ability to write, even if it had no esteem for his character. The legislators should have recognized that so flawed an epistle could never have emanated from his pen. He claimed that the house had not the "least Right to a Sight of any Part of my Correspondence," but he gave his word that the extract was not authentic.[40]

Having thus temporarily disposed of a tricky business, hoping that his indignation would serve to dissuade the assembly from pursuing the matter, he once again tried to portray himself as a man concerned only with the public welfare. He declared that his beliefs did "not entirely coincide with those of either Party," as he insisted that he was dedicated to serving both King and colony. "No Office or Honour in the Power of the Crown to bestow will ever influence me to forget or neglect the Duty I owe my Country; nor the most heinous Rage of the most intemperate Zealots induce me to swerve from the Duty I owe His Majesty." No matter how difficult the circumstances became, he was determined to serve both his masters.[41]

As the members of the assembly packed their bags and headed for home, Franklin had little to cheer about. He had barely kept the house from pressing its demands to view his correspondence, thus avoiding embarrassment, perhaps real danger, and surely the end of his effectiveness in the colony. But outside of that, the brief session had been a dismal failure. New Jersey's fate was no longer in his hands. American politics was like the whirlwind that William had seen while riding through the Maryland countryside with his father two decades earlier. Beginning as an inconsequential spiraling gust of air, it had grown ever larger and more uncontrollable as first Ben and then William had followed its crazy zigzag path through the woods. Both of them watched in amazement as it ate up dust, leaves, and even branches of trees, destroying everything in its path. It "did not keep a strait line, nor was its progressive motion uniform, it making little sallies on either hand as it went, proceeding sometimes faster, and sometimes slower, and seeming sometimes for a few seconds almost stationary, then starting forwards pretty fast again." Forward, always forward it had gone, having a life, a movement, a direction of its own. Neither man could stay its progress or divert it in another, less destructive direction.[42]

William had followed the whirlwind that day, fascinated by its unpre-dictability and its sheer power. But he was older now, and not a little frightened. He thought that this political whirlwind was likely to swerve toward him, swallowing him up and spitting him out as it continued on its ever erratic and ruinous course. To stay the tide of human events was as impossible as it was to control the force of nature itself.

10

An "Appearance of Government"

"I am loth to desert my Station, as my Continuance in it is a Means of Keeping up some Appearance of Government. . . . let the Event be what it may, I shall not attempt to quit the Province as long as I have any Chance of continuing in it in Safety."—William Franklin to Lord Dartmouth, 1775.[1]

"My Situation is, indeed, somewhat particular, and not a little difficult, having no more than one or two among the Principal Officers of Government to whom I can now speak confidentially on public Affairs."—William Franklin to Lord Dartmouth, 1776.[2]

As the governor had prepared for the ultimately futile session of the New Jersey assembly, in the spring of 1775, he had received word that Benjamin Franklin had made his long-promised return to the colonies and was in Philadelphia. William was surprised and a little hurt that his father had arrived without making any immediate effort to contact him. There had been a time when Ben had planned to travel directly to Perth Amboy as soon as he set foot on America's shores. Now it seemed that he was not so anxious to see his son. He was eager to be brought up to date on all the colonial news. But he sought the advice of men whose views were sharply different from those of New Jersey's royal governor.[3]

Still, Ben looked forward to a reunion with his son, and he longed to introduce him to Temple, who had accompanied him to America. Three days after their arrival Ben was making plans to meet William, either in Perth Amboy or Philadelphia. Only the demands of his own business, and William's impending appearance before the New Jersey legislature, kept the two men apart. As soon as his brief assembly session ended, William Franklin headed for Philadelphia. He was no doubt nervous about the meeting with his father and son. One was a total stranger; the other was growing more unfamiliar with each passing day.[4]

It was unusually hot as the governor rode into town at the end of May.

Many residents had fled in order to escape a smallpox epidemic that was running its course through the city. But most braved the heat and disease, rushing to join one of the many militia units that materialized almost from nowhere in the wake of the news of Lexington and Concord. The noise of drum and fife filled the air, as motley companies of volunteers strutted through the streets or drilled on the Commons, putting on a brave show for the throngs of spectators gathering to cheer their efforts. Everywhere Franklin saw "Uniforms and Regimentals as thick as Bees," as only the most rigid Quakers disdained the martial mania that inundated the city. When he rode past the State House, whose doors were now barred to everyone but congressional delegates, William realized that he had entered alien and hostile territory.[5]

There were, nevertheless, many men in Philadelphia with whom Franklin could comfortably share his views, and some of them were members of congress. Galloway had quit his post in disgust after the rejection of his "Plan of Union," and he refused even to consider the pleas of his old friend Benjamin Franklin that he return to Philadelphia. But there remained many moderates and conservatives, especially from the middle colonies, who still hoped for a rapprochement with the mother country. Franklin dined with some of these men on the night of the twenty-third, gleaning news about congressional activities and no doubt pushing his own plan of imperial unity to his sympathetic companions.[6] He probably argued as well for congressional approval of Lord North's proposal. His assembly had vetoed the plan, but perhaps congress would not prove so timid. Franklin's speech to the New Jersey legislature had been printed in the *Pennsylvania Ledger*, where it created quite a stir, giving heart to those delegates who still thought reconciliation a distinct possibility. Their hopes were not far-fetched. Congress was still divided in the spring of 1775, and resistance, not independence, remained the hope of most members. Even as William Franklin entered Philadelphia, the delegates had made another effort to seek a peaceful settlement of colonial grievances, although it was simultaneously preparing for war. Franklin never failed to take advantage of any opportunity to advance his own views. While he may not have been welcome in his old stomping grounds at the State House, he had access to many of the key congressional delegates. No other royal governor could boast as much.[7]

Still, his main purpose for coming to Philadelphia was to see his father and his son. At least until he talked with Ben, he harbored some illusions that the elder Franklin would help further the aims of reconciliation. He knew that his father's perspective had altered over the years, but he simply refused to believe that his attitudes had undergone a fundamental transformation. The father he knew was the defender of King and empire, the apostle of accommodation. Surely he could not have changed so much in just one decade. All William needed was a face-to-face meeting where he could make Ben see for himself the petty selfishness, the rampant emotionalism, the total unreasonableness of American radicals.[8]

Benjamin Franklin had much the same idea. He hoped that a few hours with the son he loved would be enough to convince him of his errors. If William had witnessed the perfidy of colonial leaders, Ben had tales to tell of the treachery and debauchery of the King's men. Indeed, as he had crossed the Atlantic toward home, he spent most of his time furiously writing down his thoughts and explaining his own failure to influence King, ministry, and Parliament during his final months in London. Written as a letter to his son, the treatise was his most cogent attempt to convince men like William and Joseph Galloway to use their talents in defense of American liberty.[9]

The two Franklins met for the first time in ten years at "Trevose," Galloway's palatial estate in Bucks County. As Ben and William prepared for the meeting, each nervously rehearsed the points he intended to make to persuade the other of the righteousness of his cause. Neither under-estimated the task before him. Ben was a member of the Continental Congress, and he had already admitted privately that he thought war was nearly inevitable. He had also expressed his disdain for Galloway's "Plan of Union," predicting that ties to "rotten" England would destroy America's "glorious publick Virtue." William had chosen to hold on to his seat as royal governor, was sending secret intelligence to London, and had just tried unsuccessfully to persuade the New Jersey assembly to begin separate negotiations with the government. Each man, by his actions, had already chosen sides. Neither was likely to be moved. Still, their long years of mutual service and affection made the effort worthwhile.[10]

As the three men awkwardly embraced and engaged in meaningless pleasantries, they tenderly broached the subject they anticipated and dreaded. William pulled Galloway aside, telling him that as of late he and his father had avoided all discussion of colonial affairs. But he knew it was impossible to avoid a confrontation any longer. The glass went about freely that night, as the three men reminisced about their shared victories and defeats, and talked about their hopes for the future. Galloway had already heard the elder Franklin read most of the letter he had written on his homeward voyage. But William had not. In all likelihood, Ben recounted its contents in an effort to persuade his son that it was no longer possible to hammer out a compromise between America and England. As Ben described his last days in the English capital, Galloway and William Franklin must have shifted uneasily in their chairs. This was not the voice of an affable statesman who always found a way to moderate any disagreement. This was a man who had been pushed to the limit, who had suffered humiliation at the hands of the King's ministers, and who could neither abandon his principles nor understand the value that his adversaries placed on their own dearly held beliefs.[11]

What Benjamin Franklin actually said to his two middled-aged protégés during that long, madeira-filled night remains a tantalizing mystery. But the letter written aboard Captain Osborne's *Pennsylvania Packet* provides enough clues about his mood in the spring of 1775 to give some indication of what transpired. The letter paints a picture of a bitter man, still smarting over his humiliation at the Cockpit a full year and a half earlier, still biding his time as he awaited some opportunity to seek revenge on the men who had treated him so shabbily. While he protested to all who would listen that "in truth private Resentments had no Weight with me in publick Business," just the opposite was true. He had refused to attend any of Lord Dartmouth's levees after the Cockpit incident. And while he "made no Return of the Injury" he "held a cool sullen Silence, reserving [himself] to some future Opportunity."[12]

If the desire for revenge was one theme of Franklin's letter, another involved his central role in the abortive effort to patch up the differences between England and America. Moderates in and out of Parliament made Franklin an essential component of their attempts at reconciliation. This was the role both William and Galloway had envisaged for their mentor. But both men soon realized that the elder Franklin's views were diametrically opposed to their own. While they had personally encountered the intransigence and double-dealing of colonial radicals on a daily basis, Ben blamed the King's ministers for virtually every problem facing the empire. The Americans were always willing and "ready to agree upon any equitable Terms," he thought, but "no Intention or Disposition of the kind existed in the present Ministry." Still, Franklin explained, when he was beseeched by others to aid them in their search for imperial harmony, he made the effort.[13]

As Ben described his conversations with various friends of peace, William Franklin began to suspect that his father was as stiff and unbending as the ministers he so harshly criticized. In early December he had prepared a list of seventeen "Hints" for a possible accommodation of colonial grievances. Taken together, they asked for little less than Parliament's abdication of its authority in America. In a section surely designed to make William redden, Ben demanded that all colonial governors be paid by their assemblies so that men of no estate, who used their offices for personal aggrandizement and had no "natural Regard" for the colonists they served, might be put under effective American control. Franklin's terms were bad enough, but his refusal to compromise even a little on any of his major points indicated that they were intended more in the nature of demands than as a basis for serious negotiation. To his son, it appeared that his long cherished hopes that Benjamin Franklin would lead the American forces of moderation had been based on sheer fantasy. And as he listened with a growing sense of desolation to his father's heated attacks on a venal and profligate government, he no doubt wondered how he could have so blinded himself to reality.[14]

Two subjects that the three men must have discussed that night indicated to William just how wide a chasm existed between him and his father. One was the issue of sending British commissioners to America to dispose of the differences between America and England. William Franklin had long advocated such a plan, but Ben had always contemptuously dismissed it. So far as William knew, his proposal had gone nowhere. Now, to his amazement, he found that the idea had been a live option in some circles as late as February of 1775. Thomas Pownall and Lord Howe had even asked Benjamin Franklin to accompany the commissioners to America. But Franklin discouraged his London friends from pursuing his son's pet scheme. No commissioner, he told Lord Howe, will ever be able to make "my Country men take black for white and Wrong for Right." And so he had left England alone, without giving William's cherished proposition a chance to succeed.[15]

William was also dismayed when he realized that his father scoffed at Lord North's latest proposal to the colonies. He himself had seen the proposal as an honest effort to resolve the crucial issue of parliamentary taxation. But Ben viewed it as a mere contrivance designed to pilfer American pocketbooks. It denied the colonists any voice in deciding upon the equity of Parliament's requisitions, or in judging the merits of the programs they were commanded to support. Moreover, the threat of taxation remained, hanging menacingly over their heads if they refused to comply with Parliament's "request" for funds. To Benjamin Franklin, the plan that his son saw as so fair and statesman-like was little more than highway robbery.[16]

Long before the night was through, and each man had raised his weary hand to fill his glass one more time, it was evident that compromise between Benjamin Franklin and his two beloved protégés was impossible. Ben's alienation from the British government was profound, his contempt for the motives, the values, the ideals of the men who ran that government was complete. He despised those "*Hereditary Legislators,*" as he decried "the total Ignorance" of some, "the Prejudice and Passion" of others, and the "wilful Perversion of Plain Truth in several of the Ministers" that resulted in the rejection of even the mildest attempts to appease the colonies. It "made their Claim of Sovereignty over three millions of virtuous sensible People in America, seem the greatest of Absurdities, since they appear'd to have scarce Discretion enough to govern a Herd of Swine."[17]

William must have been shocked when he heard these words. His father was plainly deceived. "Virtuous sensible People" there were in America, but they were not the men who were even then leading the colonies down the path to independence. The English government had no monopoly on stupidity and corruption. Human nature, as he had told his assembly on so many occasions, was invariably short-sighted and selfish. Passion was everywhere more readily heeded than reason. Both William Franklin and Joseph Galloway could tell their own tales of the humiliation they had suffered at the hands of the "virtuous" men who Ben so idolized but did not really know.

What about the Continental Congress's shameful treatment of the "Plan of Union," Joseph Galloway could well have asked. What of the "Insults" and "violent Opposition" he endured as he stood alone, courageously pleading with obdurate delegates who used "Art and Fraud" to thwart his attempts at accommodation? He still choked with rage when he remembered the anonymous "gift" of a halter, noose, and threatening note he had received while his "Plan of Union" remained on the congressional agenda. At a time when violence was on the rise, this had been no idle prank. How could his old crony fail to realize that blindness and corruption, stubbornness and stupidity, did not exist only in London?[18]

William, too had tales to tell of stiff-necked colonials who were more interested in private vendettas and personal aggrandizement than in principle. But as always, he acted the role of the mediator, trying to calm the tempers of both father and friend as he agreed that there was wickedness and selfishness enough on both sides of the water. What he could not understand, he said, turning to Ben, was his father's determination to see only one side of the story. If he could not support the Crown, could he not remain neutral? As William had commented earlier, he hoped that if Ben "designed to set the Colonies in a flame, he would take care to run away by the light of it."[19]

But neutrality was not the course Benjamin Franklin would take. He had bided his time when he first returned to Philadelphia, making radicals wonder and conservatives hope. But in the end, he had little choice. He had been driven from London; indeed he had narrowly foiled an attempt on his life. He, too, he said darkly, had feared a noose around his neck. It was time, Ben thought, to declare for independence. He hoped, although by now he surely did not expect, that his friend and his son would join him. Galloway, in particular, tried to convince his mentor that his course was suicidal, that a powerful England would soon rise from its lethargy, put aside all internal differences, and defeat the factious group of colonies that dared to tweak the mighty lion's tail. Benjamin Franklin simply did not agree.[20]

Neither William nor Ben should have been surprised by the views of the other. Their attitudes were the product of their separate experiences over the last decade. Ben had been ignored, humiliated, and rejected by the men who ran the empire he once loved. He had seen London at its worst, and had learned how impossible it was to expect reform from complacent English politicians. William acknowledged that all Englishmen were not perfect. He recalled with a shudder his treatment at the hands of the imperious Lord Hillsborough. But he believed that the British constitution, despite its defects, remained the best constitution in the world. He thought the empire was generally run by men of good will, and that genuine reform was still possible. Where his father had been alternately mocked and ignored by London officials, he had been maligned by colonial lawmakers during the treasury crisis and ignored during the quarrels over the Townshend and Tea acts.

Now, despite his best efforts, lawlessness prevailed; his own life was in danger; his property was threatened by rampaging mobs; and he was scarcely able to hold on to the reins of government in a colony that had once prided itself on its moderation. If his father had been rejected by the Crown, he was in very real danger of being repudiated by his country. And just as his father had not fled England until he was entirely convinced that he could do nothing to soften the hearts of the ministry toward its wayward children, so William Franklin would not quit his post until his assembly would listen to him no longer. Nevertheless, he was tempted, as no other royal governor had been, to abandon his obligations and join the rebel cause. Unlike most other Crown representatives, he had to make a deliberate choice between England and America, family and King.

And so William Franklin rode away from "Trevose" having failed to convince his father of the error of his ways. Temple, now just fifteen years old, rode with him. No doubt they were both anxious about their imminent meeting with Elizabeth, for she had only recently been told of her stepson's existence. The governor was also concerned about his political position, as he wondered how long he would be able to pretend that a legitimate government existed in New Jersey. He was riding into a confused and volatile situation. County committees and provincial congresses were proliferating and the convention at Trenton had just voted to levy taxes to support the colony's militia.[21] Franklin must have chuckled bitterly at this news, wryly recollecting his sense of victory when he managed to wring a mere £500 from the lawmakers to maintain the royal army. Once people realized the cost of their present insanity, they would be grateful for the mild yoke that London had laid on their necks. But in the meantime, true government in the colony was "nearly laid prostrate." All officials, he told Lord Dartmouth, "from the highest to the lowest are now only on Sufferance," and they would be lucky to continue even this polite pretense. He was beginning to lose control of his own council. And the colonial militia was also distintegrating. Almost daily Franklin received notes from officers resigning their commissions to join the hordes of Americans serving under the banner of the Provincial Congress. Typically, he denigrated the motives of such turncoats. It was "Ambition," not principle that made them act so shameful a part. Nevertheless, he could do nothing to stop them.[22]

Throughout the summer of 1775, Franklin tried to keep up appearances, providing a semblance of decorum to an office that was fast becoming irrelevant. He still served tea to his guests at the governor's mansion in defiance of the congressional condemnation of the unpatriotic brew. And he continued to whistle in the dark, claiming that the colonies would eventually come to their senses. Still, his only comfort came from London. At a time when he had virtually lost control of New Jersey's government, when he had endured the recriminations of his own father, it was no doubt soothing to read Lord Dartmouth's praise of his "Zeal" on behalf of the Crown. He was pleased to learn that his speech defending Lord North's offer was "highly approved" in London. And he was grateful for the paternal understanding and steadfast support of a man his father had sneeringly characterized as having "in reality no Will or Judgment of his own."[23]

Franklin was comforted, as well, by the King's determination to stand firm in the face of colonial dissent. While has father had tried to convince him that the mother country would quickly dissolve in the face of colonial unity, William Franklin was receiving a very different message. By June, Dartmouth had declared America in "open Rebellion," and in July, the King expressed his intention "to reduce His rebellious Subjects to Obedience." The governor was vastly relieved when he learned that London intended to protect all the King's men from any possible harm. He was sure that when the Americans realized that they faced such determination, their bravado would vanish. When the might of the British empire was set against a weak and disorganized band of malcontents, there was little doubt that the result would be a resounding victory for the King's forces.[24]

But all that was in the future. Franklin's immediate prospects looked bleak. Throughout the late summer and fall of 1775, both his personal and political life was troubled. While Ben continued to speak politely, even affectionately, of his son in public, the two men seldom wrote to one another and they saw each other even less frequently. Ironically, they had corresponded more often, and with greater pleasure, when they were separated by the Atlantic than they did now, when two days by coach could bring them together. True, William was still trying to salvage something of his dreams for western empire, and used his father to help him sort out some of his financial entanglements with George Croghan. But any favorable disposition of the Vandalia grant would have to wait until the current hostilities between England and America ceased. Franklin had "received the *strongest Assurances* that as soon as the present Great Dispute is settled *our Grant shall be perfected.*" But in the meantime he was helpless. The blame clearly lay with America's rebellious leaders—of whom his own father was one—not with stubborn English bureaucrats.[25]

William also continued to keep his father abreast of at least some of his own political activities in New Jersey. Perhaps from habit, perhaps because he wanted to pretend that their relationship had not fundamentally altered, he faithfully sent copies of his assembly speeches to Philadelphia, even though he must have known that their contents would only anger his already disappointed father. He no longer asked for Ben's advice, but he appeared to want to keep the lines of communication open. The night at "Trevose" had sundered the bonds between Joseph Galloway and Benjamin Franklin. But the destruction of the ties between William and his father occurred gradually, tortuously, over a longer period of time. Ben visited Perth Amboy twice during the summer of 1775. During one of those trips, the two men quarreled violently, shouting so loudly that their neighbors were disturbed by their angry voices. But their mutual pleas and recriminations were useless. Both men had a stubborn streak; both were totally convinced of the righteousness of their position. Still, even this quarrel did not separate them completely.[26]

One reason neither man was willing to dissolve the relationship was their mutual devotion to Temple. Indeed one of William's few pleasures in these chaotic days came from becoming acquainted with his only son. He assumed his fatherly role with a vengeance, trying to erase the effects of their long estrangement as thoroughly as possible. In some ways, he was an "indulgent Father." But he clearly intended to be a strict disciplinarian, resisting any temptation simply to buy his son's affections.[27]

Even their shared devotion to Temple led to competition between father and son. Ben had been the boy's "Second Parent" for so long, that William considered him a rival for his affections. And the elder Franklin still made the major decisions concerning Temple's future. The lad spent a pleasant summer with the governor and his wife, but he returned to Philadelphia in the fall where his grandfather could keep an eye on him, and where he could attend the school that Ben had helped establish. The institution was Anglican-dominated and still in the hands of his arch-enemy William Smith. But it was relatively inexpensive, close to home, and was surely a more suitable choice than New York's King's College, which fairly reeked of Tory sentiments. William evidently did not dispute this decision. When Temple began preparing to leave for Philadelphia, William asked if Ben could come to Perth Amboy to pick him up. If that could not be arranged, he tentatively suggested accompanying his son himself, but he wanted Ben's approval before he ventured into a city that was by now the seat of a hostile government. Significantly, Ben dropped everything and rushed to New Jersey. William was obviously *persona non grata* in his former home.[28]

William did not abandon his son once he left for school. He sent all sorts of fatherly advice to the lad, along with the clothes the careless Temple had left behind. But William's letters had a stiff, anxious quality as if he did not know quite what to say to this stranger who was also his son. And so he lectured him, insisting that Temple write home once a week, and sternly rebuking him for failing in his responsibilities to his stepmother. He prescribed an ambitious course of study for the boy, including Latin, Greek, French, and Math. And, because he assumed that his English-born son would live the rest of his life as an American, he suggested that Temple attend the German school at night. Knowledge of German, especially "The Colloquial Phrases," would serve him well in Pennsylvania. The classics were a prerequisite for the gentleman scholar, but the living languages had their utility. While William expected his son to follow a rigorous schedule, he also expressed concern about the boy's health. He had heard from mutual friends that Temple appeared "thin and rather melencholly" and the news disturbed him.[29]

William tried to supply his son's material needs. It was easy enough to lend Temple a book or two from his own prodigious library. Providing the free-spending lad with enough cash to fill his seemingly endless needs was a more perplexing problem. As early as October, he had already squandered the money his father had given him to last until the Christmas holidays. William reluctantly sent more. He, himself, had bitterly resented Ben's occasional reminders that he was always "behind hand" in paying his debts. Now he found himself in a similar position with his own son.[30] Temple was anxious to please both his parents, but he found the relationship a bit awkward. His first letter to Elizabeth was a disaster. Pretentious beyond belief, it was filled with "Elphinsonic" phrases that were nothing short of laughable. And so William immediately took it upon himself to explain the art of proper letter-writing. "You should consider yourself as conversing with the person to whom you write," he lectured, so "that all attempts at the Sublime, all quaint Words and Phrases, are to be as carefully avoided in Letters as in Conversation."[31]

William used his son as both a substitute for and a conduit to his own father. He often sent messages of affection to Ben, or, increasingly, simply "to the family," and reminded Temple of his grandfather's "Goodness," admonishing him to "continue to have the most grateful Sense" of the duties he owed the man who had tended to his needs over the years. At the same time, the boy's presence in Philadelphia obviated the necessity to ask Ben for often disquieting news from the city. Temple sent him all the newspapers and pamphlets that came his way. Perhaps William was a little afraid to ask Ben for political news, for his father may have suspected that much of the information the governor received, quickly found its way to London. But Temple evidently had no compunctions about indirectly supplying the mother country with intelligence.[32]

If William's personal life was strained during the summer and fall of 1775, his political fortunes were undergoing a major upheaval. Fort Ticonderoga had been taken by the rebels in May, and the British had occupied Bunker Hill the following month. By August, congress was openly gearing up for war. While Franklin did not panic, his assessment of his position was grim. Still, he stubbornly held out hope for reconciliation. His optimism was based on the commonly held loyalist belief that rebel leaders were a noisy and well-organized minority who had gotten hold of the political machinery and were using their power in a way that a vast number of their putative followers actually disapproved. His job was to revive the spirits of the King's friends and to remain in America at all costs so that there would be some legitimate government around which sensible Americans could rally. Already, many were beginning to suspect that the fomenters of rebellion were not interested in preserving American rights or even in securing independence. Their ultimate goal, their secret design, was to "establish a Republic." And Franklin was convinced that there were "Thousands" of Americans who, when they realized this, would rush to the defense of the empire. The governor did not delude himself into thinking that the Crown would have an easy time of it in the coming days. England would have to make its compromises, too. For there were none in America "who would draw their Swords in Support of Taxation." But there were many "who would fight to preserve the Supremacy of Parliament in other respects," men who longed to maintain America's "Connexion with Great Britain."[33]

As Franklin became more isolated, his resolve to remain in America and serve as the focal point for colonists who wanted reform, but not revolution, grew steadily stronger. "I am loth to desert my Station," he told Lord Dartmouth, "as my Continuance in it is a Means of Keeping up some Appearance of Government, and Matters may possibly take such a Turn as to put it in my Power to do some service." Despite fears for his personal safety, he would not, he promised, abandon his post. He trembled when he imagined himself being "led like a Bear through the Country to some Place of Confinement in New-England." But he refused to give in to his nightmarish anxieties. "Let the Event be what it may," he promised, "I shall not attempt to quit the Province as long as I have any chance of continuing it in Safety." Under any other circumstances his father would have been proud of William's determination. He was only doing what all of the Franklins had been trained to do. Ben had taken as his credo a determination never to step down from any position. Deborah had steadfastly refused to leave the Franklin home during the Stamp Act crisis. Now William Franklin was vowing to remain on the job until it was taken from him. His decision was as much a tribute to his family as it was an expression of loyalty to his King.[34]

It was also a recognition of reality. In some ways, Franklin had little choice. Dartmouth's letters to him were being intercepted and read by postal officials. Congress was planning to assume control of government throughout the thirteen colonies. The Continental Army was urging the various provincial congresses to seize royal officers for use as bargaining chips in securing captive Americans. And while Franklin had asked General Gage to place a man-of-war at the mouth of Raritan Bay so that Crown officials could "secure a Retreat there if there should be Occasion," no ship had yet appeared on the horizon. "Perhaps," he said weakly, "none can be Spared." For practical as well as for honorable reasons, William Franklin remained in New Jersey.[35]

And so he stayed in Perth Amboy, watching and waiting as his little world crumbled about him. The Provincial Congress assumed control of New Jersey's militia, and began trying to collect the £10,000 it had levied to support the colony's defenses. Franklin was grimly amused by the pretended government's efforts to collect the taxes it had voted with such nonchalance. There was "no small Confusion and Disturbance" as many New Jersey inhabitants absolutely refused to obey the new government's dictums. But there were others who paid the duties levied by the Provincial Congress, while declining to support the legitimate government. They could not afford double taxes, and they saw the governor and his men as "now little more than Cyphers." All government funds would run out by the beginning of October, and then Franklin was in real danger of losing what little salary he had. Oh to be on the King's Civil List, so that he would no longer have to grovel once a year before an indifferent or even hostile assembly for the few pennies its members deigned to throw his way![36]

Throughout the fall, many of Franklin's friends began to leave his side. No loss affected him more deeply than that of William Alexander, Lord Stirling. Alexander did not even bother to inform the governor that he had decided to throw in his lot with the rebel forces. When rumors swept the colony that he had accepted a commission as colonel of the Somerset militia, Franklin could scarcely credit the stories. He was too proud to ask his friend point-blank if they were true, asking his secretary, Charles Pettit, to do the distasteful job for him. But while Pettit may have signed the letter of inquiry, the words in the missive were clearly Franklin's own. Only he would have been sufficiently pained by Alexander's apparent disloyalty to characterize his behavior as "*Contemptible Meanness and dishonesty.*"[37]

Alexander's reply to the governor's query was equally blunt and angry. He could not believe that a man of Franklin's "Exalted Station" would treat him so insolently. Nevertheless, said Alexander loftily, "I will indulge your Excellency's Curiosity." He admitted that the people of Somerset had begged him to head their militia, and that he had accepted their offer. He pretended to assume that his former friend would look favorably upon his decision. Surely, he said with a deceptive smile, you will approve of my desire to defend American liberties. Have you not often proudly proclaimed that the "rights of the people and the prerogatives of the Crown were Equally Dear to you?"[38]

Franklin claimed to have no inclination to comment on Alexander's "extraordinary" decision. Had his friend come to him and discussed his dilemma before joining the rebel forces, he would have had plenty to say. But now it was too late. Still, the governor wanted to set the record straight. Nothing would ever induce him to attack either the Crown's prerogative or the people's liberties, for he was sworn to protect them both. But it was clearly the prerogative of the Crown, not a self-appointed Provincial Congress, to grant military commissions. To accept a commission under those circumstances was to "fly in the face of prerogative." This was not liberty. This was license. And while Franklin was a firm defender of the former, he abhorred the latter.[39]

Alexander's defection was not Franklin's only problem as fall faded slowly into winter. Elizabeth was ill, and he himself was none too well. His council was dwindling, and many of the remaining members were pursuing "a trimming Conduct."[40] Alexander was about to be suspended, and Samuel Smith, claiming that old age and infirmity had taken their toll, resigned his post. In the "present unsettled State of Affairs" it would be difficult, if not impossible, to replace either man. The courts were still open, a victory of sorts for the King's supporters. But their business had greatly diminished, and the governor frankly admitted that all he could do was "to keep up some Appearance of Government." Franklin had lost virtually all access to news from the Continental Congress. With Galloway in retirement, and other strong friends of government similarly absent from Philadelphia, the "radicals" held away. Franklin heard that most congressmen disapproved of

John Adams's public declaration in support of independence, but he doubted that this was the case. Was not Adams still welcome in Philadelphia where he continued to spew forth his treasonous rantings unmolested?[41]

In fact, Franklin had come to believe that military action alone would reunite the empire. He had hoped for so long that "all Differences would have been settled in some amicable Way," but he now realized that this would not happen. "The leaders of the People," despite their continued professions of loyalty, did not want peace, and so peace there would not be. "Were the People, even now, left to judge for themselves," were they told the truth about the Crown position and the secret intentions of America's radical minority, he had "no Doubt but their natural good sense would prevent their engaging in the Support of the present hostile and destructive Measures." But the enemies of the Crown controlled all lines of communication, and they were winning the propaganda war. Guns, not words would be needed before the "Natural good Sense" of most Americans could rise to the surface. Franklin could not help but make a weak plea for one last effort at reconciliation, as he wondered if "for the Sake of Peace" the mother country might be able to come up with some additional "Propositions" that would quiet American resentment. But he did not hazard a guess as to what those propositions might entail.[42]

Still, there was a government in New Jersey, however ineffectual it might be. Franklin was one of only four royal governors still even in nominal charge of his colony. And his position was clearly more secure than that of Tyron in New York, Dunmore in Virginia, or Wright in Georgia. Always cautious, at least parts of New Jersey were experiencing something of a conservative backlash in the fall of 1775. The Provincial Congress met in October, but while it claimed to be the effective authority in the colony, it suffered from divisions between East and West, and faced the hostility of many inhabitants who resented the financial burdens they had been called upon to shoulder.[43]

Nevertheless, it was with genuine reluctance that Franklin heeded his council's advice and called the assembly to Burlington in November. It was an audacious move, but once he had decided to challenge the claims of the provincial government, the governor doggedly prepared his remarks to what would surely be a hostile legislature. He knew this might be his final opportunity to separate New Jersey from its sister colonies, destroying the pretense of American unity. If he succeeded, the rewards he could expect from a grateful monarch would be unlimited.[44]

The delegates who came to Burlington in November were in a somber mood. And at first it looked as though few of them would bother to show up at all. But at least the assembly had consented to meet. This in itself was no small victory. Franklin's opening address to the shell of a legislature began on a firm but conciliatory note. He had asked the house to meet, he said, only because public business demanded it. Thus he declined to engage in a futile discussion of the issues that threatened the empire. He wished only to warn them of the King's firm resolve to secure colonial obedience. If Americans harbored any illusions that they would be able to continue their present activities unchecked, they were sorely mistaken. Most importantly, they should be aware of the severe consequences that would follow a threat to the safety of Crown officials.[45]

The governor shared some of his fears of the future with the men who sat grimly before him. He was pleased to report that with a couple of disquieting exceptions, New Jersey's royal servants had not yet met with "any Insults or improper Treatment." Nevertheless, he went on, "such has been the general Infatuation and Disorder of the Times," that many of his friends had urged him to follow the example of other governors, seeking asylum on one of His Majesty's men-of-war. Franklin had refused to take this well-meaning advice. He had, he claimed, the "true Interest and Welfare of the People at Heart," and were he to abrogate his duties he would be doing those people a profound disservice. If he fled the country, he would be indicating that his countrymen were in rebellion. This he would not do.[46]

Still, Franklin could not deny his own uneasiness, and he asked the legislators to use their influence to maintain order in the colony. Failing that, he begged them to inform him if they thought the King's supporters were in danger. "All I ask," he said, "is that you would tell me so in such plain open Language" that your meaning can not be misunderstood. He was aware that some men of "Consequence" had begun openly to support independence. But Franklin remained convinced that the members of the lower house had "an Abhorrence" for "Republican Government." And he challenged them to make their opposition to independence known publicly.[47]

The assembly did not respond immediately to the governor's speech. Instead it reviewed routine bills and petitions, while it waited to see if other members would make the trip to Burlington. Gradually, enough men filtered in to make the session worthwhile, and within a week they settled down to serious business. At first, Franklin piled up victory after victory. His spirits were given an immense boost on November 21, when the house agreed to consider his request for government support. Not only would this mean that he would continue to receive his salary, but it also indicated that sentiment still existed for upholding legitimate government.[48]

The following day, William shared some good news with the legislators, which he had deliberately postponed divulging until the full house was assembled. The King, he informed the assembly, had finally agreed to accept the Currency Bill, which governor and representatives alike had advocated for so long. This meant, he exulted, that New Jersey's financial worries were over, that the legislators might never have to tax their constituents again. It also removed the colony's most substantive grievance against the Crown. Pressing his luck, and following Lord Dartmouth's explicit instructions, he asked the lawmakers to grant the King's officers a permanent salary and provide for a governor's mansion. This would allow them to prove their public professions of loyalty, according them "an Opportunity of demonstrating that you mean your Actions should ever correspond with your Professions."[49]

Franklin was riding high. The assembly had listened to his remarks with attention. Its members were pleased by the long over-due acceptance of their plea for bills of credit. They had also disposed of a great deal of routine business, providing a sense of continuity in an otherwise chaotic world. Meanwhile, petitions rolled in from various freeholders in Burlington County asking the house to "discourage Independency" in America. On the twenty-second, the legislature accepted the resignations of two of its delegates to Congress. Both John de Hart and James Kinsey left their posts, claiming their "private Affairs" made the task exceedingly onerous. But Franklin thought they feared for their own safety. Significantly, the assembly replaced neither man, leaving congressional chores to the remaining three representatives. Events continued to move in Franklin's direction. On the twenty-third, the assembly rejected a move to repair the barracks, an undisguised attempt to use colony funds to help the rebel cause. The next day, the legislators asked Dennys de Berdt, Jr., to replace Benjamin Franklin as colonial agent. This surely indicated that they did not intend to sever all ties with the mother country.[50]

But the best news followed on the twenty-eighth, when the legislators appointed a committee to prepare a separate petition to the King, "to express the great Desire this House hath to a Restoration of Peace and Harmony wih the parent State on constitutional Principles." They also instructed their congressional delegates not to assent to any measures leading to independence or a "Change [in] the Form of Government" in the colonies. Two days later, the house decided to postpone indefinitely any discussion of a committee report commenting on William Franklin's excerpted letter in the *Parliamentary Register*. The delegates' forbearance was especially notable because the house had managed to obtain a copy of the entire letter. Its members had caught the governor in a palpable lie and could have used their information to devastating effect. Franklin could scarcely believe his good fortune.[51]

The session continued to run an amazingly smooth course until the end of November, when the assembly belatedly responded to the governor's opening address. The message was milder than many Franklin had received, but it was pervaded by an underlying tone of hostility and suspicion. While the legislators assured Franklin that New Jersey's Crown officers need not consider seeking asylum, they pretended to be amazed that anyone would even have suggested such an alternative. And they wondered if the governor's "best Friends" truly had the interests of the colony at heart. They assured Franklin that so long as he and the other royal officers acted prudently and did nothing to "invite any ill-Usage" they would be safe. The law itself, they said, would provide them with the only haven they needed.[52]

Franklin tried vainly to control his temper. But he was furious with the legislators' casual dismissal of his very real fears. Their feigned innocence was "extraordinary," when attacks on law and authority were everywhere "*the* FASHION *of the Times*," and Crown officers throughout the colonies had fled their homes to seek protection with the King's navy. How could they speak so blithely of the adequacy of legal protection in New Jersey, when at that very moment there were three Crown officials in Trenton, confined "by some supposed unlawful Authority," who had not been accorded any legal recourse? And how could they be so dishonest as to imply that any harrassment of government officials was the fault of the officials themselves, and not a consequence of the lawlessness that pervaded America? His officers had always acted prudently, he said, and they would continue to do so. Still, the governor did not belabor the point, for he wanted to nourish the fragile relationship still existing between himself and the legislators. He praised them for their repeated denunciations of independence, holding out hope for a peaceful future.[53]

So far, Franklin seemed to be holding the assembly together. Success was almost in his grasp. While some house members were angry at his speech and wanted to dissolve the session and call for new elections, the governor held his own.[54] But on December 4, the governor's dreams began to unravel. The first hint of disaster came from an unexpected quarter. His own council publicly broke ranks with him for the first time, berating him for his "darkly penned" comments on the character and good intentions of the people of New Jersey. At the very time when unity among the various branches of government was essential, said the councilors, the governor had initiated a gratuitous quarrel with the lower house. They could not understand how a man who prided himself on his ability to promote harmony, could have acted so recklessly. Franklin should have complimented the assembly for New Jersey's moderation instead of borrowing trouble, assuming that the violence of other colonies would spread to their own law-abiding province. Franklin was both angered and saddened by his council's hostile remarks, even though he realized that the message was partly a face-saving gesture, designed to assure suspicious assemblymen that none of its members had advised the governor to flee the colony. Still it hurt to see men upon whom he had once placed such trust, abandon him at the first hint of danger.[55]

While Franklin was still reeling from the council's attack, he received word that three members of the Continental Congress were galloping toward Burlington to plead with the assembly to reconsider sending a separate petition to the King. The governor's powers of persuasion had apparently succeeded too well. Congressional leaders feared that even the slightest break in colonial unity might signal the end of American resistance. While Pennsylvania, like New Jersey, had instructed its delegates to oppose measures leading to independence, congress saw the plan to send a separate petition to London as a singular threat. And so on December 5, John Dickinson, John Jay, and George Wythe pounded on the doors of the New Jersey assembly, demanding to be heard. After some discussion, the legislators broke with precedent, allowing the congressmen to enter their chambers, and they sat back to listen to the arguments.[56]

The three men spoke for less than an hour. The moderate "Pennsylvania Farmer" headed the delegation. For nearly thirty minutes he emphasized the absolute necessity of maintaining a united stance before the awful might of the British Crown. They see us, he said, as "a Rope of sand," easily divided and afraid to fight. Congress had acted, he argued, with remarkable restraint. In fact, had it "drawn the Sword, and thrown away the Scabbard, all lovers of Liberty, all honest and virtuous Men would have applauded them." Instead colonial leaders had drawn up petition after petition in their futile efforts to effect some sort of workable compromise. And Dickinson promised the attentive assembly that if the colonies would simply stand firm and show their willingness to fight, victory would soon be theirs; for a "Country so united cannot be conquered."[57]

After Jay and Wythe added a few words of their own to Dickinson's eloquent plea, the three men withdrew, and the New Jersey assembly was on its own once more. Its members debated the issue for "some Time," but in the end, William Franklin lost his most important battle as colonial governor. The legislators decided that because they had already sent a petition to the King, which remained unanswered, another effort would be futile. After that, William Franklin's impact on the assembly was negligible. He had battled with the Continental Congress for the hearts and minds of the New Jersey legislature. And he had lost.[58]

As the house began to wind down its business prior to the Christmas recess, it expressed its pleasure at the Crown acceptance of the paper money bill. But it declared that it would not be "prudent" to raise the salaries of the colony officers. Nor would it be "beneficial" to settle those salaries for more than a year at a time, or to begin the construction of new government buildings. They would wait, explained the legislators, until the present "unnatural Controversy" had ended before they considered any of the governor's requests.[59]

Governor Franklin almost alone represented what was left of royal government in New Jersey. At the beginning of December, General Washington and his wife had arrived in Newark to a tumultuous welcome. No one had lifted a finger to stop him. Militarily as well as politically, the King's supporters were in total disarray. The governor's council was no longer of much use. Moreover, two judges and one justice of the peace in three separate counties had been seized by "Order of Committees," for refusing to sign the Association. Franklin did not even know where they were being held, and he could do nothing to secure their release.[60]

In a long confidential letter to Lord Dartmouth, Franklin provided the ministry with his own, slightly skewed, assessment of the American scene. He remained convinced, in the face of his own evidence to the contrary, that the aims of congress were not supported by most Americans. He simply refused to believe that any but the most selfish or infatuated would voluntarily leave the protection of an empire that served the colonies so well. The problem, of course, was that rebel leaders were so insidious. "The Design," he feared would "be carried on by such Degrees, and under such pretenses, as not to be perceived by the People in general till too late for Resistance." Proof of American loyalty could be found, he thought, in the general reaction to his treatment by the council in December. Ever since he had been berated by his erstwhile supporters, he had been visited "by all Ranks of People" expressing their disapproval of the council's disrespectful behavior. Even one of Franklin's leading opponents in the assembly had indicated his disgust at the "unwarrantable, ungenerous and ungentlemanly attack." Did this sound as though New Jersey was filled with hotheads anxiously anticipating a rupture with the mother country? In spite of all his failures, the governor remained stubbornly optimistic.[61]

William Franklin's optimism was based on wishful thinking. His letter to Dartmouth, bulging with newspaper clippings and the few documents he could lay his hands on, never left America's shores. Instead, it was intercepted by his old friend, and now his sworn enemy, William Alexander, who would use its contents to help write the final chapter of the governor's long service to the people of New Jersey. There would be no more assembly sessions while Franklin remained at the helm. Instead, he faced the most painful and humiliating experience of his life. Before long, he would be arrested, imprisoned, and sent into exile by his countrymen. He would lose family and friends, property and position. But—at least from his own perspective—he would not lose his honor.

11

"An Enemy to the Liberties of This Country"

". . . No Office or Honour in the Power of the Crown to bestow, will ever influence me to forget or neglect the Duty I owe my Country, nor the most furious Rage of the most intemperate Zealots induce me to swerve from the Duty I owe his Majesty."—William Franklin to the New Jersey Assembly, 1776.[1]

"That, in the opinion of this Congress, the said William Franklin Esquire, has discovered himself to be an enemy to the liberties of this country; and that measures ought to be immediately taken for securing the person of the said William Franklin, Esquire."—New Jersey Council of Safety, 1776.[2]

In early November 1775, William had watched his father's coach roll down the long path separating the governor's estate from the bustle of Perth Amboy. He had no way of knowing that they would not meet again until after the American Revolution. Ben was headed toward Philadelphia with his sister Jane who was fleeing British-occupied Boston.[3] William had proudly given his guests the grand tour of his three-story mansion. But conversation was stilted, and even Jane's presence did little to smooth over the awkward silences. While she was duly impressed by her nephew's "very magnificent" home, Ben was anxious to be gone. The press of business awaiting him in Philadelphia was great, and he was clearly uncomfortable. One can only imagine the thoughts that flashed through his mind as he glanced up at the gilt-edged portraits of King George III and Queen Charlotte dominating the "Great Parlour" on the first floor of the governor's mansion. And William probably did not even mention his hopes for the New Jersey assembly, which would convene at Burlington in just a little over a week. He could hardly have expected his father to share his hopes that New Jersey would spearhead the drive to shatter colonial unity. Father and son had clearly reached a political impasse. There was nothing more to be said. And William was no doubt as relieved as he was saddened by his father's departure.[4]

As the new year began, Franklin wrote another one of his letters to Lord Dartmouth. He had failed to persuade the New Jersey assembly to follow an independent course. Everyday, more men who refused to sign the Association were arrested "by Order of Committee." But so long as he remained in office, he intended to do what little he could to mediate between England and America. He started the letter on its circuitous route on January 5. He evidently took none but the ordinary precautions when he sent his letter—deceptively addressed as a personal missive to Mrs. Gage—and two bundles of documents on their way to ministerial headquarters.[5]

Franklin's timing was inauspicious. On January 2, the Continental Congress had issued orders demanding that all "unworthy Americans" be disarmed, and, if necessary incarcerated or forced to give word that they would do nothing to overthrow the patriot government. As soon as William Alexander—known by colonial officialdom as "Colonel the Earl of Stirling"—received the command, he ordered all official mail intercepted, and just as quickly he began to reap rewards. On January 6, his men confiscated a bundle of suspicious letters and brought them to Stirling's headquarters at Elizabeth for inspection. As the colonel rifled through the packets, he quickly realized their value. A letter from Cortlandt Skinner to his brother, a British army officer, was "full of strong Toryism." And Stirling fairly chortled when he saw two bundles marked "Secret and Confidential" addressed to Lord Dartmouth. For "particular reasons" he dispatched the letters, documents and clippings to Philadelphia.[6]

But Stirling had no intention of waiting for congressional orders to initiate proceedings against New Jersey's "tories." Franklin had already warned Skinner that Stirling was hot on his trail, and the former speaker had fled the colony in a rowboat, clambering aboard a British man-of-war, where he barely managed to escape his former associate's clutches. His wife and thirteen children remained behind in enemy country. The governor bravely proclaimed that he intended to stay where he was. He had written nothing that was not "strictly true"; he had only done his duty when he informed Dartmouth of radical activity in the colonies; and while he fully expected the wrath of a "violent People" to descend upon him, he had decided to "let them do their worst." Still, Stirling feared that Franklin might follow Skinner's cowardly example. The colonel decided to act. Perth Amboy was well-armed with rebel soldiers, and he had a goodly number of men under his own command. There was no reason to hazard a delay. Stirling summoned his immediate subordinate, Lieutenant Colonel William Winds, and ordered him to march directly on the eastern capital. His mission was to arrest Governor William Franklin.[7]

At two in the morning, the Franklins were roused by "a violent knocking" at the front door, which so alarmed Elizabeth that William thought she was in danger of "Dying with the Fright." Leaping out of bed, he tried to calm his distraught wife as he pulled back the curtains at the chamber window and peered into the yard below. There he saw armed continentals milling about the house, cutting off all possible avenues of escape. For a moment, a tremor of real fear tingled through the governor's bulky frame. He had once voiced his apprehension that he would be captured "and led like a Bear through the Country." Now it seemed that his worst nightmares were about to become reality.[8]

At last one of the Franklins' servants opened the front door. Moments later, he rapped apologetically at the chamber entrance and silently handed Franklin a message from the soldiers. As Elizabeth wept softly beside him, William scanned the letter. It was a note from Colonel Winds, who claimed to have received some "Hints" that the governor was about to flee the colony. He wanted Franklin's word that he would not leave New Jersey without congressional approval. By now William was more furious than frightened. He could not believe that an illegitimate government would dare to give orders to a Crown official. He hastily scribbled a few words that were designed to buy some time, even while they did not acknowledge congressional authority. He was aware that his letter to Lord Dartmouth had been intercepted, he told Colonel Winds. But it was a "mere Narrative," containing "nothing but what was my Duty to write as a faithful Officer of the Crown." Consequently, he had nothing to fear. "I have not the least Intention to quit the Province," he haughtily informed Winds, "nor shall I unless compelled by Violence. Were I to act otherwise it would not be consistent with my Declarations to the Assembly, nor my Regard for the good People of the Province." With a flourish, the governor handed his reply to the waiting servant.[9]

His response had no immediate effect. Soldiers were posted about the house for the rest of the night, leaving just before dawn. One lonely sentinel remained to guard the front gate. Franklin and his nearly hysterical wife had to rely on rumors and innuendo to anticipate Winds's next move. Some of the soldiers were talking of incarcerating him in the Perth Amboy barracks while they waited further instructions from Philadelphia. The governor was convinced that congress would demand his immediate arrest and order his removal "to the Interior Part of the Country" so that he would not be able to forward further intelligence to Whitehall. He did not expect mercy from Lord Stirling, who he now counted as one of his bitterest enemies. Colonel Winds had been apologetic about arousing the Franklins "at such an improper Time of Night," laying the blame for his rudeness on his commanding officer. William had no problem crediting Winds's explanation.[10]

The threat of physical danger served almost as a tonic to the beleaguered governor. No longer did he have to play the role of moderate conciliator. Seeing all sides of every issue was not the virtue it had been when he had acted as mediator between King and colony. Even as the humiliation at the Cockpit had pushed Benjamin Franklin irrevocably into the arms of American patriots, this attack on his person and property by his own countrymen was exactly what William Franklin needed to confirm him in his devotion to the King. By their actions on the night of January 6, his adversaries had become his enemies. At least for the moment, Franklin counted himself more an Englishman than an American.

His resolve stiffened, his duty clear, he became obsessed with upholding the last remnants of royal government in New Jersey. Undaunted by the prospect of imprisonment, ignoring the guard in front of his house, he sat in his study composing another copy of the intercepted letter to Lord Dartmouth, hoping that somehow he would be able to slip it out of the house and through the network of sentinels posted throughout the eastern half of the colony. He also started a diary "of the principal Transactions, and the Treatment I received in consequence of the Interception of my Dispatches." He intended to testify fully and accurately against every person who had violated the Crown's authority. As soon as this unpleasantness was over, he would have his revenge.[11]

At the same time, he refused to back down before William Winds. Instead he put his captor on the defensive, firing off another message to the colonel, upbraiding him for his insolence, and demanding to know by what authority he dared detain the King's surrogate. Franklin had already promised not to leave the province. While he adamantly refused to swear an oath to an illegitimate government, he thought his word as a gentleman should have weight with "Those who pretend to act on Principles of honour." He also demanded the immediate removal of the guards around his house. "You will," he warned Winds, "answer the contrary at your peril." By placing an officer of the King's government under house arrest he had committed treason. And the penalty for treason was death.[12]

Winds waited anxiously for orders that would help him dispose of his unpleasant task. But Lord Stirling did not intend to let him escape his duty. While congress read the intercepted letters, and puzzled over what, if anything, to do with a royal governor who was both a spy and the son of one of its most respected delegates, Stirling forged ahead.[13] On the tenth of January he forwarded the exchange between Winds and Franklin to Philadelphia, informing congress that he was convinced the governor would not be silenced by mere house arrest. The man was dangerous, and it was only "prudent" to remove him to Stirling's headquarters at Elizabeth, some sixteen miles away. The colonel had arranged for "good, genteel private lodgings" for the governor and he had already commanded Winds to bring him there that very day.[14]

Following their orders, about one hundred soldiers and a handful of officers rode to Proprietary House to arrest William Franklin. They handed him an "invitation" from Lord Stirling requesting his presence at dinner that evening. The governor snorted contemptuously, returning the note without comment. But when he realized that he would be taken to Stirling's headquarters by force if necessary, he elected to make the "least Resistance" possible and began packing his bags.[15]

As the governor was about to deliver himself into the hands of the provincial militia, Chief Justice Frederick Smyth galloped up to the house. He had just learned that Franklin was about to be taken prisoner and was "greatly alarmed" at the news. What would be the "Ill Consequences" to the province if one of the King's ships, now stationed at New York, should demand the governor's release? Did Franklin's captors realize that either humble acquiescence to Crown authority or a pitched battle with His Majesty's men might result from their precipitous behavior? Smyth begged the officers to defer their departure. He had already dispatched a letter to Colonel Winds asking him to rescind his orders, and Winds had promised to consider the request. The officers agreed to a short delay, giving Smyth a chance to confer personally with the colonel. Still, they warned him that unless he returned quickly with countermanding orders, they would be obliged to commence their journey.[16]

While the chief justice rode frantically away in search of Colonel Winds, Franklin returned to the house. But he later insisted that he was "perfectly indifferent whether I was sent to Elizth Town or not." The threat to arrest him had already constituted a grave insult to his office, and he cared little whether the threat was actually implemented. While he was reluctant to "leave Mrs. Franklin in so dangerous a State," he would not lift a finger on his own behalf. "I was determined to ask nothing that should have the Appearance of a Favour to myself," he proudly explained, "nor would I at all interfere in the Matter."[17]

They all cooled their heels for an hour before officers and men alike grew restless. They were anxious to start for Elizabeth before dark. Franklin, too, wanted to get the journey behind him. He climbed into his coach, which had been standing in readiness by the front door. At his side sat Stephen Skinner, who intended to act as a witness to all the proceedings. The carriage lumbered slowly away from the house, surrounded by members of the provincial militia.[18]

They had not gone three hundred yards, however, when Smyth returned, one of Winds's officers at his side. The Colonel had agreed to let the governor remain in his own home, while the chief justice himself rode to Elizabeth to plead Franklin's case before Lord Stirling. Franklin almost reluctantly alighted from his coach, and when Winds visited him that evening, the governor declared that the chief justice was acting entirely on his own initiative. Despite Franklin's indifference, Smyth's mission was successful. No one knows how he persuaded Stirling to change his mind. The colonel did tell congress that Franklin had promised to give his parole to the provincial government. But whether this was a face-saving gesture on Stirling's part, or Smyth told him this was the case, remains unclear. There is no evidence that Franklin himself ever made such a promise. But, Stirling did remove the guards from around Franklin's house and made no further attempt to harass the governor.[19]

As William spent the long but uneventful winter replaying the whole episode in his mind, he claimed to regret Chief Justice Smyth's well-intended intervention. Had Stirling imprisoned him, congress would have had to acknowledge his situation and issue orders for his care. Thus the leaders of the American resistance would have been subject to punishment for treason as soon as the King's troops gained the upper hand. Besides, said Franklin bravely, "I much wanted to see how they would have behaved on the Occasion." The governor's interest was based on more than idle curiosity. Congress's reaction to his imprisonment would have provided some hint of its real views on American independence. Franklin was convinced that congress actually hoped he would flee the province. "It has long appeared to me," he told Lord Germain, the new Secretary of State for the American Department, that "some of them at least, wanted to have all the King's Governors quit the Colonies, that they might have a Pretence for forming them into separate Republics." If this was the radicals' intention, William Franklin was determined to disappoint them. Perhaps, he admitted, if there had been a ship sitting in Raritan Bay, he would have followed the example of other royal governors and sought asylum there. Had he remained in the harbor, he could claim that he had not technically relinquished his powers of government. But, he concluded, "as that was not the Case, my Language has constantly been—You may force me, but you shall never frighten me out of the Province."[20]

As long as Franklin remained at Perth Amboy, he intended to pretend that government was functioning as usual. But his bravado fooled no one. Cortlandt Skinner, his most trusted supporter was gone. "I much regret his Absence," he admitted. Moreover, he knew that he had alienated even the fence-sitters on his council with the disparaging remarks he had made about some of its members in his intercepted letter to Lord Dartmouth.[21] Despite his precarious position, Franklin remained stubbornly upbeat. He still thought that most councilors privately deplored the Continental Congress almost as much as he did. They kept quiet only because they were "under a Necessity, for the Preservation of themselves & Families, in these Times of Violence, to appear to entertain Sentiments of a different Nature." And while he reluctantly admitted that there were council members who supported congress, he insisted that they had been momentarily deluded by "artful and designing men." They were not "aware of the pernicious & destructive Tendency of those Measures" that they supported with such unbecoming naïveté. Like most Americans, they did not realize that every move the rebel leaders made was calculated to widen the breach between the mother country and the colonies so that independence would gradually appear natural, even inevitable. As he had done since the Stamp Act crisis, he simply underestimated the depth and breadth of colonial discontent.[22]

So determined was Franklin to look on the bright side of an increasingly dark future that he professed to imagine that the promulgation of Thomas Paine's *Common Sense* would help the King's cause. It was, he thought, a "most inflammatory Pamphlet," which "strongly and artfully" argued for independence. But he predicted that Paine's attempt to rally the masses would backfire. Now, he explained, the people of "Sense & Property" would understand the true intentions of the rabble rousers who led the American protest movement. Their mask had been torn off. Already, he said, the colonists had begun to "see their Danger." A few were even beginning to speak out publicly against congress. While it had grown difficult to get such sentiments printed, for the self-professed "Champions for the Liberty of the Press" were loathe to allow any real freedom in America, Franklin thought the tide was turning. Now, he argued, was the perfect time to send commissioners to America. The opportunity to secure "a lasting Reconciliation and Union" had never been greater.[23]

Nevertheless, even William Franklin must have privately wondered where the men of sense and good will had gone. No one on either side of the Atlantic seemed interested in peace, and he would hardly have been human had he not at least occasionally felt abandoned by everyone. He even suspected members of his own family of treachery, and while he did not directly accuse his father of plotting against him, the thought surely crossed his mind. His sense of isolation escalated after January, as neither Temple nor Sally sent even a word of commiseration in the wake of Stirling's abortive attempt to arrest him. Two weeks after the troops had left the Franklin's gate, Elizabeth remained prostrate. The "least sudden Noise almost throws her into Hysterics," he said. And she felt more than ever, a foreigner in an inhospitable land. She had no "relations or connexions" to whom she could turn for help; William's family evidently cared little what became of her. Even strangers, he bitterly informed his son, asked more civilly about her welfare than did her in-laws in Philadelphia. Both Sally and Temple apologized profusely for their neglect, claiming that ignorance of the Franklins' situation, not callous disregard for their feelings, accounted for their silence. But William was not appeased. He refused to believe that they had not heard "what the whole Country rang of." He knew, of course, that as a member of congress, Ben was fully aware of his difficulties. If no one in the family knew about his recent embarrassments, it was because his father had chosen to remain silent.[24]

Arguments over money also plagued Franklin's relationship with his son. William's resources were slim; he had temporarily abandoned all prospect of benefits from the Vandalia plan. He could not even be sure that he would continue to receive his salary. Consequently he viewed Temple's profligacy as a personal affront. William tried to draw up a budget for his son's expenses, asking Richard Bache, not Ben, to dole out cash as Temple's needs warranted. "You must," he lectured his son, "continue to be as saving as you can, for I have not much to offer at present."[25]

But Temple paid little regard to his father's admonitions. Some of the blame, no doubt belonged to William himself, for he constantly sent mixed signals to his son as he vacillated between his desire to play the role of paternal benefactor and his need to discipline the often careless and unthinking boy. He sent money for fencing lessons and encouraged him to begin taking instructions in horsemanship, even while he resented every unnecessary expenditure that Temple made. Part of William's indulgence resulted from his genuine concern over Temple's well-being. The boy suffered considerable strain in the months before independence was declared. The English son of a royal governor and the grandson of a leading patriot, he was vulnerable to attack from supporters and detractors of the Crown. His desire to please both his guardians made his situation even more awkward. And he was convinced that it was only Ben's prestige that kept many Philadelphians at bay. Thus in the early spring Temple was thoroughly frightened when he learned that the elder Franklin was planning a trip away from the city, and he quickly wrote to his father for guidance. William sympathized with his son, but his advice was predictable. On no account should Temple flee to Perth Amboy. He should remain where he was, and where he had every right to be, doing nothing that would give either William's or Ben's enemies an excuse to attack him. "However others behave toward you," he lectured, "be careful that your Conduct to them is as polite, affectionate & respectable as possible."[26]

Despite his concern, Franklin could be as tight-fisted as he could be generous. Indeed, he was even more exacting than his own father had been.

Whether he had inherited or acquired his ledger-book mentality from Ben, William was always determined to be given his due. If he wrote Temple a letter, he expected a prompt reply. If he sent extra spending money, he demanded an immediate expression of appreciation. And if Temple was too free with his father's money, at a time when William was fighting for his political existence, he was apt to explode. At the beginning of May, when Temple again pressed him for money, he did just that.[27]

The two had recently embarked upon a little experiment. William had reluctantly provided his son with enough cash to last until the middle of June. But by the end of April Temple was broke. "I did not imagine," William chided, "(tho' I was willing to make the Experiment) that you had Prudence enough to make it hold out for the Time it ought to have lasted." Sounding like fathers everywhere, he lectured his son for squandering his money on "Trifles." "You have much greater Allowance than I had at your Age," he moralized, "and I believe more than Nine Tenths of the Boys at the College have." And he insisted, in tones redolent of Poor Richard, that his severity only proved his concern for Temple's character. Even if I had all the money you wanted and more, he said, I would not provide you the "Means of going into Excesses that would be productive of the Ruin of your Constitution, hinder your Growth and make you miserable hereafter."[28]

The arguments over money did not cease until William became the prisoner of the rebel government. Temple continued to accuse his father of failing to provide even his barest necessities. William demanded an exact account of his son's expenditures before he agreed to advance more money. In an effort to punish his father, the boy went on strike for a time, refusing to answer William's letters and ignoring his requests for pamphlets and newspapers from Philadelphia. The governor was thoroughly disgusted and threatened to turn elsewhere for political news. But it was difficult to know who to trust, and it was impossible to ask Ben for help. And so he reiterated his request for a copy of the Evening Post, including the Strictures on Common Sense, for which he had already advanced the money. You can, he said with heavy sarcasm, get a copy of the paper in town "if it is not too much Trouble to walk so far as Front Street."[29]

It was a gloomy time for the near helpless governor. Never happy when he was inactive, his virtual house arrest weighed heavily on his nerves. His interest in Temple's finances was undoubtedly as much a product of boredom and tension as it was an indication of concern for his son's welfare. Perth Amboy had become a prison. The "joyous, social evenings" that the Franklins had enjoyed with their friends in the sumptuous governor's mansion were at an end. "Everything," sighed Elizabeth, "is now changed." Not even his wife's pathetic pleas induced the Baches to visit the Franklins to help lift the pall that hung over their silent home. Elizabeth's physical and mental condition did not improve throughout the winter. I have been, she told her sister-in-law, "so thoroughly frightened that I believe I shall never again recover my strength or spirits." Such language frightened William, who no doubt remembered that his stepmother had spoken in much the same vein the autumn before her death.[30]

When he was not sick in bed with a fever and cold or nursing his wife, who was similarly afflicted, William tried to keep busy. He continued to write in his diary, carefully noting every insult that came his way. He retained his voracious appetite for politics, and despite his disdain for the leaders of colonial resistance he tried not to let his bias interfere with his ability to appreciate a good argument or clever phrase. "I like Pieces that are well wrote," he told his son, "let them be of what Side the Question they may, especially when they abound with Wit & Humour." Many of the pamphlets he secured were, of course, intended for the eyes of royal officials. But his ulterior motives never stopped him from enjoying for themselves the political scribblings of Americans of all persuasions.[31]

Perhaps not surprisingly, William's affection for his father did not die. The two men had stopped writing by the end of 1775, and their visits were also at an end. But William could not forget the man whose guidance had meant so much to him over the years. Nearly every letter to Temple contained an anxious query about Ben. What was he doing? Was he healthy? Was there a chance that he might retire from politics altogether? But Ben, of course, was no more likely to abandon his cause than was William. When William learned that his father intended to embark upon a diplomatic mission to Canada, his concern was unfeigned. He feared the trip would be too arduous for a man of Ben's age, even though the elder Franklin was as vigorous as ever. He would do anything, William said unhappily, to dissuade his father from making the journey. One can only imagine his dismay when he heard that Ben and the other congressional delegates had passed through Woodbridge, just to the north of Perth Amboy, on their way to Canada. His father had not used the occasion to visit a son he now counted as one of the enemy.[32]

Whatever, his personal feelings William had a duty to uphold. But it was with more sadness than anger that he informed Lord Germain, without comment, that "Dr. Franklin & Mr. Chace" were on their way to Canada in order to "prevail on the Canadians to enter into the Confederacy with the other Colonies." By naming his father, he was not telling the ministry anything it did not know about Ben's role in the move for independence. But the information itself might prove valuable, and it was his job to provide it. Still his concern for his father's well-being was real. And he realized that the trip to Canada signaled a complete and final break in their relations. "Nothing ever gave me more Pain than his undertaking that Journey," he told Temple, "nor would anything give me more Pleasure than to hear he had resolved to quit all public Business."[33]

It would not be long before governor William Franklin would no longer be able to serve the Crown from the comfort of Perth Amboy. Throughout the winter of 1776, the Provincial Congress assumed *de facto* authority in the colony. It organized New Jersey's defenses, appointed officers to replace royal placeholders, held elections, and appointed its own delegates to the Continental Congress. While Whig leaders resisted an attempt orchestrated by James Witherspoon in April to go on record in favor of independence, the college president's failure merely postponed the inevitable. On May 10, congress began to lay the ground work for independence when it resolved that it was now "absolutely irreconcilable to reason and good Conscience" for Americans to swear allegiance to "any government under the crown of Great Britain." Five days later the Philadelphia delegates called for the formation of new governments in those colonies where "no government sufficient to the exigence of their affairs" existed. For Franklin, this directive was a challenge. Still convinced that most people in New Jersey opposed independence as much as they disliked parliamentary taxation, he set out to prove that in his colony, at least, government "sufficient to the exigence of their affairs" remained. Just two weeks after congress flung down the gauntlet, the New Jersey governor defiantly picked it up, commanding his assembly to convene in Perth Amboy on June 20 to discuss some "Matters of great Importance."[34]

Franklin was not merely engaging in a gratuitous gesture of defiance. He still faintly hoped to orchestrate a reconciliation between England and America. The long-awaited English peace commissioners were even then headed toward the colonies. He imagined that most members of the New Jersey assembly would be willing at least to meet with them. Franklin acknowledged that the legislature would never sign a separate peace with the mother country. But he thought that if the commissioners did their job well, the lawmakers might pressure congress to begin serious negotiations of its own. Franklin even fancied that he had "Reason to suppose" that if congress failed to yield to this pressure, then New Jersey might consider itself absolved from any further obligation to the Philadelphia regime. It was obviously a long shot. But it was, he explained simply, the "duty incumbent on every officer of Government not to quit his Post or place of Trust till the last Extremity." Thus, he continued, "I determined to stand my Ground as long as possible."[35]

Franklin never had a chance to duel with his enemies for the loyalty of New Jersey. He had underestimated the strength of the opposition, and the degree to which most Americans had come to accept, if not to embrace, the move toward independence. As soon as they learned of the governor's audacious intention to convene the assembly, the leaders of the colony's resistance sprang into action. They went forward with their planned elections for a new Provincial Congress, returning a body that was not afraid to meet the governor's challenge head-on.[36] The new congress met in Burlington at the beginning of June. On the fourteenth, its members called upon all New Jersey legislators to boycott the assembly. The following day, they declared that Franklin's latest effort to uphold royal authority was "in direct contempt and violation of the resolve of the Continental Congress." Consequently, the governor had "discovered himself to be an enemy to the liberties of this country," and they insisted that "measures ought to be immediately taken for securing the person of the said William Franklin, Esquire." At the same time they stopped the governor's salary. By discontinuing the colony's support of the King's government, they had effectively terminated Crown authority in New Jersey. "Notwithstanding the Public Faith pledged to me by the General Assembly," cried the outraged governor, this self-constituted and illegitimate government had usurped the King's power and violated the trust of the very people they claimed to serve. But for most Americans, it no longer mattered that the Provincial Congress had no legal standing.[37]

Samuel Adams himself traveled to Burlington to inform New Jersey's Provincial Government that congress would not interfere with its efforts to unseat William Franklin. Franklin had been a conspicuously active royal governor for too long, and now that congress was consolidating its position it had simply run out of patience. Any hopes that some delegates may have harbored that Benjamin Franklin's son might be won over to the colonists' side had disappeared. The time had come to act decisively.[38]

Armed with the approval of the Philadelphia government, New Jersey's new leaders moved quickly. On June 15, they ordered Colonel Nathaniel Heard to initiate proceedings against the royal governor, asking only that he act with "all the delicacy and tenderness which the nature of the business can possibly admit." It was a momentous step, and they knew it. "We are passing the Rubicon," said Jonathan Sergeant solemnly. Still, at least at first, most delegates hoped it would not be necessary to incarcerate the governor. The Provincial Congress ordered Heard to offer Franklin a chance to sign a parole promising that he would remain in Princeton, Bordentown, or on his own farm at Rancocas Creek. The choice was his. If Franklin refused this generous offer, Heard had no choice but to "put him under strong guard, and keep him in close custody."[39]

On the morning of June 17, just three days before the assembly was scheduled to convene, Colonel Heard, accompanied by Major Jonathan Deare, a native of Perth Amboy, visited the governor's mansion. Heard handed Franklin the parole and William read it carefully before returning it with an air of "contempt." He demanded to know "by what authority" such an "impertinent" order had been issued. Heard, prepared for just this response, produced two documents indicating that he was acting under orders of New Jersey's Provincial Congress. Franklin professed to be amazed. "To be represented as an Enemy to the Liberties of my Country (one of the worst characters) merely for doing my duty in calling a meeting of the legal Representatives of the People" was, he exploded "sufficient to rouse the indignation of any man not dead to human feeling." He warned Heard that he executed the orders of the Provincial Congress at his own peril. And he refused to comply with the congressional request.[40]

While Colonel Heard posted a "strong Guard" of his own Woodbridge men around the governor's mansion, Franklin strode to his library and began writing furiously. As he wrote, he overheard the muttered comments of the sentries standing outside his window, who, he realized even then did not know why they were guarding Proprietary House. It was comforting to know that the common people of New Jersey were still at the mercy of their devious leaders, and that his own popularity remained as strong as ever.[41]

But Franklin had more important concerns than any fleeting interest he may have had in the opinions of the soldiers of Woodbridge. He had a message for the council and assembly of New Jersey, whose members he suspected he would not see again in his official capacity. He was determined to justify his recent attempt to convene the assembly and to outline his general view of the relationship between America and England.

The governor acted both as a lawyer and a politician as he pled his case.[42] He began by declaring that he had in no way violated the congressional dictate of May 15. Even if he had, Franklin remarked, it surely "could not be any crime" for a royal officer to ignore the orders of an illegitimate government. The congressional resolution, which, he pointed out, was couched as a "recommendation," had suggested that the assemblies or congresses in each colony should adopt whatever form of government they thought best suited to serve the interests of their constituents. Congress had certainly implied that "where Assemblies can meet they are to consider the propriety of the measure recommended, and not a Convention." Indeed, in Pennsylvania, Delaware, and Maryland assemblies had met for just that purpose, and no one there had been accused of acting as an enemy to his country.

Had I refused to call the assembly, Franklin wryly observed, and denied the people's representatives an opportunity to consider the grave issues that lay before them, I would have been open to censure. How, he wondered, could he be faulted for allowing the legislators a chance to discuss their options and defend their constitutional rights? Was he not acting as befitted a true Whig, not a monarchical tyrant? The fact remained. Where assemblies could meet, they were obliged to do so. Because Franklin had not fled New Jersey, government there should continue in the "usual way." The Provincial Congress, by preventing the meeting of the people's own representatives, had shown itself to be contemptuous of the very liberties it so sanctimoniously professed to protect.

Franklin had another bone to pick with his persecutors, this one over their stoppage of his salary. Typically, he could not forbear running over his old complaints about his meager stipend. "If I were to quit this province tomorrow," he protested, "I should not retire one farthing the richer for anything acquired by means of my office." The people of New Jersey were fortunate, he thought piously, that "mercenary motives" had never been a part of his character. But, despite his honesty and devotion, a group of self-appointed men had chosen, without explanation, to rob him of the "pittance of the salary which their legal Representatives had granted . . . by law." By what authority, he wondered, had they usurped one of the most jealously guarded rights of any British assembly? He could not believe that the "people at large" supported "this unworthy treatment of a man who has done his duty faithfully by them during a thirteen years administration." No, he claimed, obviously warming to his subject, these impostors had actually robbed him not once, but twice. First, he said, they tried to "filch from me my good name." Then they stripped me of my property while they pretended to treat me with "*delicacy and tenderness.*"

Having disposed of the legal case against him to his own satisfaction, Fanklin offered his version of the current colonial situation. Carefully casting himself as a true Whig, he defended liberty against licentiousness, and balanced government against democratic republicanism. It was he, after all, who upheld the assembly's right to chart the colony's course at this dangerous juncture. It was the Provincial Congress, encouraged by outside agitators in Philadelphia, which had undermined the very rights it claimed to defend. This alone, thought the governor, discredited those men who would destroy his reputation. The rebel leaders were nothing but "pretended patriots" who acted from a combination of "meanness," personal animus, and a "sinister design" to replace British liberty with "an Independent Republican Tyranny." These "insidious" and "selfish" malcontents had perverted the aims of most colonists, who only wanted to rectify a few legitimate grievances, grievances that could be resolved by simple constitutional reform, not by wholesale revolution.

For Franklin, the issue was clear-cut. Shorn of all the slogans and phrasemaking of rebellious demagogues, the American people had to decide between a government that guaranteed the integrity of all its branches, or one that recognized only the liberties of the people. The one was designed to preserve both liberty and stability; the other was inevitably destined to lead to anarchy, followed quickly by democratical tyranny "the worst and most debasing of all possible Tyrannies." He could not believe that, given a real choice, the people of New Jersey would fall into the "traps of Independency and Republicanism" that had been set for them, "however temptingly they may be baited." He could not imagine that an America existing outside the protection of a strong and paternalistic empire, would result in anything but unhappiness. "Depend upon it," he predicted, "you can never place yourselves in a happier situation than in your ancient constitutional dependency on Great Britain. No Independent State ever was or ever can be so happy as we have been, and might still be, under that government." For the sake of America, not for the glory of England, he urged the people of New Jersey to wake up to reality before it was too late.

Franklin called upon the members of New Jersey's legal government to exercise the kind of leadership that could even then save the colony from disaster. He believed that good government should be for the people, but not by or of the people. A "real patriot can seldom or ever speak popular language," he said. This was what distinguished a leader from a demagogue. The latter always conformed to the "present humour and passions of the people." But the former gladly risked temporary unpopularity, for he knew that eventually his commitment to the truth would be recognized and applauded. Franklin warned against the temptation of pandering to the fickle minds of the American public. "When the present high fever shall abate of its warmth," he predicted, "and the people are once more able cooly to survey and compare their past with their then situation, they will, as naturally as the sparks fly upwards, wreak their vengeance on the heads of those who, taking advantage of their delirium, had plunged them into such difficulties and distress."

Even as he sat in his study staring through the window at the backs of armed guards, wondering how he would be able to smuggle his message out of the house, Franklin tried to present himself as a man of no rancor, who would gladly forget his humiliation at the hands of the Provincial Congress. "I bear no enmity to any man who means well," he claimed, "however we may differ in political sentiments." And he thanked those men who even "in these worst of times" had been courageous enough "to avow their loyalty to the best of Sovereigns, and manifest their attachment to their legal Constitution." As he laid down his pen, he repeated a commitment that had rung like a refrain throughout his entire administration: "*No Office or Honour in the Power of the Crown to bestow, will ever influence me to forget or neglect the Duty I owe my Country, nor the most furious Rage of*

the most intemperate Zealots induce me to swerve from the Duty I owe
His Majesty." As always he was a man in the middle, caught between conflicting loyalties, at a time when moderation was no longer considered a
virtue by men on either side of the Atlantic.

Franklin sat back to wait for congress's response to his stubborn refusal
to sign a parole. Toward sundown, some of the men from the artillery company stationed at Perth Amboy marched noisily into the yard to relieve the
Woodbridge sentries. If the governor had any fleeting thoughts of escape,
he swiftly discarded them.[43]

No one slept well that night. The loud laughter and raucous shouts of
the guards permeated the June air, making it impossible for even the sound-
est sleeper to ignore them. For three days the Franklins saw only their servants and the sentries outside their windows. No one was allowed to visit
the house. Even Mrs. Franklin's doctor and a handful of her friends were
turned away. A guard accompanied the servants whenever they ran routine
errands in town.[44]

Meanwhile, members of the Provincial Congress were deciding how to
handle the potentially dangerous and always embarrassing Governor Franklin. Upon hearing that he had absolutely refused their parole, they worried
that he would try to set himself up as a symbol around which counter-
revolutionary elements in the colony might rally. Consequently they sought
permission from the government in Philadelphia to remove him from New
Jersey. The congressional reply was quick and sure. Before it made any permanent decision, the Provincial Congress should examine the governor
thoroughly. Then, if New Jersey's officials continued to see Franklin as
a threat, the Continental Congress promised to find a suitable place for his
confinement.[45]

On June 19, Nathaniel Heard and Jonathan Deare once more knocked at
the Franklins' door, and ordered the governor to prepare for a journey to
Burlington. Outwardly unperturbed, Franklin grilled his captors. Were
they acting under orders from the Continental Congress? Heard replied
in the affirmative. His orders were disagreeable, he said, but he had no
choice but to obey them. William snorted derisively. No man was obliged
to obey "illegal Orders." And the governor assured his captor that he
would one day be held personally accountable for his treason. Heard remained unshaken by the governor's threats. He softened only enough to allow William most of the day to wind up his affairs and bid his wife good-
bye.[46]

At 3:30 Colonel Heard rode up to Proprietary House for the last time.
He was accompanied by sixteen men armed with guns and bayonets. The
guard was so heavy, suggested Franklin, because the government knew how

popular he was and feared a rescue attempt on the road to Burlington. The governor was ready for his escort. Leaving his wife "in a Condition as affecting as can be imagined," he climbed into his coach. This time, there was no last-mintue reprieve from Chief Justice Smyth. The effort to arrest the governor in January had been a mere dress rehearsal. This, it seemed, was the real thing.[47]

12

"Like a Bear Through the Country"

"If we Survive the present Storm, we may all meet and enjoy the Sweets of Peace with greater Relish."—William Franklin to William Temple Franklin, 1776.[1]

"*Pro Rege & Patria* was the Motto I assumed when I first commenced my Political Life, and I am resolved to retain it till Death shall put an end to my mortal Existence."—William Franklin to New Jersey Assembly, 1776.[2]

The journey to Burlington was not pleasant. It was a physically exhausting, and perhaps more to the point, a humiliating experience for the proud governor to be paraded through the countryside as the captive of a government whose legitimacy he did not recognize. For a man accustomed to respect, if not affection, it was excruciating to be eyed by curious farmers and shopkeepers as he made his way under armed guard along the road to the western capital. He tried unsuccessfully to shut out the laughter, the derisive catcalls, and even the muted glances of sympathy that greeted him along the way. He no doubt recalled his first trip from Perth Amboy to Burlington when, as the new governor of New Jersey, he had been welcomed with ringing church bells as he rode into town, his proud father at his side. This time his father was not there to smooth his way. Now his oath of loyalty to the Crown was the object of mockery, not a badge of honor.

The party stopped for the night at a Brunswick tavern, where the governor's room was guarded so closely that he could not even answer "a call of nature" in solitude. When a few of Franklin's friends tried to visit him, all but one were firmly turned away. That night, Colonel Heard had no trouble commandeering some of the town's inhabitants to watch the governor's room. Guards were everywhere, not only at Franklin's door but on the stairs, and at the front and back entryways to the inn. They made a party of the occasion, laughing and shouting, so that despite his fatigue the governor could not sleep. By comparison, Heard's men looked very good indeed. At least they had gone about their business with quiet efficiency and had given him "no insult."[3]

Early the next morning, the small band began the last leg of the journey. Its members "paraded along the Road to Burlington," past William's former home and toward the cottage of his cousin, Josiah Davenport. The governor remained under heavy guard. Once again, none of his old friends was allowed to visit him. Was this, Franklin wondered, the "Delicacy and Tenderness" the Provincial Government had contemplated when it ordered his arrest?[4]

At ten a.m. on Friday, the twenty-first of June, two delegates from the Provincial Congress arrived with orders to accompany Franklin to government headquarters. Franklin was ready for them. He had already devised a strategy for dealing with the colony's pretended authorities. He intended to have retribution on every man who desecrated his office. He would secure his revenge in lawyerly fashion, using the law itself against these men who so casually violated the precepts of the English constitution. Turning to his escorts, he calmly stated that he had "no Business with the Congress," and he refused to leave his room voluntarily. Nonplussed, the delegates retreated, returning with a guard of twenty or thirty men. Franklin remained unimpressed, and demanded to see their orders. His escorts sheepishly complied, even allowing him to make a copy for his records. The governor lectured the leader of the delegation, telling him that his instructions were "illegal" and that he executed them at his peril. Franklin repeated his warning to the soldiers who waited for him outside. One soldier replied that "they had their order." The rest stood silently, but William thought his words had some effect. He was convinced that many of the men were "dissatisfied with their Employment."[5]

Nevertheless they shoved Franklin into his coach and carried him to headquarters. It was a somber parade. Eighteen armed men led the way, followed by the governor's carriage. Two local officials brought up the rear. The congressional delegates awaited his arrival with a mixture of curiosity and excitement, and they fell silent as Franklin came into the room. Samuel Tucker, the president of the Provincial Congress, occupied the seat formerly belonging to the chief justice. Doctor John Witherspoon, "as hearty a friend" to the American cause as any native-born American, sat to the President's left. Tucker offered the governor a seat at the bar, and in a moment of weakness William accepted the overture.[6]

Leaning forward, Tucker indicated that he had a few questions for "Mr. Franklin." The omission of his title was not lost on the proud man seated before him. He wanted to know, Tucker began reasonably, if the governor had tried to convene the New Jersey assembly on the twentieth of June. But the members of the Provincial Congress might just as well have remained at home. Franklin refused to answer any questions emanating from an "illegal Assembly." To do so would only legitimize its proceedings. "I would," he explained two days later, "consider them in no other light than as a Body of Men who had presum'd to usurp the Government of the Province." Instead he reiterated his grievances. The provisional government had falsely accused him of being an enemy to his country, robbed him of his salary, and ordered him seized and brought before its members to answer its illegitimate charges. He was painfully aware of his captors' power, but he refused to acquiesce to his own or the Crown's demise. "Do as you please," he told them defiantly, "and make the best of it." And with that he fell silent.[7]

Tucker had no choice but to proceed. After each question, he paused briefly before continuing. Did Franklin know of the Congressional Resolves of May 15? Did he issue the call for the assembly? What "important business" did he have to discuss with the New Jersey legislature? Had he ever recommended the use of force against the colonies? Had he told Colonel Heard that "the Day was not far off when he would be made to repent what he was doing?" Franklin remained almost as silent as his own father had been when he stood before Alexander Wedderburn at the Cockpit. Only once did he respond to Tucker's interrogation. When he was accused of threatening Nathaniel Heard, he angrily demanded that the colonel be brought before him to repeat the charge.[8]

Tucker was stopped short by Franklin's unexpected request, but Witherspoon broke the silence, recommending that Heard be brought into the chamber. Two or three delegates leaped to their feet to oppose acceding to Franklin's demand. William sat back smiling. "It was the only Amusement I had for some Days," he admitted, and he was sorry when the debate came to an end. Heard was finally brought into the room, but was sent away before he had a chance to testify.[9]

Tucker finally finished his questions, and everyone looked around nervously, not sure how to proceed. The accused had refused to offer a word in his own defense. The facts in the case were in. The verdict was a foregone conclusion. But they were all a bit awe-struck by the gravity of the moment. Witherspoon's voice finally broke the uneasy silence. Railing at the governor who sat silently before them, the Scotch émigré condemned the native-born American. Not content with denigrating the prisoner's political beliefs, he became personally abusive. His arms flailing awkwardly, his flat voice rising as his "disagreeable temper" got the best of him, Witherspoon mocked Franklin's fine airs and his claims of gentility when everyone knew that he was nothing but a base-born bastard.[10] His harangue finally over, the college president moved that congress return the governor to his quarters, while its members discussed his fate. The motion passed without dissent. No one was sorry to see the obdurate William Franklin leave the room.[11]

As Franklin returned to his temporary quarters, congress decided his fate. He had scarcely departed when voices rang out clamoring for his removal from the colony. He had directly challenged congressional authority. His defiant demeanor removed the lingering doubts that anyone there may have harbored. The more moderate delegates had long since headed for home, and it was relatively easy for those remaining to declare that William Franklin was a "virulent enemy to this country, and a person that may prove dangerous" to its cause. Consequently they asked congress to designate a place for the governor's confinement, and they called for a courier to carry the results of their morning's work to Philadelphia.[12]

The "virulent" and "dangerous" Governor Franklin did not sit quietly and wait his punishment. He was fighting for his reputation as well as his freedom. He had already found a way to smuggle his June 17 letter to the legislature out of his rooms. Somehow he managed to get it to Isaac Collins, the King's printer. But after agreeing to print Franklin's letter, Collins changed his mind claiming that to do so would endanger his own life. News of the printer's negotiations with Franklin quickly reached the Provincial Congress, and its members immediately prohibited anyone from printing the governor's statements. "Poor men!" cried Franklin in frustration. "They can no more bear the light of truth, it seems, than Owls can endure the light of the sun!" Nevertheless, at least for the moment, his attempts to rally public opinion were blocked.[13]

Still, Franklin did not quit his feverish attempts to salvage his name. On Saturday, the twenty-second, he added a postscript to the letter he had begun to the New Jersey legislature in Perth Amboy, bringing his story up-to-date. But by now he was becoming frightened. He was especially worried because he understood that in their efforts to bolster their weak case, his enemies had uncovered a new and more damaging letter, purportedly written by Franklin, which they had brought before the Provincial Congress. The governor was convinced that the document was a fake, but with no access to the press, he feared that he would be convicted on the basis of a malicious lie. All he asked was a public forum, where he could seek the judgment of the entire colony instead of this "minority" that presumed to "rule over the whole people." "This," he cried, "every honest man must allow I have a right to insist on, if not as a Governor, yet, as a native of America, and a freeholder of New Jersey." He no longer stood solely on his prerogative as a Crown official. He demanded the basic rights guaranteed to any Englishmen in America.[14]

But congress was not about to lift the press ban on governor Franklin.

Undaunted, William continued writing, beginning yet another letter to the assembly on the twenty-third. While he knew that the provincial government had already asked congress to remove him from the colony, he would not be "led like a Bear through the Country" without a fight. For the first time, he wavered, hinting that he might sign a congressional parole, as he wondered why he, unlike other Crown officials, was not allowed to remain at home. He was not an enemy to America. He had never tried to raise an army to quell the resistance movement. He was willing to admit that he was powerless to reverse the trend toward independence. At worst, he was harmless. And he might even now be of some use "to the Country." Should England be willing to negotiate with the colonies, and should congress agree to work for a settlement, he was the best man available to head a peace delegation. As it was, he felt that the revolutionary government was using him to frighten other foes of independence. But he could more effectively serve the American people if he were permitted to remain free.[15]

Without actually begging, Franklin had presented his case in its most positive light. He needed only to remind all Americans that he was not their enemy, that he was simply a man of honor and moderation at a time when reason and caution had gone out of style. He loved his country and he loved his king. For him, it was impossible to separate the two. They were inextricably bound in a tightly woven tapestry made up of a common heritage and mutual interests. "Pro Rege & Patria was the Motto I assumed when I first commenced my Political Life," he explained, "and I am resolved to retain it till Death shall put an end to my mortal Existence." It was not, he thought, such a bad motto, and there was no reason to abandon it now.[16]

While Franklin wrote to a non-existent audience, the Continental Congress considered the provincial government's request. On Monday, the twenty-fourth of June, the account of the governor's interrogation was read into the record, and without apparent hesitation congress voted to remove William Franklin to the custody of Governor Jonathan Trumbull of Connecticut.[17]

On June 25, Franklin received notice of congress's decision, and he began to prepare for the journey to Hartford. But his friends, who had gathered to bid farewell to their former neighbor, took one look at the governor and rushed off to Samuel Tucker in dismay. The days of stress and uncertainty had taken their toll. Franklin was flushed with a high fever and was clearly too sick to travel. Still, it was with "great Difficulty" that they persuaded "their Low Mightinesses" to postpone his departure even for a day. No matter what his condition, Franklin had to leave Burlington by the twenty-sixth. "I leave tomorrow morning," he informed Temple. "I must go (I supposed) dead or alive." His bitterness was obvious. Congress had sent two doctors to make sure that his illness was not feigned. "Hypocrites," said Franklin, "always suspect Hypocrisy in others." But he did not wish to waste time with idle recriminations. It would be some time before he would see the son with whom he had been so recently reunited, and he did not want this last letter to be filled only with vitriol and complaints. Moreover, he had a few parting instructions. Because he feared that his incarceration might poison Temple's mind against his grandfather, he admonished his son to continue to be "dutiful and Attentive" to Ben. He also admonished the lad to watch over Elizabeth, who had grown genuinely fond of her husband's son. Finally, he wanted to offer a word of encouragement. "If we Survive the present Storm," he predicted, "we may all meet and enjoy the Sweets of Peace with greater Relish." There was still a chance that three generations of Franklin men might pass the glass between them and enjoy genuine pleasure in one another's company.[18]

On the morning of the twenty-sixth, a twenty-three-man guard arrived at the Davenport house on schedule to conduct Franklin along the two-hundred-mile trip to the Connecticut capital. Four days later, the heavily armed party had reached Hackensack where the weak and dejected governor begged to stop and rest. Claiming to regret his former obduracy, he requested permission to inform the Continental Congress that he would consider signing a negotiated parole. Robert Treat, the leader of the guard unit, agreed to go no further until congress replied to the governor's plea.[19]

Treat also allowed Franklin to scribble a few hasty words to his wife. The letter sealed his fate. Intercepted before it reached its destination, it was carried to General George Washington, who exploded when he read it. The letter contained "full evidence" that Franklin intended to escape. The governor's penitent demeanor was pure sham. He was stalling for time and hoping to be rescued. His letter to congress also appeared to be a ruse designed to produce delays. Franklin had "evidenced a most unfriendly disposition to our Cause" said Washington, and he could be coddled no longer. He advised Treat to listen to no more "frivolous Pretenses" from the wily governor, and he ordered the caravan to proceed. And so the little band went on to Hartford. Franklin's high fever continued, and the "insults" he received along the road did nothing to brighten his spirits. He was almost relieved when, on the evening of July 4, he arrived in the Connecticut capital. There, at least, he could deal directly with one of his equals, a colonial governor—albeit an elected one. There he would be accorded the respect his position deserved.[20]

But Franklin's negotiations with Governor Trumbull were not satisfactory. He admitted that Connecticut's chief executive treated him with "civility," but that was hardly the issue. The day afer the colonies declared their independence, William Franklin began the discussions that would lead to his imprisonment. Trumbull offered Franklin his choice of residence in return for a promise that he would not attempt an escape. But tired, dirty, and ill though he was, Franklin put up a fight. He continued to demand legal rights that had long since become irrelevant to his situation. He even insisted upon being returned to Perth Amboy, claiming that Connecticut officials did not have the authority to detain an officer of the King. When Trumbull summarily rejected his demand Franklin asked to go to Stratford, a town swarming with the Crown's Anglican supporters. This appeal was also denied. Stiff-necked as ever, William adamantly refused to co-operate.[21]

Exasperated, two members of Trumbull's council paid a visit to their charge. Connecticut officials had carefully followed the usual custom for dealing with prisoners of Franklin's rank. But everyone's patience was wearing thin. America had declared its independence. There was a war to be fought and won. No one had time to deal with the frivolous demands of a deposed governor. The councilors came bluntly to the point. Franklin would either sign his parole or he would be incarcerated like any common prisoner. The alternative was not a pleasant one. All colonial prisons were filthy, disease-ridden holes. And Connecticut jails were, the governor had heard, among the "worst in America." There was no point in resisting further. He would help neither himself nor the King by continued defiance. His head bowed in submission, he signed the parole.[22]

Once he had put his hand to the dreaded document, his case was disposed of rapidly. Trumbull decided to send him to Wallingford, due east of New Haven, where the governor was promised good accommodations and the company of the gentlemen of the town. But Franklin soon claimed that he had been "deceived" by the glowing promises of his captors. His quarters, were "extremely disagreeable." Only a couple of local dignitaries were allowed to visit him. Most of his conversations were with a "common Tavern Keeper." He was, moreover, in the heart of rebel country. A handbill was even then floating around the countryside, gloating over his humiliation, and drawing invidious comparisons between Benjamin Franklin and his son.[23]

As long as he stayed in Wallingford, Franklin feared for his life. Nor were his apprehensions unreasonable. On one occasion he was knocked in the head and beaten to the ground by some of the town's more "enthusiastic" rebels. A gentleman who ventured to extend him a few small kindnesses was "threatened and grossly insulted" by a band of trouble-makers. And another was fired at as he left his house by someone who mistook his figure in the dark for that of William Franklin. While he hated to beg, William found his condition intolerable, and he finally asked to be transferred to Middletown, just south of Hartford, where other loyalist prisoners were also incarcerated and he would not be so isolated or vulnerable to abuse. "As a great favor," the governor's request was granted. Washington himself had pointed out that men like William Franklin occupied a special category. Their social position commanded a certain respect. They were able to pay for their own expenses. Moreover, they had been apprehended "merely on Suspicion arising from a General line of Conduct unfriendly to the American Cause." They had been convicted of no crime, and while they had to be kept away from the coast and from post towns, they could nevertheless be accorded every "indulgence."[24]

There is no reason to believe that William harbored any hopes that his father would use his influence to alleviate his own condition. If such thoughts occurred to him, he shared them with no one. He was wise to do so, for Ben had no intention of coming to his son's rescue, and was even reluctant to provide succor for his daughter-in-law. William's loyalist friends suspected that, if anything, his special relationship to one of the leading American patriots made the governor's treatment that much worse. "His Father," said one, "is and has been every way his misfortune." Ben had "thrown off all natural affection for him," and William could expect no sympathy from his captors.[25]

Indeed Ben appeared to view William and Elizabeth's situation with singular detachment. He reluctantly allowed Temple to continue visiting Perth Amboy and did not interfere when Sally invited Elizabeth to stay with the Bache family in Philadelphia. But he was no doubt relieved when Mrs. Franklin refused the invitation. She was in a pitiable state. All her mail was intercepted and not so much as a newspaper was permitted entry to the governor's mansion. "I can do nothing," she said, "but Sigh & Cry; and even now my Nerves are so weak that my Hand shakes to such a degree that I can Scarcely hold a Pen." Still, she bravely vowed to stay on in Perth Amboy. But her spirits were low, and she was obviously weakened by the ordeal. Unruly soldiers marched through the streets at all times of the day and night. They delighted in shouting "rude" and "Insolent" abuse at the unprotected governor's wife. Despite orders to the contrary, they roamed over the grounds of Proprietary House plucking the apples off the trees and throwing them about the orchard with reckless abandon. They even tried to steal Temple's pet dog before Elizabeth tearfully dissuaded them from taking a canine captive for the rebel cause. Most unsettling was the dearth of news she had about her "dear *Prisoner's*" condition. She received one first-hand report from two men who saw him at New Haven in July, but their account of William's "horrid journey" hardly comforted her. She did not expect to hear from William himself. "I doubt," Elizabeth snorted, that the "saints" will allow the "Sinners" to write. My heart, she told her stepson, "is almost broke." William was an "Honest, upright Conscientious Man" and she could not understand why he was being treated so shamefully.[26]

She was even less able to comprehend her father-in-law's silence. No one knew more than she, the depth of affection that had for so long existed between Benjamin and William Franklin. Ben's apparent indifference seemed almost inhuman. When he finally sent her sixty dollars in response to her request for help in meeting her barest expenses, he brusquely belittled her pleas for sympathy. There were many others, he sternly lectured, whose sufferings were much greater than her own. Elizabeth was taken aback by Ben's cold retort. She acknowledged that her misery was small compared with that endured by others. But she was no abstract supplicant, nor was she some casual acquaintance. She was the living, breathing wife of his only son. Others might have more troubles, she admitted, "yet that does not lessen the Weight of mine, which are really more than so weak a Frame is able to Support." And she remained convinced that it was even then in Ben's power to alleviate her pain. Was there not, she asked hopefully, some way that William could give his parole without bringing dishonor to himself? And if that could be arranged, would it not be possible for William to return to his family? "Consider, my Dear and Honored Sir," she cried, "that I am now pleading the Cause of your Son and my Beloved Husband."[27]

But if Ben was moved by his daughter-in-law's tears, he gave no indication of it. In September he was one of a three-man congressional peace delegation designated to discuss Anglo-American relations with Lord Howe. He thought the meeting might take place in Perth Amboy. If it did, he told his grandson to arrange for private lodgings in the town. He wanted no personal contact with the denizens of Proprietary House. While he sent his love to Elizabeth by way of Temple throughout the summer and fall of 1776, and even asked for news of William—perhaps to indicate how little involved he was in determining his son's fate—more than this he would not, or could not, do.[28]

He seemed more concerned about Temple than about his own son. Ben had already lost William to the "enemy" and he was determined not to lose his grandson as well. He felt obliged to let the boy travel to New Jersey when school closed for the summer holidays. Yet the dangers there were real. An Englishman born and bred, the boy could hardly be expected to identify with the claims of the rebellious colonists. The British army was securely ensconced in New York, just across the water from Perth Amboy. Temple's sympathies would naturally be touched by the pitiable specter of his stepmother, and he would almost inevitably resent his father's rough treatment by colonial authorities. Moreover, so long as he remained under

Elizabeth's roof, his constant companions would surely be hostile to the rebel cause, and they would ply the impressionable boy with spurious loyalist propaganda at every opportunity.[29]

Ben grew increasingly alarmed in mid-September. As he waited anxiously for the start of the school year when he would have an excuse to bring his grandson back to Philadelphia, he received a letter from Temple requesting permission to visit William at Middletown. Elizabeth had been unable to get any letters to her husband and she wanted Temple to carry some messages directly to him. Ben's reply was immediate and negative. He instructed Elizabeth to send a sealed letter to her husband, enclosing it inside one addressed to Governor Trumbull. If she gave him permission to peruse its contents, there was no reason why Trumbull would not forward it to Middletown. He even sent Temple some franked paper to smooth the way for Elizabeth's letters. But Franklin was clearly worried. He hoped his grandson's request did not imply any "Reluctance" to resume his studies at a time when he should be laying the basis for his "future Improvement," and "Importance among Men. If this Season is neglected," he admonished, "it will be like cutting off the Spring from the Year." It was not Temple's studies that most concerned Benjamin Franklin. Above all he wanted to spirit the boy away from that "Tory House" where "Treason" and intrigue were as natural as breathing.[30]

But Temple had apparently inherited the Franklin obduracy, and he remained determined to travel to Connecticut. Elizabeth needed help in dealing with the family's complex finances. She had always left such details to William, and now she was helpless before the entangled state of her husband's far-flung speculative ventures. She had already tried twice to send letters to Connecticut, using Governor Trumbull as a mediator, but her efforts had been futile. Temple reacted angrily to his grandfather's references to the "Treason" swirling about the Franklins' "Tory House." And he assured Ben that he had neither the intention nor the opportunity to use his proposed trip as an opportunity to enlist as a spy in the loyalist cause.[31]

Ben was beside himself, and he quickly fired back a conciliatory response to his grandson's letter. He had only a "tender Concern" for Temple's welfare, he explained. Still, he continued to believe that Temple simply had a youthful longing for adventure, an aversion to school, and a "Desire I do not blame of seeing a Father you have so much Reason to love." In fact, Ben should not have been altogether surprised at his grandson's longing to strike out on his own. It was, after all, something of a family tradition.[32]

Temple never did visit his father. At the end of September, Benjamin Franklin was designated one of three American commissioners to France.

Immediately disregarding his own arguments for the importance of his grandson's education, Ben decided to take Temple with him as his personal secretary. In France he could insulate the boy from the blandishments of loyalist propaganda, and woo him away from any lingering sympathy he might have for his father's cause. On September 28 he sent terse instructions to Perth Amboy, telling Temple to return to Philadelphia immediately, cryptically promising that it would be to his advantage to do so. Four days later Temple bade a hurried farewell to his mother and friends, and rushed away from his New Jersey home.[33] Ben had kept William from joining a privateer by giving him his start in a career of service to King and country. He was now doing the same for his grandson, putting him in the pay and service of an American government dedicated to abolishing the Crown's control of its colonial possessions. He had "rescued a valuable young man from the danger of being a Tory, and fixed him in honest republican Whig principles."[34]

It was some time before William learned that his father had stolen his only son away from him. Two days after Temple left Perth Amboy, Franklin wrote to him, endeavoring as always to appear optimistic. He knew that other rebel prisoners had already been exchanged, and he hoped that a similar fate awaited him. One of his fellow inmates, a Mr. Irving of South Carolina, had just been allowed to return home, and William had lent him his sulky and horses to carry him as far as Perth Amboy. His slave Thomas would bring the horses back, and he hoped Temple might decide to accompany Thomas when he made the return trip to Middletown. Little did he know that his son was already preparing to re-cross the Atlantic, where he would serve as an enemy to his native country and to the King to whom William had sworn his allegiance. But if he was hurt or surprised when he finally learned of Temple's precipitous departure, he remained philosophical. "If the old gentleman has taken the boy with him," he told Elizabeth, "I hope it is only to put him in some foreign University."[35]

Franklin's term in captivity had barely begun. And much of the blame for his long confinement rested on his own shoulders. His treatment at Middletown was not unduly harsh. Like many prisoners under similar circumstances, he was given the freedom of the town and even allowed to ride in the countryside where both his health and spirits were considerably revived.[36] His old partner in land speculation, Thomas Wharton assumed responsibility for much of his expenses, so that his financial worries were minimal. The Anglican church was active in Middletown, and its presence no doubt attracted many quiet Crown sympathizers. And on occasion he and his fellow prisoners celebrated the news of British victories with so much "hallooing and shouting" that they were punished with stints in the rebel guard house. How much Franklin participated in these drunken acts of defiance is unclear. But he felt no sadness when he heard the Americans derided as "Cowards," and he joined with those who prayed loudly for a British victory. Having done his duty, he now felt free to lash out at everyone responsible for his present humiliation.[37]

Franklin continued to hope for an exchange throughout most of the winter. His old friend Cortlandt Skinner, living safely in New York, busily contacted confidants of General Howe on his behalf, as he assured those who were still suspicious of this son of Benjamin Franklin that the breach between the two men was deep and irreparable. A string of British victories made congress amenable to prisoner exchanges, as the King's forces captured more and more of their men and American morale sank to its lowest ebb since the fighting had begun. In November, congress instructed Washington to consider trading Franklin for Brigadier General William Thompson, and on December 1, Washington formally suggested the trade to the British commander. But three days later, congress abruptly told Washington to suspend all negotiations indefinitely. John Hancock thought the release of so important and personable a loyalist as William Franklin might be "prejudicial" to American interests and "attended with bad consequences."[38]

Even while Franklin's supporters were angling for his exchange, William was engaged in clandestine activities that would make his release impossible. Having committed himself to serve the King, Franklin was determined to use his name and the relatively lax security at Middletown to their best advantage.[39] He always shared his dwindling savings with other, less fortunate supporters of the loyalist cause, but he wanted to do more than render individual acts of kindness to his compatriots. If this meant the violation of his parole, then so be it. A gentleman had no obligation to honor a forced agreement with liars and thieves.[40]

In September, William Livingston, now governor of New Jersey, openly expressed his suspicion that even in captivity William constituted a danger to the rebel cause. He accused his predecessor of absconding with a box of valuable documents belonging to the New Jersey government, claiming that he planned to use them as evidence against rebel leaders should the American move for independence founder. The Connecticut assembly promptly instructed the governor's guards at Middletown to search his quarters for the missing papers. But though they ransacked his room, the documents were never found. Still, Livingston vowed to keep a sharp eye on his former political opponent.[41]

It was Livingston who first unearthed evidence that Franklin was using his Middletown headquarters to render covert aid to the British army. He discovered that "by some means or other" Franklin had managed to begin an illicit correspondence with New York loyalist Hugh Wallace. Even worse, by the spring of 1777, rumor had it that William had "granted protections to such as would take them in Connecticut." His innocent rides in the countryside had apparently been used as a cover to disguise Franklin's real activities. He had been trying to persuade the farmers of Connecticut to swear allegiance to the British government, and as the American position grew steadily weaker he had apparently been successful. Livingston's flimsy evidence was based on heresay. But Washington took it seriously, instructing Governor Trumbull to have his charge more "narrowly watched".[42]

By the middle of April, the rebel authorities were convinced of the veracity of Livingston's allegations. Washington was outraged at Franklin's "truly reprehensible" behavior, and he saw it as a serious threat to the new nation's survival. "Thro' the intrigues" of men like Governor Franklin, he informed congress, "the Enemy have found a means to raise a spirit of disaffection." If known culprits were allowed to continue unchecked, others would be encouraged to follow their example.[43] Congress agreed, and on April 22 it informed an embarrassed Jonathan Trumbull that his most famous prisoner had "scandalously" dispersed the protections of William and Richard Howe throughout Connecticut, and that he had "otherwise aided and abetted the enemies of the United States." To guarantee that Franklin's nefarious activities would cease, congress ordered Trumbull to keep him in "close confinement, prohibiting him the use of pen, ink, and paper, or the access of any person or persons," save for those who received explicit written permission from the Connecticut governor himself.[44]

Thus began the most painful and degrading experience of William Franklin's life. On May 2, 1777, the sheriff and a number of armed men marched into his chamber room. As they grabbed William's shoulders and shoved him roughly out the door, a musket fired and a shot whizzed by just inches from his head. While everyone protested that the incident was accidental, Franklin was not convinced. Later he almost wished that the musket had not missed its mark.[45]

The sheriff informed Franklin that his days as a spy were over, and he allowed him no time to gather up his belongings or to bid his friends goodbye. He was marched forty miles to Litchfield, Connecticut, where he was thrown unceremoniously into a "most noisome filthy Room." It was, he exaggerated, "the very worst gaol in America." There he would reside for the next eight months. The one-windowed room, situated above a tavern, was overrun with flies, lice, and rats who became the governor's sole companions during his protracted confinement. Throughout the spring, rumors circulated that he would be hanged. Almost as bad, for a man who always took pen and paper in hand whenever he suffered unusual stress, he was allowed no writing materials. Moreover, the naturally gregarious governor had virtually no contact with anyone in the outside world. His own servants were seldom allowed to see him, and then his jailer watched the prisoner's every move, making sure that no secret messages passed between them. It was, thought Franklin, like being buried alive. His food, which he choked down with difficulty, was shoved through a hole carved out in the door. Board was five pounds a week, and his expenses were higher than that, for he often sent Thomas to scrounge provisions from local farmers to replace the lice-ridden fare supplied by his host.[46]

Franklin continued to insist that the charges against him were bogus, and demanded that Trumbull give him a chance to prove his innocence at a public hearing. When the Connecticut governor refused even to acknowledge his request, Franklin's suspicions were aroused. He was certain that congress was trying to break his will and persuade him to declare his support for American independence. Despite the obvious advantages of such an about-face, the governor stood his ground. While he was persuaded that with his father's influence he would obtain "anything [he] could in reason require" if he only renounced his allegiance to the King, Franklin would not succumb to American pressure.[47]

In June, his faithful slave Thomas brought him news that made him forget his wretched surroundings. His wife was in New York, where she had been forced to flee when the British army abandoned Perth Amboy the previous month. She had barely had time to pack her husband's papers and books, and the accumulated possessions of a lifetime before making the journey. There she had managed to secure quarters in a city already overflowing with frightened refugees. The trip had proved too much for her. Always weak, she had barely withstood the shock of her husband's imprisonment, and, particularly after Temple's abrupt departure she had been "truely Miserable," as she struggled to cope "in a strange Country without a Friend or Protector." She had endured the hostility of the rebel army as it had paraded through Perth Amboy. She had survived the equally nerve-shattering experience of living with a "friendly" army of British and Hessian soldiers who converted her once lovely showplace into a military headquarters. She had even born the pain of knowing that her husband lived in solitary confinement at Litchfield jail. But the cumulative effect of these repeated assaults on her system proved too much. Elizabeth Franklin lay near death in New York.[48]

William roused himself, demanding, and for once receiving, pen and paper. While his jailer stood by impassively, he wrote directly to George Washington, begging to be released on parole for a few short weeks to visit his dying wife. Washington's reply was sympathetic, but noncommittal. Whatever his personal inclination might be, he explained, congress handled all such decisions. Nevertheless, he promised to forward the governor's request to the civilian authorities, and he even extended himself, recommending a favorable response to Franklin's plea. William's situation was "distressing" and Washington had no doubt that his concern for Mrs. Franklin was unfeigned. "Humanity and Generosity," he thought, "plead powerfully in favor of his application."[49]

But congress was not so easily moved. It had in its hands a copy of a certificate of protection Franklin had given one Robert Betts when the governor still resided in Middletown. Why, the congressmen wondered, should they trust any man who could so blithely violate as "sacred a tie as that of honor." It was not, they argued, "consistent with the safety of the States, to permit him to have an opportunity of conferring with our open enemies under any restrictions whatsoever."[50]

Not long thereafter, Franklin learned that his wife of fifteen years had "died of a broken heart." The news caused him to sink into a dangerous depression. He lost all interest in his future prospects, caring only about putting his effects in order and preparing for his own death, "an Event," he told Governor Trumbull, "that I am convinced cannot be far off, unless there should be some speedy Relaxation of the unparall'd Severity of my Confinement." The absence of good food, fresh air, and exercise, coupled with the remorse he felt over the death "of one of the best of Women," had made his life "quite a Burthen." His once large frame was gaunt, his body wracked with fever. As he contemplated what he believed would be a lingering death, he began to think it an act of mercy to be "immediately taken out and shot."[51]

Still, there were a few details that Franklin needed to dispose of before he died. He wanted Thomas to go to New York, look after his remaining possessions, and forward all his business records either to Benjamin Franklin or to an attorney. He also requested permission to write to both his father and his son, while he was still capable of holding a pen. He would, he promised, be willing to have the contents of all his letters perused before they were forwarded to France. Franklin also wanted to clear his name. To disprove some of congress's charges against him, he needed some of the documents, now in Trumbull's possession, which he had left behind in Middletown. And he asked to be moved from his present quarters, where the noise from the revelers in the tavern below was so loud that he could not concentrate. Both he and the sheriff agreed that a carefully guarded room in a private house would guarantee his security. There he could write in solitude. The paper he used could be counted as it entered and left his room, ensuring that he did not smuggle out any subversive material.[52] The tone of Franklin's request revealed a man much altered by his imprisonment. Gone, apparently, was the stiff-necked adversary who demanded all his legal rights and refused to acknowledge his captors' legitimacy. Now he begged only for a quiet room, a piece of paper and a pen. He agreed to be watched; he offered his private letters for inspection. His will to continue fighting for his due was diminished, if not destroyed. William Franklin was a more chastened and humble man than he had been a year earlier. Still, he did not offer his captors the one thing he was convinced they wanted most: the surrender of his allegiance to the Crown.

Although Franklin remained determinedly loyal to the mother country, Trumbull allowed him to leave Litchfield some time in December of 1777. He was taken to East Windsor, confined in a private house, and was even allowed to take infrequent short rides in the country so long as he remained under guard. He was able to send an occasional letter to the Baches. He also enjoyed the company of other loyalist captives. As his health improved and his isolation diminished, the worst symptoms of his depression lifted. Still, East Windsor was a jail, and Franklin's chances for obtaining his freedom seemed no greater than ever.[53]

But behind the scenes, some efforts on his behalf were finally being made by those who felt that the son of Benjamin Franklin should not be treated so cruelly, or by those who simply thought that the former governor had suffered enough. For a long time these efforts went nowhere.[54] There were still many congressional leaders who viewed William with undisguised hostility. They thought his accommodations in East Windsor were better than he deserved, and they argued that his anti-Americanism put him in the same odious category as a William Howe or a Henry Clinton. Until he was released, Governor Franklin would be treated as a most dangerous political prisoner. One person did not lift a finger in William's behalf; Benjamin Franklin refused even to discuss his son's plight, much less to intercede for him. While his old friend William Strahan was shocked when he heard of the governor's continued ordeal, Franklin himself remained silent.[55]

It was not until the spring of 1778, two years after William Franklin had been taken into custody, that serious plans were in the works for his release. While William Livingston's recommendation that he be exchanged for Brigadier General William Thompson fell through, another opportunity materialized in August when congress began to consider swapping Franklin for Governor John McKinly of Delaware. But there were still those skeptics who doubted that freeing one of America's most determined enemies was "consistent at present with the interest of the United States." Some thought that "much evil" would come from an exchange, especially so long as William's own son acted as Ben's private secretary and confidant. After three hours of debate, the proposal was set aside.[56]

The deal hit another snag in September when congress reconsidered

McKinly's situation. Hugh Wallace, a loyalist prisoner, had recently left his Connecticut jail and traveled to New York on parole. Once safely behind British lines, Wallace refused to return. At the same time, McKinly had been granted a parole by his British captors so that he could arrange for his own exchange. As a means of putting pressure on Wallace, congress advised McKinly not to return to British hands. Thus there was no need for him to seek an exchange with Franklin. Once again, William's hopes for freedom were dashed. But on September 14, after a prolonged and vigorous discussion, congress finally agreed to exchange Franklin for McKinly. Even then, the governor's departure from East Windsor was delayed for over a month.[57]

Franklin finally left Connecticut for the protection of British-controlled New York at the end of October. He had suffered more than any other royal governor for his steadfast allegiance to the Crown, and might have been excused for retiring immediately to England where he could live in peace, building a new life for himself on the ashes of the one destroyed by the rebel government. His wife was dead, his property confiscated, his salary discontinued. Both his father and his son were dedicated to the destruction of the empire he continued to love. He had paid a heavy price for his loyalty.

But William Franklin was not a quitter. The war between England and America had only begun, and in 1778, Franklin believed that he was on the winning side. He now had a chance to work for the Crown instead of merely to suffer for it. He had proved beyond doubt that his "connexions" to his patriot father would not dampen his allegiance to the King. Now he would be able to use his military and administrative experience in the service of the royal army. His health was returning. He was still young enough to make a name for himself by serving King and country. He could rally "true" Americans to his side, offering himself as a mediator between the English bureaucracy, with which he had a vast reservoir of experience, and the American loyalists whose special concerns he understood.

It would be easier, he thought, than the task of royal governor had ever been. As governor he had been forced to reconcile competing, sometimes antithetical interests. He had been viewed with a certain mistrust by both the ministry and the colonists he had tried to serve. With one foot in each camp, he had belonged nowhere. But all that was about to change. Now he was serving Americans and Englishmen who were united in a common cause, men who recognized the mutuality of interest between the mother country and its colonies. There would be no more distrust. The time for selfish bickering and demagogic pandering was over. At last, thought Franklin as he rode away from East Windsor, it would be to his advantage to be both an Englishman and American.

He did not even consider fleeing the country and leaving the work of defeating the rebels to others. He stayed because he had been taught never to leave any battle voluntarily. He remained, as well, because he hoped to be rewarded for his services to King and country. Perhaps his dreams of a western empire would be fulfilled when, at war's end, British power returned to colonial soil. And he stayed because he had a few scores to settle with the men who had stolen his position, his name, and his freedom.

13

"An Unwillingness to Quit the Scene of Action"

"But an unwillingness to quit the scene of action where I think I might be of some service, if anything is intended to be done, has induced me to remain till I can discover what turn affairs are likely to take."—William Franklin to Joseph Galloway, 1778.[1]

"Will the day never again dawn? Shall the tide always run Ebb? Shall the poor Tories after being so long in Purgatory, not see better days?"—David Sproat to Joseph Galloway, 1779.[2]

William Franklin must have been shocked when he first rode into New York. American refugees, British soldiers, and Hessian mercenaries clogged the streets, competing for shelter and fuel, food and water.[3] A fire of unknown origins had swept through New York in September of 1776, leaving one-fourth of the city a charred ruin. No effort had been made to rebuild the area, as blacks and campfollowers, vagabonds, drunks, and displaced refugees erected temporary shelters on the remains of the burned-out area.[4] British officers claimed the best homes in town for themselves, even confiscating the property of loyal Americans in the process. Troops crammed into churches, hospitals, and every other available space. Refugees poured into the city, and people who had been reduced from affluence to penury overnight, fought desperately for any tiny, dirty, and expensive spot to rest their bones and store their pitiable belongings. As garbage piled up in the streets and water was contaminated, the stench grew unbearable, even to normally insensitive colonial noses.[5]

Despite the best efforts of the authorities to control it, inflation rose steadily.[6] And food and fuel were difficult to get at any price, as the rebels controlled most of the countryside surrounding New York, and the needs of a growing population put ever increasing pressure on dwindling supplies. Overcrowding and poverty brought disease and lawlessness. Respectable citizens were the easy prey of New York's new underclass. Even worse, they had to contend with the depredations of the King's own soldiers, who filled long periods of inactivity with carousing and gambling, plundering and even murdering helpless civilians.[7]

The ever optimistic General William Howe had done little to alleviate the distress of American loyalists. But when Sir Henry Clinton replaced him in May of 1778 he made at least some effort to ease the worst suffering of the refugees. While Clinton had little faith in the loyalists' ability to contribute decisively to the war effort, he recognized that he would lose American allegiance if he abandoned them completely. He appointed two American advisers, diverted some military provisions to loyal citizens, and tried to secure jobs for those who wanted more than handouts from the British government. It was never enough. Every day as he left his house he was surrounded by desperate men and women, pleading for help and clinging to his coattails as he pushed his way through the tattered throng and into his waiting coach.[8]

William Franklin was understandably curious about the condition of rebel prisoners in the city, for New York and Long Island were the centerpieces of the royal prison system. Honesty forced him to acknowledge that his enemies fared little better than he had. Officers had the freedom of the city if they could afford their room and board in designated accommodations sprinkled throughout the town. But if a prisoner languished in the Provost or in one of the three sugar houses strung along the waterfront, his condition was deplorable and his future grim. The British were generally not intentionally cruel or vindictive, but William should have been assured that the King's foes were not coddled.[9]

Franklin arrived in New York anxious to make up for lost time. Thin and still weak though he was, in the first heady days of freedom his spirits soared. He knew that most of the juiciest political plums had already been claimed by others. Moreover, unlike many loyalists, he could not rely on family connections to secure position or fortune.[10] Most of William's influential friends had already fled the country for the safety of London, and everyone fully expected the governor to follow their prudent example. No one but Franklin himself thought there was much future for him in America.[11]

Still, William was determinedly optimistic. As he was wined and dined, admired and "much carressed" by his admirers, he never questioned his ability to secure a position that would serve the King's cause as well as his own considerable ambitions. He had no doubt that with his military training, administrative talents, and record of loyalty, British officials would recognize his expertise and treat him as their equal. Despite the bitter memories he harbored of his sufferings at the hands of his rebel captors, despite the death of his wife and the loss of his job, salary, and possessions, Franklin viewed his future with enthusiasm. He was free for the first time in his life to act with single-minded conviction. No longer did he have to assume the role of mediator between England and America. No longer was he torn apart by his duty to King and country. He could serve the Crown, and the loyal Americans who loved the empire as he did, without worrying about the divisiveness that had always plagued him as governor. Now the Americans and Englishmen with whom he had thrown in his lot were of one mind—and shared one goal. The time for moderation, for seeing both sides of every issue, was blessedly over.[12]

But Franklin had not taken into account the suspicions that soured relations between the loyalists and their British protectors. Ironically, the King's officers distrusted the loyalists even more than they did their enemies in the rebel camp. These were men, after all, who had turned their backs on their own countrymen. Would they remain steadfast in their devotion to the Crown? The Continental army may have been composed of "rebels" but the King's friends, thought many British officers, were "damned traitors and scoundrels." Moreover, they were convinced that even the best Americans were hopelessly ignorant of correct military procedure, and particularly after Saratoga, they were reluctant to put much faith in loyalist promises.[13] As Ambrose Serle, William Howe's private secretary, explained, "Alas, they all prate & profess much; but when you call upon them they will *do* nothing."[14]

Part of the problem, of course, was that loyalists like William Franklin had painted such an unrealistic picture of their strength that disappointment was inevitable. But the issue was more fundamental than inflated claims of American prowess. The very attitude that had troubled American soldiers throughout the eighteenth century confounded Crown supporters during the American Revolution. A smug belief in British superiority made it impossible for royal officers to view their American compatriots as equals, and they treated men who had lost friends, family, and possessions because of their loyalty, with scarcely concealed contempt. British commanders regularly disdained the advice of loyal Americans, loftily asserting that "information from Head Q^ters is always the best." Obduracy, bureaucratic mismanagement, and dissension in the upper ranks combined to destroy loyalist hopes at every turn. Benjamin Franklin had lodged such complaints against the North ministry before the war. As time dragged on, William found himself sounding increasingly like the father whose cause he abhorred.[15]

None of this should have surprised the loyalists. It was just this attitude that had helped sow the seeds of distrust that made the war for independence possible. But for men like William Franklin, it came as a rude

shock. He and others like him had voluntarily abandoned their own countrymen. They were fighting on their soil for their conception of what was
best for the American people. They, not the British soldiers, would be the
true losers if the mother country failed to suppress the "unnatural rebellion." If the rebels were victorious, they alone would forfeit their property,
their position and their influence, and be forced to start life anew in some
alien land. They would lose *their* America, the America that was part of
the British empire, but the America whose distinctiveness they cherished
almost as much as did the men who led the rebel forces.

If the British distrusted the Americans, the loyalists held serious grievances against the King's men. By the time William Franklin escaped captivity, most had succumbed "to a lethargy very nearly bordering on despair."
They had railed against Howe's indecisiveness and complained bitterly that
neither Howe nor Clinton made proper use of American potential. Convinced of Washington's weakness, and always sure that "one vigorous Campaign properly conducted" would send the rebel government to its well-
deserved grave, they grew increasingly critical of the King's men.[16] New
Yorkers in particular resented "military gentlemen" who amused themselves and their ladies with "trifles and diversions" while honest Americans
suffered.[17]

Franklin had his work cut out for him, and it soon became apparent that
his dream of working with a united cadre of men dedicated to a single
cause was illusory. He would have to continue to use his skills to mediate
between the conflicting interests of Americans and Englishmen. This time,
however, as he picked his way carefully among men whose vanities, interests, ideological proclivities, and personal idiosyncracies constantly muddied
the waters, his sympathies lay more clearly with his own countrymen than
they did with the King's officers.

Henry Clinton never had much faith in the British ability to win the
war. Resentful of Lord Germain's rosy view of loyalist strength, he assured
his American supporters that he would not abandon them to the rebel
wolves, even while he harbored deep misgivings about their usefulness and
often saw them as a real nuisance. He could neither control the independent loyalist units operating outside established channels, nor incorporate
them successfully into the regular army. He was irritated by constant demands of "over-sanguine refugees" for a more aggressive war, and he never
really understood the frustrations of men who were virtually imprisoned in
New York while rebel units roamed at will through the New England countryside. He only saw that their zeal had "too often out-run their prudence"
and he refused to listen to their "ill-founded suggestions."[18]

Some of Clinton's problems were self-inflicted. Jealous, quarrelsome, and
insecure, he shared neither power nor confidences easily, often refusing to

see even his closest advisers for days at a time. Taciturn and possessed of a "Procrastinating Disposition," he was afraid to lose the war but reluctant to take the risks to win it. He feared embarrassment and consequently demanded total control of his forces, viewing anyone trying to act independently as a personal threat.[19]

The people surrounding Clinton did nothing to mitigate Franklin's difficulties. Admiral Mariot Arbuthnot was incompetent, frequently ill, and temperamentally erratic. Moreover, he quarreled often with the thin-skinned commander, and by 1780 the two men were not even on speaking terms. The men closest to Clinton were a mixed lot, often advocating mutually contradictory programs. New Yorker Wililiam Smith, former Philadelphian Andrew Elliot, and Scottish-born James Robertson cast themselves in the role of conciliators. Arguing that most Americans would flock to the King's banner if given the slightest encouragement, they bolstered Lord Germain's fond belief that the war could be won without significant increases in British arms or money. Smith, one of the empire's most Whiggish supporters, was virtually consumed by his desire to return civil rule to New York, convinced that a display of British good faith would rally reluctant rebels everywhere.[20] Oliver De Lancey and William Tryon, on the other hand, had both suffered immensely at rebel hands and hungered for revenge. They argued that a policy of terror and destruction by the "true loyalists" would frighten the rebels into submission. From the beginning, William Franklin's sympathies lay with the hard liners.[21]

In the first few months of his freedom, the governor gave no overt indication that he was aware of the obstacles that confronted him as he tried to find some way to contribute to the King's cause and improve his own fortune. To the contrary, he scarcely took time to draw a breath before plunging feverishly into action. After so many months of quiet brooding, he could not sit still. Almost immediately he reported to Clinton's headquarters and offered his services in either a military or civilian capacity. One of Franklin's first concerns was making ends meet in a town whose greatest enemy was spiralling inflation. The New Jersey legislature had cut off his salary in 1776. His property had been confiscated. He had no family to help him. His prison expenses had been hefty and had been made worse because he had tried to share his own meager resources with men even poorer than he. The few possessions his wife had managed to bring to New York, worth, he thought, about £5000 sterling, had been destroyed by fire. He was, in fact, nearly destitute. And like any other American supporter of the Crown, he looked to the British for help.[22]

He sought justice, not charity. By the time of the American Revolution, he was the only royal governor whose livelihood remained entirely dependent on his assembly. Whitehall had taken steps to put him on the Civil

List in the spring of 1776, but before all the paper work had been completed, he had been arrested. Every other Crown surrogate had remained on the government payroll after independence had been declared. By an unfortunate quirk of fate, he alone had been cut off without a penny. Because of his losses, his sufferings, and his continued willingness to serve the British cause he had earned the right to compensation.[23]

Franklin's pleas were not ignored. Clinton, in concert with the two remaining peace commissioners, William Eden and Lord Carlisle, agreed to reward him £1200 New Jersey currency. And at the end of January, Carlisle informed him that the Treasury would grant him £500 immediately, and an additional £500 per year thereafter. Although this was less than half of what he had earned as governor, Franklin was undaunted. He immediately set to work recruiting Anglican ministers Samuel Seabury of Connecticut and his old friend Jonathan Odell to write propaganda pieces for the New York newspapers.[24]

Almost naturally, he became the unofficial leader of the loyal Americans. As he publicly inveighed against the lethargy of the Crown's supporters, he breathed new life into the despondent loyalist population. He spent much of his time securing aid for needy refugees. But his first significant venture was, not surprisingly, made on behalf of loyalist prisoners of war. When the rebels captured a group of refugees during a wood cutting expedition in Connecticut, Franklin demanded that Clinton take an equal number of Connecticut captives as hostages. After considerable foot-dragging, Clinton agreed. The governor's success was cheered by Americans everywhere, who hoped that the government would "no longer tamely see some of the King's best subjects sacrificed with impunity." At last someone with influence, who understood the problems of loyalist prisoners, was willing to speak on their behalf. And there were many who fervently agreed with Isaac Ogden's wish that the governor would be made "*Super Intendent General of Refugees.*"[25]

As always, Franklin was most interested in currying favor and influencing opinion at the top. And he could hardly wait to offer his typically up-beat assessment of the American situation to Whitehall. He was as convinced of his own correct analysis of current events now, as he had formerly been when he discussed the empire's needs with his assembly, and his letters to Lord Germain were devoid of the obsequious tone with which provincials customarily addressed their London superiors. He quickly passed over Burgoyne's disastrous defeat at Saratoga, admitting only that it had momentarily "elevated the favourers of Rebellion." Despite the promise of French and Spanish aid, the rebel forces, insisted Franklin, were in disarray. Nine-tenths of the people were tired of war and longed to reconcile with Great Britain if they could only return the empire to its 1763 status. The Continental currency was worthless. Congress was split over the question of how to dispose of the western lands. The selfishness that Franklin had always seen as the root cause of independence was apparent everywhere, as each colony seemed more concerned with its own interests than it was in American victory.[26]

Even more pleasing was the condition of George Washington's army. The general reportedly had less than 10,000 men serving under him, and most of those had been drafted for terms not exceeding nine months. His regiments were riddled with untrained boys, Indians, and negroes, many of whom were dangerously close to mutiny. Obviously the British were on the verge of victory. Only two obstacles remained. First, and not surprisingly, congressional leaders continued their old tricks of deceiving the American people. When the peace commissioners had announced their conditions for ending the war, offering the colonists everything short of independence, the "Champions of Independency" refused even to discuss the terms. They lied, held out false hopes of imminent victory, and in keeping with their usual "tyrannical" methods, proclaimed that anyone who so much as talked to the commissioners would be branded as a traitor.[27]

Franklin expected this kind of perfidy from his rebel enemies. What he could not understand was the lackluster performance of the King's own army. All the British needed, he cried in exasperation was one "Capital Stroke," and there would be clamors for surrender throughout the land. Franklin had some specific suggestions. He wanted the navy to begin blockading American harbors. He argued that Clinton should concentrate his efforts on the middle provinces, where the patriot position was demonstrably weakest. And he urged the army to follow up each military victory by establishing civil governments headed by loyal Americans in the captured territory. Americans were better equipped than British officers to win the affection of moderates who might accept the authority of known civilians but who would resent the rule of military "foreigners." Moreover, each "liberated" province would serve as an asylum for disaffected Americans everywhere, and would provide a base for further attacks on rebel strongholds.[28]

Franklin was clearly angling for greater personal responsibility. He was working unofficially for the British government. His contacts had enabled him to gather considerable rebel intelligence. He had spoken as a successful advocate for loyalist prisoners. He had also met with peace commissioners Eden and Carlisle. But he was doing all this as a private citizen. To be effective, he needed official sanction. Otherwise he had no authority or leverage. If he were to be asked to head a civilian government in one of the middle provinces, his usefulness would be immeasurably enhanced.[29]

But Franklin had other irons in the fire. Within a month of his arrival in New York, he had helped establish a Refugee Club composed of the "first characters" of the various provinces. A substantial number of separate loyalist units already existed, but William always dreamed of uniting the King's supporters under one umbrella. In fact, the little group, which met once fortnightly at Hick's Tavern, was remarkably successful in its efforts to boost the morale of New York's loyalists even though its members did little more than share information and discuss the latest political news. But William Franklin wanted to do more than raise the spirits of American refugees. By November he had formulated an ambitious proposal for a semi-autonomous Board of Loyal Refugees, an intelligence gathering operation directed by men like himself, which would engage in covert activities and retaliatory raids against the rebel forces. Franklin showed his plan to Carlisle and Eden, asking them to take it directly to Lord Germain upon their return to London.[30]

There was some reason to believe that the plan, or something like it, would be approved. William Tryon wanted to give the governor a high profile position, arguing that it would be foolhardy to ignore the propaganda benefits to be derived from dramatizing Franklin's willingness to defy his influential father in order to serve the Crown. William did not discourage Tryon's efforts on his behalf. He had suffered long enough on account of his father. He was convinced that he had remained in captivity for so long because of his filial bonds. The British had questioned his loyalty, and the rebels had been reluctant to release him, all because of an accident of birth. Even now there were those who professed to believe that William's devotion to his father was stronger than it should be. It was time to reap some benefits from his relationship with Benjamin Franklin.[31]

Nevertheless, throughout the winter and early spring of 1779, the governor remained in limbo. New York had its share of diverting amusements. The Royal Theater opened in January. Occasional concerts and the Dancing Assembly were entertaining. And, when the weather permitted, there was always his beloved horse racing to help him while away a pleasant afternoon. But none of this was enough. By January, Franklin had developed a plan for "retaliatory" raids on rebel strongholds. Despite Tryon's enthusiastic approval of what one historian has labeled a "joint stock company for plunder," Clinton ignored the proposal. And so Franklin continued to act without official sanction, trying to help the loyalists who turned to him for advice, procuring arms, collecting information, and encouraging raids in Connecticut and New Jersey. As the governor remembered how he had once denounced rebel leaders for their extra-legal activities, he must have been aware of the irony of his position. And as he saw Clinton ignoring what seemed to be golden opportunities for winning the war, he grew increasingly disgusted with the commander and the "Parcel of Blockheads" around him.[32]

At the end of May, William wrote to John André[33] explaining that he had begun a detailed plan for a "Board of Intelligence" which he hoped the major would convey to Clinton. The two men discussed the basic parameters of Franklin's proposal, agreeing that a board utilizing the expertise of loyalist leaders from all the colonies, could provide immeasurable support for the war effort. The following day, William sent André a tentative plan. Franklin envisioned a virtually autonomous role for his board. It would be able to subpoena and examine on oath any one entering New York from behind enemy lines. It could inspect and copy all letters and papers captured by the King's troops. And it would be able to reward informants. Franklin modestly suggested that Clinton might want to offer some "Allowance or Consideration" to the board members, but he declined to designate any precise figure. André liked Franklin's proposal, but Clinton was leery of any plan that gave so much authority to American civilians.[34]

The governor was nothing if not determined. After waiting a month without receiving even an acknowledgment of his proposal, he tried again. At the end of June he drafted another plan, sending this one to General Tryon, commander of the Provincial Forces in America. Formerly a royal governor, Tryon seemed likely to give Franklin's project a sympathetic hearing. He was known to admire the "zeal" of the loyal refugees and to think that their superior knowledge of the American countryside would "render them useful." Once again, Franklin argued for considerable autonomy. The head of the proposed organization would nominate and appoint all officers. The board itself would be a military as well as a civilian body and would be furnished with enough supplies to enable its members to "distress the Enemy in any Quarter not expressly forbid by the Commander in Chief." While Franklin promised that his men would not indulge in excessive cruelty, "unless by Way of Retaliation," he wanted them to share in all the plunder that fell their way. Finally, the board would have absolute control over its own prisoners. In return, Clinton would receive the finest enemy intelligence and he would enjoy the help of a band of men who were familiar with the land, and were utterly dedicated to destroying the rebel army.[35]

Franklin's proposal was audacious, although he seemed totally unaware of just how unrealistic it was. In effect he demanded equality with England's military establishment. He envisioned an authority more absolute and independent than he had dared even to contemplate as governor of New Jersey. His expectations are symptomatic of the naïveté that characterized many leaders of the loyalist community. These men had once held powerful positions in America and while they had been aware of the imperfections of English rule, they had never failed to believe in the essential good will of the mother country. Imperial differences, they assumed, were simply the result of English ignorance of American circumstances. Consequently, loyalists like William Franklin imagined that once leaders from home came to America and confronted colonial reality head on, they would be only too happy to recognize the validity of their own superior advice, which, after all, was based on a lifetime of valuable experience. They saw themselves as equal partners with the English in the battle to subdue the rebel government, and were genuinely shocked to discover that the King's men viewed them as "mere" Americans.

But in the spring of 1779, William Franklin was unwilling to admit that he could find no acceptable position from which to serve the empire. He was a little discouraged that Clinton did not respond immediately to any of his suggestions. Still, he had impressed two of the general's advisers. Tryon went so far as to draw up his own proposal, based largely on Franklin's, which he delivered personally to General Clinton in July.[36] Tryon specifically designated William Franklin as the head of the loaylist organization. But he toned down the governor's blueprint in many particulars. He insisted that the proposed board be held accountable for the military supplies it used, set upper limits on the number of men it employed, and restricted the money allocated for its activities. He was also reluctant to grant the loyalists a free hand. He gave Clinton more control over the board's routine operations. And he forbade the members from engaging in any "Excesses" or "Barbarities." Still, Tryon had not gutted the plan, and William had every reason to be happy with it.[37]

But Franklin continued to spin his wheels as he waited in vain for a response from Clinton and watched the British army suffer defeat after embarrassing defeat at the hands of an inferior American army. The summer of 1779, a dismal one for all supporters of the King's cause, was especially frustrating for William Franklin. At the end of June, having handed Clinton his proposal for the loyalist association, Tryon left for an expedition in Connecticut. Ignoring Clinton's orders, Tryon's troops burned New Haven, Fairfield, and half of Norwalk on the raid, an action which displeased the commander as much as it invigorated the militant refugees. After that, Clinton was in no mood to listen to any schemes that might result in similar outrages. Unfortunately, Franklin and his friends had been so confident of the viability of Tryon's plan that they had already purchased a rebel frigate, the *Oliver Cromwell*, to be used in expeditions along the New England coast.[38]

Still, the governor refused to abandon hope. If anything, he worked even harder to reverse the trend of defeatism that permeated the air. He sent copies of critical newspaper articles to William Strahan. He continued to write to Lord Germain, offering advice and demanding harsher treatment for rebel prisoners. And he helped Major André gather intelligence on rebel positions in Connecticut and New Jersey. The more Frankiln learned from his various contacts, the more frustrated he became. There were loyalist prisoners to be freed, defenseless towns ripe for guerilla raids, demoralized militia men who were waiting only for a sign of British strength to abandon the patriot cause. Yet Franklin could do nothing to take advantage of American weaknesses. While he no doubt enjoyed the occasional honors that came his way, he hungered after much more than empty expressions of regard.[39]

At times he reluctantly ignored proper channels entirely. By July he was actively organizing "Companies of Safety" composed of refugee farmers looking for revenge and plunder. Calling themselves the "King's Militia Volunteers," they took orders from Franklin and performed their duties without pay. William hoped that if they were successful, thousands like them would flock to the King's banner. Still, he was clearly uncomfortable with this kind of ad hoc organization, and he continued to angle for a permanent and totally legal appointment. The role of guerilla leader was not really suited to a man of Franklin's temperament and aspirations, and he knew it.[40] William was given an official role in July, when, at Eden's suggestion, Clinton formed a council of advisers to help him deal with American affairs. But while Franklin leaped at the chance to be of official use, making himself the most conspicuous member on the council, the commander viewed the appointment as mere window dressing.[41] By now it was obvious to all observers that the two men were incompatible. The governor described Clinton as "weak, irresolute, unsteady, vain, incapable of forming any Plan himself & too weak or rather proud and conceited to follow that of another." Clinton, characterized Franklin as "sanguinary and Mercenary." Still, William had little choice but to make the best of a bad situation, and he continued to apply pressure on the men around the British commander, hoping to accomplish indirectly what he obviously could not do any other way.[42]

By fall, Franklin was desperate. Many men upon whom he had counted to join his loyalist organization were deserting the ranks in disgust. Those who remained were scattered throughout the area, their numbers fluctuating daily. Once more he went to Major André begging for help in securing Clinton's approval of Governor Tryon's proposal. William denied that he had personal reasons for preferring Tryon's plan to any possible alternative. He knew that some of his detractors assumed that he liked Tryon's suggestions because they promised him so much power. But Franklin insisted that although he had "No Objection to undertake the Office, troublesome" as he knew it would be, he "was so far from a Desire of Emolument" that he would "take equal Pains in forwarding the Measure if the Commander in Chief would appoint any other Person to the Command who was agreeable to the Refugees." He was convinced that some variation of Tryon's plan was essential to the British war effort. If Clinton wanted only to attach a few Americans to various military posts, where they would be used "for occasional Excursions at the Pleasure and under the Directions and Restraints of the Commanding Officers," then Franklin thought that the royal army might just as well abandon any effort to utilize the loyalists' talents. "So few men of Consequence" would submit to these strictures, he predicted, that "so little will be done by them in that Way, as not to deserve Attention."[43]

A chance remained that some worthwhile organization could be devised. In October, Major André tried his hand at a rough draft that contained many elements of the two plans already on the table. There were significant differences. André's proposal gave Clinton more control over prisoners; it prohibited the loyalists from capturing or plundering rebel supporters "excepting when in Acts of Absolute Rebellion." Anyone disregarding these regulations would be regarded as "a disaffected person or a robber." When Franklin read André's proposal, he tactfully remarked that it contained elements that actually improved on Tryon's plan. And he offered to make a stab at combining the best aspects of all the proposals. But by the end of the year Clinton, who was putting together his southern strategy, had no inclination even to listen to Franklin's schemes. It was clear by now that he would never voluntarily form any loyalist organization.[44]

There was some possibility that force could succeed where requests had failed. William knew that loyalist exiles in London had begun meeting regularly at the end of May. With men of the caliber of Joseph Galloway on hand to lobby personally for their counterparts in America, Whitehall might be convinced of the value of Franklin's proposals. The governor tried to exert his own pressure on the ministry, persuading George Leonard, one of the King's most selfless American friends, to sail for London with a proposal for a loyalist organization.[45]

While he waited, Franklin remained active, though largely ineffective. He had evidentally inherited his father's organizational genius, for he was tireless in his ability to turn out proposals for every conceivable project. And although his ideas were often rejected or ignored, his productivity continued unabated.[46] Nevertheless, by the spring of 1780 the governor's patience had worn thin. Clinton was engaged in an all-out assault on Charleston. Leonard was in London trying to catch the ear of the ministry. Meanwhile, New York's refugees had reached their nadir, having barely endured one of the city's most frigid winters. Franklin continued to gather intelligence and act as a self-appointed advocate for loyalist prisoners. He also joined in an ill-fated military attack on New Jersey, which naturally infuriated General Clinton.[47]

As summer faded slowly into fall, and rumored plans of an assault on rebel strongholds never materialized, William was convinced that Clinton was a disastrous choice as the British commander in chief. When John André was captured by the rebels at the end of September, as a result of Benedict Arnold's bungled attempt to turn West Point over to the British, Franklin's spirits were as low as they had been since his release from his Connecticut jail. He was irritated by André's failure and thought the whole business had been poorly handled. As his frustation mounted, his former ebullience gave way to bitterness, and his public pronouncements became more heated. New York's self-styled moderates seized on his every intemperate outburst to prove that he was "dangerous to himself" and totally unsuited "for his old Station or any other in this Country." Even the usually sympathetic William Tryon remarked on the governor's ill humor, noting that his self-pity grew almost daily, and he was now given to "magnifying his Sufferings." Increasingly he could be found in the company of refugees like himself who fed his desire for revenge. As his early optimism faded, and his personal aspirations as well as his dreams of British victory dimmed, he became convinced, like many another displaced American, that Clinton's tendency to rely on moderates was inimical to both his own and his country's interests.[48]

There was only one bright spot sustaining William Franklin throughout most of 1780. In April, George Leonard obtained the King's formal approval of a plan for organizing America's loyalist refugees. The ministry drew up some general guidelines, designating Franklin and eight other loyalist leaders as the first "directors" of the organization. Orders to Henry Clinton, describing the proposal and commanding his cooperation, were soon on their way to New York. And Leonard, who intended to return to America shortly, wrote to Franklin promising to bring a copy of the King's orders with him.[49] Meanwhile, news of the plan appeared in *Rivington's Royal Gazette*. The way was at last being prepared for the acceptance of Franklin's pet project.[50]

William was elated by Leonard's news. While he would be sharing power with a sizable group of men, his name was at the top of the King's list, and it was to him that Leonard had communicated His Majesty's approval. But while he was anxious to get started, he remained silent, awaiting official confirmation before he shared the good news with any of the other board members. A couple of weeks after he received Leonard's letter, Franklin visited headquarters on routine business. There, Clinton's secretary called him aside, showing him a copy of Lord Germain's instructions.

Franklin perused the letter carefully before silently returning it. The governor had to be pleased with Germain's instructions. They were couched in sufficiently general terms to allow him to claim a good deal of power for the proposed Association. The Secretary envisioned an autonomous organization whose members would receive neither rank nor pay as military officers. They would be rewarded with shares in their plunder, and if they served until the end of the war, they would receive 200 acres of American land. Both Clinton and Admiral Arbuthnot were obliged to provide the loyalist forces with the necessary supplies to conduct raids on enemy strongholds. No enterprise, however, could be undertaken without Clinton's approval.[51]

Franklin bided his time until September 10, when, once again at headquarters, he ran into Clinton, who casually asked him if he had made any progress in fulfilling the terms of Germain's instructions. Taken aback, William explained that he had not received a copy of the minister's letter and had no authority to organize the loyalist association. Indeed he had not received one official word about the project from any one in America. Clinton appeared cooperative, insisting that he wanted to "afford Encouragement to the Design" and ordered a copy of Germain's letter to be sent to Franklin's quarters. The period of endless waiting was almost over.[52]

In less than a week Franklin convened a meeting of as many of the designated board members as he could locate on such short notice. By October 21st, Leonard himself was in New York. He waited on Clinton immediately, hoping to press him into action. The general had little choice but to obey Germain's orders, but despite his repeated promises he dragged his feet. He finally convened Germain's board of directors, but when the men arrived at headquarters, he announced that he had no "particular Commands" of his own for the organization and asked them to devise a proposal, which he promised to approve with possible alterations.[53]

The task of designing such a proposal fell naturally to Franklin, who presented the draft of "a Commission and Instructions for Establishing and Regulating a Board of Directors of Associated Loyalists" to his fellow directors on October 26th. The draft was adopted after a few minor changes the next day. On October 28, Franklin forwarded the plan to Clinton. But the commander was unhappy with the Board's proposals, which embodied most of the elements he had found so distasteful in the original plans drawn up by Franklin and Tryon. Board members would assume almost complete control of all loyalist operations. No loyalist anywhere could conduct raids without securing approval of the Board or the commander in chief. The "associators" would enjoy many perquisites. They would be guaranteed arms, supplies, and ships and would have access to British army hospitals. They would be accorded equal treatment in the royal army whenever they rendered temporary service to His Majesty's forces. No soldier could be impressed. Most importantly, the board would excercise control of its own prisoners. Franklin did include some limits on the board's wide powers. It had to seek Clinton's general approval for its enterprises. And the Associators were advised to avoid plundering or molesting neutrals.[54]

Clinton had no intention of granting so much independence to a coterie of vengeful refugees. He immediately showed Franklin's proposal to Andrew Elliot and William Smith, both of whom were dismayed by the draft, fearing that the Board would unleash a band of cut-throat terrorists on the American countryside, alienating moderates and ending all chances of reconciliation with the rebel forces. Securing Clinton's promise to keep their work secret, they began to develop a counter-proposal that would significantly pare down the Associated Loyalists' powers. While the two men worked on the draft, Franklin complained bitterly about Clinton's "inertia," even threatening to return to England if the general did not act soon.[55]

While he waited, Franklin was constantly reminded of his anomalous position. The situation at Bergen Point in New Jersey was typical. At the end of October, the governor had inspected the loyalist forces there, and had been appalled by their vulnerability. Only a small stockade, less than ten feet high, stood between the refugees and a potential rebel invasion. The men who occupied the area had already been removed from the Hudson River area against their will, and, despite the weakness of their position, they stubbornly refused to move again. Moreover, these refugees, like so many of their counterparts, were destitute. Consequently, instead of heeding Franklin's advice to shore up their defenses, they took to the woods to fell trees, earning just enough money to help them survive the long winter looming ahead.[56]

Roughly two weeks after Franklin's visit to Bergen Point, Major Oliver De Lancey, John André's replacement, told Franklin that the Point was untenable. Franklin promised to relay De Lancey's opinion to Captain Ward, but he reminded his superior that so long as he held no official position he could do little more than serve in an advisory capacity. By refusing to extend himself further, he was undoubtedly engaging in a bit of not-so-subtle blackmail, as he tried to impress his superiors with the potential value of his services. Despite De Lancey's continual remonstrances, Franklin refused to assume authority over Ward and his men. It was not "proper," he insisted, for him to do otherwise, for the King himself had "strongly" recommended that loyalist operations be directed by the entire board. He wished neither to risk the displeasure of the King, nor to offend the other potential Board members by accepting authority that adhered collectively to all the directors.[57]

With Franklin refusing to honor any but the commander's most basic requests, Clinton gave in to the inevitable and met secretly with Elliot and Smith, approving their revised version of the Board's proposal, and forwarding it to Franklin with virtually no changes. When the directors met to peruse Clinton's plan, they were stunned.[58] The commander's commission and accompanying regulations for the Board were not, as its members had expected, a set of counter-proposals offered as the basis for negotiation. Instead, Clinton had forwarded a "Commission signed and sealed in a manner that implied *Either this or none.*" Even worse, the proposal gutted Franklin's original draft, so vitiating the directors' powers that the Association could now "answer no valuable End."[59] While Clinton did not invite any comments, the members of the Board were so unhappy with his blueprint that they decided to make an effort to retrieve some of the authority they had envisioned for themselves.[60] As it now appeared, they were to be mere "ciphers," members of a weak and insignificant arm of Clinton's operations. They would be administrators with no power to make decisions of any "consequence." Franklin himself had exercised more discretion as governor of New Jersey than he would have as president of the Board of Associated Loyalists.[61]

Franklin scarcely knew where to begin enumerating his objections. The Commission was riddled with restrictions on the Board's activities. Moreover, the first article indicated that the organization might be even more circumscribed in the future, for it allowed the commander or his successors to issue unilaterally "other new Instructions altering enlarging or changing" its original powers "from time to time."[62]

Franklin was especially discouraged because Clinton gave the Board of directors no authority over the prisoners captured by the Associators. The question of the treatment of rebel captives was the most divisive issue facing Clinton and the Board, for it highlighted the nebulous position of America's Crown supporters. It was a problem that was never resolved to anyone's satisfaction. It was a problem, moreover, in which William Franklin had keen personal interest. At the heart of the disagreement was the issue of retaliation.

It was a matter of "notoriety" that the rebels subscribed to an invidious double standard in their policy toward their captives. The King's soldiers received all the privileges accruing to prisoners of war. But the loyalists were viewed as traitors to their country, or even as common criminals, not as prisoners. They were, claimed the loyalists, "treated with almost every Species of Cruelty." They were malnourished, shut up in cells where the windows were opened wide "in the severity of winter" and nailed tightly shut in the summer so that there was "scarcely light enough to pick off the vermin which swarm in abundance." They were beaten, tortured, and even wantonly executed without benefit of trial. Some were sent to labor in Connecticut's notorious Simsbury mines from which few returned.[63]

To men like Franklin, this was an outrage. To be viewed as rebels, traitors, and "Bandetti" by an illegitimate government was a humiliation almost as painful as the physical abuse the prisoners suffered. Even worse was the "indulgent" attitude of the British army toward rebel captives, an indulgence that seemed particularly inexplicable because legally the patriots were nothing more than traitors. Yet, although the British refused to recognize the rebel government's existence, it treated its prisoners as legitimate prisoners of war.[64]

There were solid reasons for Britain's paradoxical position. Clinton clearly did not want to follow any course that invited harsh treatment for his own men. To treat rebel prisoners as traitors, or to engage in a rapidly escalating war of retaliation with the Americans, might easily have this undesirable result. Moreover, the general had leverage that did not necessitate retaliation. The rebels were anxious to have Clinton treat American captives as prisoners of war. This would imply an acceptance of the legitimacy of the United States government, and would be an important step toward independence. So long as there was the slightest chance that Clinton might recognize its prisoners as POWs, the American government handled its British prisoners with a modicum of civility.[65]

There was obviously no need to deal kindly with the loyalists. Just the reverse was true. To underscore its own legitimacy, congress had to treat its loyalist captives as traitors to the one true government in America. Thus the refugees found themselves in the humiliating position of being viewed as rebels by men that they themselves regarded as treasonous. They were treated as traitors by the United States congress, and as useless and slightly bothersome Americans by British officers. They existed in limbo, with no country they could truly call home. Under the circumstances, Franklin and the other board members were obliged to fend for themselves. They wanted complete control of their own prisoners.[66] And they incessantly tried to persuade the commander in chief of the necessity of a "Discretionary Power of Retribution." For them, retaliation was a matter of self-defense and "strict justice."[67]

Franklin and his companions also objected to the fifth and seventh provisions of Clinton's commission. The Board could not undertake any enterprize without securing the explicit permission of the commander in chief. The directors had to describe each operation in "minute" detail, allowing for no alteration in plans, no maneuverability. There were times, Franklin believed, when the "suddenness of the operation" required prompt action, not an adherence to burdensome "Formalities." The governor predicted that no one would associate under the terms Clinton suggested. To be so circumscribed at every step would totally undermine any officer's authority, destroying his usefulness. Some "Latitude of Command" was essential, argued Franklin. Officers often had to adapt to circumstances, utilizing their superior knowledge of the local situation. This knowledge he thought, could be used "much more advantageously than can possibly be directed by any Orders given at New York."

Finally, the Board objected to Clinton's method for protecting neutral Americans from attack by loyalist raiders. The general feared that the Associators would use their commissions to engage in private vendettas or as licenses to plunder. He was genuinely concerned that the Americans, out of anger, frustration, or ignorance, would engage in acts of "barbarity" that would be detrimental to the long-term aims of the British army.[68] Thus he insisted that the Board reimburse any innocent victim of loyalist zeal. Franklin thought this was neither practical nor fair. Clinton apparently did not understand that the Associators would be divided into discrete groups, whose sole connection was their relationship to the Board. Yet the commander was, in effect, asking one group to pay for the excesses of another. This system would not make the Associators more responsible; instead, it would anger law-abiding members and would invite abuse by rebels who might callously use it to discredit the entire Association.

This was especially likely because Clinton had completely ignored Franklin's suggestion that all non-associating loyalists be barred from making excursions against the enemy. Franklin's "main object" had always been to place all loyalist operations under the aegis of a central, American-dominated body. Only this would stop the "parties and Dissention, Confusion and Disorder" that occurred when each band of refugees acted on its own. Unless the general actively discouraged ad hoc action, Franklin feared that the excesses of independent operators would destroy the Board.

The over-all tone of Clinton's regulations was as distressing as any of its provisions. Franklin had assumed that he would have some hand in negotiating the final terms of the Board's instructions. The general's decision to dictate terms displayed a level of contempt for the Board that was profoundly disturbing. And his restrictions implied a distrust of Franklin's integrity that was difficult for the proud governor to swallow gracefully. Germain's letter had indicated that the King had considerable confidence in the Board's directors. Clinton had rendered that confidence meaningless.

The commander exploded when he read the Board's "rude" complaints. When he replied to Franklin's objections on December 10, he pretended "surprise" at the directors' unhappiness, assuring them that he had framed his instructions "with the strictest Regard to the Minister's letter," making them as "nearly conformable" to the Board's proposal as he had, in conscience, been able to do. He insisted that he wanted to give the Board "every aid and support." But he refused to alter his instructions. A week later, the directors meekly submitted to Clinton's commission. They had no alternative.[69]

Despite his disappointment, Franklin set out to turn Clinton's blueprint into full-bodied reality. It apparently never occurred to him to resign his commission. He complained, often bitterly, about the strictures that hemmed him in at every juncture. He never ceased arguing for more autonomy. He railed against the bureaucratic red tape that threatened his most innocuous enterprises, as he insisted, in words that echoed his old arguments with Lord Hillsborough, that ends were more important than means, and that knowledge of a particular situation should take precedence over "Formalities."[70]

But while he criticized his superiors, he neither ignored nor disobeyed them. His trust in the law was too ingrained for him to strike out on his own. He ached for independence, autonomy, equality almost as much as did his enemies in the patriot camp. But he needed to exercise his independence with the approval of his superiors. He was simply unable to grab power on his own, or to lead a little band of guerilla warriors in raids against the enemy. Moreover, he needed the support of the English government in order to accomplish his aims. However unsatisfactory Clinton's aid was, it was better than no aid at all. Franklin's weapons, rations, ships, and supplies came from the royal army. Whatever respect he garnered from Englishman and American alike, he derived in large measure as president of the Board of Associated Loyalists.

Still, the time he spent as head of the Board was one of the most frustrating periods he endured in the King's service. The Board met often, sometimes daily, and Franklin seldom missed a session. In between formal meetings he could constantly be found in and about New York, lobbying for supplies, arguing for a pet project or two, arranging the exchange of prisoners, and writing letter after letter to civilian authorities and loyalist sympathizers in London, hoping to effect changes in British military policy.

A perusal of the Board's minutes provides a small indication of the numerous and disparate activities in which Franklin and the other directors engaged. They collected and analyzed military intelligence, inspected points of defense and served as a sounding board for all refugee complaints. They procured passes for people traveling to and from rebel territory. They recruited and organized loyalist companies and helped plan raids on rebel strongholds. The directors also arranged prisoner exchanges and adjudicated quarrels over rival claims to the fruits of plunder. They tried to secure supplies, and they helped the Associators survive between forays against the enemy. Not surprisingly, Franklin had little time to dwell on his personal affairs. The press of business and his insatiable thirst for an English victory consumed him. But when he did manage a few minutes to scribble a short note to Sally, who remained in Philadelphia throughout the war, he asked faithfully for news of his father. Ben never returned the favor.[71]

14

"Deprived of Their All"

"If I took a Rebel Prisoner, he was subject to be exchanged, according to the Laws of War and of nations—if I should happen to have fallen into the hands of Rebels, my life was subject to be taken as a Rebel to a Rebel state. The Laws of War and of nations have been wrested from the protection of subjects of an established Empire, & held sacred to those who have no national Character, & who are consequently not proper objects of the protection of those Laws."—Court-Martial Proceedings for Richard Lippincott, 1782.[1]

"But alas, your infatuated rulers have tied up the hands of your army and sent over a General not impowered to avail himself of circumstances as they arise, but on the contrary, ordered to make almost unconditional submission, and prostrate the honor of Great Britain at the feet of a Banditti."—William Franklin to William Strahan, 1782.[2]

Franklin's duties as president of the Board of Directors for the Associated Loyalists were awesome. Some of his tasks were mere housekeeping chores. He had to find suitable accommodations for the Board.[3] He lobbied for an assistant to Secretary Sampson Blowers and persuaded General Clinton to pay for the Board's stationary. Under normal circumstances these time-consuming tasks would have been minor irritants, almost beneath Franklin's notice.[4]

But, the governor faced a number of difficulties that promised to destroy the very purpose of the Board of Associated Loyalists. At bottom was Clinton's attitude. The general clearly distrusted the entire organization, and felt that its usefulness was vastly outweighed by the trouble it caused and the potential dangers it posed.[5] Consequently he restricted its activities whenever he could. When that was impossible, he simply hid behind bureaucratic red tape. Franklin always complained that he was "shackled by Forms of Office and other Restraints," as he was shunted from one agency to another and back again on a daily basis. What support he obtained was often as not, too little and too late.[6]

Franklin faced roadblocks whenever he tried to secure support for the men who united under the aegis of the Associated Loyalists. Almost as soon as the Board announced its existence, the directors received word from behind rebel lines that there were hundreds of men who were eager to associate if they could be guaranteed support. Franklin thought Lord Germain's instructions implied that Clinton was responsible for providing minimum subsistence to anyone in the Board's employ. But the commander disagreed, arguing that he was obliged to succor loyalist volunteers only when they were directly assisting the royal army. This seemed unreasonable to the governor, who maintained that he wanted only enough rations to sustain new recruits until they were "able to subsist themselves out of the Estates of those who have so unfeelingly deprived them of their all." It seemed such a small favor. And yet he was shuffled from Clinton to the commandant of New York and back again, pleading for rations that he was sure he deserved. Wherever he went, the door slammed in his face. This sort of treatment damaged the Board's credibility, making it difficult to recruit new members.[7]

Franklin solved the problem by going over Clinton's head. He complained to Galloway, hoping that loyalists in London would pressure the ministry into examining the Board's difficulties. He also applied directly to Lord Germain. The governor's appeals paid off. Galloway and his cohorts lobbied effectively for their American counterparts. And Germain, who always had more faith in potential loyalist contributions than Clinton, ran interference for the Board, inducing the reluctant general to supply rations for the new recruits.[8]

Still Franklin and the other directors were usually on their own and they could do little to get out from under Clinton's thumb. When they asked for control over their own weapons and ammunition, they were firmly refused. The commander himself insisted upon approving all expeditions and ordering the Board's supplies on a case-by-case basis. When the directors requested blank commissions for prospective volunteers, they were politely turned away. There was solid evidence that Clinton's policies actually damaged the Board's efforts, for there were many who simply refused to work under the commander's strictures. But while he claimed a desire to offer "every Encouragement" to the Board, Clinton remained convinced that he could follow both the letter and spirit of Germain's instructions "without creating any new or separate Establishment." For him, as for Franklin, the real issue was the degree of autonomy that would be accorded the Board of Associated Loyalists.[9]

If William Franklin had his quarrels with General Clinton, his relations with the army looked amicable compared with his dealings with naval commander Admiral Marriot Arbuthnot. Arbuthnot made it clear from the start that he had no use for Franklin and his Board, and he made almost no effort to cooperate with them. Almost as soon as he received Clinton's commission, Franklin went directly to the admiral, assuming that a personal conversation would be more effective than official channels. He had always been proud of his ability to conduct quiet diplomacy, but in this case he overestimated his talents. Arbuthnot obviously had "conceived Prejudices" against the Association and had "a Disinclination" to offer it any assistance. But Franklin was undaunted. He showed the admiral his commission and explained the Board's plans, emphasizing the tight restrictions under which the loyalists would be operating. Arbuthnot appeared mollified, admitting that some of his earlier suspicions had been unfounded. He even promised to have a "Stout Vessel" fit up for Franklin's use.[10]

The governor was elated. Once again his charm had reaped solid achievements, and he could hardly wait to inform the others of his success. The directors applauded their president's efforts, and decided to wait upon Arbuthnot en masse, hoping to nail down the verbal agreements he had made. But the erratic admiral had already changed his mind. He had no vessel to spare, he said shortly, and he doubted that he would ever be able to furnish the Board with much material aid. He "would not promise any thing, for nothing was in his Power—but what he could do he would do." There was not, he maintained, "a single Board or Plank in the Yard" and he "could not and would not expend a single shilling for the Refugees." He had no authority to allow such expenditures. Moreover, he added, retreating into the bureaucratic excuses that Franklin always detested, he did not "know any Account to which he could place it."[11]

Franklin was red-faced, but there was little more to say. Hoping to salvage something from the debacle, he requested Arbuthnot's word that none of the Associators would be impressed by the King's navy. He also asked him to allow the loyalists to pass to and from the rebel lines without being molested. The admiral agreed, even offering naval protection to any friendly vessel if it "should happen to be going the same Way with Refugees." It was hardly a sterling victory, and Franklin knew it.[12]

Relations never improved. Arbuthnot always ignored the requests for vessels and supplies, hampering the Board's efforts to disrupt the sea coast trade of the rebel forces.[13] The admiral's assurances that the navy would not impress the Associators were not always honored. And when the directors sought restitution for men who were forced to serve in the King's navy, the admiral dallied, referring their complaints to the admiralty court.[14]

Franklin did win one victory in his ongoing struggle with his military superiors. Gradually, and with some misgivings, Clinton gave the directors one of the powers they most desired: control over their own prisoners. Clinton had always promised the Board that its prisoners would be exchanged only for Associators, but this provision was seldom observed. Moreover, it was hardly sufficient to the directors' aims. If the Board was to protect its own men, and to wreak vengeance on the enemy for its inhumane treatment of loyalist captives, then the directors required direct control of their prisoners. Above all, they must have the right of retaliation. If the Associators were routinely "treated with almost every Species of Cruelty," justice demanded that they be able to deal with rebel prisoners in the same way.[15]

At the end of January 1781, Clinton agreed to set aside a separate section of the provost to house the men captured by the Associated Loyalists. This would protect the Board from having its prisoners exchanged for British soldiers. It would also allow the Associators some voice in determining their prisoners' fates. The Board still had to secure Clinton's permission before any exchange could be effected, and it had to observe all rules of civilized warfare. But Franklin viewed Clinton's decision to allow the Board greater autonomy as a meaningful concession. He was especially pleased when, in April, Walter Chaloner was commissioned to act as the Commissary of Prisoners for the Board.[16]

Still, the Associators never ceased to rail at the treatment loyalist captives received at the hands of the rebels. And Franklin could never convince Clinton of the need for retaliation, even when he warned—in words that proved all too prophetic—that if the Associators were not allowed a measure of "just vengeance," a "Spirit of resentment" would develop and the refugees would take matters into their own hands. Should this occur, he said, "no Authority will be able to govern or restrain" them. Nevertheless, throughout most of the war, the Board managed to keep its men in line.[17]

The Board of Associated Loyalists never lived up to Franklin's expectations. The organization did little more than harass the enemy, striking at isolated villages and keeping the inhabitants of rural Connecticut and New Jersey on their guard.[18] Nothing it did was calculated to bring the American army to its knees. Much of its activities were accomplished with an eye to plunder or a desire for revenge. But the Board had a symbolic significance that far outweighed its military contributions. It was one official organization that was run entirely by Americans and that could speak for their needs. Despite their love of the empire, the loyalists were as much Americans as they were Englishmen. They preferred to take orders from their own kind, not from British soldiers who never seemed to understand their needs or to sympathize with their plight. The Board remained a source of pride for these men and women who had so little to sustain them after 1776. And William Franklin, who led the fight to establish the Board and worked tirelessly to expand its powers, was more responsible than anyone for giving Americans what little self-respect they enjoyed during the long, and ultimately disastrous war. It was entirely fitting that the refugees at Lloyd's Neck named their post "Fort Franklin" in honor of the president of the Board of Associated Loyalists.[19]

Whatever the Board's contributions may have been, they were clearly not enough. The defeat of Cornwallis at Yorktown ultimately put an end to the effort to suppress the "unnatural rebellion" and return America to its rightful owners. But Yorktown was more than a military defeat. It underscored more than anything how deep the chasm was between loyal Americans and the British army they tried to serve. At no time was William Franklin so disillusioned—and so American—as when he viewed the terms of Cornwallis's defeat and watched the British will to continue fighting evaporate.

Cornwallis surrendered on October 17, 1781. By the end of the month, handbills were floating around New York announcing the British defeat. Official word of the disaster was not long in coming. The news brought into the open all the frustrations that had bubbled so long just beneath the surface. Throughout the summer and early fall, New York loyalists had grown nervous, and then angry, as Washington's troops had marched south, traveling virtually unmolested through the American countryside. While Cornwallis courted disaster in Virginia, Clinton wined and dined Prince William Henry, the King's third son, in New York. The commander's behavior was a "Scandal," said some, and the Yorktown debacle was the direct result of his "willful neglect." Like everyone else in the city, Franklin had anticipated a rebel attack that summer. He had almost welcomed a decisive, head-to-head engagement with the Continental Army. But as Washington went south and Clinton did nothing to stop him, the governor became openly hostile toward the British general.[20]

Up until the disaster in Virginia, in spite of many British "Blunders" and Clinton's "shameful inactivity," the military situation had looked promising. In the south, Wilmington, North Carolina, had been subdued and all of Virginia appeared to be in British hands. In the north, Ethan Allen's Green Mountain Boys had created the sovereign state of Vermont and had begun negotiating a military treaty with the British. Clinton's army boasted 18,000 men "in high health and good Spirits," while at best Washington's dwindling forces numbered 7000. Franklin could not understand how the miserable American army had been allowed to move "unmolested" for so long. He laid the blame at Clinton's feet, claiming that it was impossible even to attempt to understand the "deep laid schemes" of the commander in chief. "For deep laid they must be," he sniffed, "because they are unintelligible."[21]

But Franklin did not blame Clinton alone for England's military failures. All British commanders, routinely ignored intelligence that loyal Americans had garnered at considerable personal risk. Officers refused to believe reports of Washington's weakness. When Franklin's old friend Cortlandt Skinner had arrived from Staten Island to report that Washington's forces numbered a little more than half the troops that Clinton insisted were there, the commander simply "swore it was false, turned upon his Heel and Shutt himself from all the World for two or three days." In the face of such pig-headed arrogance how could the loyalists continue to trust in the British army?[22]

Had Franklin stopped to analyze his criticisms of the military establishment, he could not have failed to notice how much like his father he sounded. His disgust at the obduracy, bureaucratic bungling, and dissension in the army's upper ranks was uncannily similar to Ben's anger at the North ministry in the days following his humiliation at the Cockpit. Neither man could tolerate incompetence. Both resented arrogant superiors who disregarded their own advice. If it was true that familiarity bred contempt, then both Franklins should have expected to grow contemptuous of British leaders the longer they attempted to work with them.

Nowhere did William sound more like his father than when he attacked the "Evil" English system of selling officers' commissions. Under Clinton, the practice had reached a "pernicious height" so that "a man of moderate fortune," no matter how deserving, could never hope to advance, while men of means, with no experience or skill, could move up the ranks with ease. From a military standpoint, this was disastrous. While the rebel army grew progressively more efficient, the British forces stagnated, as officers paid "no attention to improving in their profession because it cannot promote them." But the problem went deeper. Both Franklins believed almost instinctively in a system that awarded merit more than birth and fortune. The one was the son of an immigrant candlemaker, the other the illegitimate child of a Philadelphia printer. Neither could have aspired to his present heights had class or financial standing been essential to his success.[23] Even while Franklin criticized British leaders, he could not suppress a note of provincial pride as he contemplated American victories in the field. When he analyzed Colonel Tarleton's defeat at Cowpens he grudgingly admitted that the battle was a tribute to an army that fought off an enemy nearly twice its size. The soldiers had managed to "make a virtue of necessity" choosing to stand and fight instead of sticking to the rule books and retreating in despair. It was the British who broke ranks, and fled the sight of the "shameful" battle.[24]

For Franklin, the defeat at Yorktown was simply another in a long string of deplorable and unnecessary British failures. It was a battle that should never have taken place, and once begun, one that should not have been lost. But he was even more dismayed when he learned the terms of Cornwallis's surrender, especially when he examined the notorious "Article Ten."[25] The terms of surrender were negotiated in a hurry. The British general made a half-hearted attempt to protect the loyalist soldiers who fought beside the regular army during the siege, asking in Article Ten of the Capitulation that Americans not be "punished" for their part in the battle. Washington summarily rejected Cornwallis's request, arguing that the treatment of the loyalist forces was "altogether of civil resort.'[26] Thus the American prisoners would not be treated as honorable prisoners of war, but would be subject to the individual state governments. As Franklin saw it, they would be treated as traitors by traitors. To the loyalists' dismay, Cornwallis did not quarrel with Washington's decision.[27]

The outcry against the Tenth Article was vociferous and immediate, as Americans on both sides of the Atlantic proclaimed their sense of betrayal. Clinton himself said it was "impossible to describe the indignation, horror, and dismay with which the American refugees who had either taken up arms in our cause or flown to us for protection read the *tenth article* of that convention." To be "excluded from the same conditions of surrender with their fellow soldiers," to be "most cruelly abandoned" to the care of the pretended state governments, was a humiliation that most loyalists would not suffer lightly. The Americans had voluntarily joined Cornwallis's forces at the general's urging. Now they were the only people abandoned "to the vindictive resentment of a set of people whose tender mercies are cruelty." If, said one dismayed Crown supporter, "Great Britain thus permits her friends to be sacrificed, she may bid adieu to America."[28]

The governor was thoroughly disgusted. General Clinton was now worse than useless. Obsessed with defending his own record, he spent all his time in "wild and distressed" recriminations against anyone who he could conceivably blame for the disaster at Yorktown. All Franklin's efforts seemed wasted, and he resolved to quit the country for London. He remained convinced that the war was winnable. But to reverse England's fortunes, bold leadership and a totally different attitude toward loyal Americans were essential. He yearned for a new "Spirit of Enterprise, and a Firmness of Temper capable of rising as Dangers increased." This required more than a mere change in personnel. The entire army and navy had to be placed under central control, so that the debilitating competition between the two branches would cease. And commissions had to be granted not to those who could afford them, but to those who, because of their "local knowledge and influence in the Country," deserved them. Without such wholesale policy changes, Franklin despaired of America's future.[29]

Typically, while Franklin longed to leave for England, he would not make a move without securing Clinton's permission, even though he viewed the general with scarcely masked disdain. To his surprise, the commander begged him to remain where he was. Even Clinton recognized the respect with which Franklin was held by many loyalists, and he feared that the governor's abrupt departure would be highly "prejudicial" to his own position. Franklin alone could hold loyalist resentment in check. Reluctantly, William agreed to remain in New York, primarily, he said, because he recognized that his exodus would signal an open breach between the British command and the president of the Board.[30]

Once he had decided to stay in America, Franklin did what he could to mollify his loyal compatriots. As president of the Board of Associated Loyalists, he naturally led the opposition to the disposition of the Tenth Article. He feared that Washington would take advantage of American disaffection, offering such favorable terms to repentant loyalists, that there would be a wholesale flood of defections to the rebel banner. To hold loyal Americans in line, Franklin embarked on a campaign to convince them of British good will and to assure them that Clinton would not tolerate any further treatment of the kind they had received from Lord Cornwallis. When the general asked for Franklin's "sentiments" on how best to rectify the damage done at Yorktown, William eagerly replied. In the first place, he argued, Cornwallis had begun his negotiations in a "degrading" manner. When he had asked that the loyalists under his command not be "*punished*" for their service to the King, the general had implicitly conceded their separate and inferior status. He seemed to "*admit guilt* and a *consequent right* in the revolted colonists" to persecute loyal Americans "for acts of allegiance to their lawful sovereign." Worse yet, Cornwallis had meekly abandoned even this weak attempt at protecting the loyalists, and he had submitted to Washington without even one "spirited effort" on behalf of the American prisoners.[31]

In mid-November, Franklin delivered a series of suggestions to General Clinton designed to prevent any further "pernicious effects" from the terms of the Yorktown capitulation. He wanted, above all, a "Solemn Publick Repudiation of the Principle of Discrimination on which the Tenth Article" was founded. He pressed, as well, for a promise that future British commanders would guarantee equal treatment for all captives. No "distinction or Discrimination" should ever be allowed, he said, "it being always to be understood that as they at least run equal risks with the King's Troops, they are justly entitled to equal Advantages on Such occasions." While Clinton had already explained that he personally deplored Cornwallis's disposition of the Tenth Article, this was not enough. Private expressions of regret and confidential promises of future protection for American supporters of the Crown were worthless if neither the loyalists nor the rebels knew anything about them.[32]

But there was more. Franklin asked Clinton to issue a "publick Proclamation" to be sent both to congress and General Washington warning that if any American prisoner taken at Yorktown was executed by "any of the Revolted Provinces," retaliation against American prisoners would be carried out "to the fullest Extent possible." If Clinton refused to accept the general principle of retaliation, then Franklin asked at the very least that he empower the loyalists to take rebel hostages and to use them to respond to the "particular Injuries they or their friends may sustain." Nothing short of this, he insisted, would quiet the "present ferment."[33]

Franklin's demands went far beyond anything that Clinton could accept. To ask him to repudiate one of his own generals publicly and to allow the Associated Loyalists unlimited freedom to wreak vengeance on their rebel captives was impossible. Clinton did discuss the situation with his board of advisers. Claiming that a policy of military retaliation would be suicidal, he even listened to arguments for reopening New York's courts, preparing the way for the use of "civil weapons of terror." After considerable debate, however, the board rejected the proposal. Instead, Clinton promised to issue an order prohibiting discriminatory treatment, hoping that this would assuage loyalist fears. In March, he repeated his assurances, directing them—at the King's behest—directly to the members of the Board of Associated Loyalists. But he postponed a general promulgation of his policy.[34]

With the British defeat at Yorktown, the loyalists were plunged into "extreme Dejection." There was a "dead calm" everywhere, as the directors met less and less often, and engaged in only the most routine business when they did convene. Everyone seemed to be going through the motions. The North ministry had fallen in March. Lord Rockingham, North's replacement, was ready to sue for peace. The House of Commons had issued an order proclaiming all Englishmen who engaged in offensive warfare as enemies to their country. The loyalists were in such a state of "Agitation" that it was almost impossible for them "to come to any fix'd Determination with Regard to the Conduct they should pursue."[35]

Franklin, himself, felt betrayed. When he discovered that Clinton was to be replaced by Sir Guy Carleton, and that the new commander was hemmed in by Parliament's "extraordinary" restrictions, he exploded. "With the force under his command," he told William Strahan, Carleton could be victorious in less than three months. "There never was a more glorious opportunity for striking a decisive stroke against Washington," he insisted, "who may in fact be said to have no army at all." Instead, England's "infatuated rulers" had tied the hands of their generals and ordered them to "make almost unconditional submission, and prostrate the honor of Great Britain at the feet of Banditti."[36]

Still, Franklin made every effort to revive the flagging spirits of the King's supporters. The loyalists continued to see him as their spokesman. Ironically, it was during this period, that the governor came closest to acting as a popular leader. He was, as always, caught between his respect for authority and his sympathy with the people whose interests he also served. But now, as it became apparent that Clinton's days were numbered, he listened more to the pleas of the Associators in his care than he did to the words of caution emanating from headquarters.[37]

The growing weakness of British authority, Franklin's bitterness after Yorktown, and his sense of desperation as he saw the British will to fight steadily dwindle, all contributed to his involvement in one of the most infamous terrorist incidents of the war.[38] The reasons for the Huddy-Lippincott affair are not difficult to fathom. After Cornwallis's surrender, New York was in total disarray. Discipline broke down. Clinton eagerly awaited his replacement. The loyalists were convinced that they were about to be abandoned to the questionable mercies of the rebels. Clinton and Washington had even begun to discuss future prisoner exchanges.[39]

Two options were open to the loyal Americans. They could submit meekly to British policy, accepting the loss of their country with quiet dignity. Or they could escalate the level of hostilities so that rapprochement would be impossible. The Board chose the second option, deciding to make one last effort to keep the war alive. The associators needed a show of force, some proof of the vitality of the King's cause, an indication that the rebel government was too weak to protect its supporters from enemy attack. Terrorism and retribution were essential if the loyalists were not to abandon hope.[40]

The Board's quest for vengeance led to an isolated spot in northern New Jersey. On the early morning of April 12, Timothy Brooks, a tailor from Bucks County, Pennsylvania, stood on the mainland shore looking across the bay at a strange tableau. Twenty-five men disembarked from a sloop anchored by Sandy Hook, a thin, finger-like peninsula jutting out into the water. A prisoner was shoved roughly off the boat, his hands bound tightly behind him. Silently, one of the men rolled a barrel from the sloop, placing it upright under a tree. Another led the prisoner to the barrel and ordered him to stand on it, while a third placed a rope around a sturdy branch and put the other around his captive's neck. One of the participants, obviously in charge of the operation, stepped forward, mumbled a few words to his helpless victim, shook his hands, and stepped back. He held a piece of paper, but he did not even glance at it. A black man checked the noose and rope, then pushed the barrel away. The prisoner swung slightly in the morning breeze.[41]

The men, their numbers reduced by one, returned to their sloop, leaving their victim hanging from the tree. Before they left, the leader took the paper he had been carrying and pinned it to the dead man's chest. It read:

> We, the Refugees, have with grief long beheld the cruel murders of our brethren, and finding nothing but such measures daily carrying into execution, we, therefore, determine not to suffer without taking vengeance for the numerous cruelties, and having made use of Captain Huddy as the first object to present to your view, and further determine to hang man for man, as long as a refugee is left existing. UP GOES HUDDY FOR PHILIP WHITE.[42]

The gruesome little drama that culminated in the death of Joshua Huddy of the Jersey State Artillery had begun sometime in early April of 1782 when Samuel Taylor, a New Jersey farmer and a loyal refugee, called on Governor Franklin at number four Nassau Street. He reported that one of the Associators, Philip White, had recently been taken from Monmouth jail and executed without trial by his rebel captors. Taylor said that the Monmouth rebels also held Clayton Tilton, one of the Board's most effective Associators, and were threatening him with a similar fate. He wanted the Board to arrange Tilton's immediate exchange. He also urged retaliation for the execution of White, suggesting that rebel prisoner Joshua Huddy be targeted as the Board's victim. Huddy had been captured during a bloody rebel raid on the Block House at Tom's River at the end of March, and was being held in one of the Sugar Houses down by the docks. Franklin momentarily expected his transfer to the provost where he would be in the hands of the directors.[43]

The choice of Huddy was no accident. Already notorious, he had loudly boasted of his earlier role in executing loyalist prisoner Stephen Edwards. With the help of General David Forman, or "Black David" as he was known in New York, Huddy claimed to have "Greased the Rope well," and "pulling the Rope hand over hand," had helped hang the unfortunate Edwards from an oak tree near Monmouth Court House.[44]

Franklin was furious when he learned of White's death, although his informant's tale was by no means an unusual one. Eastern New Jersey was nearly equally divided between patriots and loyalists. As a result, says one historian, it was a "grim twilight zone of random violence and increasing insecurity." Constantly the scene of bloody guerilla warfare, it was a virtual state of nature whose inhabitants were never safe from marauding bands of cutthroats. Franklin was used to hearing horror stories about his former home. Moreover, Taylor's report was still unconfirmed, and indeed no one ever knew for sure why, or how, Philip White died.[45]

But William Franklin was in no mood to quibble about technicalities. According to Taylor, Franklin not only agreed to execute Huddy, but he also promised to order future retaliatory executions if necessary. Taylor was pleased with the governor's response and recommended that Captain Richard Lippincott be appointed to deal with Huddy. Lippincott, who had received his captain's commission from the Board in 1781, was a dedicated Associator. A New Jersey native, he had lost all of his property to the pretended state government, and many of his neighbors had been cruelly treated and even "executed in cold blood" by the rebels. He was a perfect choice to carry out the act of revenge that Franklin had in mind.[46]

The governor lost no time in arranging for Lippincott to come to the Board to receive his instructions. But when the captain reported on April 8, Franklin was not present, in itself a rare occurence. Daniel Coxe was there, however, serving as president in the governor's absence. Robert Alexander and Edward Lutwycke were also present, as was the secretary, Sampson Blowers. Upon entering the room, Lippincott asked for an order to attempt an exchange, using Huddy, Daniel Randolph, and Jacob Fleming to free Clayton Tilton and Aaron White from Monmouth jail. Coxe ordered Blowers to prepare a requisition asking for permission to essay the exchange.[47]

According to Blowers, Lippincott returned to the Board the next day. This time Franklin was there along with Coxe and Anthony Steward. A few minutes later, Edward Lutwycke strolled into the chambers, just in time to hear Lippincott outline a more ambitious plan than the one he had earlier proposed. He wanted to attack Monmouth jail and rescue Tilton instead of trying to secure him through an exchange. If that failed, he proposed to capture "Black David" Forman and use him as a hostage to force Tilton's release. The directors promised to ask Clinton for sufficient ammunition and provisions to carry out Lippincott's plan. Franklin signed the request, and Blowers drew up a new set of instructions. While Blowers worked, Lippincott drew their attention to a "paper" he held, saying that he planned to take it with him into New Jersey. Franklin looked at it, while Steward tried to read it over the governor's shoulder. But Coxe "hastily" intervened, shouting, "We have nothing to do with that Paper. Captain Lippincott keep your papers to yourself the Board do not wish to see them or hear them read."[48] Blowers did not know if anyone actually read the document. He himself had seen nothing. When Steward tried to discuss the matter after Lippincott left the room, Coxe abruptly changed the subject. Nevertheless, Blowers later insisted that there was no reason to assume that anyone in the room had prior knowledge of Lippincott's plans.[49]

Lippincott never implemented his scheme to capture Forman. Instead, sometime on the 9th of April, he called at the home of Walter Chaloner with an order to release Huddy, Randolph, and Fleming to his custody. On the way to the provost, Lippincott boasted that Huddy would be murdered to avenge White's death. And after Lippincott had left the prison, Chaloner remarked to William Foster, the deputy provost marshall, that "if Captain Huddy knew what was intended against him or what his fate was to be he . . . would not go out so joyfully as he did."[50]

Two days later, Lippincott brought his three prisoners to Captain Richard Morris's ship the Britannia, asking the British commander to hold them temporarily. He returned the next day, and requested that Huddy alone be released to his custody, openly declaring that he intended to hang his prisoner, and claiming that he was acting on Board orders. He even produced papers purporting to authorize the execution. Morris glanced at them, but later insisted that he did not read them carefully. He remembered a phrase that proclaimed "Up goes Huddy for White," but he did not recall seeing any signature on the documents. Nevertheless, he allowed Lippincott to get a rope from one of his officers before leaving the ship. The royal navy was now implicated, at least peripherally, in the events that would follow. According to Clinton, this was exactly what the Associated Loyalists desired. The entire execution, he argued, was intended to create an incident that would make further talk of peace impossible.[51]

Huddy was hanged on Sandy Hook, and Lippincott, well pleased with his work, returned to New York. But the murder of Joshua Huddy was immediately greeted with cries of outrage from all sides. The residents of Monmouth demanded justice for the perpetrators of this "wanton and cruel act" against an American hero who had died "with the Firmness of a Lion." Clinton was furious when he heard about the incident, and General Washington immediately terminated all negotiations with the British. He demanded that Lippincott be turned over to the Americans for punishment, threatening to execute a captured British officer of equal rank if Clinton did not comply. The commander resented Washington's peremptory interference in his army's affairs and refused to accede to his demands. But he agreed that Huddy's murderers should be punished, and he ordered an investigation, asserting that "Such an outrage against the laws of Nations to the Army I commanded—to Humanity—could not pass unnoticed."[52]

While Washington began the unpleasant task of selecting by lot a British captain to be executed if justice was not done, Clinton proceeded with his investigation, asking the Board for a thorough account of the Association's involvement in Huddy's execution. At first the directors' response to his urgent queries was almost insolent. Lippincott, they casually explained, "was gone to the Races" and they had to delay their report until he returned. In the meantime, the captain began preparing his defense, but on the evening of the twenty-fourth he was arrested and hauled off to the provost. Consequently, he claimed that he was not able to forward a complete account of his actions to headquarters.[53]

The next day, after Clinton repeated his demand for the Board's version of events, its members reluctantly issued a "very bold" statement to headquarters. They did not forgo a chance to attack the commander's policies head-on, enclosing a "State of Facts" that purported to explain Lippincott's actions. They provided details of rebel atrocities against the King's supporters in New Jersey, highlighting Huddy's own terrorist record.[54] And they asserted that Clinton had never made so much as "one spirited attempt" to defend loyal Americans from enemy attack. The Board's remarks were a desperate attempt at damage control. Already Clinton had forbade any further expeditions by the Associated Loyalists pending the outcome of his investigation. But the directors feared even worse consequences should Lippincott's case go to trial.[55]

The Board followed two courses of action. First, its members tried to avoid military proceedings against Lippincott, arguing that as a private citizen, the captain could only be tried in a civil court. Second, they attempted to persuade Lippincott to sign a prepared statement indicating that he had acted on his own initiative when he executed Joshua Huddy. Lippincott nearly signed the document, changing his mind only at the last minute. Instead he used it in his own defense, as evidence that the Board was aware of and had authorized Huddy's death.[56]

General Clinton was in an impossible position. If he proceeded against Lippincott, he would totally lose whatever remained of his loyalist support. But if he spared the captain's life, he would alienate the King's officers, who knew that Washington planned to hang one of their own comrades, Captain Charles Asgill, if Lippincott was freed. They were more than willing to sacrifice an American Associator to rescue a commissioned man. Washington had "the best Blood of England" in his power, and it seemed the height of folly to risk the life of an innocent officer to save a "mere" American.[57]

Part of the problem was that most, if not all, of Clinton's advisers assumed that Lippincott had acted with the Board's blessing. The directors, claimed Andrew Elliot, had conducted themselves in this instance with "a singular Blackness of Heart." The "Street Talk of the Day" held that the

Board had ordered Huddy's execution and was now trying to wriggle out of its responsibility. If the directors were so cowardly as to leave one of their own men in the "lurch," it was difficult for many to sympathize with their plight.[58]

On April 25th, Clinton told a group of high-ranking officers to begin its own investigation of Huddy's death. He also asked his council for its views. The council decided that because there were no civil courts operating in New York, Clinton should request a court-martial. And so, with the advice of "all the Principal Officers both Sea and Land British and Provincial and Foreign" the commander ordered Richard Lippincott to stand trial in the military courts for murder.[59]

Clinton immediately advised William Franklin of his decision, demanding more information about the Board's involvement in Huddy's death, and forbidding the directors from removing any more prisoners from the provost. Franklin's response was defiant. While he insisted that Lippincott had exceeded his instructions, he proclaimed that Huddy had nevertheless been "disposed of in a Manner which the Board are clearly of Opinion was highly justifiable from the general Principles of Necessity and the peculiar Nature and Circumstances of the Case."[60]

Fortunately for Henry Clinton, he was spared the task of proceeding against Lippincott. On April 27th, news spread through New York that he was about to be relieved of his command and replaced by Sir Guy Carleton.[61] Carleton arrived in New York on the afternoon of May 5, just as Richard Lippincott's trial was getting under way. The new commander sympathized with the loyalists and at first he hoped to negotiate a rapprochement with the rebel government without granting American independence. In this vain hope he was encouraged by the loyalists, who swiftly offered him their myopic view of the British position. One thing was clear. If Carleton's aspirations were to have any chance, he had to defuse rebel anger over the murder of Joshua Huddy.[62]

Within four hours of his arrival in New York, Carleton called William Franklin and William Smith to headquarters. Smith insisted that Lippincott was not a murderer and spoke eloquently against the court-martial.[63] Franklin obviously agreed, and early the next morning submitted a written request for a delay of Lippincott's trial. But from the beginning, the governor and the general were at cross-purposes and their relationship was never cordial. Carleton thought Franklin was a war-mongering extremist. And, like his predecessor, he was leery of anybody who threatened his own authority. Franklin blamed Carleton's coldness on the "exaggerated misrepresentations" that he presumed had emanated from Clinton. As he saw it, Clinton had always regarded the Board as an "obnoxious Institution," and he had seized upon this opportunity to kill it once and for all. This, not Washington's threat of retaliation, was the real reason for the court-martial.[64]

Lippincott won a delay of his trial. Meanwhile, Carleton set to work trying to find a graceful way out of the dilemma his predecessor had left him. He established contact with rebel leaders, attempting to reach some agreement whereby both parties would call a halt to atrocities perpetrated by their own men. Unless Americans and Englishmen alike repudiated the destructive policy of retaliation, everyone would be "involved in one common Dishonor."[65] He also sought the opinion of members of his own board of advisers, asking them if Lippincott's military trial should be continued. Many suspected that Carlton would "get rid of Lippincott's affair by Procrastination." Nearly everyone assumed that once the case was disposed of, the general would "break the Board of Refugees."[66]

Throughout all the discussions, William Franklin worked feverishly to quash the court-martial. His concerns were both practical and philosophical. He feared the results of a trial, knowing that evidence presented there would seriously embarrass the Board. Any verdict would be a disaster. If the trial resulted in Lippincott's conviction, Franklin's ability to maintain the trust of the Associators would be damaged beyond repair. But if Lippincott was cleared, the Board and its president would no doubt be viewed as accessories to murder. Franklin hoped that a decision against a military trial would mean no trial at all, for there were no civil courts in New York capable of proceeding against Lippincott.

But Franklin had other concerns as well. If Lippincott was tried in a military court, the Board of Associated Loyalists would lose any claim to autonomy. The directors had always maintained that the Associators were entirely separate from the British army, that they were civilian volunteers whose only legal obligation was to the Board itself. If Lippincott was accorded the same treatment as a British officer, the fiction of loyalist independence would be forever buried. Thus William Franklin, royal governor, defender of the King's prerogative, and president of the Board of Associated Loyalists, found himself arguing that a court-martial would violate Richard Lippincott's rights. Like his father, he talked now, almost desperately, of the rights of Englishmen and the tradition of Magna Carta. As William Smith noted, with a certain degree of maliciousness, "Governor Franklin, poor Man, had Reason to be greatly embarrassed."[67]

Despite Franklin's pleas, Carleton eventually arrived at the same conclusion that Henry Clinton had reached before him. It was "Manifest" he announced, that the court-martial of Richard Lippincott must go forward. Lippincott pled "not guilty" to the charge of murder, and the trial began in earnest on June 14. The captain offered two basic lines of defense. First he argued that retaliation against rebel atrocities was a form of self-defense. Without the threat of retaliation, rebel iniquities would continue unchecked. To prove his contention, he called a number of witnesses—and claimed to have even more waiting in the wings—who told grizzly tales of "barbarities" against loyal Americans. They told of loyalists who were "tried by Rebels as Rebels to their usurped form of Government" and of other men who were simply "executed in cold blood." Lippincott bemoaned his "unequal" situation. "If I took a Rebel Prisoner," he explained, "he was subject to be exchanged, according to the Law of War and of nations—if I should happen to have fallen into the hands of Rebels, my life was subject to be taken, as Rebel to a Rebel state. The Laws of War and of Nations have been wrested from the protection of Subjects of an established Empire, & held sacred to those who have no national Character, & who are consequently not proper objects of the protection of those Laws." This was the kind of defense that William Franklin and the other directors entirely approved. Lippincott was using his trial as a public forum from which to attack British policy toward rebel prisoners. Had it occurred earlier, it might even have done some good. But Lippincott's complaints were too late, and they were summarily rejected by his fourteen-member jury.[68]

He had better luck with his second line of defense, which, unfortunately for William Franklin, was extremely damaging to his own and the Board's image. Lippincott claimed to be acting under orders from the Board in general and Franklin specifically. He admitted that he had never received a written command to execute Joshua Huddy, but he argued with the help of a goodly number of witnesses that the order had been issued in terms that could not possibly be misunderstood. The evidence was impressive. Clinton certainly believed it.[69] The members of the jury, who included Franklin's old friend Cortlandt Skinner, agreed. They assumed that, however wrongfully, Lippincott thought Huddy's execution was legally sanctioned. The implication behind the ruling was that Franklin himself was responsible for Huddy's murder.[70]

It is ironic that the man who set such store by the law should have been involved in such a sordid little affair as the execution of Joshua Huddy. It did more to ruin Franklin's name than anything he ever did. One historian has referred to the incident as the "most blatant act of premeditated cruelty on record during the Revolution." And most contemporaries, except for loyal Americans themselves, no doubt agreed.[71]

Franklin's role in the death of Joshua Huddy seems most uncharacteristic. He had chafed under General Clinton's restrictions from the moment the Board of Associated Loyalists had been founded. Yet he had never rebelled against them or disobeyed his orders. He had not become the leader of a band of terrorists. Even when he had supported terrorist activity, he had always assumed that he was acting with the King's blessing.

Franklin was also a man of moderation, who, even at war's end was desperately seeking some means of accommodating the differences that split the empire in two. As late as May, he remained convinced that the American people, if not their leaders, longed to resume the old relationship with the mother country. He argued that if Guy Carleton would only draw up some "clear Specific Propositions founded on Liberal Principles," print them on handbills, and spread them throughout the countryside, Americans would flock to the British banner, emancipating themselves from "Congressional Tyranny" and returning to the true liberty guaranteed by the British constitution.[72]

But, Franklin by the spring of 1782, was a tired, bitter, and disillusioned man. The capitulation of Cornwallis had depressed him as nothing since the death of his beloved Elizabeth had done. He recalled Lord Germain's early promises that his sacrifices would be rewarded, and almost laughed to think that he had believed them. Germain was gone; Shelburne had taken his place. Most of his friends and connections were out of power. And despite his own "unflagging" efforts to serve the King he was not materially better off now than he had been when he first arrived in New York. Meanwhile, he observed, the men who were responsible for the failure of what should have been an easy effort to quash the American rebellion, were being promoted.[73]

He was disillusioned by what he saw on both sides of the Atlantic. The rebels were still weak, their numbers pitifully small compared with the mighty British army that even now had only to sweep through the countryside, take Baltimore and Philadelphia, and win the war. In England a few short-sighted men had been so intent upon achieving recognition of all the empire's claims, that they had ended in losing everything. In America, a handful of malcontents had been, from the beginning, so dedicated to American independence and republican tyranny, that they would stop at nothing less than total victory. Minorities on both sides had pursued their dangerous course, disregarding the welfare of either England or America, and had thus destroyed the empire. "Human Nature," sighed Franklin, "is the same every where." Perhaps it is not after all so surprising that William Franklin, this man of moderation, succumbed, if only for a second, to the temptation to strike back at the rebel enemy. He was still prudent enough—and lawyer enough—not to put his orders to Richard Lippincott in writing. But there is little doubt that he enjoyed a bit of momentary satisfaction when he learned of Joshua Huddy's death.[74]

His satisfaction was costly. When General Washington heard of Lippincott's acquittal, he furiously threatened to proceed with Captain Asgill's execution. He insisted that if Lippincott was innocent, then his superiors were guilty. In effect, Washington was demanding the death sentence for William Franklin. Many observers agreed, arguing that the results of the court-martial indicated that "Govr Franklin was the Culprit & should have been punished."[75] Meanwhile, General Carleton and his closest American advisers were contemplating dissolving the Board of Associated Loyalists. While they knew that such a move was risky, for it could alienate Americans whose aid might one day be needed, even the Board's defenders had little stomach for continuing its operations.[76]

Franklin's influence in America was over. There was no point in remaining in New York, and with Washington calling for his head it began to be dangerous for him to linger there. As early as May he began selling his possessions and putting his financial affairs in order. On August 10, the refugees gathered at Assembly Hall. They drew up a number of petitions, one of which was addressed to the King, begging for continued support. And they unanimously voted to ask William Franklin to carry their petition to London.[77] William Smith thought the arrangement was a mere "Pretext" for spiriting Franklin out of the country, and he may have been right. But it allowed the governor to depart the country of his birth with his dignity intact.[78]

Franklin sailed for London in August, the cloud of the Huddy affair still hanging over his head. He had never really belonged completely to America. He had fled Philadelphia at his first opportunity. He had returned to the colonies as the surrogate of the King of England and he owed his position to royal authority. Yet he had always prided himself on his understanding of the American people, and he had honestly tried to serve their interests as he interpreted them. Nevertheless, if he ruled "for" the people, he was never really "of" the people.

As Franklin left for England, he was convinced that little hope remained for a Crown victory. Guy Carleton was a "spirited General" but he was "bound Neck and Heels," by the House of Commons. The activities of the Associated Loyalists had been indefinitely suspended. Moreover, his own fortunes had been destroyed, his hope for honor, wealth, and power gone with them. New York was growing more expensive by the day, and his small salary was in no way sufficient to his needs. He could no longer even afford to ask a friend to dinner. You know, he told Joseph Galloway, "how mortifying this must be to me who lived in the Stile you know me formerly" to have enjoyed. He had submitted "patiently to this Degradation" for so long because he always expected a "speedy and honourable" conclusion to the war, and because he had continued to hope for some monetary recognition of his services. But now those expectations had proven false, and it was time to quit the country and sail for England.[79]

Even as he prepared to leave New York, he must have harbored some instinctive fears that he would be no more comfortable in England than he had been in America. He had surely heard of the disillusionment and heartbreak suffered by the loyal refugees in the mother country as the war effort sputtered and died, and they realized that they would probably exist as permanent exiles from their native land.[80] And he knew by now that he could not count on the reward he deserved from a ministry that seemed neither to understand nor to care about the Americans who had served its interests so loyally for so long.

Franklin clung to one lingering hope for personal happiness. He still dreamed of being named governor of Barbados, a post he had always coveted. There he could live where "dear Mrs. Franklin was born, and had near Connections with the first-Families on the Island." Perhaps, there, he could make a new life for himself. He had no roots, no sense of belonging anywhere. In Barbados he could use his wife's connections to gain at least an illusory attachment to the world around him.[81]

Epilogue

William Franklin never went to Barbados. Instead he died in exile in the England he had always honored and loved. There, despite repeated disappointment, he tried to win respect for himself and compensation for the sacrifices endured by his fellow Americans. No longer the head of a royal colony, no longer the legitimate leader of His Majesty's loyal forces, he acted out his role on the periphery of England's public stage. Like most other American refugees, he was an outsider in the land he had chosen to call his own.

His first years of exile were especially difficult. He had departed America's shores with the sound of his enemies' denunciations reverberating in his ears. He had lost his position, his property, his country, and even, it seemed, his honor. His £500 government pension had not stretched very far in New York and would be worth even less in London. And the ocean crossing had taken its toll; his tall and once portly frame was gaunt, revealing the effects of the strain of the last few months. Still, William Franklin did not wallow in self-pity. He soon found lodgings on Suffolk Street in London and set to work renewing his contacts with Lord Shelburne, the King's new first minister. Unlike the more organized New England loyalists, Franklin did not have a solid base from which to operate. But this did not deter him. Many Americans still viewed him as a man of considerable prestige, and loyalist leaders trusted him to argue their cause at Whitehall. The governor accepted the challenge with alacrity. Work had always acted as a tonic for him, and he plunged into London politics with enthusiasm.[1]

His first effort involved an abortive attempt to influence the terms of any peace settlement hammered out between the English and American delegations in Paris. If "independency" was granted, he argued, the mother country had an obligation to protect the loyal Americans. The former colonies should honor all outstanding debts to the loyalists. They should return all unconfiscated property to the original owners, compensating the King's supporters for any property already sold. And they should guarantee the safety of those who chose to remain in America, promising them equal justice before the law. Franklin also hoped that the British government would provide financial assistance to Americans who had no choice but to flee their native land and resettle in an alien country.[2]

Unfortunately for William Franklin, the loyalists were not the Crown's highest priority. Moreover, his own father was a chief negotiator in Paris, and he proved to be one of the refugees' most implacable foes. He fought every attempt to force the new government to compensate the King's supporters, and opposed any proposal that lessened the burden of his American enemies.[3] England wrung what few concessions it could from the American delegation. Congress agreed to recommend that the individual state governments return the property of passive loyalists. Refugees and active supporters of the King were granted twelve months to settle their estates and leave the country for good. And the British government promised to help those individuals who did not receive restitution from the former colonies. To make sure that a financially strapped and penurious Parliament did not engage in dilatory tactics, loyalist leaders from all over England traveled to London in February 1783 to consider lobbying efforts on behalf of the refugees. Named, along with former governors James Wright, John Wentworth, and Robert Eden to present the loyalist view to the government, Franklin began to work on behalf of the "suffering" Americans.[4]

Arguing that their claims were a matter of natural and legal right, Franklin and his fellow petitioners put "their Case in the strongest light." But Parliament was divided on the issue of loyalist compensation, and was reluctant to spend a great deal of money on the refugees. While William's sympathizers viewed this attitude as a "Disgrace," and bemoaned the government's "tyrannical unjust treatment of All America," the loyalists were virtually helpless to influence Parliament's deliberations. It was not until mid-summer that the government established a five-member commission to examine refugee claims on a case-by-case basis. Petitioners would have to prove their unconditional devotion to the Crown and provide detailed evidence that any losses they claimed were a direct consequence of their loyalty.[5]

Franklin worked diligently to help loyal Americans prepare their cases for the commission, gathering information, serving as a witness, and lobbying for financial rewards. Even as an exile he exhibited a sense of *noblesse oblige*, and he continued to see himself as a leader of the refugees. While his theater of action had been severely restricted since his glory days as the King's servant in New Jersey, he threw himself into his new role with as much energy as ever.[6]

While he worked to secure restitution for others, and waited to present his own claims to the commission, he tried without much success, to put his personal affairs in order. When he first arrived in England, William made no attempt to contact either his father or his son. Temple exerted some influence on his father's behalf, suggesting to Benjamin Vaughan, Lord Shelburne's representative in Paris, that because he was "the only Governor who gave his court plain & wholesome advice before the war," that William deserved some emolument. Vaughan harbored no illusions about Temple's motives. He presumed the lad imagined that if his father was well-provided, than Ben would feel no obligation to him and he himself would inherit the lion's share of his grandfather's fortunes. Still, Vaughan did not reject the suggestion out-of-hand, arguing that a "seasonable compliment in that quarter" might prove useful. But nothing came of Temple's overtures.[7]

If Temple had not forgotten William Franklin, Ben apparently had. So long as he resided in Paris he did nothing to help his son. And William proudly refused to write either to his father or his son, even when fellow loyalists asked him to use his influence on their behalf. Only after the Peace of Paris, when Ben was preparing to sail for home and William faced the possibility that he might never see his father again, did he try to "revive that affectionate Intercourse and Connexion which till the Commencement of the late Troubles had been the Pride and Happiness of my Life." While he knew that Ben still resented the "decided and active Part" he had taken in the war, he hoped his father would respect his views even if he could not share them. Claiming that "I uniformly acted from a Strong Sense of what I conceived my Duty to my King and Regard to my Country," Franklin refused to apologize. "If I have been mistaken, I cannot help it," he said. "It is an Error of Judgment that the maturist reflection I am capable of cannot rectify, and I verily believe were the same Circumstances to occur Tomorrow, my Conduct would be exactly similar to what it was hertofore." Still, William was willing to let bygones be bygones, and he hoped his father would agree. He had "broken the Ice" and he now begged for a "personal Interview." The two men had so much to discuss that he thought a letter would not suffice to cover all the ground they had lost. He was even willing to go the extra mile, offering to meet Ben and Temple in Paris if his father did not want to come to England.[8]

William's desire to mend fences was painfully sincere, and many of the Franklins' mutual friends, including William Strahan, took it for granted that Ben would welcome William's overtures. But Ben was unmoved. His response to his son's proposal was unbending. "Nothing has hurt me so much," he cried, "and affected me with such keen Sensations as to find myself deserted in my old Age by my only Son; and not only deserted, but to find him taking up Arms against me, in a Cause wherein my good Fame, Fortune and Life were all at Stake." While he admitted that all mortals were "subject to Errors," he simply could not countenance William's active support of the King. "Your Situation was such," he argued, "that few would have censured your remaining Neuter, *tho' there are Natural Duties which precede political ones, and cannot be extinguish'd from them.*" Strange sentiments, indeed, from a man who had always placed his own devotion to public affairs above the needs of his family. Myopic sentiments from a man who had not raised his son to sit quietly on the sidelines or to avoid his duty as he saw it.[9]

Still the elder Franklin promised to confer with William when he found time to arrange a visit. For the moment he forbade his son to visit him in France, agreeing to send Temple to London instead, to act as an intermediary. Even this concession was difficult for him to make. "I trust," he caustically admonished, "that you will prudently avoid introducing him to Company that it may be improper for him to be seen with." Temple and William were united in the fall of 1784. William sent messages of affection to Ben through his son. And Temple appeared to enjoy his father's company, while William tried to cram in as many days of pleasure as he could with the foppish young man he scarcely recognized. Ben almost immediately regretted letting Temple out of his sight, peevishly demanding that the lad write more often and begging him to return to France. Once more Temple was the prize in a tug of war between his father and grandfather, but if he found his position distasteful or awkward, he gave no sign of it.[10]

Temple finally returned to France in December, and William continued to be solicitous of Ben's welfare. But it was not until the following summer that the three generations of Franklins met face-to-face for the first time in nearly ten years. It was not a cordial visit. They met at Southhampton as Ben was making final preparations for his journey home. The elder Franklin was accompanied by Temple, his nephew Jonathan Williams, and Sally's son and his namesake, Benjamin Franklin Bache. It was a hurried affair. Ben professed to have only enough time to tend to the most urgent business. And he left no doubt that Temple had replaced William in his affections. He had already demanded that his son reimburse him for all the debts he had accumulated over the years. Knowing that William could not possibly come up with such a sum on so short notice, he proposed an alternative plan. He insisted that William sell Temple his New Jersey lands for £2000 sterling, much less than their current value. He also forced his son to hand over his New York holdings as payment for a debt of £1500. The few days at Southampton were used to validate the land sales and, one assumes, to catch up on news from home. But Ben was busy and William was uncomfortable. If he had hoped for a real rapprochement he was sadly disappointed.[11]

William remained in Southampton for a few days after Ben and Temple sailed for America. He was disconcerted by his experience, and not a little homesick. The sight of his nephew brought back painful memories of his sister, who he had not seen since before the war. And he knew that he would almost surely never see his father or his native land again. "My fate," he told Sally, "has Thrown me on a different side of the Globe."[12]

In 1788—a full five years after the body had been convened—the Parliamentary Commission on Loyalists finally agreed to consider William's claims. He had better luck arguing for the requests of others than he did when he pled his own case. Once more, his paternal connections weakened his position. There were those who pretended to question Franklin's loyalty, claiming that he and his father had been in collusion from the beginning, deliberately supporting opposite sides in the war so that no matter what the outcome, the Franklins would come out on top. Despite his sacrifices and his long record of devotion, he had to prove his unqualified loyalty to the Crown.[13]

William Franklin repeated his well-worn litany of the services he had rendered and the sufferings he had endured in the name of the King. From the beginning, he claimed, he had "openly and uniformly oppos'd" colonial "Republicans," making himself "extremely obnoxious to the principal promoters of that measure." As a consequence of his loyalty he had been imprisoned, treated with "extraordinary rigor and severity" by the rebel government, and had lost his property, his wife, and his health. Upon his release from prison he had not quit the American scene, but had worked without pay as president of the Board of Associated Loyalists. So great had been his "zeal" that Lord Germain had promised him a reward as compensation for his services. Neither the King in England nor the loyalists in America had questioned his integrity or his commitment, and William was at a loss to understand why the Parliamentary Commission doubted his word.

To bolster his case, Franklin trotted a number of eminent witnesses before the commission, all of whom stated what the governor thought should be obvious to any impartial observer. Isaac Ogden, George Leonard, Cortlandt Skinner, and Joseph Galloway all praised his "Spirit" and his "Exemplary conduct." They assured the commissioners that William's quarrel with his father was genuine, and based on profound political differences, not on a desire to outwit partisans on both sides of the Atlantic. Even Sir Henry Clinton, never one of the governor's greatest admirers, vouched for his unfeigned devotion to the King's cause.

But such words of praise were of little comfort to a man who resented their necessity. To have to prove his loyalty at this late date was humiliating. The commission's disposition of his case merely added to Franklin's sense of injury. Of the £48,000 he claimed as losses, the Board disallowed all but £1800. He received compensation only for the goods lost in the New York fire of 1778. In addition, he was one of 204 loyalists guaranteed a pension of £300 a year on top of the £500 he had won in New York. All told, this was only £50 more than he had received annually as New Jersey's governor. It was a comparatively paltry sum, about what other royal governors had been receiving since the war began. And it seemed to be an insult, not the badge of honor and the "Mark of the Royal Favour" he craved. As he saw it, the commission's decision was nothing more than "Discrimination" and he felt only "Mortification" as a result.[14]

Franklin did not obtain what he thought he deserved from the Parliamentary Commission. He was even less successful in his attempts to reap any profits from his speculative ventures. William hoped to be able to retrieve some of the money he had lent to George Croghan over the years, and to realize some profits on the land he claimed from his various real estate investments. The American West might yet prove to be his salvation. Croghan was dead, but he thought he had a chance to win some recompense from the Indian traders' estate, even though many of the papers he needed had been destroyed in the New York fire. Even he was no longer sure of the particulars. William's dealings with Croghan had been so complicated, and his wartime activities so distracting, that he found the entire affair "in a manner obliterated from my mind." Still, he was willing to make a stab at getting what he assumed was his due, and almost immediately upon his arrival in London he had begun to try to put his financial affairs in order.[15]

Typically, while Franklin frequently threatened to abandon his efforts and quit throwing good money after bad, he never stopped seeking recognition of his claims. But the deck was stacked against him. His papers were scattered, destroyed, and lost. He had to use intermediaries to look after his American interests and thus was not able to argue his case for himself.[16] "I cannot think of becoming a Resident in America," he told his friend John Taylor. And he was convinced that even if he recovered some of his claims, they would be heavily taxed by a hostile American government. Moreover, Franklin's affairs were extremely complex. His rivals included Thomas Wharton as well as the remaining members of the Burlington Company. And much of Croghan's land had already been settled by a "great body of intruders" who had no intention of recognizing William Franklin's claims. Nor was it likely that the new state governments would force them to do so. Finally, Franklin was simply too financially strapped to carry out a more vigorous campaign.[17]

Only his desire to get "what is due to me" and his determination to avenge real or imagined wrongs prompted William to continue fighting. As always, he saw personal plots, "secrecy," and affronts to his honor in every move made by rival claimants. Members of the Burlington Company were, he thought, engaged in "some collusive design" and they took "undue advantage of my situation and the circumstances of the Times." Honor and justice, not financial reward, were, he insisted, his only goals. And so he badgered friends and family alike in his almost obsessive hunger for vindication, endlessly iterating the details of his case to an often benumbed audience. But then, he really had little else to do.[18]

With the exception of his devotion to his American real estate interests, William Franklin was often at loose ends after the closing of the Parliamentary Commission on Loyalist Claims. A former governor and military man, a lawyer who had never practiced law, an American with no patrons in the British government, his glory days were behind him. He could hobnob with old friends, travel through the English countryside, staying as long as he wanted wherever he happened to be. There was no pressing business to call him home, no meetings with the assembly or reports to send to the King's minister. Only lack of money and a growing tendency toward "Indolence" cramped his style.[19]

Averse to a solitary life, he married Mary D'Evelyn, his landlady, in 1788. An Irish gentlewoman of solid connections, she helped ease his loneliness and provided him with a substitute family. But he never cut the bonds that tied him to America. While he insisted that with the end of the war he had "buried all my American Hatchets," this simply was not the case. So long as Ben lived, William inquired after his father's health and spirits. And he begged Sally for news from home, asking for any details she could provide about her family and their mutual acquaintances.[20]

But if William wished that political differences would not intrude upon his personal life, Benjamin Franklin had no interest in patching up their quarrel. Two years before his own death, he added a codicil to his will, effectively disinheriting his only living son. He left William some worthless lands in Nova Scotia and the books and papers he already had in his possession. He also forgave him his remaining debts. "The part he acted against me in the late War," he explained tersely, "which is of public Notoriety, will account for my leaving him no more of an Estate he endeavored to deprive me of."[21]

William was stung by this final public humiliation. Most of the books and papers Ben left him had been destroyed in the fire. He had assumed that he had already paid his financial obligations to his father when he had sold him his American land. Even in his death Ben had not forgiven him— and the bulk of his father's fortune had ended up in the hands of that "fortune hunter," Richard Bache. It was time to declare his independence from his father, and the pleasant memories he still cherished, once and for all. "The Revolution in America and the Shameful Injustice of my Father's Will have in a manner dissolved all my Connexions in that Part of the World of a private as well as publick Nature," he told Jonathan Williams. And perhaps, at least for a moment, he meant it.[22]

Temple returned to England in 1792. He was a roué and a spendthrift, who possessed all of his father's and grandfather's charms, but had inherited none of their dedication or principles. The farm in New Jersey had bored him. He was a European, not an American, and even Philadelphia was a stodgy backwater town by his exacting standards. London was little better. His father was virtually a stranger; he was also a bit of a nag. He urged his son to settle down and get married; but Temple was not interested. Not, at least, unless it "was to some Woman possessed of such a Fortune as he could have no reasonable Pretensions to expect." William also begged his son to take full advantage of the letters and papers Ben had bequeathed him to write a biography of the American statesman before someone less qualified to tell the story beat him to the punch. But the young man had neither the inclination nor the energy for such a prodigious task.[23]

Worse yet, Temple followed in William's and Ben's footsteps, fathering an illegitimate child, Ellen, in 1798. Ellen Franklin's mother was Ellen Johnson D'Evelyn, Mary's sister-in-law, who lived in the Franklin household. Like Ben before him, William assumed responsibility for the little girl, telling friends only that "we have a child." But the strain proved too much. Temple was soon on his way to Paris, living with another woman, and all contact between the two men abruptly ended. William was devastated. You can be sure, he told Jonathan Williams, that Temple's conduct had to be greatly offensive to overcome the affection I had for him. "In short it hurt my Feelings and occasion'd me more Trouble of Mind than I had ever before experienced or can be expressed." Still, William waited nine years before he changed his will, leaving most of his small estate to his granddaughter.[24]

Much of Franklin's life was devoted to his family. In 1792, the Baches visited Europe, and William showed them the sights of the English countryside, visiting many of the haunts he and his father had once enjoyed together. He loved having them there, even though in his straitened financial circumstances he could not entertain them properly. "Time was," he sighed, thinking of his magnificent house in Perth Amboy, "but no more of that!" Two years later, Sally's son and William's namesake came to London to study medicine, and his uncle helped him make the right contacts in the capital city. It was the kind of task he enjoyed and at which he excelled.[25]

After twenty years of a happy marriage, Franklin's wife fell seriously ill in 1808. Confined to her chambers, she required William's constant attention and not a little of his money to help her. She recovered a little the following spring, but by December she was "totally deprived of her Reason and refused every kind of Nutriment and Medicine." Force-feeding was the only solution. But despite the efforts of the best doctors, even that failed, and on September 3, 1811. Mary Franklin mercifully died.[26]

William was more alone than he had ever been. Joseph Galloway had died in 1803. Sally was gone in 1808. He and Temple were estranged. After Mary's death he went to the seaside to recover his health and his spirits. But his mood was low. "I must resign myself," he said, "for the remaining Days of my Existence to that Solitary State which is most repugnant to my Nature." Only his beloved Ellen, upon whom he doted, and his memories of happier times, helped ease the pain.[27]

Not surprisingly, his thoughts turned as often as not to his father. His letters were dotted with references to Benjamin Franklin. He fretted because Temple continued to put off writing his long-awaited biography. And he began plans for writing one of his own, instead. He thought that with the help of friends and the aid of his own memory, he might be able to amass enough material to make a respectable effort. He wanted to show the world "the Turn of [Ben's] Mind and the Variety of his knowledge." Whenever he looked at Ellen, who, he thought had "every Promise of making a fine sensible Woman," he was reminded of his father to whom he insisted she bore a remarkable resemblance. And no matter what dark thoughts he may have harbored against Ben, except for his own outburst when he heard of the "Shameful Injustice" of his father's will, he kept them to himself. When Jonathan Williams criticized Ben for the way he raised Temple, blaming the boy's upbringing for a life "spent in sensuality and all the frippery of living," William remained pointedly silent.[28]

Actually, William Franklin never wanted a complete rupture with any member of his family. In 1812, Temple wrote asking for permission to visit England. He was finally getting down to the business of writing Ben's biography and needed William's help. Unlike his own father, William was almost pathetically eager to make amends. "I shall be happy to see you," he said, "whenever you can make it convenient. I would not have you, however, much as I long for the Meeting, make any Sacrifice of Consequence to your Interest." And, with just a touch of cynicism, he reminded his son that his own pension died with him. He hoped Temple would remember his daughter in his will.[29]

Franklin was eighty-two years old. He claimed to be in good health for a man his age. He looked forward to seeing Temple's volumes published. And he was delighted that their quarrel had been set aside, for he could not "bear the thoughts of dying at enmity with one so nearly connected." But William never saw Temple again. He died in 1814 still awaiting his son and chafing at the interminable delays that kept him from crossing the Channel. He left the bulk of his estate to Ellen, asking only to be buried "with as much frugality as is consistent with decency."[30]

Selected Bibliography:
A Note on Sources

Manuscript Sources

Many of William Franklin's private papers have been lost; others were destroyed in the New York fire in 1778. Nevertheless, the remaining public and private papers present a clear, coherent, and consistent portrait of the governor. His correspondence has holes in it as the result of unavoidable accident, not because the author altered the record with an eye fixed on future generations of historians.

The most complete collection of Franklin Papers is located at the American Philosophical Society in Philadelphia. Letters to and from William Franklin of both a personal and political nature are in the Franklin Papers and in the Bache Collection. They include letters to and from his father, son, and sister. The David Hall Papers, containing letters from William Strahan to his former colleague, provide valuable information concerning young Franklin's first trip to London. The Jonathan Williams Collection (obtained on microfilm from the University of Indiana Library) offers a good deal of data concerning Franklin's land speculations as well as letters dealing with the years he spent in exile.

Also in Philadelphia is the Pennsylvania Historical Society, which has some Franklin Papers, among its holdings. The Gratz Collection contains some Franklin Papers, as well as a few letters to Elizabeth Graeme Fergusson. The Penn Papers are useful in documenting the relationship between the Franklins and the proprietary interests. The Cadwallader Collection, Croghan Papers, the Wharton Papers (especially the Wharton Letterbook, 1773–84) and the Byars Papers throw additional light on the Franklin involvement in western land deals.

Second only to the Franklin holdings at the American Philosophical Society are the Franklin Papers at the Stirling Library, Yale University, New Haven, Connecticut. This is also the home of the ongoing project to complete the multivolume *Papers of Benjamin Franklin*.

The New Jersey Historical Society, in Newark, New Jersey, has some miscellaneous letters written by William Franklin. It also contains the Jacob Spicer Papers, the Ely Papers, the Sherwood Papers, and the Revolutionary Era MSS. collection, all of which have some relevant items.

The William L. Clements Library in Ann Arbor, Michigan, has a number of invaluable collections. The Amherst Papers, the Gage Papers (both the

American and the English Collections) and the Shelburne Papers all contain correspondence between Franklin and English officialdom. Even more crucial are the Clinton Papers. These include letters between Franklin and the Commander in Chief of the British forces, some of the Minutes of the Associated Board of Loyalists (Jan. 4, 1781–Aug. 1781, and Nov. 1781), and a copy of the proceedings of Richard Lippincott's trial for the murder of Joshua Huddy. They also include many papers dealing with the Board of Associated Loyalists, including various proposals for alternative versions of the Board.

In the New York Public Library, in New York, can be found the Varick Papers, each of which has a handful of documents concerning William Franklin. It also contains a photostat copy of the British Headquarters Papers, available on microfilm, which is a treasure trove of documents dealing with British military policy and practice, including much pertinent information dealing with the Lippincott case. The New-York Historical Society contains the Reed Papers, the Early Papers, and the Duane Miscellaneous Manuscripts, which also have a few documents of interest. More valuable are the William Alexander Papers, which include many letters between the governor and "Lord Stirling."

The Houghton Library, at Harvard University, Cambridge, Massachusetts, has the Jared Sparks manuscripts, containing some helpful documents relevant to loyalist studies in general.

For scholars who find a trip to London economically prohibitive, the Library of Congress, in Washington, D.C., is a godsend. The library has excellent transcripts of Public Records Office and British Museum manuscripts containing letters to and from William Franklin. These include essential Minutes of the Board of Associated Loyalists that are not in the Clinton Papers. The library also holds some miscellaneous William Franklin letters, the Boudinot Papers, and the Force Papers, all of which contain items of interest.

Printed Sources

Many excellent printed sources deal with various aspects of William Franklin's personal and public life. While I have consulted the original manuscripts, whenever possible I have cited the printed documents in the chapter notes, realizing that they are more readily accessible to scholars who do not wish to make the rounds of the various manuscript collections.

The best place to begin is with Yale University's excellent *Papers of Benjamin Franklin* edited successively by Leonard W. Labaree, William B. Willcox, and Claude-Anne Lopez. These papers are beautifully edited and contain a wealth of information concerning both William Franklin and his more illustrious father. Because the series is not yet completed, scholars will also wish to consult the appropriate volumes of Albert Henry Smyth's, *The Writings of Benjamin Franklin* (New York, 1905–07). While these are less useful than the Yale edition, in part because they contain letters written by, but not written to, Benjamin Franklin, they do contain some valuable items, especially those letters written after the War of Independence. Also important are Labaree, ed., *The Autobiography of Benjamin Franklin* (New Haven, 1964); William Duane, ed., *Letters to Benjamin Franklin from His Family and Friends, 1751–1790* (Freeport, N.Y., 1970); George Simpson Eddy, "Account Book of Benjamin Franklin Kept by Him During His First Mission to England as Provincial Agent, 1757–1762," *PMHB* 55 (1931): 97–133; Carl Van

Doren, *Letters and Papers of Benjamin Franklin and Richard Jackson, 1753–1785*, (New York, 1945), and Van Doren, *The Letters of Benjamin Franklin and Jane Mecom* (Princeton, 1950). For insights into William Franklin's relationship with Elizabeth Graeme, see Simon Gratz, "Some Material for a Biography of Mrs. Elizabeth Fergusson, Née Graeme," *PMHB* 39 (1915): 257–321. C.H. Hart's "Letters From William Franklin to William Strahan," *PMHB* 35 (1911): 415–62, is replete with information concerning Franklin's personal and public life. And "The Correspondence Between William Strahan and David Hall, 1763–1777," *PMHB* 10 (1886); 11 (1887); and 12 (1888) contains pertinent tidbits about both Benjamin and William Franklin.

Many Europeans traveled through the middle colonies in the mid-eighteenth century, and their descriptions of the countryside are useful in giving today's readers a sense of the political, economic, social, and geographical milieu in which William Franklin existed. Among the best such descriptions are James Birket, *Some Cursory Remarks Made by James Birket in His Voyage to North America, 1750–1751* (New Haven, 1916); Oral S. Coad, *New Jersey in Travelers Accounts, 1524–1971: A Descriptive Bibliography* (Meutchen, N.J., 1972); Alexander Hamilton, *Gentleman's Progress: The Itinerarium of Dr. Alexander Hamilton, 1744*, Carl Bridenbough, ed. (Chapel Hill, 1948); Peter Kalm, *Travels in North America*, John R. Forster, ed. (Barre, Mass., 1972); Newton D. Mereness, ed., *Travels in the American Colonies* (New York, 1916); and Andrew Burnaby, *Travels Through North America* (New York, 1904). For a first-hand description of William Franklin's trip through the Ohio country, see Conrad Weiser, "Journal of a Tour to the Ohio, August 11–October 2, 1748," in Reuben G. Thwaites, ed., *Early Western Journals, 1748–1765* (Cleveland, 1904). A good sense of the environment at London's Middle Temple can be gained from H. Trevor Colbourn, ed., "A Pennsylvania Farmer at the Court of King George: John Dickinson's London Letters, 1754–1756, Part I," *PMHB* 86 (1962): 241–86, and from John Hancock, "Letters from London, 1760–1761," Massachusetts Historical Society, *Proceedings* 43 (1909/10): 193–200. And for details concerning Pennsylvania politics, see the "Diary of James Allen, Esq., of Philadelphia, Counsellor-at-Law, 1770–1778," *PMHB* 9 (1885): 176–96; 278–98; 424–41, as well as Lewis B. Walker's *Burd Papers: Extracts from Chief Justice William Allen's Letterbook* (n.p., 1897).

There are a number of good printed sources concerning the official business of New Jersey's colonial government. F. W. Ricord, ed., *Documents Relating to the Colonial History of the State of New Jersey* is a good place to begin. Volumes 5 and 6 (Newark, 1892, 1893) deal with the activities of the governor and his council. Volumes 9 and 10 (Newark, 1885, 1886) focus on the assembly, and also include many pertinent letters to and from Crown officials. These documents, valuable as they are, must be supplemented by the *Votes and Proceedings of the General Assembly of the Province of New Jersey*, which are available on microfilm. Also helpful is Clarence Edwin Carter, ed., *The Correspondence of General Thomas Gage with the Secretaries of State, 1763–1775*, 2 vols. (Hamden, Conn., 1969). New Jersey could not support a newspaper in the years prior to the Revolution, but items relevant to New Jersey politics can be found in the newspapers of the neighboring colonies of New York and Pennsylvania. The most useful papers are the *Pennsylvania Gazette*, the *Pennsylvania Journal*, the *New York Gazette*, and the *Pennsylvania Chronicle*. For the years in New York, see especially *Rivington's New York Gazeteer* and *Rivington's Royal Gazette*. Other sources include the *Pennsylvania Packet*, the *New York Gazette or Weekly Post Boy*, the *New York Gazette and Weekly Mercury*, and the *New York Journal or General Advertiser*.

For information concerning New Jersey's Provincial Congress, which operated beside the legitimate government and was responsible for making William Franklin a prisoner of the rebel government, see *The Minutes of the Provincial Congress and the Council of Safety of the State of New Jersey* (Trenton, 1879). Pertinent insights concerning the private side of New Jersey politics can be found in C. E. Prince, ed., *William Livingston Papers*, Vol. One (Trenton, 1979), and William Thompson Read, ed., *Life and Correspondence of George Read* (Philadelphia, 1870).

There are a number of printed sources that document the official proceedings of the rebel government's activities in the years immediately preceding the Declaration of Independence. Especially useful are Worthington Chauncey Ford, ed., *Journals of the Continental Congress, 1774–1789*, Vol. One (Washington, D.C.: 1904); and Paul H. Smith, ed., *Letters of Delegates to Congress* (Washington, D.C., 1976–   ). Also useful is John C. Fitzpatrick's multivolume *The Writings of George Washington* (Washington, D.C., 1931–44).

For the war years, begin by looking at some of the personal observances of people who lived in and around New York during the British occupation of the city. Useful pieces of information can be found in William Abbatt, ed., *Memoirs of Major General William Heath* (New York, 1968); Elias Boudinot, *Journal or Historical Recollections of American Events During the Revolutionary War* (Philadelphia, 1894); "Letters to Joseph Galloway from Leading Tories in America," *Historical Magazine* 5 (1861): 271–73, 295–301, 335–38, 356–64; and 6 (1862): 177–82, 204–6, 237–39; Gustav Schaukirk, "Occupation of New York City by the British," *Pennsylvania Magazine* 10 (1886): 418–45; and Ambrose Serle, *The American Journal of Ambrose Serle, Secretary to Lord Howe, 1776–1778*, Edward H. Tatum, Jr., ed. (San Marino, Calif., 1940).

To understand the political machinations of those who were close to the centers of power, see William Smith, *Historical Memoirs of William Smith, from 12 July 1776 to 25 July 1778* (New York, 1958) and Smith, *Historical Memoirs of William Smith, 26 Aug. 1778 to 12 Nov. 1783* (New York, 1971), both edited by William H. W. Sabine. Both volumes are obviously slanted, but are nevertheless replete with valuable details concerning the day-to-day activities of British leaders and their American supporters. For Clinton's perspective, see William Willcox, ed., *The American Rebellion: Sir Henry Clinton's Narrative of his Campaign, 1775–1782* (New Haven, 1954). Also useful is Milton M. Klein and Ronald W. Howard, eds., *The Twilight of British Rule in Revolutionary America: The New York Letterbook of General James Robertson, 1780–1783* (Cooperstown, N.Y., 1985). For the view from the British side of the Atlantic, see John Fortescue, ed., *The Correspondence of King George the Third from 1760 to December, 1783*, 5 (London, 1928).

Secondary Works

A study of William Franklin should properly begin with an understanding of the phenomenon historians currently designate as "loyalism." Fortunately, within the last decade and a half, interest in loyalist studies has burgeoned and has become correspondingly more sophisticated. We have come a long way from the time when loyalists were "tories" who were either ignored, vilified, or perhaps worse, praised by a handful of nineteenth-century reactionaries who detested the very idea of reform. Moses Coit Tyler was one of the first scholars who insisted upon dealing with loyalism more-or-less on its own terms in his landmark "The Party of the Loyalists in the American Revolution," *American Historical Review* 1 (1895): 24–45. Two years later, he reiterated his concern in his *Literary History of the American Revolution* (New York: 1897). Claude H. Van Tyne's *The Loyalists in the American Revolution* (New York, 1902) took up Tyler's challenge. Although his work was more descriptive than analytical, it was remarkably free of the bias characterizing earlier studies. The imperial school, for obvious reasons, was implicitly sympathetic to loyalist views. This is especially noticeable in Lawrence H. Gipson's *Jared Ingersoll: A Study of American Loyalism in Relation to British Colonial Government* (New Haven, 1920). But the "progressive" historians once more relegated the King's American supporters—erroneously—to the role of elitist reactionaries whose economic self-interest impeded the progress of the masses. And the "consensus" school was generally uncomfortable with the notion that there were indeed those Americans who, for whatever reason, chose to remain outside the revolutionary "mainstream." It was not really until the 1960s, and even more the seventies and eighties, that loyalist studies came into their own. Any student of loyalism in New Jersey should consult Larry R. Gerlach, "Loyalist Studies in New Jersey: Needs and Opportunities," *New Jersey History* 95 (1977): 69–84. And although they are slightly dated, no one should neglect Wallace Brown, *The King's Friends: The Composition and Motives of the American Loyalist Claimants* (Providence, 1965); *The Good Americans* (New York, 1969); or William Nelson, *The American Tory* (Boston, 1968). A more recent general study of loyalism is Robert M. Calhoon, *The Loyalists in Revolutionary America, 1760–1781* (New York, 1973). Philip Ranlet, *The New York Loyalists* (Knoxville, Tenn., 1986) argues that New York was not the "tory" stronghold that it was once suspected to be.

I found two approaches to the analysis of loyal Americans particularly useful in helping to establish the conceptual framework of this book. Both biographical studies and analyses of the ideology of the loyalists, particularly of members of the colonial elite, were essential to my understanding of William Franklin and his world. There are a number of excellent biographies of loyal members of the colonial elite. Bernard Bailyn's *The Ordeal of Thomas Hutchinson* (Cambridge, Mass., 1974) is superb, as it not only places loyalism within the mainstream of British-American thought, but also helps us understand the "tragic" dimensions of the American Revolution. There are other good depictions of upper-class loyalists, as well, most of which agree that American supporters of the King were not reactionary ideologues but, rather, shared many similarities with their patriot counterparts. In this vein are Carol Berkin's *Jonathan Sewall: Odyssey of an American Loyalist* (New York, 1974); John E. Ferling, *The Loyalist Mind: Joseph Galloway and the American Revolution* (University Park, Pa., 1977) and Elizabeth P. McCaughey, *From Loyalist to Founding Father: The Political Odyssey of William Samuel Johnson* (New York, 1980). Anne Zimmer, in *Jonathan Boucher: Loyalist in Exile* (Detroit,

1978), even manages to turn that arch-conservative into an American whose views were markedly similar to those held by the leaders of the cause he so vehemently opposed.

This same tendency to see, even to emphasize, the Whig antecedents of loyalist thought is apparent in many recent examinations of the ideology of the King's supporters. Especially fruitful are William A. Benton, *Whig Loyalism: An Aspect of Political Ideology in the American Revolutionary Era* (Rutherford, N. J., 1969); Jeffrey M. Nelson, "Ideology in Search of a Context: Eighteenth-Century British Political Thought and the Loyalists of the American Revolution," *The Historical Journal*, 20 (1977): 741–49; Mary Beth Norton, "The Loyalists' Critique of the Revolution," in *The Development of a Revolutionary Mentality: Library of Congress Symposia on the American Revolution* (Washington, D.C., 1972), 127–48; and Janice Potter, *The Liberty We Seek: Loyalist Ideology in Colonial New York and Massachusetts* (Cambridge, Mass., 1983). An interesting effort to reconstruct the psychological differences between loyalists and patriots is Thomas S. Martin's *Minds and Hearts: The American Revolution as a Philosophical Crisis* (Lanham, Md., 1984).

It is as difficult to study any loyalist without putting him or her in the general context of the revolutionary era, as it is unwise to attempt to understand the American Revolution without taking into account the loyalist view of the events preceding the Declaration of Independence. It would be impossible and no doubt fruitless to list all the interpretations of the American Revolution consulted for this study. A few are deserving of special attention, however, for they contributed heavily to the conceptual framework that informs my understanding of William Franklin. These include, especially, Bernard Bailyn, *The Ideological Origins of the American Revolution* (Cambridge, Mass., 1967) and his *Origins of American Politics* (New York, 1968); Pauline Maier, *From Resistance to Revolution: Colonial Radicals and the Development of American Opposition to Britain, 1765–1776* (New York, 1972), and her *The Old Revolutionaries: Political Lives in the Age of Samuel Adams* (New York, 1980); Caroline Robbins, *The Eighteenth-Century Commonwealth Man* (Cambridge, Mass., 1959); and Gordon Wood, *The Creation of the American Republic, 1776–87* (Chapel Hill, 1969). Jack P. Greene's *The Quest for Power: The Lower Houses of Assembly in the Southern Royal Colonies, 1689–1776* (Chapel Hill, 1963) remains a solid portrayal of the importance of the colonial assemblies in the years preceding the Revolution. Michael G. Kammen's *A Rope of Sand: The Colonial Agents, British Politics and the American Revolution* (New York, 1968) provides an understanding of the relationship of the colonial agents, the American colonies, and Whitehall.

A number of historians have attempted to understand the British perspective on the events preceding the American Revolution. Particularly interesting is the frankly revisionist analysis by Robert W. Tucker and David C. Hendrickson, *The Fall of the First British Empire: Origins of the War of American Independence* (Baltimore, 1982), which offers a view of English policy and practice with which William Franklin would easily have agreed. Also notable are Ian R. Christie and Benjamin W. Labaree, *Empire or Independence, 1760–1776: A British Dialogue on the Coming of the American Revolution* (New York, 1976); Alison Gilbert Olson, *Anglo-American Politics, 1660–1775: The Relationship Between Parties in England and Colonial America* (New York,

1973); and Charles Ritcheson, *British Politics and the American Revolution* (Norman, Okla., 1954). See, too, the essays in Peter Marshall and Glyn Williams, eds., *The British Atlantic Empire Before the Revolution* (London, 1980).

Every study of William Franklin begins with his more illustrious father. And if historians have paid little attention to William Franklin over the years, the wealth of material on the ever fascinating Benjamin Franklin is nothing short of daunting. Nevertheless, some studies do stand out. Carl Van Doren's *Benjamin Franklin* (New York, 1938) remains a solid, dependable and thorough biography and is as good a place as any to begin. It should be supplemented by the more readable Esmond Wright, *Franklin of Philadelphia* (Cambridge, Mass., 1986). Studies that give greater insight into Franklin's private life and his relationship to his family and friends include Thomas Fleming, *The Man Who Dared the Lightning: A New Look at Benjamin Franklin* (New York, 1971); Claude-Anne Lopez and Eugenia W. Herbert, *The Private Franklin: The Man and His Family* (New York, 1975); and Willard S. Randall's *A Little Revenge: Benjamin Franklin and His Son* (Boston, 1984). Many scholars have attempted to get inside the mind of Benjamin Franklin. Among the more interesting and successful of such efforts are Richard L. Bushman's "On the Uses of Psychology: Conflict and Conciliation in Benjamin Franklin," *History and Theory* 5 (1966): 225–40; Hugh J. Dawson, "Fathers and Sons: Franklin's 'Memoirs' as Myth and Metaphor," *Early American Literature* 14 (1979/89): 269–92; Norman S. Fiering, "Benjamin Franklin and the Way to Virtue," *American Quarterly* 30 (1978): 199–223; Gary Lindberg, *The Confidence Man in American Literature* (New York, 1982); and Robert F. Sayre, *The Examined Self: Benjamin Franklin, Henry Adams, and Henry James* (Princeton, 1964). An excellent analysis of Franklin's political views is Paul W. Conner's *Poor Richard's Politicks: Benjamin Franklin and His New American Order* (New York, 1965). Jack Greene's "The Alienation of Benjamin Franklin, British-American," *Journal of the Royal Society for the Encouragement of the Arts, Manufactures, and Commerce,* 124 (1976): 52–73, brilliantly synthesizes Franklin's psychology and his political views, highlighting the Doctor's pro-empire bent while explaining his ultimate decision to break with the empire he loved. Also valuable is Gerald S. Stourzh's "Reason and Power in Benjamin Franklin's Political Thought," *American Political Science Review* 47 (1953): 1092–1116. To understand Franklin's role in the fragmented world of Pennsylvania politics, the reader should consult Benjamni H. Newcomb, *Franklin and Galloway: A Political Partnership* (New Haven, 1972); John J. Zimmerman, "Benjamin Franklin and the Quaker Party," *WMQ* 3rd ser. 17 (1960): 291–313; and William S. Hanna, *Benjamin Franklin and Pennsylvania Politics* (Stanford, 1964). While Hanna's book is refreshingly iconoclastic, it should be read in conjunction with James H. Hutson's *Pennsylvania Politics 1746–1770: The Movement for Royal Government and Its Consequences* (Princeton, 1972).

It is surprising that no major scholarly biography of Governor William Franklin has yet been written. William A. Whitehead's "A Biographical Sketch of William Franklin," *New Jersey Historical Society Proceedings* 1st ser., 3 (1848): 137–59 contains useful kernels of information, but is decidedly dated. William H. Mariboe, "The Life of William Franklin, 1730–1813: *Pro Rege et Patria*" (Ph.D. diss., U. of Pennsylvania, 1962), is valuable, although it suffers from lack of organization and needs a tighter conceptual framework. Gerlach's brief *William Franklin: New Jersey's Last Royal Governor* (Trenton, 1975) provides an excellent overview of the governor's life, but it is not a comprehensive study. Randall's *A Little Revenge* is a lively attempt to analyze the relationship between the patriot father and the loyal son. Unfortunately, Randall is given to unfounded generalizations about both of the Franklins and vastly underestimates the close relationship that existed between the two men until at least 1774. A good short political analysis of William Franklin's term as governor is Catherine Fennelley's "William Franklin of New Jersey," *WMQ* 3rd ser. 6(1949): 361–82. Also useful are Randall, "William Franklin: The Making of a Conservative," in Robert A. East and Jacob Judd, *The Loyalist Americans: A Focus on Greater New York* (Tarrytown, N.Y., 1975), 56–73; Glen H. Smith, "William Franklin: Expedient Loyalist," *North Dakota Quarterly* 42 (1974): 57–75; and Calhoon's analysis of governors Franklin, Bull, and Wentworth in chapter 10 of *The Loyalists in Revolutionary America*. Kenneth S. Lynn's psychological portrayal of Franklin in *A Divided People* (Westport, Conn., 1977) is thought-provoking although it is not always on target.

Information dealing with William Franklin's youth and young adulthood is frustratingly sketchy. Yet recent studies of the relation between the early experiences of eighteenth-century children and their later political beliefs indicates that this is an area that can be neglected only at the biographer's peril. A good conceptual framework for understanding this crucial relationship is Jay Fliegelman's *Prodigals and Pilgrims: The American Revolution Against Patriarchal Authority, 1750–1800* (Cambridge, Mass., 1982). It should be supplemented by Edwin G. Burrows and Michael Wallace, "The American Revolution: The Ideology and Psychology of National Liberation," *Perspectives in American History* 6 (1972): 167–306; Winthrop D. Jordan, "Familial Politics: Thomas Paine and the Killing of the King, 1776," *Journal of American History* 60 (1973): 294–308; and Bruce Mazlich, "The American Revolution: The Ideology and Psychology of National Liberation," E. H. Kegan, compiler, *Leadership in the American Revolution* (Washington, D.C., 1974), 113–33. Also see Melvin Yazawa, *From Colonies to Commonwealth: Familial Ideology and the Beginnings of the American Republic* (Baltimore, 1985). For an understanding of the changing methods of child-rearing in the eighteenth century, see especially, Philip J. Greven, Jr., *The Protestant Temperament: Patterns of Child-Rearing, Religious Experience and the Self in Early America* (New York, 1977); Greven, *Child-Rearing Concepts, 1628–1861: Historical Sources* (Ithaca, Ill., 1973); J. H. Plumb, "The New World of Children in Eighteenth-Century England," *Past and Present* 67 (1975): 64–93; Daniel Blake Smith, "Autonomy and Affection: Parents and Children in Eighteenth-Century Chesapeake Families," *The Psycho-History Review*, 6 (1977/8): 32–51; Smith, *Inside the Great House: Planter Family Life in Eighteenth-Century Chesapeake Society* (Ithaca, 1980); and John F. Walzer, "A Period of Ambivalence: Eighteenth-Century American Childhood," in Lloyd de Mause, ed., *The History of Childhood* (New York, 1974). For the connection between John Locke's views on child-rearing and the development of personality and political beliefs in later life, see, in addition to the works mentioned above, R. W. K. Hinton, "Husbands, Fathers, and Conquerors: Patriarchalism in Hobbes and Locke," *Political Studies* 16 (1968): 55–67, and Geraint Perry, "Individuality,

Politics, and the Critique of Paternalism in John Locke," *Political Studies* 12 (1964): 163–77. The essays in John W. Yolton, ed., *John Locke: Problems and Perspectives: A Collection of New Essays* (Cambridge, Mass., 1969), are useful, especially Gordon J. Schochet's "The Family and the Origins of the State in Locke's Political Philosophy," pp. 81–98.

Only a smattering of information concerning Franklin's youth exists. For a dependable description of Philadelphia in the eighteenth century, see Carl Bridenbaugh's *Rebels and Gentlemen* (New York, 1942). Sister Joan de Lourdes CSJ, offers a nice description of the Pennsylvania assembly, where William worked as a clerk, in "The Organization and Procedure of the Pennsylvania Assembly, 1682–1776," *PMHB* 72 (1948): 215–39. G. B. Warden's "The Proprietary Group in Pennsylvania, 1754–1764," *WMQ*, 3rd ser. 21 (1964): 367–89, paints a clear picture of the Franklins' political enemies in pre-revolutionary Philadelphia. For material on Franklin's fiancée, Elizabeth Graeme Fergusson, see C. P. Keith, "The Wife and Children of Sir William Keith," *PMHB* 56 (1932): 1–8; John J. Loeper, *Elizabeth Graeme Fergusson of Graeme Park* (Philadelphia, 1974); and Martha Slotten, "Elizabeth Graeme Fergusson: A Poet in the 'Athens of North America,'" *PMHB* 108 (1984): 259–88.

For information on William Franklin's London, M. Dorothy George's *London Life in the Eighteenth-Century* (New York, 1926) provides a reliable overview. C. E. A. Bedwell's "American Middle Templars," *American Historical Review*, 25 (1919): 680–89 is valuable, as it points out that future patriots as well as future loyalists studied at London's Middle Temple. Both John Clive and Bernard Bailyn, "England's Cultural Provinces: Scotland and America," *WMQ* 3rd ser. 1 (1954): 200–213, and J. Bennett Nolan's *Benjamin Franklin in Scotland and Ireland, 1759 and 1771* (Philadelphia, 1956) help flesh out the emotional impact that the trip to Scotland must have had for the two Franklins. Little is known about Franklin's first wife, Elizabeth, but interested readers should consult Vernon Stumpf, "Who was Elizabeth Downes Franklin?" *PMHB* 94 (1970): 533, 534.

The best place to begin a study of New Jersey politics is Larry Gerlach's *Prologue to Independence: New Jersey in the Coming of the Revolution* (New Brunswick, 1976). Gerlach's approach is solid and his mastery of New Jersey politics is impressive. Moreover, he devotes considerable effort to understanding the role that William Franklin played in the colony as the revolutionary crisis developed. Other general works on the colony include Donald L. Kemmerer, *Path to Freedom: The Struggle for Self-Government in Colonial New Jersey, 1703–1776* (Princeton, 1940) and John E. Pomfret, *Colonial New Jersey: A History* (New York, 1973). There are a number of more specific topics that a student of pre-revolutionary New Jersey should master. James J. Nadelhaft, "Politics and the Judicial Tenure Fight in Colonial New Jersey," *WMQ* 3rd ser. 28 (1971): 46–63, is helpful in understanding the controversy that allowed William Franklin to secure his position as governor. Nadlehaft's study, along with John F. Burns's *Controversies Between Royal Governors and Their Assemblies in the Northern Colonies* (Boston, 1923) gives an indication of just how formidable a task Franklin faced as he tried to preserve both royal prerogatives and assembly rights in the colony of New Jersey. For an understanding of the troublesome controversy over paper money, see Joseph A. Ernst, *Money and Politics in America, 1755–1775: A Study in the Currency Act of*

1764 and the Political Economy of Revolution (Chapel Hill, 1973), and Thomas L. Purvis, Proprietors, Patronage, and Paper Money: Legislative Politics in New Jersey, 1703–1776 (New Brunswick, 1986). John Shy's "Quartering His Majesty's Forces in New Jersey," New Jersey Historical Society Proceedings 78 (1960): 82–94, and his Toward Lexington: The Role of the British Army in the Coming of the Revolution (Princeton, 1965) are especially useful in analyzing the quarrels over the Mutiny Act that chronically plagued Franklin and his assembly. For the governor's protracted quarrels with Customs Collector John Hatton, see Gerlach, "Customs and Contentions: John Hatton of Salem and Cohansey," New Jersey History 89 (1971): 69–92. And for the all-important robbery of the East Jersey treasury, see the slanted but still useful, Whitehead, "The Robbery of the Treasury of East Jersey in 1768," New Jersey Historical Society, Proceedings 5 (1851): 51–65; and the more judicious "Politics and Prerogatives: The Aftermath of the Robbery of the East Jersey Treasury," New Jersey History 90 (1972): 133–68 by Larry Gerlach. Background for the land riots in Monmouth and Essex counties can be found in Edward Countryman, " 'Out of the Bounds of the Law': Northern Land Rioters in the Eighteenth-Century," in A. F. Young, ed., The American Revolution: Explorations in the History of American Radicalism (Dekalb, Ill., 1976).

A number of individuals influenced Franklin and helped shape his existence during his long tenure as New Jersey's royal governor. His continued friendship with his old law tutor and political crony, Philadelphian Joseph Galloway, was especially important. For an understanding of Galloway see Ferling, Joseph Galloway, as well as Julian P. Boyd, Anglo-American Union: Joseph Galloway's Plans to Preserve the British Empire, 1774–1788 (Philadelphia, 1941); Calhoon, " 'I Have Deduced Your Rights': Joseph Galloway's Concept of His Role, 1774–1775," Pennsylvania History 35 (1968): 356–78, and Robert L. Schuyler, "Galloway's Plans for Anglo-American Union," Political Science Quarterly 57 (1942): 281–85. In New Jersey, Franklin was especially close to William Alexander, or as he preferred to call himself, Lord Stirling. Alan Valentine's Lord Stirling (New York, 1969) helps put this friendship in perspective, and is more accurate than the effort by Alexander's grandson, William Alexander Duer, The Life of William Alexander, Earl of Stirling (New York, 1847). Duer's work does contain many letters to and from Alexander, however, which makes the edition worth pursuing.

Any biographer of William Franklin must make some sense out of his confusing and entangling forays into land speculation. Jack M. Sosin's Whitehall and the Wilderness: The Middle West in British Colonial Policy, 1760–1775 (Lincoln, Neb., 1961) puts the question of land speculation into perspective, showing how the American—and the British—fascination with the West affected Anglo-American relations before Independence. Cecil Currey's Road to Revolution: Benjamin Franklin in England, 1765–1775 (New York, 1968) provides a good overview of the Franklins' wheelings and dealings, as it emphasizes the seamier side of western land speculation. Robert F. Oaks's "The Impact of British Western Policy in the Coming of the American Revolution," PMHB 101 (1977): 171–89, is also helpful. And Peter Marshall's "Lord Hillsborough, Samuel Wharton and the Ohio Grant," English Historical Review 80 (1965): 717–39, sheds some light on the American Secretary's role. Good biographies of the main characters involved in the Franklin's speculative adventures are hard to come by, but Sewell Elias Slick's William Trent and *the West* (Harrisburg, Pa., 1947), Albert T. Volwiler's *George Croghan and the Westward Movement, 1741–1782* (Cleveland, 1926), and Nicholas B. Wainwright's *George Croghan: Wilderness Diplomat* (Chapel Hill, 1959) are all worthwhile.

For Franklin's experiences as a prisoner of the rebel forces, see the appropriate sections of Randall's *A Little Revenge* as well as Joseph F. Folsom's "Governor Franklin in Litchfield Jail," New Jersey Historical Society, *Proceedings* 3 (Jan. 1918): 45–48. There are a number of good secondary sources describing New York during the war. Especially helpful are Oscar T. Barck, *New York City During the War for Independence* (New York, 1931) Alexander C. Flick, *Loyalism in New York During the American Revolution* (New York, 1901). See as well, Thomas J. Wertenbaker's *Father Knickerbocker Rebels: New York City During the Revolution* (New York, 1948).

Military histories of the American Revolution abound. Most useful for this study, because they focus either on the loyalist experience or on the politics of war as it was practiced in New York City, are W. O. Raymond, "Loyalists in Arms," New Brunswick Historical Society, *Collections* 4 (1904): 189–223; Paul H. Smith, *Loyalists and Redcoats: A Study in British Revolutionary Policy* (Chapel Hill, 1964); Edward H. Tebbenhoff's "The Associated Loyalists: An Aspect of Militant Loyalism," *New-York Historical Society Quarterly*, 63 (1979): 115–44; and Carl Van Doren, *Secret History of the American Revolution* (New York, 1941).

One aspect of the military experience, in particular, needs more attention. The treatment and politics of prisoners of war, especially of loyalist prisoners of war, merit further study. A few attempts are worthy of notice. John K. Alexander, "Forton Prison During the American Revolution," Essex Institute *Historical Collections* 103 (1967), Olive Anderson, "The Treatment of Prisoners of War During the American War of Independence," *Bulletin of the Institute of Historical Research* 28 (1955): 63–83, and Oaks's "Philadelphians in Exile: The Problem of Loyalty During the American Revolution" *PMHB* 96 (1972): 298–325, are all solid, though narrowly focused, studies of the problem. Larry G. Bowman, *Captive Americans: Prisoners During the American Revolution* (Athens, Ohio, 1976) is a good study of American prisoners. Charles H. Metzger's *The Prisoner in the American Revolution* (Chicago, 1971) provides the best general analysis of the issue, but it barely scratches the surface.

There are some good studies of the personalities with whom Franklin was involved in New York. At the top of the list is William B. Willcox's *Portrait of a General: Sir Henry Clinton in the War of Independence* (New York, 1964). Also helpful are Eugene Devereux, "Andrew Elliot: Lieutenant-Governor of the Province of New York," *PMHB* 11 (1887): 129–50; Robert Ernst, "Andrew Elliot, Forgotten Loyalist of Occupied New York," *New York History* 57 (1976): 285–320; Ira Gruber, *The Howe Brothers of the American Revolution* (New York, 1972); Paul H. Smith, "Sir Guy Carleton, Peace Negotiations and the Evacuation of New York," *Canadian Historical Review* 50 (1969): 245–64; and L. F. S. Upton, "William Smith of New York and Quebec" (Ph.D. diss., University of Minnesota, 1957). For insights into Lord Germain's policies, see Gerald S. Brown, *The American Secretary: The Colonial Policy of Lord Germain, 1775–1778* (Ann Arbor, 1963).

Mary Beth Norton's *The British Americans: The Loyalist Exiles in England,*

1774–1790 (Boston, 1972) remains as far and away the best complete account of the loyalists' exile experience. Norton's "Eighteenth-Century American Women in Peace and War: The Case of the Loyalists," WMQ 3rd ser. 33 (1976): 386–409, is helpful in understanding the effect her husband's captivity had on Elizabeth Franklin.

Common Abbreviations

A full citation of each work cited appears in the Notes.

ABF	Leonard Labaree, ed., *The Autobiography of Benjamin Franklin*
APS	American Philosophical Society
BF	Benjamin Franklin
BM Add. MSS.	British Museum Additional Manuscripts
BHQP	British Headquarters Papers
Clements	William L. Clements Library, University of Michigan
DF	Deborah Franklin
EG	Elizabeth Graeme
GW	George Washington
GW, *Writings*	John C. Fitzpatrick, ed., *The Writings of George Washington*
Houghton	Houghton Library, Harvard University
HSP	Historical Society of Pennsylvania
JG	Joseph Galloway
JW	Jonathan Williams
JW Coll.	Jonathan Williams Collection
LC	Library of Congress
NJA	F. W. Ricord, ed., *Documents Relating to the Colonial History of the State of New Jersey*
NJHS	New Jersey Historical Society
NJPCS	*Minutes of the Provincial Council of Safety of the State of New Jersey*
NYHS	New-York Historical Society
NYPL	New York Public Library
PBF	Leonard Labaree, et. at., ed., *The Papers of Benjamin Franklin*
PMHB	*Pennsylvania Magazine of History and Biography*
PRO AO	Public Record Office, Audit Office
PRO CO	Public Record Office, Colonial Office
PRO Treas.	Public Record Office, Treasury

Stirling	Stirling Library, Yale University
SW	Samuel Wharton
TW	Thomas Wharton
V & P	*Votes and Proceedings of the General Assembly of the Province of New Jersey*
WF	William Franklin
WMQ	*William and Mary Quarterly*
WS	William Strahan
WTF	William Temple Franklin

Notes

1. An "Indulgent" Father, a Loyal Son

1. Benjamin Franklin (BF) to Jane Mecom, [June] 1748, Leonard Labaree, et al., eds., *The Papers of Benjamin Franklin* (New Haven, 1959–   ), 3: 303 (hereafter, *PBF*).
2. BF to Jane Mecom, 24 Oct. 1751, *PBF*, 4: 199, 200.
3. See Robert F. Sayre, *The Examined Self: Benjamin Franklin, Henry Adams and Henry James* (Princeton, 1964), 13.
4. Leonard W. Labaree, ed., *The Autobiography of Benjamin Franklin* (New Haven, 1964), 128 (hereafter *ABF*).
5. Both contemporaries of the Franklins and historians have guessed at the identity of William's mother. See Anon., "What is Sauce for a Goose is also Sauce for a Gander" (Philadelphia, 1764; Rev. Bennett Allen, *London Morning Post*, 1 June, 1779; Charles H. Hart, "Who Was the Mother of Franklin's Son," *Pennsylvania Magazine of History and Biography* (hereafter *PMHB*) 35 (July 1911): 308–14; Theodore Parker, *Historic Americans*, ed. Samuel A. Eliot (Boston, 1908), 29; Paul L. Ford, *Who Was the Mother of Franklin's Son, A Conundrum Hitherto Given Up, Now Partly Answered* (New York, 1889), 24, 25.
6. See, for example, Van Doren, *Benjamin Franklin* (New York, 1938), 91; *PBF*, 4:447; William E. Mariboe, "The Life of William Franklin, 1730 (1)—1813: 'Pro Rege et Patria' " (Ph.D. dissertation, University of Pennsylvania, 1962), 24; Richard Morris, *Seven Who Shaped Our Destiny: The Founding Fathers as Revolutionaries* (New York, 1973), 13.
7. George Roberts to Robert Crofton, 9 Oct. 1763, Charles Morton Smith MSS, Volume 2, Historical Society of Pennsylvania, Philadelphia (hereafter, HSP).
8. Anon., "Sauce for a Goose"; John Penn Esq. to Earl of Stirling, 3 Sept. 1762, William Alexander Duer, ed., *The Life of William Alexander Earl of Stirling* (New York, 1847), 70, 71; John Watts to Sir Charles Hardy, n.d., *Letterbook of John Watts 1762–1765*, New-York Hist. Soc., *Coll.* 61 (1928): 101–3; John Adams, *Diary and Autobiography*, ed. L. H. Butterfield, 4 vols. (Cambridge, 1961), 4:151.
9. Ford, *Who Was the Mother of Franklin's Son?*, 16; Morris, *Seven Who Shaped Our Destiny*, 13; "Extracts from the Diary of Daniel Fisher, 1755," *PMHB* 17 (1893): 276 ff. Deborah's hostility cannot be shrugged off. D. B. Smith argues that children whose parents acted as a "collective unit" in relationship to their children had offspring who "could form a clearer, and more secure self-identity." Smith, *Inside the Great House: Planter*

Family Life in Eighteenth-Century Chesapeake Society (Ithaca, N.Y., 1980), 35; Smith, "Autonomy and Affection: Parents and Children in Eighteenth Century Chesapeake Families," *The Psycho-History Review* (1977–78), 32–51. See also Tess Forrest, "The Paternal Roots of Male Character Development," *Psychoanalytic Review* 54 (1967): 54.

10. *Pennsylvania Gazette*, 30 Dec. 1736; Deborah Franklin (DF) to BF, 13 on 15 June 1770, *PBF*, 17:175, BF to Jane Mecom, 13 Jan. 1772, *PBF*, 19:29.

11. Until William was nine, the family lived above Ben's printing and stationery shop; in 1739 they moved four doors closer to the river, where they occupied the second floor and the attic of their new residence, leaving the ground floor for the post office that was established in the fall of 1737. Even then their quarters were not spacious. Mariboe, "William Franklin," 26, 27; *Pa. Gazette*, 27 Oct. 1737; Van Doren, *Benjamin Franklin*, 125.

12. See, for example, Peter Kalm, *Travels into North America* (Barre, Mass., 1972), 28.

13. Thomas Scharf and Thomas Westcott, *History of Pennsylvania, 1609–1884*, 3 vols. (Philadelphia, 1884), 1:234, 238; Van Doren, *Benjamin Franklin*, 117, 118, 138–41; *ABF*, 171–82. BF probably attained the clerkship, a non-elective position, with the help of speaker Andrew Hamilton. Sister Joan de Lourdes Leonard, "The Organization and Procedure of the Pennsylvania Assembly, 1682–1776, Part I," *PMHB* 72 (July 1948): 234.

14. Thomas Fleming, *The Man Who Dared the Lightning: A New Look at Benjamin Franklin* (New York, 1971), 106. There is some evidence to indicate that a child's ability to interact easily with many adults has a positive effect in helping him adjust to the adult world. See Philip J. Greven, *Four Generations: Population, Land and Family in Colonial Andover, Massachusetts* (Ithaca, N.Y., 1970), 254–58; D. B. Smith, "Autonomy," 39 .

15. Evarts B. Green and Virginia D. Harrington, *American Population Before the Federal Census, 1780* (Gloucester, Mass., 1916), 117, 118; Alexander Hamilton, *Gentleman's Progress: The Itinerarium of Dr. Alexander Hamilton, 1744*, ed. Carl Bridenbaugh (Chapel Hill, 1948), 21; Willard S. Randall, "Boom Town Grows Along the Delaware," in David R. Boldt and W. S. Randall, eds., *The Founding City* (Philadelphia, 1976), 19; Grant Miles Simon, "Houses and Early Life in Philadelphia," *Transactions of the American Philosophical Society* 43 (1953): 286.

16. See for example, Hamilton, *Gentleman's Progress*, 19–23, 29; James Birket, *Some Cursory Remarks Made by James Birket in His Voyage to North America 1750–1751* (New Haven, 1916), 63–69; Andrew Burnaby, *Travels through North America*, ed. Rufus R. Wilson (New York, 1904), 89–98; Kalm, *Travels*, 25–37.

17. Simon, "Houses," 282; G. B. Warden, "The Proprietary Group in Pennsylvania, 1754–1764," *William and Mary Quarterly* (hereafter WMQ) 3rd ser. 21 (1964): 379, 380.

18. Cecil B. Currey, *Code Number 72: Ben Franklin: Patriot or Spy* (Englewood Cliffs, N.J., 1972), 20; Benjamin H. Newcomb, *Franklin and Galloway: A Political Partnership* (New Haven, 1972), 11; Paul W. Conner, *Poor Richard's Politicks: Benjamin Franklin and His New American Order* (New York, 1965), 213–15; *ABF*, 43, 53, 58.

19. See W. S. Randall, A Little Revenge: Benjamin Franklin and His Son (Boston, 1984).

20. See ABF, 64, "Proposals Relating to the Education of Youth in Philadelphia (1749)," PBF 3:397–421, for direct evidence that BF endorsed Locke's educational theories.

21. Edwin G. Burrows and Michael Wallace, "The American Revolution: The Ideology and Psychology of National Liberation," Perspectives in American History 6 (1972): 255–67; Geraint Perry, "Individuality, Politics and the Critique of Paternalism in John Locke," Political Studies 12 (1964): 172, 173; J. H. Plumb, "The New World of Children in Eighteenth Century England," Past and Present 67 (May 1975): 69; R. W. K. Hinton, "Husbands, Fathers and Conquerors: Patriarchalism in Hobbes and Locke," Political Studies 16 (1968): 55–67; Gordon J. Schochet, "The Family and the Origins of the State in Locke's Political Philosophy," 81–98, in John W. Yolton, ed., John Locke, Problems and Perspectives: A Collection of New Essays (Cambridge, 1969); John Dunn, "The Politics of Locke in England and America in the Eighteenth Century," 45–80, in Yolton, Locke; Jay Fliegelman, Prodigals and Pilgrims: The American Revolution against Patriarchal Authority, 1750–1800 (Cambridge, 1982), 12–35; Bernard Wishy, The Child and the Republic: The Dawn of Modern American Child Nurture (Philadelphia, 1968), 18, John Locke, Two Treatises on Government, ed. Peter Laslett (Cambridge, 1960), 1:52, 53; 2:55, 56, 58; Sheila L. Skemp, "William Franklin: His Father's Son," PMHB 109 (April 1985): 145–78. See also Melvin Yazawa, From Colonies to Commonwealth: Familial Ideology and Beginnings of the American Republic (Baltimore, 1985).

22. BF to DF, 3 Oct. 1770, PBF, 17:239. See also BF to Jane Mecom [June] 1748, 21 May 1757, PBF, 3:303; 7:215.

23. ABF, 69n.

24. Hugh J. Dawson, "Fathers and Sons: Franklin's 'Memoirs' as Myth and Metaphor," Early American Literature 14 (Winter 1979–80): 273. D. B. Smith has argued that the attention and affection showered upon children in upper-class Chesapeake households enabled them to absorb parental values and to develop a strong sense of duty to their parents that dominated them throughout their adult lives. Children raised in an atmosphere of love were more likely to remain obedient and respectful to their parents than were children whose early lives were characterized either by harsh authoritarianism or mere indifference. Paradoxically, that same care and attention provided the basis for the child's autonomy. Smith, "Autonomy," 50; Smith, Great House, 82, 86, 88, 102.

25. Pa. Gazette, 26 Dec. 1734, 17 June 1742; Mariboe, "William Franklin," 27; Claude Anne Lopez and Eugenia W. Herbert, The Private Franklin: The Man and His Family (New York, 1975), 60; Van Doren, Benjamin Franklin, 200, 201; PBF, 2:29n, 388, 388n; Glen H. Smith, "William Franklin: Expedient Loyalist," North Dakota Quarterly 42 (1974): 58; William A. Whitehead, Contributions to the Early History of Perth Amboy and Adjoining Country (New York, 1856), 85; BF to Jane Mecom [June] 1748, PBF, 3:303.

26. Ibid; ABF, 53, 57, 170.

27. Van Doren, Benjamin Franklin, 18; Mariboe, "William Franklin," 36.

28. *PBF*, 3:89n; Joseph F. Folsom, "Colonel Peter Schuyler at Albany," New Jersey Historical Society, *Proceedings*, n. ser. 1 (1916): 161, 162; Carl Woodward, *Ploughs and Politics: Charles Read on New Jersey and His Notes on Agriculture: 1715–1774* (New Brunswick, N.J., 1941), 65; Fred Anderson, *A People's Army: Massachusetts Soldiers and Society in the Seven Years' War* (Chapel Hill, 1984).

29. *Pa. Gazette*, 7 May 1747; W.F. Papers, MSS., Gratz Collection, HSP; WF to Peter Schuyler, 19 June 1759, *PBF*, 8:406.

30. BF to [John Franklin], 2 April 1747; BF to Cadwallader Colden, 5 June 1747; BF to William Strahan (WS), 28 Nov. 1747; 19 Oct. 1748, *PBF*, 3:119, 142, 213, 321.

31. BF to WS, 19 Oct., 1748, *PBF*, 3:321. Under the circumstance, W. S. Randall's implication that Ben's penury kept William from continuing his military career seems more than a little unfair. Other Americans, including an equally ambitious George Washington, were rudely turned away whenever they sought to attain preferments in the British army. Randall, *Revenge*, 56.

32. W. Neil Franklin, "Pennsylvania-Virginia Rivalry for the Indian Trade of the Ohio Valley," *Mississippi Valley Historical Review* 20 (1934): 465, 466.

33. Sewell Elias Slick, *William Trent and the West* (Harrisburg, Pa., 1947), 4–9; Albert T. Volwiler, *George Croghan and the Westward Movement, 1741–1782* (Cleveland, 1926), 110–13; Clarence W. Alford, *The Illinois Country* (Springfield, Ill., 1920), 263.

34. How Franklin managed to wangle an invitation to join the expedition is unclear. Volwiler maintains the trip was arranged by BF "as part of William's education." Volwiler, *George Croghan*, 66. But it is just as likely that he made the deal for himself. He may have known Trent before he left Philadelphia, and almost surely had some contact with him at Albany. Randall, *Revenge*, 56.

35. Slick, *William Trent*, 9; Conrad Weiser, *Journal of a Tour to the Ohio, Aug. 11-Oct. 2, 1748*, Reuben G. Thwaites, ed., *Early Western Travels, 1748–1765* (Cleveland, 1904), 12, 19, 24, 14n.

36. BF to Peter Collinson, 18 Oct. 1748, *PBF*, 3:320. Unfortunately, the journal no longer exists.

37. Ibid.

38. *ABF*, 195; Richard Morris, *Seven Who Shaped Our Destiny*, 15. See William Franklin (WF) to BF, 13 Nov. 1766, *PBF*, 13:501, for an indication that WF saw printing as a relatively lowly activity.

39. John T. Faris, *The Romance of Old Philadelphia* (Philadelphia, 1918), 121; G. B. Warden, "Pennsylvania Proprietors," 379; John F. Watson, *Annals of Philadelphia and Pennsylvania in the Olden Time*, 2 vols. (Philadelphia, 1860), 1:284, 285. Despite its proprietary flavor, BF did not initially view its activities with hostility. In fact, DF's name was included on a 1757 list of "Belles Dames of Philadelphia fashionables," along with the Graemes, Franks, Shippens, Burds, and Steadmans. Watson, *Annals*, 1:285.

40. Fleming, *Lightning*, 3, 24; "Extracts from the Diary of Daniel Fisher, 1755," 276ff; Mariboe, "William Franklin," 146, 147; Thomas Collinson to His Uncle, 12 Sept., 1760, *PBF*, 9:212; Lopez and Herbert, *Private*, 62; BF to Abiah Franklin, 12 April 1750, *PBF*, 3:474, 475.

41. *ABF*, 195; Morris, *Seven Who Shaped Our Destinies*, 15.
42. *ABF*, 171, 172, 196, 197. William Hanna is no doubt correct in maintaining that at least until 1750 BF was "an obscure provincial Philadelphian" whose acquaintances "had no reason to be awed by him or to imagine that they lived in the age of Franklin." Hanna, *Benjamin Franklin and Pennsylvania Politics* (Stanford, 1964), 23; see also pp. ix, 51, 72.
43. *ABF*, 197.
44. Randall argues that BF found his son's interest in law distasteful. Randall, *Revenge*, 64. In fact BF encouraged both WF and later his grandson to enter the legal profession, and he found the law a "reputable" occupation. BF to WF, 1 Aug. 1774, *PBF*, 21:266.
45. Robert M. Calhoon, " 'I Have Deduced Your Rights': Joseph Galloway's Concept of His Role, 1774–1775," *Pennsylvania History* 35 (1968): 359; Newcomb, *Franklin and Galloway*, 6, 131. In 1753, Galloway (JG) would marry Grace Growden, daughter of Lawrence Growden, a member of Penn's council and second justice of the Supreme Court of Pennsylvania. Thus JG had important connections with the proprietary party, whose pretensions to power he would one day adamantly oppose. G. B. Warden, "Pennsylvania Proprietors," 373.
46. BF to WS, 6 Dec. 1750, *PBF*, 4:76; Edw[ar]d Shippen to Joseph Shippen, 17 Jan. 1753, Shippen Papers, American Philosophical Society, Philadelphia (hereafter APS). William's name was entered in the Middle Temple on 11 Feb. 1751. *PBF*, 4:78n; Edward Alfred Jones, *American Members of the Inns of Court* (London, 1924), 78; Carl Bridenbaugh, *Rebels and Gentlemen* (New York, 1942), 193; Jones, *Inns of Court*.
47. BF to Jane Mecom, 24 Oct. 1751, *PBF*, 4:200, 201.
48. The clerk was kept very busy. Among his other duties, he maintained all records, called out the election returns and the qualifications of members, drafted bills, transcribed acts, made the sessions laws and searched journals for precedents. Leonard, "Pennsylvania Assembly," 235.
49. *ABF*, 197; WF, "The Belles of Philadelphia," n.d., Franklin MSS, New Jersey Historical Society, Newark, N.J. (hereafter, NJHS); James H. Hutson, "BF and Pennsylvania Politics, 1751–1755: A Reappraisal." *PMHB* 92 (July 1969): 353; *Votes of the Assembly* 5, in *Pennsylvania Archives*, 8th ser. 5:3903, 3904, 3913.
50. WF to BF, 28 June 1753, *PBF*, 4:513. Larry R. Gerlach, *William Franklin: New Jersey's Last Royal Governor* (Trenton, 1975), 10.
51. Gerlach, *William Franklin*, 9, 10; Mariboe, "William Franklin," 50; Lopez and Herbert, *Private*, 53.
52. *PBF*, 4:116; Mariboe, "William Franklin," 54; "Extracts from the Diary of Daniel Fisher, 1755," 272; Bridenbaugh, *Rebels and Gentlemen*, 334; BF to Abiah Franklin, 12 April, 1750, *PBF*, 3:475.
53. *PBF*, 4:367; *ABF*, 244; Fleming, *Lightning*, 1–6; Priestly's Account, *PBF*, 4:367–69; WF to BF, 28 June, 12 July 1753, BF to WF, 23 July 1753, BF to Peter Collinson, Sept. 1753, *PBF*, 4:513, 514; *PBF*, 5:4–7, 15, 69, 70. See Randall, *Revenge*, 60–63, for evidence that BF did not always give WF full credit for his contributions.
54. *ABF*, 229, 230; Burnaby, *Travels*, 99. For analyses of the complex issues characterizing Pennsylvania politics in this period, see Hutson, *Pennsylvania Politics, 1746–1770: The Movement for Royal Government and Its*

Consequences (Princeton, 1972), 19–40; Newcomb, *Franklin and Gallo-way*, 18–24; Hanna, *Benjamin Franklin and Pennsylvania Politics.*

55. *ABF*, 212–14; BF to Peter Collinson, 26 June 1755, *PBF*, 6:86. WF's connections were forged in the social circles he frequented after King George's War. But BF, too, had his proprietary contacts. Chief Justice William Allen and college provost William Smith were close friends of both BF and JG, and were also staunch advocates of proprietary privilege. BF also had ties with Dr. Thomas Cadwalader, a member of the Penns' council who joined the Philosophical Society and BF's Society for Promoting Useful Knowledge. Newcomb, *Franklin and Galloway*, 21; Warden, "Pennsylvania Proprietors," 374.

56. See Ralph L. Ketcham, "Conscience, War and Politics in Pennsylvania, 1755–1757," *WMQ* 3rd ser. 20 (July 1963): 416–39, especially p. 419.

57. Lopez and Herbert, *Private*, 62; *ABF*, 209; *PBF*, 5:392–417—see especially p. 399 for indications that BF blamed colonial disunity for the continued French threat.

58. *ABF*, 216.

59. Ibid., 216–25.

60. BF to Peter Collinson, 25 Aug., 1755, *PBF*, 6:167, 168; Van Doren, *Benjamin Franklin*, 228; Broadside 156, 30 May 1755, APS; *ABF*, 219, 221, 222, Van Doren, *Benjamin Franklin*, 228, 230; Fleming, *Lightning*, 43, 45; Whitfield J. Bell, Jr., and L. W. Labaree, "Franklin and the 'Wagon Affair,' 1755," American Philosophical Soc. Proc. 101 (1957): 554–57.

61. William Buchanan Carlisle to Gen. Braddock, 21 July 1755; Officers Account, 15 July 1755, Misc. Coll., HSP; *ABF*, 224, 225; Daniel Dulany, "Letter to [Charles Carroll?]," 9 Dec. 1755, *PMHB* 3 (1879): 24.

62. See Zimmerman, "Benjamin Franklin and the Quaker Party," 292, 293, for a brief analysis of the division *within* the Quaker party at this time. See also Burnaby, *Travels*, 99; Newcomb, *Franklin and Galloway*, 23–26.

63. *ABF*, 229.

64. Ibid., 229, 230; Dulany, "Letter," 24; William Allen to Ferdinando Paris, 25 Nov. 1755; to William Beckford, 27 Nov. 1755; to D. Barclay and Sons, 17 Dec. 1755, William B. Walker, *Burd Papers: Extracts from Chief Justice William Allen's Letter Book* (n.p., 1897), 30–34; Votes of the Assembly 5: 4094ff; Newcomb, *Franklin and Galloway*, 26–28; Zimmerman, "Benjamin Franklin and the Quaker Party," 306, 307.

65. William Smith, *A Brief State of the Province of Pennsylvania* (London, 1755); Joseph Shippen to Edward Shippen, Sr., 13 Dec. 1755, Balch Papers, Shippen MS., HSP; "Humphrey Scourge," *Tit for Tat, or The Score Wip'd Off* (Philadelphia, 1755); Ketcham, "Benjamin Franklin and William Smith: New Light on an Old Philadelphia Quarrel," *PMHB* 87 (April 1964): 146; Pa. Gazette, 1 Jan. 1756; Pa. Journal, 25 March, 22 April, 17 June 1756.

66. Watson, *Annals* 2:165.

67. Hamilton, a former friend of BF's was Chief Justice William Allen's brother-in-law. He was no doubt sent to keep an eye on BF's activities, and in fact the entire mission was characterized by fighting between the Franklins and the proprietary forces. See Randall, *Revenge*, chap. 4; J. Bennett Nolan, *General Benjamin Franklin: The Military Career of a Philosopher* (Philadelphia, 1936), 35–37, 49, 50.

68. *ABF*, 231–37; Provincial Commissioners Instructions to William Parsons, *PBF*, 6:313, 314.
69. *ABF*, 231; WF to Timothy Horsfield, 21 June 1756, *PBF*, 6: 401, 462; *PBF*, 6: 342–48.
70. *ABF*, 232, 233; Thomas Lloyd to [?], 30 Jan. 1756, Franklin Papers, 1:141, APS.
71. Ibid.
72. Ibid., *ABF*, 233–35; Mariboe, "William Franklin," 64.
73. *BF* to George Whitefield, 2 July 1756 *PBF*, 6:468, 469; Fleming, *Lightning*, 58, 59.

2. Father, Brother, and Companion

1. WF to Elizabeth Graeme (EG), 17 July 1757, Emmett Collection, New York Public Library (hereafter, NYPL).
2. WS to DF, 13 Dec. 1757, *PBF* 7:297.
3. See especially *PBF*, 6:409–12; 415–20, for an analysis of the battle over the militia commission and its significance in Pennsylvania politics.
4. BF himself won re-election. John Hughes and JG, both BF protégés, were among the new members of the assembly who would be instrumental in forging BF's coalition. See especially Newcomb, *Franklin and Galloway*, 32–36; Zimmerman, "Benjamin Franklin and the Quaker Party," 311, 312.
5. *ABF*, 238, 239; *PBF*, 6: 425n; Cadwallader Colden to Peter Collinson, 23 April 1756; Richard Peters to Thomas Penn, 1 June 1756; BF to Peter Collinson, 5 Nov. 1756, *PBF*, 7:13n, 73, 13, 14. Both Mariboe and Fleming claim that WF "probably" instigated the incident, but there is no evidence to substantiate this charge. Mariboe, "William Franklin," 65; Fleming, *Lightning*, 55, 56.
6. *ABF*, 248; Newcomb, *Franklin and Galloway*, 37–40; Fleming, *Lightning*, 59–61.
7. BF to Isaac Norris, 9 Feb. 1763, *PBF*, 10:194; *ABF*, 93–95, 115.
8. WF to EG, 26 Feb. 1757, Simon Gratz, "Some Material for a Biography of Mrs. Elizabeth Fergusson, née Graeme," *PMHB* 39 (1915): 260; Martha Slotten, "Elizabeth Graeme Fergusson, A Poet in the 'Athens of North America,'" *PMHB* (1984): 259, 260; Warden, "Proprietary Group," 373: *PBF*, 7: 177n; Bridenbaugh, *Rebels and Gentlemen*, 192; WF to EG, 7 April 1757, *PBF*, 7: 178.
9. EG to Benjamin Rush, 23 Dec. 1797, *PBF*, 7:177n. Attempts to show that BF totally disapproved of his son's involvement with a representative of "aristocratic" privilege and proprietary leanings are misleading. BF was no less immune to the charms of Philadelphia's elite than was WF. See Randall, *Revenge*, 102, 106.
10. *ABF*, 80–82; Slotten, "Elizabeth Fergusson," 272; Warden, "Proprietary Group," 385.
11. WF's illegitimacy was probably not an issue, as Ann Graeme's father had sired two illegitimate children of his own. The Graemes were certainly in no position to cast moral aspersions on WF on this account. Charles P. Keith, "The Wife and Children of Sir William Keith," *PMHB* 56 (1932): 3.

12. WF to Mrs. Abercrombie, 24 Oct. 1758; Mrs. Ann Graeme to EG, 3 Dec. 1762, Gratz, "Elizabeth Graeme," 265, 267, 269. Gratz incorrectly indicates that the October letter to Mrs. Abercrombie was addressed directly to EG.

13. WF to Mrs. Abercrombie, 24 Oct. 1758, ibid., 265.

14. *ABF*, 107.

15. WF to EG, 7 April 1757, *PBF*, 7:177, 178.

16. *ABF*, 250, 251.

17. G. S. Eddy, ed., "Account Book of Benjamin Franklin Kept by Him During His First Mission to England as Provincial Agent, 1757–1762," *PMHB* 55 (1931): 97–133; WF to EG, 11 April 1757, William Franklin Papers, Simon Gratz Autograph Collection, HSP. Both Fleming and Bernard Fay indicate that WF admired Temple because of his "aristocratic" pretensions and his "ability to drop the names of England's great and near great." This is totally speculative. Fleming, *Lightning*, 66; Bernard Fay, *Franklin, the Apostle of His Times* (Boston, 1929), 262.

18. WF to EG, 12 May 1757, *PBF*, 7:213; WF to EG, 16 May 1757, Gratz, "Elizabeth Graeme," 262; BF to [Peter Franklin?], 21 May 1757, *PBF*, 7:214; Adam Gordon, "Journal of Lord Adam Gordon," in Newton D. Mereness, ed. *Travels in the North American Colonies* (New York, 1916), 413, 414; Thomas Pownall, "A Topographical Description of . . . Parts of North America," in Oral Coad, ed., *New Jersey Travelers Accounts, 1524–1971: A Descriptive Bibliography* (Meutchen, N.J., 1972), 19.

19. WF to EG, 16 May 1757, Gratz, "Elizabeth Graeme," 262.

20. WF to EG, 2 June, 17 July 1757, *PBF*, 7:234, 243, 244; *ABF*, 258, 259.

21. Ibid., 261. Fothergill, physician, amateur scientist, and influential lobbyist for the Society of Friends, would prove an extremely useful contact. Botanist Peter Collinson, with whom BF had communicated most of the results of his electrical experiments, was also a Quaker. His close ties with Dr. John Pringle and Joseph Priestly made him an equally valuable friend. *PBF*, 4:126n; Dorthea W. Singer, "Sir John Pringle and His Circle, Part I," *Annals of Science* 6 (1949): 164.

22. *ABF*, 259. See J. A. Cochrane, *Dr. Johnson's Printer: The Life of William Strahan* (Cambridge, 1964), 10, 61, 67, and Robert D. Harlan, "William Strahan's American Book Trade, 1744–1776," *Library Quarterly* 31 (1961), 235, 236, for an explanation of the Franklin-Hall-Strahan connection.

23. Verner W. Crane, "The Club of Honest Whigs," *WMQ* 3rd ser. 23 (1966): 211–19. Pringle, who would shortly become King George III's personal physician, was well known at court. He also had connections with London's non-conformist, literary, and scientific circles. And, as a member of the Royal Society, he had international connections as well. Like so many of BF's London friends, he was a Scotsman who received his early training at the University of Edinburgh. Singer, "Pringle," 129, 142, 160.

24. *ABF*, 205n, 261; WF to EG, 9 Dec. 1757, *PBF*, 7:289; BF to Isaac Norris, 9 Feb. 1763, *PBF*, 10:194. See M. Dorothy George, *London Life in the Eighteenth Century* (New York, 1926), 110, 114–40, 160, 273, and Ian R. Christie and Benjamin W. Labaree, *Empire or Independence, 1760–1776* (New York, 1976), 1, 2, for a picture of London at this time.

25. Lorenzo Sabine, *Loyalists of the American Revolution*, 2 vols. (Boston, 1864), 1:438; William Alexander Duer, ed. *The Life of William Alexan-*

der, *Earl of Stirling* (New York, 1847), 80n; Glen Smith, "Expedient Loyalist," 59; Fay, *Franklin*, 272, 293; Van Doren, *Benjamin Franklin*, 272.

26. Philip Livingston to William Alexander, 25 Oct. 1762, Duer, *William Alexander*, 68; Dr. Thomas Graeme to EG, 1 Jan. 1763; Gratz, "Elizabeth Graeme," 272; Sabine, *Loyalists*, 1:438.

27. John Dickinson to Mary Dickinson, 19 Jan. 1754; to Samuel Dickinson, 18 Jan., 25 May 1754, in H. Trevor Colbourn, ed., "A Pennsylvania Farmer at the Court of King George: John Dickinson's London Letters, 1754–1756, Part 1," *PMHB* 86 (1962): 253, 251, 269; John Hancock to Thomas Hancock, 14 Jan. 1761; to Ebenezer Hancock, 31 March 1761, "Letters from London, 1760–1761," Mass. Hist. Soc., *Proceedings* 43 (1909–10): 196–98; William Franklin Accounts, 1757, Franklin Papers, 67:111, APS; David Hall to WF, 18 Jan. 1759; 5, 31 March, 18 April 1760; 9 Feb., 20 July 1761; David Hall to WS, 18 Jan. 1759, David Hall Letterbook, APS; Eddy, "Accounts," 104ff; Van Doren, *Benjamin Franklin*, 272; C. E. A. Bedwell, "American Middle Templars," *American Historical Review* 25 (1919): 680, 681; William Allen to D. Barclay and Sons, 15 Feb., 12 April 1762; 25 Sept. 1764, Walker, *Burd Papers*, 49, 50, 56.

28. *ABF*, 118, 125, 126, 145; BF to Isaac Norris, 9 Feb. 1763, *PBF*, 10:194; William Allen to D. Barclay and Sons, 15 Feb. 1762, Walker, *Burd Papers*, 49; Van Doren, *Benjamin Franklin*, 272; Eddy, "Accounts," 102; BF to DF, 19 Feb. 1758, *PBF*, 7:380; Currey, *Code Number* 72, 24, 41, 73.

29. BF to Hugh Roberts, 26 Feb. 1761, *PBF*, 9:280.

30. See, for example, Jack Greene, "The Alienation of Benjamin Franklin, British American," *Journal of the Royal Society for the Encouragement of the Arts, Manufactures and Commerce* 124 (1976): 53–56; Hanna, *Benjamin Franklin and Pennsylvania Politics*, 174; Fleming, *Lightning*, 174, 176; Yehoshua Ariel, *Individualism and Nationalism in American Ideology* (Cambridge, 1964), 46, 47; Fay, *Franklin*, vi; Ralph Ketcham, "Benjamin Franklin and William Smith," 162.

31. WF to EG, 9 Dec. 1757, *PBF*, 7:290; WF to Col. Peter Schuyler, 19 June 1759, *PBF*, 8:407.

32. Newcomb, *Franklin and Galloway*, 50n; *ABF*, 261, 262.

33. *ABF*, 262–64. Paris was a good friend of William Allen, a political enemy of BF.

34. WF to EG, 9 Dec. 1757, *PBF*, 7:291, 255–63. See also Lopez and Herbert, *Private*, 81; Van Doren, *Benjamin Franklin*, 283; Fleming, *Lightning*, 76.

35. Isaac Norris to WF, [?] Feb. 1758, Franklin Papers Facsimiles, Stirling Library, Yale University, New Haven (hereafter, Stirling); Thomas Penn to Richard Peters, 13 May 1758, Penn Papers HSP; WF to EG, 9 Dec. 1757, *PBF*, 7:291.

36. BF to JG, 7 April 1759, *PBF*, 8:309, 310; BF to JG, 17 Feb. 1758; to Isaac Norris, 9 June 1759, *PBF*, 7:374; 8:401, 402; WF to JG, 28 Dec. 1759, Franklin Papers, Stirling. No one ever took credit for the highly incendiary publication.

37. BF to DF, 22 Nov. 1757, *PBF*, 7:272–74; WS to DF, 13 Dec. 1757, *PBF*, 7:297. See also Thomas Collinson to his Uncle, 12 Sept. 1760, *PBF*, 9:212.

38. WS to DF, 13 Dec. 1757, to DF, [Jan? 1758], *PBF*, 7:297, 369.
39. BF to [Isaac Norris], 14 Jan. 1758, *PBF*, 7:360–62; BF to JG, 7 April 1759, *PBF*, 8:313; WF to Mrs. Abercrombie, 24 Oct. 1758, Gratz, "Elizabeth Graeme," 265.
40. Ibid., 265; WF to JG, 28 Dec. 1759, Franklin Papers, Stirling; WF to JG, 26 Aug. 1760, *PBF*, 9:191.
41. Ibid., 125–31.
42. *ABF*, 265, 266; WF to JG, 16 June 1760, *PBF*, 9:124; Newcomb, *Franklin and Galloway*, 66, 67; Hanna, *Benjamin Franklin and Pennsylvania Politics*, 130, 131, 138; PBF, 9:196–211; Fay, *Franklin*, 290.
43. BF, knowing that his London sojourn was at the colony's expense, claimed he needed to travel to improve his health and to "increase Acquaintance among Persons of Influence." But this excursion, at least, was purely pleasureable. BF to JG, 6 Sept. 1758, *PBF*, 8:146.
44. BF to DF, 10 June, 6 Sept. 1758; to John Lining, 17 June 1758, ibid., 90, 133–35, 108.
45. Ibid., 136–38; BF to Mary Fisher, 31 July 1758, ibid., 117–19.
46. BF to DF, 6 Sept. 1758, ibid., 137, 138; *ABF*, 45–48.
47. BF to DF, 6 Sept. 1758; WF to BF, 3 Sept. 1758, *PBF*, 8:138–46; 132, 133.
48. WF to BF, 3 Sept. 1758, ibid., 131–33; BF to DF, 19 Feb. 1758, *PBF*, 7:380. Indeed WF was still in Tunbridge Wells three weeks later. BF to DF, 21 Sept. 1758, *PBF*, 8:168. He did, however, move with Jackson to cheaper lodgings.
49. John Clive and Bernard Bailyn, "England's Cultural Provinces: Scotland and America," *WMQ* 3rd ser. 11 (1954): 208.
50. Ibid., 200, 203–9; J. Bennett Nolan, *Benjamin Franklin in Scotland and Ireland* (Philadelphia, 1956), 56–72; WS to David Hall, 6 Oct. 1759, David Hall Papers, APS; Cochrane, *Dr. Johnson's Printer*, 105; Alexander Carlyle, *Autobiography of the Rev. Dr. A. Carlyle, 1722–1805* (Edinburgh, 1860), 414. It was not, as Randall suggests, simply a crass search for political connections that drove them to Scotland, and the secretive visit to Lord Bute's home he describes could not have taken place. Randall, *Revenge*, 140–43.
51. Nolan, *Travels in Scotland*, 56–68, 72, 78; Cochrane, *Dr. Johnson's Printer*, 3, 105. The nature of WF's gift is not known.
52. BF to Lord Kames, 3 Jan. 1760; *PBF*, 9:9.
53. WS to David Hall, 17 Nov. 1760, David Hall Papers, APS; Hinton Brown to Goldney Smith and Co., 16 Sept. 1760; Thomas Collinson to his Uncle, 12 Sept. 1760; WF to Sally Franklin, 10 Oct. 17[61], *PBF*, 9:218; 211, 211n; 365–68. WF's journal has not been preserved.
54. Van Doren, *Benjamin Franklin*, 300; Mariboe, "William Franklin," 106.
55. See, for example, WS to David Hall, 22 July 1758; 13 March, 12 June, 10 Aug. 1762, David Hall Papers, APS. Perhaps if DF had not been so frightened of the ocean crossing, BF would have decided to remain in the England he loved. BF to WS, 7 Dec. 1762, *PBF*, 10:169.
56. David Hall to WF, 20 April 1760; David Hall to BF, 15 Dec. 1769; 1 June 1761, David Hall Letterbook, APS; Hugh Roberts to BF, 15 May 1760, *PBF*, 9:113, 115.
57. WF to EG, 9 Dec. 1757, *PBF*, 7:288–292; WF to Mrs. Abercrombie, 24

Oct. 1758, Gratz, "Elizabeth Graeme," 263–67; WF to JG, 28 Dec. 1759, Franklin Papers, Stirling; WF to JG, 26 Aug. 1760, *PBF*, 9:192; Charles Thomson to WF, 12–15 March 1758, Franklin Papers 48:122, APS.

58. WF to EG, 9 Dec. 1757, *PBF*, 7:292.
59. EG's letter no longer exists. The summary of its contents comes from WF's synopsis in his missive to Mrs. Abercrombie, 24 Oct. 1758, Gratz, "Elizabeth Graeme," 263–67.
60. Margaret Abercrombie to Ann Graeme, 4 April 1759, ibid., 267.
61. WF to Mrs. Abercrombie, 24 Oct. 1758, ibid., 265.
62. WS to David Hall, 17 Dec. 1759, 5 April, 17 Nov. 1760, 6 Oct. 1761, David Hall Papers, APS; WF to WS, 5 April 1760, Franklin Papers, 66:99, APS; WF to Sally Franklin; 10 Oct. 17[61], *PBF*, 9:368. See also John Hancock to Daniel Perkins, 29 Oct. 1760, Hancock, "Letters," 194.
63. There is no evidence that BF had to force WF to assume responsibility for his son. It is true that BF, not WF, took over the financial burden of raising Temple (WTF). WF's modest income form the Post Office was hardly sufficient to the task. Fleming, *Lightning*, 93.
64. Again, no none knows who WTF's mother was; and the date of his birth is even hazier than WF's. Van Doren says he was born in 1760. Labaree et al. note that his Paris tombstone puts the date at 22 Feb. 1762. Van Doren, *Benjamin Franklin*, 290; *PBF*, 1:ixii.
65. Vernon Stumpf, "Who Was Elizabeth Downes Franklin?" *PMHB* 94 (1970): 533, 534; BF to Mary Stevenson, 20 Aug. 1758, 11 Aug. 1762, *PBF*, 8:122, 123; 10:142; Herman R. Lantz, Raymond Schmitt, Margaret Britton, and Eloise C. Snyder, "Pre-Industrial Patterns in the Colonial Family in America: A Content Analysis of Colonial Magazines," *American Sociological Review* 33 (June 1968): 421, 422; Fliegelman, *Prodigals and Pilgrims*, 136–48; BF to Lord Kames, 2 June 1765, *PBF*, 12:159.
66. Mariboe, "William Franklin," 111. Thomas Bridges, Richard Jackson's brother-in-law, referred to her as an "Old Flame." Thomas Bridges to Jared Ingersoll, 30 Sept. 1762, *PBF*, 10:155n.
67. The average age of marriage for young men in New England, and probably in the rest of the colonies, was going down in the eighteenth century. In Hingham, Mass., it was 26.4 and in Andover it was 25.2. At the age of 31 or 32, WF was definitely past the average. Carl Degler, *At Odds: Women and Family in America from the Revolution to the Present* (New York, 1980), 7; Greven, *Four Generations*, 229. Still his "late" marriage was by no means extraordinary. Patriots Thomas Jefferson, John Jay, and John Adams all remained unmarried until they were nearly thirty. Other patriots who married late were James Madison, Eldridge Gerry, and Samuel Osgood. WF's late marriage did not indicate a reluctance to act independently, nor did it reveal a "loyalist personality." Greven, *Protestant Temperament*, 248; Jack N. Rakove, *The Beginning of National Politics: An Interpretive History of the Continental Congress* (New York, 1979), 229.
68. Lopez and Herbert, *Private*, 93; Fleming, *Lightning*, 93–98; Randall, *Revenge*, 179; BF to Jane Mecom, 25 Nov. 1762, *PBF*, 10:154, 155; WS to David Hall, 20 Oct., 1 Nov. 1762, David Hall Papers, APS; Peter Collinson to BF, 21 Oct. 1762, *PBF*, 10:151.

69. BF to Jane Mecom, 25 Nov. 1762, *PBF*, 10:154, 155; WS to David Hall, 20 Oct., 1 Nov. 1762, David Hall Papers, APS; Peter Collinson to BF, 21 Oct. 1762, *PBF*, 10:151.

70. Thomas Penn to James Hamilton, 11 March 1763, Penn Papers, HSP.

71. John Penn to William Alexander, 3 Sept. 1762, Duer, *William Alexander*, 70; Ian Christie, *Myth and Reality in Late Eighteenth Century British Politics* (Berkeley, 1970), 33, 34; Thomas Penn to James Hamilton, 11 March 1763, Penn Papers, HSP. BF was so proud of his friendship with Bute that he had a picture of the King's adviser displayed prominently in his Philadelphia home.

72. BF to John Morgan, 16 Aug. 1762, *PBF*, 10: 146; James Hamilton to Thomas Penn, 21 Nov. 1762, Penn Papers, HSP; Fleming, *Lightning*, 98; Newcomb, *Franklin and Galloway*, 71n; Robert M. Calhoon, *The Loyalists in Revolutionary America, 1760–1781* (New York, 1973), 121; Peter Oliver, *Origin and Progress of the American Revolution: A Tory View*, ed. Douglass Adair and John A. Schutz (Stanford, 1961), 81; Whitehead, "A Biographical Sketch of William Franklin," N.J. Hist. Soc., *Proc.* ser 1, 3:141; North Callahan, *Royal Raiders: The Tories of the American Revolution* (New York, 1963), 102; Randall, *Revenge*, 176, 178; Fay, *Franklin*, 293, 296.

73. Adam Gordon observed that New Jersey governors had "very trifling salaries" making it virtually impossible to lure men of "great Character or reputation" to the colony. Perhaps WF was simply the best man the King could find for the job. Gordon, "Journal of Lord Adam Gordon," in Mereness, *Travels*, 414. Moreover, WF's predecessor, Josiah Hardy, had no previous experience in the colonies, a further indication that the government was not always demanding where New Jersey was concerned. Gerlach, "Anglo-American Politics in New Jersey on the Eve of the Revolution," *Huntington Library Quarterly* 39 (1976):294.

74. Thomas Bridges to Jared Ingersoll, 30 Sept. 1762, *PBF*, 10:147n; Whitehead, "Biographical Sketch," 141; Frederick W. Ricord, ed., *New Jersey Archives, Documents Relating to the Colonial History of the State of NJ.*, 1st ser. 9:366 (hereafter, NJA); WF to WS, 4 Sept. 1762, C. H. Hart, "Letters from William Franklin to William Strahn," *PMHB* 35 (1911): 421; *Pa. Journal*, 18 Nov. 1762. A partial copy of WF's commission is at the NJHS.

75. WF to WS, Nov. 1762, Franklin Papers, Stirling; When he wrote to WS announcing his marriage, he hoped that the printer would insert an announcement of the event in the *Chronicle*. But, he warned his friend, "don't stile me Excellency, as I think it not quite so proper as I have not yet kissed hands." He was going to take his oath a mere four days after his marriage. WF to WS, 4 Sept. 1762, Hart, "Letters," 421.

76. WF to WS, Nov. 1672, Franklin Papers, Stirling; WF to WS, 14 Dec. 1762, Hart, "Letters," 422–24. The experience did encourage WF to make a will, which he forwarded to WS.

77. Ibid., 423, 424.

3. An Easy Agreeable Administration

1. BF to Jane Mecom, 25 Nov. 1762, *PBF*, 10:154, 155.
2. WF to WS, 14 Oct. 1763, Hart, "Letters," 430, 431.
3. WF to WS, 25 April 1763, ibid., 424, 425.
4. Ibid., 425; *Pa. Journal*, 10 Feb. 1763; *Pa. Gazette*, 17 Feb. 1763; WF to EG, 16 May 1757, Gratz, "Elizabeth Graeme," 262.
5. WF to WS, 25 April 1763, Hart, "Letters," 425.
6. *Pa. Gazette*, 24 Feb. 1763; WS to David Hall, 20 Oct. 1762, David Hall Papers, APS; BF to Jane Mecom, 25 Nov. 1762, *PBF*, 10:155.
7. See, for example, Bernard Bailyn, *The Origins of American Politics* (New York, 1967), 59–105; Robert W. Tucker and David C. Hendrickson, *The Fall of the First British Empire: Origins of the War of American Independence* (Baltimore, 1982), 60, 156; Jack P. Greene, "An Uneasy Connection: An Analysis of the Preconditions of the American Revolution," in Stephen G. Kurtz and James H. Hutson, eds., *Essays on the American Revolution* (Chapel Hill, 1973), 43; John F. Burns, *Controversies Between Royal Governors and Their Assemblies in the Northern Colonies* (Boston, 1923), 16, 18.
8. See Francis B. Lee, *New Jersey as a Colony and a State* (New York, 1902), 1:176–224; Larry R. Gerlach, *Prologue to Independence: New Jersey in the Coming of the Revolution* (New Brunswick, N.J., 1976), 3–25; Birket, *Some Cursory Remarks*, 46.
9. In fact the East Jersey proprietors dominated the council. When Josiah Hardy, WF's predecessor, was governor, he professed not to be able to find a single West Jersey man qualified to serve on the council. Jerome J. Nadlehaft, "Politics and the Judicial Tenure Fight in Colonial New Jersey," *WMQ* 3rd ser., 28 (1971): 57.
10. Gerlach, *Prologue*, 4–6.
11. Burnaby, *Travels*, 110.
12. Gerlach, "Anglo-American Politics in New Jersey on the Eve of the Revolution," 291, 292, 297, 299; Nelson R. Burr, *The Anglican Church in New Jersey* (Philadelphia, 1954), 74; Alison Olson, *Anglo-American Politics 1660–1775: The Relationship Between Politics in England and Colonial America*, (New York, 1973), 148, 149. Morris's allies included William Shirley of Mass., George Clinton of N.Y., Gov. Horatio Sharpe of Md., Gov. Robert Dinwiddie of Va., and Gov. Arthur Dobbs of N.C. The Franklins counted among their supporters Thomas Pownall, Israel Pemberton, William S. Johnson, and James de Lancey. Morris's coalition was loosely allied with the Duke of Bedford; the Franklins' was connected with the Duke of Newcastle. Olson, *Anglo-American Politics*, 149.
13. John Watt to Sir Charles Hardy, 1 Dec. 1762, *Letter Book of John Watts, 1762–1765*, 102, 103; John Penn to Earl of Stirling, 3 Sept. 1762, Duer, *William Alexander*, 70, 71; Gov. Hamilton to Thomas Penn, 21 Nov. 1762, Penn Papers, HSP; Peter Collinson to BF, 21 Oct. 1762, *PBF*, 10:151.
14. Jesse Lemisch, "Jack Tar in the Streets: Merchant Seamen in the Politics of Revolutionary America, *WMQ* 3rd ser., 25 (1968): 371–407; Thomas Thompson, " 'A Letter from New Jersey': Monmouth County in the Mid-

Eighteenth Century," Fred Shelley, ed., N.J. Hist. Soc., *Proc.*, ser. 8 (1923): 302.

15. The proprietors were locked into an ongoing battle with the settlers at Monmouth and Elizabeth who claimed that land grants handed to their families in the 1660s freed them from proprietary interference. Nadlehaft, "Judicial Tenure Fight," 50, 56.

16. WF to WS, 25 April 1763, Hart, "Letters," 425; *Pa. Gazette*, 24 Feb. 1763; *N.Y. Gazette*, 7 March 1763; *Pa. Journal*, 10 March 1763; see also *ABF*, 74, 112, 113.

17. Ibid.; *N.Y. Gazette*, 14 March 1763; WF to WS, 25 April 1763, Hart, "Letters," 426. The house had just been completed that September. Maxine Lurie and Joanne Walroth, eds., *The Minutes of the Board of Proprietors of the Eastern Division of New Jersey from 1764–1794* (Newark, 1985), 4:13n.

18. *N.Y. Gazette*, 14 March 1763.

19. Ibid.

20. BF to WS, 28 March 1763, *PBF*, 10:236; WF to Jonathan Williams, Sr., 7 April 1763, Franklin Papers, MSS, APS; WF to WS, 25 April 1763, Hart, "Letters," 426; *Votes and Proceedings of the General Assembly of the Province of New Jersey*, 65:40 (hereafter, V & P).

21. Kalm, *Travels*, 122; Birket, *Cursory Remarks*, 49; Thompson, "A Letter," 297; Bamyfylde Moore Carew, "Life and Adventures (1745)," in Coad, *New Jersey in Travelers Accounts*, 15; Ambrose Serle, *The American Journal of Ambrose Serle, Secretary to Lord Howe, 1776–1778*, ed. Edward H. Tatum, Jr. (San Marino, Ca., 1940), 66; Burnaby, *Travels*, 105.

22. Kalm, *Travels*, 321; Carew, "Life and Adventures," 15; John Smith Diary, HSP; Birket, *Cursory Remarks*, 52; Hamilton, *Gentleman's Progress*, 33; WF to WS, 25 April 1763, Hart, "Letters," 426.

23. WF to Jonathan Williams, Sr., 7 April 1763, Franklin Papers MSS, APS; WF to WS, 25 April 1763, Hart, "Letters," 426. When WF nominated his first two councilors, both of West Jersey, their fears grew. But it soon became clear that the new governor posed no threat to their interests. Nadlehaft, "Judicial Tenure Fight," 62.

24. SF to DF, 12 April 1763, Franklin Papers, Bache Collection, APS; WS to David Hall, 21 Feb. 1763, Hart, ed., William Strahan, "Correspondence Between WS and David Hall 1763–1777," *PMHB* 10 (1886): 89; WF to WS, 27 June 1763, Hart, "Letters," 429; John Sargent to BF, 8 Nov. 1763, *PBF*, 10:366.

25. Alan Valentine, *Lord Stirling* (New York, 1969), 97, 162 (see pp. 80–207 for a more detailed description of Alexander's quest for a Lordship).

26. Ibid., 56–59, 102, 103.

27. Ibid., 46; WF to WS, 18 June 1764, Hart, "Letters," 438. See also WF to Earl of Stirling, 2 April 1767; Earl of Stirling to WF, 26 May 1767; Earl of Stirling to Col. Samuel Ogden, 3 Dec. 1773, Duer, *William Alexander*, 86, 87, 105.

28. WF's interest in his home echoed that of his father. BF was as obsessed with controlling the decor of his home in Philadelphia as WF was in Burlington. BF to DF, 4 June 1765, *PBF*, 12:167; DF to BF [Oct. 8–13 1765?], *PBF*, 12:303, 304.

29. WF to WS, 27 June, 15 Nov., 18 Dec. 1763, Hart, "Letters," 428, 432–

35; G. M. Hills, *History of the Church in Burlington, New Jersey* (Trenton, 1876), 304; Lopez and Herbert, *Private*, 178.

30. WF to Gov. Sharpe, 7 April 1763, Dreer Collection, Governors, HSP; *Pa. Gazette*, 26 May, 16 June, 11, 25 Aug. 1763; *Pa. Journal*, 19 May 1763; WF to WS, 25 April 1763, Hart, "Letters," 427.

31. SF to DF, 12 April 1763, Franklin Papers, Bache Collection, APS; Lee, *New Jersey*, 291; WF to Lords of Trade, 10 May 1763, *NJA*, 9:385.

32. V & P, 63A:4, 5.

33. Ibid., 13; BF to Richard Jackson, 10 June 1763, *PBF*, 10:286; WF to Lords of Trade, 10 May, 27 June 1763, *NJA*, 9:384, 389.

34. WF to WS, 14 Oct. 1763, Hart, "Letters," 430, 431.

35. WF to Lords of Trade, 10 May, 27 June 1763; WF to Earl of Halifax, 21 Feb. 1765, *NJA*, 9:384, 389, 488, 489.

36. Former Gov. Jonathan Belcher complained that the assembly was "tolerably honest, but stingy." Burns, *Royal Governors*, 405.

37. See Joseph A. Ernst, *Money and Politics in America, 1755–1775: A Study in the Currency Act of 1764 and the Political Economy of Revolution* (Chapel Hill, 1973), 246–71; Thomas L. Purvis, *Proprietors, Patronage and Paper Money: Legislative Politics in New Jersey, 1703–1706* (New Brunswick, 1986), 145–55.

38. See Gerlach, *Prologue*, 42–45; D. L. Kemmerer, *Path to Freedom: The Struggle for Self-Government in Colonial New Jersey 1703–1776* (Princeton, 1940), 280; Catherine Fennelly, "William Franklin of New Jersey," *WMQ* 3rd. ser. 6 (1949): 363, 364. Significantly, a loan office was supported by merchants, farmers, and the gentry and cut across ethnic, class, and sectional divisions. Purvis, *Proprietors*, 148.

39. WF to Lords of Trade, 10 May 1763, *NJA*, 9:385, 386; Purvis, *Proprietors*, 161–66.

40. WF to Lords of Trade, 8 Feb. 1764, *NJA*, 9:404. The Board of Trade had been moving in this direction for over three decades. WF's predecessors had generally managed to ignore the ministry's strictures on paper money emissions, but by the time WF took office, the Board and the assembly were on a collision course. See Purvis, *Proprietors*, chap. 6.

41. Lords of Trade to WF, 21 Oct. 1763, *NJA*, 9:396. See also, Gerlach, *Prologue*, 43.

42. See Purvis, *Proprietors*, 63, 65.

43. John Shy, "Quartering His Majesty's Forces in New Jersey," N.J. Hist. Soc., *Proc.* 78 (1960): 86; Jeffrey Amherst to WF, 30 Oct. 1763; WF to Jeffrey Amherst, 1 Nov. 1763, Amherst Papers, Clements Library, Ann Arbor, Mich. (hereafter, Clements). Indeed the colony had already raised 90 Morris county militia men to defend its inhabitants from further attack.

44. WF to Jeffrey Amherst, 14 Nov. 1763, Amherst Papers, Clements; WF to JG, 28 Dec. 1759, Franklin Papers, Stirling.

45. WF to Jeffrey Amherst, 14 Nov. 1763, Amherst Papers, Clements; Thomas Gage to WF, 22 Nov. 1763, Gage Papers, American, Clements.

46. WF to Lords of Trade, 20 Jan. 1764, *NJA*, 9:401; WF to Thomas Gage, 30 Nov. 1763, Gage Papers, American, Clements, V & P, 63B:170, 19–21, 35–37.

47. WF to Thomas Gage, 7 Dec. 1763; Gage Papers, American, Clements; WF to Lords of Trade, 5 Dec. 1763, *NJA*, 9:398–400.

48. *NJA*, 5:361–63.
49. Ibid., 350, 351, 370, 372, 376, 377; WF to Thomas Gage, 24 Feb. 1764, Gage Papers, American, Clements; WF to Lords of Trade, 6 March 1764, *NJA*, 9:428, 429; V & P, 64:7, 19–22.
50. Secretary Halifax to WF, 12 May 1764, *NJA*, 9:439; Thomas Gage to WF, 6 March 1764, *NJA*, 9:432, 433.
51. WF to Lords of Trade, 6 March 1764, *NJA*, 9:429.
52. WF to Lords of Trade, 28 April 1764; Lords of Trade to WF, 13 July 1764, *NJA*, 9:433, 444, 445.
53. Gov. F. to Lords of Trade, 4 Oct. 1764, *NJA*, 9:458.
54. WF to WS, 18 Dec. 1763, 1 May 1764, Hart, "Letters," 434, 436; WF to Lords of Trade, 8 Aug. 1765, *NJA*, 9:491; John Sargent to BF, 8 Nov. 1763, *PBF*, 10:366; BF to Sir Alexander Dick, 11 Dec. 1763, *PBF*, 10:385; see also WF to Joseph Reed, 23 Sept. 1764, Reed Papers, New York Historical Society, New York, N.Y. (hereafter NYHS).
55. BF to DF, 16 June 1763, *PBF*, 10:290; WF to WS, 18 Dec. 1763, 1 May 1764, 18 Feb. 1765, Hart, "Letters," 434, 436, 444; Adam Gordon, "Journal," 414; James Parker to BF, 22 March 1765, *PBF*, 12:88; DF to BF [7 April 1765], ibid., 102.
56. Thompson, "A Letter," 297, 298; W. J. Mills, ed., *Glimpses of Colonial Society and the Life at Princeton College* (Philadelphia, 1903), 16; Leonard B. Rosenberg, "William Paterson: New Jersey's Nation Maker," *New Jersey History* 85 (1967): 9; Mark Edward Lender, "The Social Structure of the New Jersey Brigade: The Continental Line as an American Standing Army," in Peter Karsten, ed., *The Military in America from the Colonial Era to the Present* (New York, 1980), 30; WF to WS, 25 April 1763, Hart, "Letters," 427.
57. Ibid.

4. "Times of Ferment and Confusion"

1. WF to Lords of Trade, 8 Aug. 1765, *NJA*, 9:491.
2. WF to BF, 13 Nov. 1765, *PBF*, 12:367.
3. WF to Lords of Trade, 8 Aug. 1765, to Earl of Halifax, 21 Sept. 1764, *NJA*, 9:491, 454.
4. Brook Hindle, "The March of the Paxton Boys," *WMQ* 3rd ser. 3 (1946): 461–86; Warden, "Proprietary Group," 367, 387; Robert F. Oaks, "The Impact of British Western Policy on the Coming of the American Revolution," *PMHB* 101 (1977): 174; BF to WS, 1 May 1764, *PBF*, 11:189; BF, *Cool Thoughts* . . . (1764), ibid., 162–72; Hutson, "The Campaign to Make Pennsylvania a Royal Province, 1764–1770, Part I," *PMHB* 94 (1970): 450.
5. WF to WS, 1 May, 23 Sept. 1764, Hart, "Letters," 436, 437, 439; John Penn to Thomas Penn, 19 Oct. 1764, Penn Papers, HSP. See also J. Philip Gleason, "A Scurrilous Colonial Election and Franklin's Reputation," *WMQ* 3rd ser. 18 (1961): 78; Anon., *Sauce for a Goose*, 2–7.
6. See Newcomb, *Franklin and Galloway*, 92–100; W. Allen to D. Barclay & Sons, 24 Oct., 20 Nov. 1764, Walker, *Burd Papers*, 62, 63; George S. Wycoff, ed., "Petter Collinson's Letter Concerning Franklin's 'Vindica-

tion:' Notes and Documents II," *PMHB* 66 (1942): 102; W. Allen to D. Barclay and Sons, 24 Oct. 1764, Walker, *Burd Papers*, 62. In fact as early as May, BF was already preparing to leave for England to argue against the proprietors. WF to WS, 1 May, 18 June 1764, Hart, "Letters," 436, 438.

7. Only these circumstances, and BF's determined opposition to the proprietors, could have induced him to enlist the propaganda efforts of Rhode Island's proto-loyalists Dr. Thomas Moffatt and Martin Howard, in his cause. BF to Richard Jackson, 1 May 1764, *PBF*, 11:186, 186n.

8. Joseph Sherwood, New Jersey's London agent, was inclined to agree. Indeed he went even further in his support of the Sugar Act, saying that in most instances its provisions were favorable to the colonists. Significantly, BF was equally cavalier in his response to the Sugar Act. Joseph Sherwood to Charles Reed, Samuel Smith and Jacob Spicer, 13 May 1765, N.J. Hist. Soc., *Proc.* 1st Ser., 5:149; Joseph Sherwood to Samuel Smith, 20 April, 4 Aug., 1763; 4 Feb. 1764, Sherwood Papers, NJHS; BF to Richard Jackson, 25 Sept. 1764, *PBF*, 11:359.

9. Kemmerer, *Path to Freedom*, 282; Gerlach, *Proglogue*, 93–96; Ernst, *Money and Politics*, 249, 250; W. Allen to D. Barclay and Sons, 20 Nov. 1764, Walker, *Burd Papers*, 65; V & P, 65A:6, 8, 9; *Pa. Gazette*, 27 Dec. 1764.

10. Circular Letter from the Earl of Halifax to the Governors in North America, 11 Aug. 1764, *NJA*, 9:448; WF to Earl of Halifax, 28 Oct. 1764, ibid., 479–82.

11. David Ogden to Cortlandt Skinner, 24 Aug. 1764, ibid., 449–51.

12. WF to the Earl of Halifax, 21 Feb. 1765, ibid., 488, 489; Secretary Conway to WF, 14 Sept. 1765, ibid., 492; *Pa. Gazette*, 30 May 1765; *Pa. Journal*, 15 Aug. 1765; Jane Mecom to BF, 30 Dec. 1765, *PBF*, 12:417.

13. Cecil Currey, *Code Number 72*, 142; Hanna, *Benjamin Franklin and Pennsylvania Politics*, 175, 176. BF did offer an alternative to Grenville's proposal, the so-called "paper money scheme." It was not, however, seriously considered and had major flaws. Newcomb, *Franklin and Galloway*, 110–12. For a more generous assessment of BF's activities prior to the Stamp Act crisis, see P.D.G. Thomas, *British Politics and the Stamp Act Crisis* (Oxford, 1975), 78, 142. Still, BF's opponent, William Allen, did more to modify and delay the Stamp Act than he did. Warden, "Proprietary Group," 377. See also, Esmond Wright, *Franklin of Philadelphia* (Cambridge, Mass., 1986), 189.

14. BF to Charles Thomson, 11 July 1765, *PBF*, 12:207, 208. See also BF to John Ross, 14 Feb. 1765; BF to WF [26 July 1765], ibid., 67, 68, 222; Hanna, *Benjamin Franklin and Pennsylvania Politics*, 174, 175; Newcomb, *Franklin and Galloway*, 112–16. Even Richard Jackson, as a member of Parliament did more to combat both the Sugar and the Stamp Act than BF did. Thomas, *Stamp Act Crisis*, 57; Richard Jackson to Colony of Connecticut, 10 March 1764; Richard Jackson to Thomas Fitch, 27 Nov. 1764; 9 Feb., 9 March, 5 June 1765, Conn. Hist. Soc., *Coll.* 18 (1929): 300–3, 316, 340–42, 349–51.

15. *Pa. Gazette*, 6 June 1765. Significantly, the celebrants included members of the council and assembly who were in Burlington for the spring legislative session.

16. *V & P*, 65A:1, 2, 24, 41, 58. The assembly did refuse WF's request for help with his personal expenses, and for a higher salary for the new chief justice.

17. Robert Ogden to S. White, 20 June 1765, *NJA*, 9:496. The assembly later pretended that Ogden, under pressure from WF, had accorded its members little opportunity to discuss a response to the Mass. circular letter, implying that New Jersey assemblymen were not as conservative as the vote indicated. But there is reason to believe that the assembly hoped Great Britain would change its mind voluntarily and that most members were indeed reluctant to become involved in the Stamp Act congress in the summer of 1765. See Jacob Spicer to William Bayard, 2 July 1765, Jacob Spicer Papers, NJHS. The minutes of the spring session do not mention any discussion of the Stamp Act congress.

18. See Hutson, "Campaign, Part II," *PMHB* 95 (1971): 32–38; Hanna, *Benjamin Franklin and Pennsylvania Politics*, 174–77. There are, admittedly, indications that BF was working behind the scenes to secure repeal of the Stamp Act. WS described his "assiduity" in buttonholing MPs, "throwing out Hints in the Public Papers," claiming that he was busy day and night in his efforts to get rid of the obnoxious legislation. WS to David Hall, 11 Jan. 1766, Hart, "Correspondence," 92, 93.

19. BF to John Hughes, 9 Aug. 1765, *PBF*, 12:234, 235. See also BF to WF, 9 Nov. 1765; to Jane Mecom, 1 March 1766, ibid., 361–65; ibid., 13:188.

20. *N.Y. Gazette*, 22 Aug. 1765. A week later, the *Pennsylavnia Journal* repeated the story, wondering, "who will underwrite on such Houses." *Pa. Journal*, 29 Aug. 1765.

21. William Coxe to WF, 3 Sept. 1765, *NJA*, 9:497. Two days later the *Pa. Journal* printed the rumor that Coxe was resigning his commission; the *N.Y. Gazette* followed on Sept. 12.

22. WF to William Coxe, 4 Sept. 1765, *NJA*, 9:497, 498; WF to BF, 7 Sept. 1765; *PBF*, 12:260, 261.

23. John Hughes suggested that his son be named as Coxe's replacement, but there is no indication that WF ever seriously considered this alternative or even that he was aware of Hughes's recommendation. John Hughes to BF [8–17 Sept. 1765], ibid., 265. See also WF to BF, 7 Sept. 1765, ibid., 260, 261.

24. WF to Gage, 14 Sept. 1765, *NJA*, 9:494, 495. Gage obligingly assured WF that he would have 100 soldiers at his disposal. Gage to WF, 16 Sept. 1765, ibid., 495, 496.

25. See John Hughes to BF [8–17 Sept. 1765], *PBF*, 12:265.

26. *N.Y. Gazette or Weekly Post Boy*, 24 Oct. 1765; *Pa. Journal*, 3 Oct. 1765.

27. WF to WS, 18 Feb. 1765, Hart, "Letters," 441–43. DF to BF, 22 Sept. 1765, *PBF*, 12:270–72; David Hall to BF, 6 Sept. 1765, *PBF*, 12:256–59.

28. DF to BF, 22 Sept. 1765, *PBF*, 12:271, 272.

29. Samuel Wharton to WF, 29 Sept. 1765, Franklin Papers, 1:159, APS; *Pa. Journal*, 3 Oct. 1765.

30. WF to BF, 30 April 1766, *PBF*, 13:256.

31. *Pa. Journal*, 3 Oct. 1765; *Pa. Gazette*, 3 Oct. 1765.

32. WF to Secretary Conway, 23 Sept. 1765, *NJA*, 9:492–94.

33. Even when advice from home finally arrived, it was totally useless. Conway told him to exercise his "prudence" and to act with "Caution and Cool-

ness," but left all specific decisions to his discretion. On Nov. 5, Secretary of the Treasury Grey Cooper told him to "take care" that all stamps were distributed and gave him by now meaningless permission to appoint an interim distributor. Conway to WF, 24 Oct. 1765, ibid., 501–3; Grey Cooper to WF, 5 Nov. 1765, BM ADD. MSS. 33030 fo. 51, Newcastle Papers, Library of Congress, Washington, D.C. (hereafter LC).

34. WF to Lords of Trade, 10 Oct. 1765; WF to Secretary Conway, 30 Nov. 1765, NJA, 9:499, 500, 508.
35. WF to Lords of Trade, 10 Oct. 1765, NJA, 9:499–500.
36. WF to Lords of Trade, 18 Dec. 1765, NJA, 9:524; Pa. Gazette, 3 Oct. 1765; V & P, 65B:6. There is no evidence that Ogden called the meeting when and where he did because he was trying to circumvent WF's power. The meeting was probably called extra-legally because the speaker had delayed requesting an assembly session for so long that a formal meeting was impossible. The rump session did not indicate any "radicalism" in New Jersey. Just the opposite, it reveals the reluctance with which men like Ogden approached the Stamp Act congress.
37. Pa. Journal, 10 Oct. 1765; NJA, 9:514, 515.
38. The four who failed to arrive no doubt opposed the Stamp Act, but their reasons for staying away were probably legitimate. NJA, 9:509–11; Gerlach, Prologue, 121.
39. Lord Stirling to WF, 3 Nov. 1765, NJA, 9:509–11; Gov. Colden to WF, 29 Sept. 1765; Capt. Archibald Kennedy to WF, 4 Oct. 1765; Capt. James Hawker to WF, 3 Oct. 1765, ibid., 511–14; see also ibid., 517, 518.
40. WF to Capt. Hawker, 9 Nov. 1765, NJA, 9:519, 520; WF to BF, 13 Nov. 1765, PBF, 12:369.
41. NJA, 9:518, 519; WF to BF, 13 Nov. 1765, PBF, 12:368, 369.
42. Ibid., 367.
43. WF to Lords of Trade, 13 Nov. 1765; WF to Secretary Conway, 30 Nov. 1765, NJA, 9:505–8.
44. WF to BF, 13 Nov. 1765, PBF, 12:367, 368; Pa. Journal, 1 May 1766; N.Y. Gazette or Weekly Post Boy, 29 Oct., 21 Nov. 1765.
45. WF to Lords of Trade, 18 Dec. 1765, NJA, 9:525.
46. V & P, 66:36, 37, 49, 50; ibid., 65B:3; WF to BF, 13 Nov. 1765, PBF, 12:369.
47. V & P, 65B:4–8. The document was "surprisingly radical," attacking parliamentary taxation on constitutional rather than on economic foundations. Ironically, it was the only colony to protest the Stamp Act as an infringement of freedom of the press. Gerlach, Prologue, 112, 113; Pa. Journal, 5 Dec. 1765; N.Y. Gazette or Weekly Post Boy, 12 Dec. 1765.
48. V & P, 65B:10. This of course was a palpable falsehood, as his letter to BF on Nov. 13 indicates.
49. V & P, 65B:10; WF to Lords of Trade, 18 Dec. 1765, NJA, 9:525.
50. V & P, 65B:10, 11.
51. Indeed Coxe had recently been visited by a "delegation" from the Woodbridge Sons of Liberty to secure his renewed promise to refuse to perform all duties associated with the Stamp distributorship. Coxe received them courteously. Satisfied with his pledge, they returned home, meeting up with a group of men from New Brunswick, Piscataway, and Woodbridge who were also intent on keeping the stamps out of New Jersey. The gath-

ering drank the health of Coxe and the King, but, more ominously, they wished confusion to every stamp distributor. Under such circumstances, WF's assessment was on target. *N.Y. Gazette or Weekly Post Boy,* 9 Jan. 1766.

52. WF to Grey Cooper, 15 Jan. 1766, PRO. Treas. 1 Bundle 452, fo. 65, LC. See also WF to Lords of Trade, 13 Nov. 1765; WF to Secretary Conway, 30 Nov. 1765, *NJA,* 9:505–8 for other examples of WF's tendency to place the blame elsewhere.

53. WF to Lords of Trade, 18 Dec. 1765, *NJA,* 9:525; *N.Y. Gazette or Weekly Post Boy,* 27 Feb. 1766.

54. *Pa. Journal,* 10 April 1766; JG to WF, 29 April 1766, Franklin Papers, 48:123, APS; WF to BF, 30 April 1766, *PBF,* 13:254, 255. WF complained that his father had not received sufficient credit for securing the Stamp Act's repeal, but there is reason to doubt that BF's testimony was essential in moving Parliament to act as it did. Economic and political pressure, not the Doctor's quick-witted replies to Parliament's queries, no doubt carried the day. See Hanna, *Benjamin Franklin and Pennsylvania Politics,* 184, 185; Thomas, *Stamp Act Crisis,* 370, 233, 224; WS to David Hall, 7 April, 10 May, 14 June 1766, Hart "Correspondence," 97, 220, 221, 228.

55. BF's letter of 25 Feb. has been lost. Its contents can be deduced from WF's reply on 30 April 1765, *PBF,* 13:254–58.

56. Ibid., 256.

57. Ibid.

58. *Pa. Gazette,* 29 May 1766; see, for instance, BF to Joseph Fox, 1 March 1766; BF to [JG], 12 April 1766, *PBF,* 13:186, 187; 242, 243. See also BF to WF, 9 Nov. 1765, *PBF,* 12:361–65; Samuel Wharton (SW) to George Read, 14 Nov. 1766, William Thompson Read, ed. *Life and Correspondence of George Read* (Philadelphia, 1870), 25.

59. V & P, 66:4.

60. Ibid., 5.

61. Ibid., 13, 14.

62. Ibid., 24, 25, 34–39.

63. Ibid., 50–53.

64. [WF] to BF [Dec. 1766], *PBF,* 13:539; Sir Alexander Dick to BF, 28 Oct. 1766; Thomas Wharton to BF, 2 March 1766, ibid., 478, 192.

65. WF to BF, 27 June 1766, [13 July 1766], ibid., 322, 323, 334, 335.

66. Shelburne to WF, 13 Sept. 1766, *NJA,* 9:571.

67. Randall, "William Franklin: The Making of a Conservative," in Robert A. East and Jacob Judd, eds., *The Loyalist Americans: A Focus on Greater New York* (Tarrytown, N.Y., 1975), 64; WF to Lords of Trade, 18 Dec. 1765, *NJA,* 9:525. Thomas Hutchinson suffered from a similar problem in Massachusetts. See Bernard Bailyn, *The Ordeal of Thomas Hutchinson,* (Cambridge, Mass., 1974).

5. The Letter of the Law

1. WF to BF, 23 Oct. 1767, *PBF,* 14:293.

2. WF to Lord Hillsborough, 23 Nov. 1768, *NJA,* 10:70.

3. See Burrows and Wallace, "The American Revolution," for a description of the "loyalist personality." See also Kenneth A. Lynn, A Divided People (Westport, Conn., 1977).

4. WF to BF, 2 March, 11 May 1769, PBF, 16:61, 127, 128; N.Y. Journal or the General Advertiser, 10 Nov. 1774; Frederick Tolles, "A Literary Quaker: John Smith of Burlington and Philadelphia," PMHB 65 (1941); Assignment of Land Deeds from WF to WTF, 26 July 1785, Franklin Papers, APS.

5. WF to BF, 31 Jan., 2 March, 11 May 1769, PBF, 16:38, 61, 128.

6. WF to WS, 25 April 1763, 29 Jan. 1769, Hart, "Letters," 427, 445; WF to BF, 10 May 1768, 11 May 1769, PBF, 15:120, 16:126–30; WF to Cortlandt Skinner, 22 Jan. 1768, Ely Papers, NJHS.

7. Burr, Anglican Church, 88, 495, 629, 630; Hills, History of the Church in Burlington, 276n, 291, 297, 300.

8. PBF, 16:125, 125n; Thomas Jefferson Wertenbaker, Princeton 1746–1896 (Princeton, 1946), 48, 49, 87; John Wallace to Archibald Wallace, 4 Dec. 1766; Samuel Purviance to Ezra Stiles, 13 Dec. 1766, in L. H. Butterfield, ed., John Witherspoon Comes to America (Princeton, 1953), 16, 17; 19, 20. Actually, Rutgers was inspired by Dutch-Reform, not Anglican interests; and it was more a product of New Jersey's personality than it was of WF's machiavellian plots. See George P. Schmidt, Princeton and Rutgers (New York, 1964), 6.

9. Butterfield, John Witherspoon, x, 1, 10; Pa. Journal, 24 March, 21 April 1768; N.Y. Gazette or Weekly Post Boy, 28 March 1768; N.Y. Gazette and Weekly Mercury, 4 April 1768; BF to Jane Mecom, 23 Feb. 1769, PBF, 16:50, 51. See also Carl Bridenbaugh, Mitre and Sceptre: Transatlantic Faiths, Ideas, Personalities, and Politics (New York, 1962).

10. NJA, 6:2; Pa. Journal, 12 Oct. 1769; Hills, History of the Church in Burlington, 296. Interestingly, BF's first "do-good" project had been his society for the relief of poor widows in Boston. See J. A. Leo Lemay, "Benjamin Franklin," in Everett Emerson, ed., Major Writers of Early American Literature (Madison, Wis., 1972), 209.

11. Pa. Journal, 12 Oct. 1769; Pa. Packett and the General Advertiser, 12 Oct. 1772; Hills, History of the Church in Burlington, 296. Rev. Jonathan Odell was Secretary of the Corporation from 1769 to 1774 (p. 297n.).

12. WF to Lord Stirling, 2 April 1769, William Alexander Papers 3, NYHS; DF to BF, 10 Feb. [1765], [7 April 1765]; Thomas Wharton (TW) to BF, 16 July 1765; WF to BF, 10 May 1768, 1 Sept. 1769; Cadwalader Evans to BF, 27 Nov. 1769, PBF, 12:44, 102, 216; 15:125, 125n; 16:189, 242; Pa. Chronicle 25 May, 1 June 1767; James Allen, Diary, 180, 180n.

13. DF to BF, 8 Jan. 1765; 16 May 1767, 20–27 Nov. 1769; David Hall to BF, 17 March 1770, PBF, 12:13, 14:156; 16:230; 17:101. SF, in particular, profited from the social connections she made through WF. But even on her own she was adept at making friends, enjoying favors from opposers and supporters of the Pennsylvania proprietors. DF to BF, 2[20–25, 1767], ibid., 14:137.

14. Jane Mecom to BF, 8 Nov. 1766, ibid., 13:490; Van Doren, Letters and Papers of Benjamin Franklin and Richard Jackson 1753–1785 (New York, 1945), 142; WF to BF, Fragment [Jan. 1769], PBF, 16:5, 6.

15. BF clearly took care of the details of raising WTF, charging all expenses to WF's account; see ibid., 13:443, 444.
16. WF to BF, Fragment [Jan. 1769], ibid., 16:5.
17. DF to BF [Fall 1765?], ibid., 12:298; see also DF to BF, 10 Feb. [1765], ibid., 44.
18. DF to BF, 2 [20–25 April 1767], [13–18? Oct. 1767]; WF to BF [May? 1767], ibid., 14:136, 137, 280, 174, 175.
19. WS to David Hall, 9 March 1745, Hall Letterbook, APS; Cochrane, *William Strahan*, 106, 107; BF to DF, 23 May, 13 Oct., 5 Aug. 1767; to Richard Bache, 5 Aug. 1767, *PBF*, 14:166, 281, 225, 220, 221. WF to DF, 12 Sept. 1767, Franklin Papers, 48:103, APS; *Pa. Chronicle*, 2 Nov. 1767.
20. To his sister Jane, BF tersely remarked, "She has pleas'd herself and her Mother, and I hope she will do well: but I think they should have seen some better Prospect. BF to Jane Mecom, 21 Feb. 1768, *PBF*, 15:57.
21. WF to BF, 10 May 1768, ibid., 123.
22. DF to BF, 10 Feb. [1765]; 16 May 1767, ibid., 12:44; 14:157; WF to BF, 1 Sept. 1769, ibid., 16:189.
23. WF to BF, 13 Nov. [1766]; David Hall to BF, 27 Jan. 1767, ibid., 13: 499–502; 14:18; W.S. to David Hall, 8 Aug. 1770, Hart, "Correspondence," 349, 350.
24. British sentiment was "strong against America" even before Lord Hillsborough took office. BF to JG, 14 April 1767, *PBF*, 14:125. It should be emphasized that despite WF's understandable concern, New Jersey's violation of the Quartering Act was always a sideshow in Whitehall's eyes. There, attention was focused on New York's defiance, and there was a conscious effort to limit the ministry's response to American disobedience as much as possible. Thomas, *Stamp Act Crisis*, 151ff; Christie, *Empire or Independence*, 96–99.
25. Ernst, *Money and Politics*, 263. New York, which categorically refused to comply with the Mutiny Act, only intensified ministerial hostility, making London more determined than ever to defend Crown prerogative from all encroachments.
26. See his first letter to the colonial governors, which set the tone for his administration. Lord Hillsborough to the Governors in America, 23 Jan. 1768, *NJA*, 10:10, 11.
27. Christie, *Empire or Independence*, 120.
28. WF to BF, 22 Aug. 1767, *PBF*, 14:235, 236; *NJA*, 9:581, 618; V & P, 68:11; WF to Lord Shelburne, 21 Feb., 12 April 1767, Shelburne Papers, 55:153, 193, Clements.
29. WF to BF, 22 Aug. 1767, *PBF*, 14:235, 236.
30. WF to Lord Hillsborough, 24 Aug. 1768, 28 Jan. 1769, *NJA*, 10:48–50, 100, 101; Lord Hillsborough to WF, 7 June 1768, C.O. 5/1003, LC; *Acts of the Privy Council, Colonial Series*, 5:196, 197; 6:471, 485; V & P, 69:4, 14.
31. The bill called for a loan of £100,000 in paper currency at 5% interest, redeemable at the loan office for the next 20 years. The currency would be immediately retired. Ibid., 75, 77.
32. Christie, *Empire or Independence*, 76; Verner W. Crane, ed., *Benjamin Franklin's Letters to the Press* (Chapel Hill, 1950), 27; Ernst, *Money and Politics*, 99; New Jersey Committee of Correspondence to BF, 7 Dec.

1769, *NJA*, 10:137; WF to Lord Hillsborough, 29 Sept. 1770, ibid., 200; *V & P*, 71:4, 33.

33. Shy, "Quartering," 87, 89. See also Bailyn, *Origins of American Politics*.
34. Thomas, *Stamp Act Crisis*, 107.
35. Gen. Gage to WF, 24 April 1765, 3 July, 15 Aug. 1766; WF to Gen. Gage, 29 April 1765, 6 June, 18 July, 25 Aug. 1766, 1 Aug. 1767; WF to John St. Clair, 13 July 1767; John St. Clair to Gen. Gage, 15 July 1767, Gage Papers, American, Clements.
36. Shy, *Toward Lexington: The Role of the British Army in the Coming of the Revolution* (Princeton, 1965), 161, 162, 219–23; *New York Journal or General Advertiser*, 6 Aug. 1767.
37. WF to Earl of Shelburne, 18 Dec. 1766, Shelburne Papers, 51:786–790, Clements.
38. Indeed at least one impartial visitor to New Jersey inspected the barracks there and found them quite acceptable. Coad, *New Jersey in Travelers Accounts*, 23.
39. *V & P*, 67:4; WF to Lord Hillsborough, 23 Nov. 1768, *NJA*, 10:86, 88, 89; WF to Lord Shelburne, 22 Aug., 22 Oct. 1767, Shelburne Papers, 51:797, 798, Clements; Lord Shelburne to WF, 18 July 1767, ibid., 54:63.
40. WF to Lord Shelburne, 22 Oct. 1767, ibid., 51:798, 799.
41. Lord Hillsborough to WF, 23 Feb. 1768, *NJA*, 10:12, 13; *V & P*, 68:5, 9, 31, 40.
42. WF to BF, 10 May 1768, *PBF*, 15:125; WF to Lord Hillsborough, 14 June 1768, *NJA*, 10:32, 33.
43. Ibid., 43; Lord Hillsborough to WF, 16 Aug. 1768, ibid., 47; WF to Lord Hillsborough, 23 Nov. 1768, ibid., 83, 88.
44. Ibid., 88–94.
45. WF to BF, 11 May 1767, *PBF*, 16:126, 127; Gen. Gage to Lord Hillsborough, 16 Dec. 1769, Gage Papers, American, Clements; WF to Lord Hillsborough, 29 Sept., 5 Nov. 1770, *NJA*, 10:200–205.
46. *V & P*, 68:3, 7.
47. WF to Lord Hillsborough, 23 Nov. 1768, *NJA*, 10:73, 74. No record of the discussion or final vote appeared in the minutes. The petitioners expressed their "utmost Concern" about the Townshend Acts, but also reaffirmed their due "Subordination" to Parliament. *V & P*, 68:26–39.
48. Lord Hillsborough to the Governors in America, 21 April 1768, *NJA*, 10:14, 15; WF to Charles Read, 13 June 1768, to Lord Hillsborough, 16 June 1768, ibid., 28, 34, 35.
49. WF to Lord Hillsborough, 11 July 1768, ibid., 36, 37.
50. Lord Hillsborough to WF, 16 Aug. 1768, ibid., 45, 46.
51. Ibid., 46.
52. Ibid., 46, 47.
53. WF to WS, 18 June 1771, Hart, "Letters," 447, WF to Lord Hillsborough, 23 Nov. 1768, *NJA*, 10:64.
54. WF was not exaggerating. Even conservatives like William Allen were convinced that the Townshend Acts were unconstitutional. W. Allen to D. Barclay & Sons, 8 Nov. 1767, 7 Nov. 1769, Walker, *Burd Papers*, 74, 75; 77, 78. WF to Lord Hillsborough, 23 Nov. 1768, *NJA*, 10:64–69.
55. Ibid., 69, 70.
56. Ibid., 70–72.

57. Ibid., 75, 76.
58. Ibid., 81, 83–92; V & P, 68:33; WF to Cortlandt Skinner, 22 Jan. 1768, Early Papers, *NYHS*. See above, pp. 90, 91.
59. WF to Lord Hillsborough, 23 Nov. 1768, *NJA*, 10:74–78.
60. Ibid., 77, 78.
61. Ibid., 74, 75, 70; WF to BF, 31 Jan. 1769, *PBF*, 16:36.
62. WF to Lord Hillsborough, 23 Nov. 1768, *NJA*, 10:70, 85, 86, 88.
63. Ibid., 78, 79. The same fears troubled WF during the quarrel over the currency bill, when the Pennsylvania and Maryland assemblies both enacted bills that were virtually identical to New Jersey's. Yet their laws had not been disallowed. In fact, WF's fears had been unduly paranoic, but they continued to haunt him so long as Hillsborough remained in power. WF to Lord Hillsborough, 29 Sept. 1770, ibid., 200; Ernst, *Money and Politics*, 283; Tucker and Henderickson, *The Fall of the First British Empire*, 234–237.
64. Ibid., 77.
65. Ibid., 94.

6. Walking a Tightrope

1. WS to David Hall, 8 Aug. 1770, Hart, "Correspondence," 348.
2. WF to WS, 18 June 1771, Hart, "Letters," 448, 449.
3. V & P, 71A:32.
4. WF to BF, 22 Aug. 1767 [31 Jan. 1769], *PBF*, 14:238; 16:35; John Temple to WF, Franklin Papers, 43:136, APS; *Pa. Chronicle*, 8–15 Oct. 1770. Actually the 1768 exercises had been, if anything, even more volatile. See Larry Gerlach and Sheldon Cohen, "Princeton in the Coming of the American Revolution," *N.J. History* 92 (1974): 74; *N.Y. Journal or General Advertiser*, 6 Oct. 1768.
5. WS to David Hall, 12 March 1768, Hart, "Correspondence," 333; Conner, *Poor Richard's Politicks*, 145, 148; BF to JG, 14 April 1767, *PBF*, 14:125. Sometime in 1767, BF actually asked Thomas Pownall to introduce a bill calling for American representation in Parliament, but nothing ever came of his proposal.
6. WF to BF, 22 Aug. 1767, ibid., 237, 238.
7. Conner, *Poor Richard's Politicks*, 141–44. BF had always exhibited a desire to bequeath a landed estate in the new world to his progeny. BF to Richard Jackson, 1 May 1764, *PBF*, 11:186, 187.
8. WF to WS, 14 Dec. 1762, Hart, "Letters," 423.
9. V & P, 63:153, 154; *N.Y. Gazette*, 14 Nov., 12, 19 Dec. 1763.
10. See Anne H. Wharton, "The Wharton Family," *PMHB* 1 (1877): 325–29; Alvord, *The Illinois Country*, 283; Warden, "Proprietary Group," 381; Currey, *Road to Revolution*, 201, 206; Abernethy, *Western Lands*, 16. The initial group also included Joseph Galloway and John Hughes, *PBF*, 13:257n.
11. They included Croghan, William Trent, and the rival firms of Simon, Levy and Franks, and Baynton, Wharton and Morgan.
12. WF to BF, 17 Dec. 1765, *PBF*, 12:403–6; Currey, *Road to Revolution: Benjamin Franklin in England, 1765–1775* (New York, 1968), 199–205; Jack Sosin, *Whitehall and the Wilderness: The Middle West in British Colonial Policy, 1760–1775* (Lincoln, Neb., 1961), 145, 146.

13. Nicholas Wainwright, *George Croghan: Wilderness Diplomat* (Chapel Hill, 1959), 225, 226; William Johnson to George Croghan [4 April 1765], to John Penn, 12 April 1765, Johnson, *Papers*, 4:710, 711; Franklin, "Pennsylvania-Virginia Rivalry," 474–78; Abernethy, *Western Lands*, 29; George Croghan to BF, 25 Feb. 1766, WF to BF, 30 April 1766, *PBF*, 13:171, 172, 257.

14. Johnson and both Franklins were silent partners in the project. Croghan thought they could "be of more Service by Nott being thought Concerned in the Plan." Gen. Thomas Cadwallader Coll., Croghan Papers, Box 6, HSP.

15. Wainwright argues that WF had Croghan in mind for the job; others insisted it was Sir William Johnson. He clearly did not wish to commit himself to anyone at this juncture. Wainwright, *Croghan*, 230; Abernethy, *Western Lands*, 29.

16. William Johnson to WF, 3 May 1766, Johnson, *Papers*, 4:196, 197; to Messrs. Wharton, et al., 20 June 1766, ibid., 276, 278; George Croghan to William Johnson, 30 March 1766, Copy, Gen. Thomas Cadwallader Coll., Croghan Papers, Box 6, HSP.

17. George Croghan to BF, 12 Dec. 1765; WF to BF 17 Dec. 1765, 30 April 1766, *PBF*, 12:395–400, 403–6; 13:257.

18. BF to Baynton, Wharton and Morgan, WF, and JG, [10 May 1766], to WF, [12 Sept.], [11 Oct.], [8 Nov. 1766], ibid., 275, 276, 414, 415, 446, 447, 486; WF to BF, [Dec. 1766], ibid., 540, 541.

19. Gen. Gage to George Croghan, 2 March 1765; WF to George Croghan, 15 April 1776, Gen. Thomas Cadwallader Coll., Croghan Papers, Box 6, HSP; Lord Shelburne to Governors in America, 13 Sept. 1766, NJA, 9:569, 570; V & P, 66:32, 33; 67:4; WF to Gen. Gage, 24 July 1766, Gage Papers, American, Clements; WF to Lord Shelburne, 16 Dec. 1767, NJA, 9:575, 576; WF to Shelburne, 23 Dec. 1767, Shelburne Papers, 51:782, Clements; Frank John Esposito, "Indian-White Relations in New Jersey, 1609–1802," Rutgers University Ph.D diss., 1976, pp. 305, 306.

20. BF to WF, [14 Feb.], 13 June, 28 Aug., [9 Oct.] 1767, *PBF*, 14:40, 180, 242, 243, 275.

21. WF to BF [13 Nov. 1767], ibid., 302, 303; see also 302n.

22. WF to Cortlandt Skinner, 22 Jan. 1768, Ely Papers, NYHS; BF to WF, 9 Jan., 13 March 1768, *PBF*, 15:15, 74.

23. BF to WF, 13 March 1768; WF to BF, 10 May 1768, *PBF*, 15:74; 124.

24. His explanation for attending the conference indicated a certain reluctance to attend. He claimed that the council persuaded him to go because it was too late to call the assembly and elect a delegation. In fact nothing could have kept him from Fort Stanwix. WF to Lord Hillsborough, 27 Aug. 1768, NJA, 10:55, 56.

25. Randall, *Revenge*, 222; [SW] to BF, 2 Dec. 1768, *PBF*, 15:275–79.

26. There were those who did complain about the inconvenience his long absence caused. William Paterson to John MacPherson, 16 Nov. 1768, Mills, *Glimpses*, 60, 61.

27. [SW] to BF, 2 Dec. 1768, *PBF*, 15:275–79; Jonathan Williams Coll., Microfilm at APS; Wainwright, *Croghan*, 259, 269.

28. Lord Hillsborough to Gen. Gage, 24 March 1769, Gage Papers, English, Clements; WF to WS, 29 Jan. 1769, Hart, "Letters," 445, 446; WS to

George Croghan, 28 May 1769, William Trent to George Croghan, 10 June 1769, Gen. Thomas Cadwallader Coll., Croghan Papers, Box 7, HSP.

29. BF to WF, 17 March 1770, *PBF*, 17:97, 97n.

30. George Croghan to William Trent, 30 Nov. 1769, Gratz Coll., Croghan Papers, Vol. 1, HSP. Hillsborough assumed the Treasury would raise the price of the land to an unacceptable level, thus killing the project once and for all. Sosin, *Whitehall and the Wilderness*, 187.

31. Currey, *Road to Revolution*, 252–54; Byars Papers, 13, HSP.

32. Claims from the Grand Ohio Company of Virginia, the Mississippi Company (represented by BF's rival Arthur Lee), and George Washington all had to be examined before the Board would give its imprimatur to the Franklins and their cohorts. Currey, *Road to Revolution*, 256–58; Byars Papers, 14, HSP; *PBF*, 18:75n.

33. WF to William Trent, 14 Jan. 1771, *NJA*, 10:228; Mariboe, "William Franklin," 315, 324; WF to George Croghan, 21 Nov. 1772, George Croghan to WF, 26 Dec. 1772, WF to TW, 28 Oct., 5 Nov. 1771, William Franklin Papers MSS., HSP; Byars Papers, 14; SW and William Trent to WF, 13 Aug. 1771; TW to WF, 12 Oct. 171, Franklin Papers, 3:70, APS.

34. *NJA*, 10:29–32; WF to BF, [31 Jan.], 2 March 1769, *PBF*, 16:37, 58. In fact when the Barbados governorship fell vacant in the summer of 1766, WF mentioned it to BF, perhaps hoping for a more lucrative appointment in his wife's native land. But no such reward materialized. WF to BF, [13 July 1766], ibid., 13:336.

35. WF to Boston Customs Commissioners, 29 March, 30 July [Oct.-Nov.] 1768; Customs Commissioners to WF, 8 July, 13 Oct. 1768; WF to George Trenchard and Grant Gibbon, 10 April 1769, Franklin Papers, 48:135, 136, APS.

36. John Williams to Customs Commissioners, 17 June 1769, *NJA*, 10:295–97; WF to Customs Commissioners [Oct.-Nov. 1768]; WF to John Williams, 10 April 1769, Franklin Papers, 48:135, APS.

37. WF, "A Proclamation," *NJA*, 10:205; Gerlach, "Customs and Contentions: John Hatton of Salem and Cohansey 1764–1776," *N.J. History* 89 (1971): 83, 84. In fact this was only Hatton's version of the story. Another observer claimed that Hatton's son provoked the fight "when he could find nothing to seize." William Logan to John Smith, 14 Nov. 1770, Smith, Correspondence, HSP. See Gerlach, "Customs and Contentions," 69–92, for the complete account of both of WF's run-ins with Hatton.

38. Franklin, "A Proclamation," *NJA*, 10:205, 207–9.

39. "Notes and Observations Made by the Deputy Secretary of New Jersey," *NJA*, 10:276–84; Cortlandt Skinner to John Hatton, 25 Dec. 1770, Cortlandt Skinner to Charles Petit, 25 Dec. 1770, ibid., 216–18; John Hatton to Customs Commissioners, 30 Dec. 1770, ibid., 218, 219; WF to Lord Hillsborough, 19 May, 21 Oct. 1771, ibid., 275, 276, 314; Customs Commissioners to WF, 26 March 1771, ibid., 286, 287.

40. WF to Customs Commissioners, 10 April 1771, ibid., 287–95.

41. John Williams to Customs Commissioners, 17 June 1769, ibid., 295–97; Lord Hillsborough to WF, 19 July 1771, ibid., 304.

42. *Pa. Journal*, 20 April 1769; WS to David Hall, 10 Nov. 1768, Hart, "Correspondence," 463–65; WF to WS, 29 Jan. 1769, Hart, "Letters," 446;

Lord Hillsborough to Governors in America, 13 May 1769, *NJA*, 10:110; BF to Pa. Assembly Committee of Correspondence, 10 June 1766; BF to JG, 14 April 1767; BF to Cadwalader Evans, 5 [Aug.] 1767, *PBF*, 13:298, 299; 14:124, 125, 223, 224.

43. *V & P*, 69:5.

44. Ibid., 15, 16, 87, 88.

45. *NJA*, 10:148n, 149n; Gerlach, *Prologue*, 185, 186; *Pa. Gazette*, 19 Oct. 1769; *V & P*, 69:15, 19, 20, 22, 25–46. In fact, they dismissed most of the petitions and they actually reduced the cost of debt action, assuring further multiplication of lawsuits and increasing the likelihood that debtors would lose their property.

46. See especially Norman S. Cohen, "The Philadelphia Election Riot of 1742," *PMHB* 92 (1968): 306–19, and Edward Countryman, " 'Out of Bounds of the Law': Northern Land Rioters in the Eighteenth Century," in Alfred Young, *The American Revolution: Explorations in the History of American Radicalism* (Dekalb, Ill. 1976), 37–70, for background on the land riots.

47. *N.Y. Gazette or Weekly Post Boy*, 26 Feb.–5 March 1770; *N.Y. Gazette and Weekly Mercury*, 22 Jan. 1770; *NJA*, 6:108.

48. WF to Cortlandt Skinner, 28 Jan. 1770, *NJA*, 10:148, 149; *V & P*, 70A:6, 7.

49. *V & P*, 70A:5, 6.

50. Ibid., 5, 7.

51. Ibid., 8.

52. Ibid., 11, 14, 24, 25. WF had asked them to revive the militia bill, had recommended new anti-riot legislation, and had requested help in repairing the colony's prisons (Ibid., p. 8). Their few stabs at reforming the legal system were internally contradictory. While they discouraged creditors from trying to recover debts under £50, they also facilitated the recovery of arrears from insolvent debtors.

53. Ibid., 14, 23, 24; WF to Lord Hillsborough, 28 April 1770, *NJA*, 10:192.

54. WF to BF, 22 Aug. 1767, *PBF*, 14:236.

55. WF to Lord Hillsborough, 20 July 1771, *NJA*, 10:307, 308; *V & P*, 71A:11, 22–25.

56. Lord Hillsborough to WF, 4 Dec. 1771, 6 April 1772, *NJA*, 10:318, 334–336; *V & P*, 71C:18, 27. WF's interpretation of the assembly's rights was ultimately upheld in the summer of 1772. *NJA*, 10:369.

57. *V & P*, 71A:4, 5.

58. Ibid., 9; Stephen Crane to BF, 22 June 1771, *PBF*, 18:134, 135.

59. WF to WS, 18 June 1771, Hart, "Letters," 447–50.

60. *V & P*, 71A:12–16.

61. Stephen Crane to BF, 22 June 1771, *PBF*, 18:134; *V & P*, 71A:18–21; Ernst, *Money and Politics*, 289n, 290n; WF to Lord Hillsborough, 30 April 1771, *NJA*, 10:237, 238. See also ibid., 269–273.

62. WF to Lord Hillsborough, 1 June 1771, ibid., 299. See Ernst, *Money and Politics*, 277, 278, 290, 291.

63. Gen. Gage to Lord Hillsborough, 2 July 1771, Clarence Edwin Carter, ed., *The Correspondence of General Thomas Gage with the Secretaries of State, 1763–1775*, 2 vols. (Hamden, Conn., 1969), 1:303; Lord Hillsborough to WF, 3, 19 July 1771, *NJA*, 10:303, 304; Lord Hillsborough

to Gen. Gage, 19 July 1771, Carter, *Gage Correspondence*, 2:135; WF to Gen. Gage, 28 Oct. 1771, Gage Papers, English, Clements.

64. WF to WS, 18 June 1771, Hart, "Letters," 449.

65. See V & P, 71C:4–36, 65, 69, 72–79; Gen. Gage to Lord Hillsborough, 6 Nov. 1771, Gage Papers, English, Clements; WF to Gen. Gage, 26 Dec. 1771, Gage Papers, American, Clements; NJ Assembly Committee of Correspondence to BF, 21 Dec. 1771, *PBF*, 18:270.

66. WF to WS, 18 June 1771, Hart, "Letters," 448, 449; Stephen Crane to BF, 22 June 1771, *PBF*, 18:134.

67. Hillsborough's approach was not new. But ministers had habitually recognized agents selected solely by the assembly throughout the 1760s. It was this flexibility and lack of attention to detail that the Secretary intended to arrest. He may also have hoped to do away entirely with the colonial agents, who had grown increasingly unpopular in ministerial circles after the Stamp Act crisis. See BF to Thomas Cushing, 5 Feb. 1771, *PBF*, 18:28; Michael Kammen, *A Rope of Sand* (Ithaca, N.Y., 1968), 67, 233–35; Olson, *Anglo-American Politics*, 177, 178.

68. *PBF*, 18:11; BF to Samuel Cooper, 16 Jan. 1771, ibid., 12–16; Lords of Trade to WF, 21 June 1771, *NJA*, 10:301.

69. WF to BF [Sept. or Nov.] 1771, *PBF*, 18:218; WF to Lords of Trade, 21 Oct., 21 Dec. 1771, WF to Lord Hillsborough, 27 Dec. 1771, *NJA*, 10:317, 320, 323. He had made this kind of promise to them in the past. See above pp. 89, 111.

70. BF to Thomas Cushing, 5 Feb. 1771, *PBF*, 18:28; WF to BF, 6 Jan. 1772, ibid., 19:3.

71. BF to WF, 30 Jan. 1772, ibid., 51.

72. WF to BF, [31 Jan.], 2 March 1769, *PBF*, 16:34, 35, 58.

73. WF to BF, 10 May 1768; [2 Jan.], 2 March, 11 May 1769, ibid., 15:122; 16:5, 60, 129, 130; *Pa. Gazette*, 7 May 1767; *Pa. Chronicle*, 25 July–22 Aug. 1768; Newcomb, *Franklin and Galloway*, 195.

74. DF to BF, 13 [15] June, 16 Aug., 14 Oct. 1770, *PBF*, 17:175, 205, 255; Thomas Bond to BF, 7 June 1769, ibid., 16:153; WF to BF, 3 Aug. 1771, ibid., 18:195.

75. WF to BF [31 Jan.], 2 March, 11 May 1769, 30 March, [Sept. or Nov.] 1771, ibid., 16:35, 36, 59, 127, 128; 18:64, 64n, 218; BF to George Read, 12 June 1766, ibid., 13:313; BF to WF, 13 March 1768, ibid., 15:77; Abel James to WF, 16 May 1767, Franklin Papers, 58:133, APS; SW to George Read, 14 April, 14 Nov. 1766; BF to George Read, 12 June 1766, Read, *Life and Correspondence of George Read*, 22, 23, 25; WF to WS, 18 June 1771, Hart, "Letters," 448; BF to WF, 20 April 1771, 19 Aug. 1772, *PBF*, 18:74, 76; 19:256. Some critics contend the "Autobiography" was aimed at wooing the "elegant and snobbish William" away from his longing for advancement in the empire, and toward the pleasures of a simple life of industry, virtue, and self-reliance. See Fleming, *Lightning*, 205, 206; Lopez and Herbert, *Private*, 2; BF to Mathew Carey, 16 Aug. 1786, Smyth, *Writings*, 9:733, 734. For another view see Lemay, "Benjamin Franklin," 238, 239, or Sayre, *Examined*, 19.

76. BF to WF, 20 April 1771, 30 Jan. 1772, *PBF*, 18:75; 19:52.

77. Lopez and Herbert, *Private*, 181; WF to WS, 29 Jan. 1769, Hart, "Letters," 446; WF to BF, 22 Aug. 1767, *PBF*, 14:235–37.

78. Green, "Alienation," 60–64, 72; Hutson, "Reappraisal," 310; Caroline Robins, *The Eighteenth-Century Commonwealth Men* (Cambridge, Mass., 1959, 16, 276; Newcomb, *Franklin and Galloway*, 181, 198; BF to John Ross, 11 April 1767; BF to JG, 14 April 1767; 20 Aug. 1768, *PBF*, 14:117, 124, 125; 15:189, 190.

79. *PBF*, 14:114, 115; BF to WF, 25 Nov. 1767; 13 March 1768, ibid., 326; 15:75, 76.

80. Gerald Stourzh, "Reason and Power in Benjamin Franklin's Political Thought," *American Political Science Review* 47 (1953): 1108, 1112; Conner, *Poor Richard's Politicks*, 144; Greene, "Alienation," 65; Fleming, *Lightning*, 174; BF, "Causes of the American Discontent before 1768," 5–7 Jan. 1768, *PBF*, 15:8, 12; WF to BF, 10 May 1768, ibid., 124; BF to Samuel Cooper, 27 April 1769, ibid., 16:118.

81. BF to WF, 2 July 1768, *PBF*, 15:159–64.

82. WF to BF, [31 Jan.], 2 March 1769, 30 June 1772, *PBF*, 16:34, 35; ibid., 19:194, 195; BF to WF, 20 April 1771, ibid., 18:74, 75. See also Franklin Papers, 3:108, APS.

83. Arthur Lee to Samuel Adams, 10 June 1771, ibid., 18:128; BF to WF, 30 Jan. 1772, ibid., 19:50. It was an argument whose logic he could not pursue too vigorously, for he, too, held a royal post.

84. WS to WF, 3 April 1771, Franklin Papers, 48:139a, APS; WF to WS, 18 June 1771, Hart, "Letters," 448, 449.

85. WS to WF, 3 April 1771, Franklin Papers, 48:139a.

86. WF to WS, 16 June 1771, Franklin Papers, 48:139b, APS. Historian Peter Marshall agrees with WF's assessment of the relative importance of BF and SW to the project. Peter Marshall, "Lord Hillsborough, Samuel Wharton and the Ohio Grant, 1769–1775," *English Historical Review*, 80 (1965): esp. 719, 738.

87. WF to WS, 18 June 1771, Hart, "Letters," 449.

7. Seeds of Controversy

1. V & P, 72:92.

2. Ibid., 73:139.

3. Ibid., 70B:29, 24.

4. Ibid., 22–30.

5. Glen Smith, "Expedient Loyalist," 69; WF to BF, 23 Oct. 1767, *PBF*, 14:293.

6. *NJA*, 5:519. The investigation took place July 25. There seemed no doubt that a robbery had occurred, and there was no direct evidence of Skinner's negligence. Ibid., 520–24; 10:37–39.

7. V & P, 70B:25; 69:5; N.Y. Gazette and Weekly Mercury, 25 July 1768; *NJA*, 5:519; 6:8, 9; WF to Henry Moore, 29 July 1768, Ely Coll. NYHS; Broadside 131, APS; Pa. Gazette, 28 July, 25 Aug. 1768.

8. V & P, 69:14. The assembly attempted to get both treasurers to give security for the funds entrusted to their care. And when the legislation got tied up in council, both Skinner and the western treasurer, Samuel Smith, voluntarily posted security bonds. Gerlach, "Politics and Prerogatives: The Aftermath of the Robbery of the East Jersey Treasury in 1768," *N.J. History* 90 (1972): 139.

9. V & P, 69:74.
10. See Gerlach, *Prologue*, 179.
11. V & P, 70B:21–30, 35.
12. See Gerlach, "Treasury Robbery," 142.
13. Kinsey was a Quaker lawyer, son of James Kinsey, former attorney general and speaker of the New Jersey house, as well as chief justice of Pennsylvania. The son made his reputation as a popular leader because of his prominent role in the treasury affair. Gerlach, *Prologue*, 31, 32.
14. V & P, 72:49–51, 56, 57.
15. Ibid., 64–66.
16. Ibid., 75–77. Once more, Kinsey drafted the message.
17. Ibid., 78, 80, 83; *NJA*, 6:295, 431.
18. Chief Justice Smyth to Lord Hillsborough, 5 Oct. 1772, *NJA*, 10:380.
19. V & P, 72:84, 86.
20. See ibid., 84–92.
21. Ibid., 94. See ibid., 99, for the assembly's belated and negative response to Skinner's request.
22. Ibid., 95, 96.
23. Ibid., 99–103. For Franklin's assessment of the assembly's "secret" motives, see especially p. 100.
24. *N.Y. Gazette*, 26 July 1773; *Pa. Chronicle*, 26 July, 4 Oct. 1773; *Rivington's N.Y. Gazette*, 14 Oct. 1763; *NJA*, 6:357–59; 10:361, 362.
25. Ibid., 361, 362; V & P, 73:3, 6, 7, 9, 10, 12, 13.
26. Ibid., 57. Franklin's presentation of the case against Ford is in ibid., 28–58.
27. Ibid., 57–60, 66, 67; Cortlandt Skinner to Philip Kearney [18 Nov.], 5 Dec. 1773, *NJA*, 10:412–14.
28. Cortlandt Skinner to Philip Kearney, 19 Dec. 1773, ibid., 415; V & P, 73:85–112. The final vote was 24–5. Ibid., 115, 116. On the same day, the council unanimously rejected the assembly's request that Skinner be removed. *NJA*, 6:375, 376.
29. V & P, 74:125. One of those was Charles Pettit, WF's clerk.
30. Ibid., 120, 123, 153, 170, 172, 180. Only two petitions asked that the treasurer be tried while he still held office. Ibid., 152.
31. Ibid., 135–37, 139.
32. Ibid., 138, 143, 151.
33. Ibid., 138, 139.
34. Ibid., 166, 167.
35. Ibid., 176, 177; *NJA*, 6:381–84. He did not even get to name his first choice as Skinner's replacement. WF wanted to appoint Philip Kearney, Cortlandt Skinner's father-in-law, to the post, but the council, questioning Kearney's integrity and ability, strongly advised against it. John Smyth got the job.
36. V & P, 74:184, 185, 188, 193–95; *NJA*, 6:387–89.
37. For an attack on the assembly's behavior in general and Kinsey's behavior in particular, see W. A. Whitehead, "The Robbery of the Treasury of East Jersey in 1768," in N.J. Hist. Soc., *Proc.* 5 (1850–51): 51–65.
38. For criticism of WF's stance, see Duer, *Lord Stirling*, 100. Even Mariboe, generally sympathetic to WF, gives him low marks on his handling of the treasury crisis. Mariboe, "William Franklin," 393.

39. BF to WF, 7 Oct. 1772, *PBF*, 19:323; N.Y. *Gazette and the Weekly Mercury*, 18 Oct. 1773.
40. See Lord Hillsborough to WF, 11 Jan. 1772, *NJA*, 10:323; Gen. Gage to WF, 12 Jan. 1772, Franklin Papers, 58:41, APS; V & P, 72:22, 24, 25, 27, 52, 66; ibid., 73:61, 65, 113; WF to Gen. Gage, 19 Aug. 1772, 5 May 1773; David Ogden to WF, 20 May 1773, Gage Papers, American, Clements; WF to Gen. Haldiman, 15 June 1773, PRO CO5, 90, p. 341, LC.
41. V & P, 72:22, 24, 25, 27, 52, 66; ibid., 73:65, 113; WF to Gen. Gage, 29 Aug. 1772; 5 May 1773; David Ogden to WF 20 May, 1773, Gage Papers, American, Clements; WF to Gen. Haldiman, 15 June 1773, PRO CO5, 90, p. 341, LC.
42. V & P, 72:6. The governor of New Hampshire was the only other royal governor still completely at the mercy of the legislature for his salary by 1772.
43. Lord Hillsborough to WF, 6 June 1772, WF to Lord Dartmouth, 13 June 1774, *NJA*, 10:361, 362, 462; V & P, 72:5, 6, 19, 20; ibid., 74:179, 186, 189. See also *NJA*, 10:383–85, 697, 698.
44. WF to BF, 13 Oct. 1772, *PBF*, 19:336.
45. WF to Lord Dartmouth, 5 Jan. 1773, *NJA*, 10:392, 393.
46. WF to Lord Dartmouth, 31 May 1773, Lord Dartmouth to WF, 4 Aug. 1773, ibid., 405, 406, 408.
47. Lord Dartmouth to WF, 1 July 1772, Franklin Papers, 48:142, APS; WF to BF, 13 Oct. 1772, *PBF*, 19:333; WF to Lord Hillsborough, 5 May 1772, *NJA*, 10:337, 338. See also WF to Lord Hillsborough, 15 March 1771, Franklin Papers, 45:81, APS, for a similar conflict between the governor and Lord Hillsborough.
48. Marshall, "Lord Hillsborough," 730; Sosin, *Whitehall and the Wilderness*, 202–4; Kenneth P. Bailey, *The Ohio Company of Virginia and the Westward Movement, 1748–1792* (Glendale, Calif.), 246; Currey, *Road to Revolution*, 294; Randall, *Revenge*, 245, 246; Byars Papers, 18, 19, HSP; BF to WF, 17 Aug. 1772, *PBF*, 19:243; Ohio Book, Etting MSS., HSP.
49. WF to Michael Gratz, 28 Sept. 1772, Etting MSS, HSP. WS agreed. He had heard that Hillsborough was still trying to obstruct the land grant, but thought he had no chance of succeeding. WS to David Hall, 7 Oct. 1772, Hart, "Correspondence," 244.
50. BF to WF, 17 Aug. 1772, *PBF*, 19:243, 244. Ironically, Lord Hillsborough blamed BF for his downfall. BF to WF, 14 July 1773, ibid., 20:309.
51. BF to WF, 17 Aug. 1772, *PBF*, 19:243, 244; Currey, *Road to Revolution*, 301.
52. In fact Dartmouth was considering none of the partners as governor, not even William Johnson who reputedly had the inside track. He planned to give the job to his cousin, Major William Legge. Abernethy, *Western Lands*, 55–58.
53. WF to BF, 13, 29 Oct. 1772; BF to WF, 14 Feb., 14 July 1773, *PBF*, 19:333, 334, 349–52; 20:60–62, 304; SW to George Croghan, 3 Feb., 3 Nov. 1773, TW to George Croghan, 4 May 1774, Gen. Thomas Cadwallader Collection, Croghan Papers, Box 7, HSP; TW to SW, 24 Nov. 1773, Wharton Letterbook, 1773–1784, HSP; JG to WF, 25 Nov. 1773; WF to JG, 25 Nov. 1773, Franklin Papers, 48:144a, 144b, APS; Currey,

Road to Revolution, 301. See Alvord, *The Illinois Country*, 299, for SW's self-serving analysis of the quarrel with the Franklins.

54. WF to BF 30 April 1773; BF to WF 14 July 1773, *PBF*, 20:184; 304, 305; WF to SW, 21 Dec. 1770; WF to TW, 5 Nov. 1771, 27 April 1772, William Franklin Autograph Collection, HSP.

55. BF to WF, 14 Feb. 1773; WF to BF, 29 Oct. 1772, 5 Jan., 30 April 1773, *PBF*, 20:60–62; 19:349–52; 20:12, 185; SW to George Croghan, 24 Dec. 1772, Gen. Cadwallader Collection, Croghan Papers, Box 7, HSP; Earl of Stirling to WF, 5 Dec. 1772, Franklin Papers, 48:143, APS; Chief Justice Smyth to Lord Hillsborough, 5 Oct. 1772, NJA, 10:380, 381. Franklin had reason to be concerned, especially where Virginia's Governor Dunmore was involved. At the end of 1773, Dunmore began surveying sections of the Ohio Valley, touching off a short-lived war with the Shawnee. Virginia's victory gave Dunmore some leverage in pursuing his claims to Vandalia. Mariboe, "William Franklin," 338; Byars Papers, 26, HSP; TW to SW, 7 May 1774; TW to George Croghan, 17 March 1774, Wharton Letterbook, 1773–1784, 73–84, HSP.

56. BF to WF, 14 Feb., 6 April 1773, *PBF*, 20:62, 148; Currey, *Road to Revolution*, 298.

57. See BF to Thomas Cushing, 10 June 1771, *PBF*, 18:121, 122; BF to WF, 14 July 1773, ibid., 20:310 for evidence of BF's deep hostility toward Lord Hillsborough.

58. BF to WF, 30 Jan. 1772; WF to BF, 13 Oct. 1772, *PBF*, 19:47–49; 333. BF's version was quite different. He claimed that he had tried on several occasions to see Hillsborough, but had been abruptly turned away on every attempt. BF to WF, 19–22 Aug. 1772, ibid., 257, 258.

59. WF to BF, 13 Oct. 1772, *PBF*, 19:335, 336.

60. WF to BF, 5 Jan. 1773, *PBF*, 20:12; BF to Samuel Cooper, 13 Jan. 1772, to WF, 6–[9] April 1773, ibid., 19:13, 14; 20:147.

61. WF's one terse reference to the dispute came in January 1774, when the assembly had recessed for the Christmas break before returning to demand Skinner's resignation. He simply said he was "a good deal engaged" with assembly business, an obvious understatement under the circumstances. WF to BF, 5 Jan. 1774, *PBF*, 21:11.

62. BF to WF, 19–[22] Aug. 1772, *PBF*, 19:259, 260. See also BF to WF, 14 July 1773, ibid., 20:303, 312, 313.

63. BF to Josiah Davenport, 14 Feb. 1763, to WF, 14 July 1773; WF to BF, 4 May 1773, *PBF*, 20:56, 57, 307; 196, 197.

64. BF to WF, 14 July 1773, *PBF*, 20:303, 308, 309.

65. WF to BF, 13 Oct. 1772; BF to WF, 2 Dec. 1772, *PBF*, 19:336, 337; 418. Randall claims that BF's reference to WF's sociable relations with neighboring governors is intended to be read as sarcasm. There is nothing in the context of the letter, or in the context of their relationship in 1772, to justify such a reading. See Randall, *Revenge*, 243.

66. BF to WF, 19–[22], 3, [4] Nov. 1772, 14 Feb. 1773, *PBF*, 19:256, 360, 361; ibid., 20:60, 62; WF to BF, 13 Oct. 1772, 5 Jan. 1773, ibid., 19:336; 20:12.

67. See, for instance, BF to WF, 14, 25 July 1773, *PBF*, 20:309, 327.

68. BF to WF, 30 Jan. 1772, 14 July, 3 Aug. 1773, *PBF*, 19:52, 20:311, 312, 339, 340; Cochrane, *William Strahan*, 93, 94.

69. BF to WF, 30 Jan. 1772, *PBF*, 19:53.
70. BF to WF, 6 [9] April, 3 Nov. 1773, to Jane Mecom, 1 Nov. 1773, *PBF*, 20:147, 461, 457, 458.

8. A Government Man

1. BF to WF, 6 Oct. 1773, *PBF*, 20:437.
2. WF to Lord Dartmouth, 31 May 1774, *NJA*, 10:458, 459.
3. *PBF*, 19:399–401; BF to Thomas Cushing, 2 Dec. 1772, ibid., 409–13. The letters are printed as an Appendix in ibid., 20:539–80.
4. Samuel Cooper to BF, 14 [15] June 1773, *PBF*, 20:233. They were printed on June 10 in the *Mass. Spy* and by the end of June they had been disseminated everywhere. Ibid., 539n.
5. WF to BF, 29 July 1773, BF to WF, 1 Sept. 1773, *PBF*, 20:332, 387; Lopez and Herbert, *Private*, 190.
6. Temple was the former Surveyor General of the Customs for the Northern Colonies. He was an enemy of Hutchinson, a radical leader in Boston, and a long-time friend of both Franklins.
7. BF to Thomas Cushing, 25 July 1773, WF to BF, 29 July 1773, Samuel Cooper to BF, 10 Nov. 1773; *PBF*, 20:323, 332, 480.
8. BF to WF, 1 Sept. 1773, *PBF*, 20:387. See also BF to Thomas Cushing, 2 Dec. 1772; to Samuel Cooper, 7 July 1773; to Lord Dartmouth, 21 Aug. 1773, ibid., 19:412; 20:270, 271; 372, 373; BF to Samuel Cooper, 25 Feb. 1774, ibid., 21:124, for other indications that this indeed was BF's motive. Most historians agree that BF sincerely wanted to reconcile differences between England and America when he sent the letters to Boston. See for example, Newcomb, *Franklin and Galloway*, 240; Greene, "Alienation," 52, 53. It seems likely that he was also motivated by a desire to ingratiate himself with Boston's radicals, who remained suspicious of his moderation.
9. BF to WF, 1 Sept., 6 Oct. 1773, *PBF*, 20:387, 439. See also BF to Thomas Cushing, 6 May 1773, ibid., 200; Tucker and Hendrickson, *Fall of the First British Empire*, 305, 305n.
10. He could not even be absolutely sure that BF wanted anonymity. It is conceivable that BF used the letter as a vehicle to acknowledge his part in sending the Hutchinson-Oliver letters. He knew his mail was often intercepted by British authorities and could not have been certain that this letter would escape detection. See Randall, *Revenge*, 266.
11. WF to BF, 29 July 1773, BF to WF, 1 Sept. 1773, *PBF*, 20:332, 387. At some point, WF actually wrote a letter to WS indicating his disapproval of BF's conduct, and implying that he wanted his views made public. But his attempt at covering himself did little good, as his father's enemies assumed BF had suggested this stratagem himself to give his son more credibility at home. Hutchinson, *Diary*, 1:219.
12. BF to WF, 14 Feb. 1773, *PBF*, 20:63, 64. See B. W. Labaree, *The Boston Tea Party* (New York, 1964), 70–73. BF was correct, for once, in predicting the negative reaction the Tea Act would have in America. Unlike the MPs he knew that principle was by now as important as financial self-interest to a substantial and growing number of colonists. BF to Thomas Cushing 4 June 1773, *PBF*, 20:228.

13. BF to Thomas Cushing, 9 March 1773, to Mass. House of Representatives, 7 July 1773, *PBF*, 20:99, 279–83.
14. BF to WF, 6 Oct. 1773, *PBF*, 20:437.
15. *PBF*, 20:437–39; V & P, 73:5.
16. Labaree, *Boston Tea Party*, 109–41; Samuel Cooper to BF, 17 Dec. 1773, *PBF*, 20:500–505.
17. *Pa. Packet*, 9 Jan. 1775; *NJA*, 10:530–32; Gertrude Wood, *William Paterson of New Jersey 1745–1801* (Fair Lawn, N.J., 1933), 22; *Pa. Journal*, 16 Feb. 1774; Cohen and Gerlach, "Princeton," 80–81; V & P, 73:122; WF to Lord Dartmouth, 31 May 1774, *NJA*, 10:458. New Jersey was the last mainland colony to form a Committee of Correspondence.
18. BF had publicly acknowledged his role in December. *London Public Advertiser*, 25 Dec. 1773.
19. *PBF*, 20:278, 279; BF to Mass. House of Representatives, 7 July 1773, ibid., 282. See Greene, "Alienation" and Fleming, *Lightning*, 240–250, for two excellent accounts of the event.
20. Wedderburn had long been a thorn in BF's side. He had opposed repeal of the Stamp Act and had been instrumental in thwarting the Vandalia project.
21. See BF to Jane Mecom, 30 Dec. 1770, *PBF*, 17:314, and *ABF*, 247, for BF's expression of his philosophy of personal independence.
22. BF to WF, 2 Feb. 1774, to Jane Mecom, 17 Feb., 28 July 1774, *PBF*, 21:75, 103, 264, 265; Alexander Carlyle, *Autobiography of the Rev. Dr. Alexander Carlyle* (Edinburgh, 1910), 458.
23. *ABF*, 185.
24. BF to WF, 18 Feb. 1774, *PBF*, 21:107, 108.
25. *N.Y. Journal or the General Advertiser*, 26 May 1774; Hanna, *Benjamin Franklin and Pennsylvania Politics*, 199; Conner, *Poor Richard's Politicks*, 161.
26. TW to SW, 3 May 1774, Wharton Letterbook, 1773–1784, HSP.
27. WF to BF, 3 May 1774, *PBF*, 21:207. Actually BF had begun to make plans for returning to America, landing in New York and stopping at Burlington before reaching Philadelphia, right before the Cockpit incident. He wanted, he said, to retire from politics, to offer what advice he could, but to avoid the spotlight as much as possible, BF to WF, 5 Jan. 1774, ibid., 9.
28. WF to BF, 3 May 1774, *PBF*, 21:207.
29. Ibid.
30. BF to WF, 7 May [1774], *PBF*, 21:212.
31. *PBF*, 21:457–59.
32. WF to Lord Dartmouth, 31 May 1774, *NJA*, 10:458, 459.
33. *Pa. Gazette*, 29 June 1774; *NJA*, 10:459, 460, 465–67. One by one, the other New Jersey counties followed suit. *N.Y. Journal or General Advertiser*, 30 June, 7, 21 July 1774; *Pa. Gazette*, 13 July 1774; *Rivington's N.Y. Gazette*, 14 July 1774; *Pa. Journal*, 20 July 1774.
34. WF to Lord Dartmouth, 28 June 1774, *NJA*, 10:464.
35. WF to Lord Dartmouth, 13, 28 June 1774, *NJA*, 10:461–64; *Pa. Gazette*, 8 June 1774; WF to Lord Dartmouth, 28 June 1774, *NJA*, 10:464. James Kinsey had seen WF's negative response as almost inevitable from the

start. The Brunswick petition had specifically stated that it wanted the
assembly to discuss the events in Boston. WF could not allow this without
risking his commission, and Kinsey thought this quite unlikely. He favored
an alternate petition, which he himself had composed, asking the assembly
to discuss "public Business." Kinsey to Elias Boudinot 14 June, 2 July
1774, Boudinot Papers, Box 1, LC.

36. Thomas Wharton to Thomas Walpole, 7 Jan. 1774, Wharton Letterbook,
1773–1784, HSP; BF to Mass. House Committee of Correspondence, 2
Feb. 1774, to Thomas Cushing, 22 March 1774, to WF, 30 June 1774,
PBF, 21:76, 77, 153, 235.

37. WF to Lord Dartmouth, 28 June 1774, *NJA*, 10:465; WF to BF, [July
1774], *PBF*, 21:237, 238.

38. WF to Lord Dartmouth, 28 June 1774, *NJA*, 10:465.

39. *Pa. Journal*, 27 July 1774; *NJA*, 10:469–72; *Minutes of the Provincial
Congress and the Council of Safety of the State of New Jersey* (Trenton,
1879), 25–27 (hereafter, *NJPCS*).

40. TW to Thomas Walpole, 27 Dec. 1773, Wharton Letterbook, 1773–
1784, HSP; TW to George Croghan, 4 May 1774, Gen. Cadwallader Collection Box 7, HSP; BF to WF, 7 Sept. [1774], *PBF* 21:288. In July, Sir
William Johnson died with WF at his side. Ibid., 287n, 288n.

41. See especially WF to WS, 18 June 1771, Hart, "Letters," 447–49.

42. After WF had seen one version of the letter's contents, he declared it was
an altered copy, significantly different from the original. TW to SW, 25
Oct. 1774, Wharton Letterbook, 1773–1784, HSP.

43. Thomas Coombe, Jr., to BF, 24 Sept. 1774, *PBF*, 21:314. It is true that
both Walpole and SW rushed excerpts of the letter to America as soon as
possible.

44. TW to SW, 23 Sept. 1774, Wharton Letterbook, 1773–1784, HSP. The
"Hored lie," as BF's sister called it, had spread to Boston. Jane Mecom to
BF, 3 [–21] Nov. 1774, *PBF*, 21:349. Even BF expressed some concern
over the rumors, although he insisted that he did not "blame" WF for the
views attributed to him. TW to SW, 23 Sept. 1747, Wharton Letterbook,
1773–1747, HSP.

45. TW to Thomas Walpole, 23 Sept. 1774, Wharton Letterbook, 1773–
1784, HSP.

46. By this time it was even being said that the embarrassing letter had been
sent, not to WS, but to the ministry itself. *Boston Gazette*, 3 Oct. 1774.

47. TW to SW, 23 Sept., 25 Oct. 1774, Wharton Letterbook, 1773–1784,
HSP.

48. TW to SW, 25 Oct. 1774, ibid.

49. BF to WF, 1 Aug. 1774, *PBF*, 21:266.

50. Ibid.

51. BF to WF, 7 Sept. [1774], *PBF*, 21:286, 287.

52. Ibid., 287.

53. WF to Lord Dartmouth, 28 June 1774, *NJA*, 10:464–72.

54. See Randall, *Revenge*, 283; Mary Beth Norton, *The British-Americans:
The Loyalist Exiles in England 1774–1790* (Boston, 1972), 7.

55. WF to Lord Dartmouth, 6 Sept. 1774, *NJA*, 10:473–94. Confidentiality
was essential, for the delegates had decided that the "doors be kept shut"

and members were "under the strongest obligation of honour, to keep the proceedings secret." Worthington Chauncey Ford, ed., *Journals of the Continental Congress, 1774–1789* (Washington, 1904), 1:26.

56. WF to Lord Dartmouth, 6 Sept. 1774, NJA, 10:474, 475. [JG to WF], 3 Sept. 1774, ibid., 475–77. A copy of JG's pamphlet is in ibid., 478–492. See also H. J. Henderson, *Party Politics in the Continental Congress* (New York, 1974), 39–40; Robert M. Calhoon, "Galloway," 356–78.

57. WF to Lord Dartmouth, 6 Dec. 1774, NJA, 10:504; Ford, *Journal*, 1:48, 49; E. C. Burnett, ed., *Letters of Members of the Continental Congress* (Washington, 1921), 1:51n.

58. [WF to JG] 12 March 1775, NJA, 10:578.

59. Calhoon, "Galloway," 359, 375; Henderson, *Party Politics*, 23, 24, 32–34; [JG to WF], 5 Sept. 1774, 26 March 1775, NJA, 10:477, 478, 582–84; WF to Lord Dartmouth, 6 Dec. 1774, ibid., 503. JG's insinuations of a conspiracy does not square with the facts. Congress probably discussed the plan, but never actually voted on it before laying it on the table by a vote of 6–5. While Thomson did not enter the plan on the official minutes, this was often his procedure. Indeed, the following July, BF's proposal of some Articles of Confederation received the same treatment. See Paul H. Smith, *Letters of Delegates to Congress, Aug. 1774–1775* (Washington, 1976), 1:116, 643n, 664n.

60. [WF to JG] 12 March 1775, NJA, 10:578, 579.

61. See Lord Dartmouth to WF, 4 May, 6 July, 7 Sept., 2 Nov. 1774, NJA, 10:456, 468, 496, 497, 501.

62. WF to Lord Dartmouth, 29 Oct., 6 Dec. 1774, NJA, 10:500, 503, 504.

63. BF to WF, 7 Oct. 1772, PBF, 19:323; *N.Y. Gazette and the Weekly Mercury*, 18 Oct. 1773; Lurie and Walroth, *The Minutes of the Board of Proprietors of the Eastern Division of New Jersey from 1764 to 1794*, 4:181, 191; Mariboe, "William Franklin," 389, 390; Randall, *Revenge*, 279, 280.

64. *N.Y. Gazette and the Weekly Mercury*, 24 Oct. 1774.

65. WF to BF, 24 Dec. 1774, PBF, 21:403.

66. PBF, 21:402, 403.

67. Ibid., pp. 403, 404.

68. The letter to which he referred in his Dec. 24 missive has been lost. It was a "long letter," dealing at least in part with WTF's education. Whether or not he tried to defend himself or his views is, unfortunately, not clear.

69. PBF, 21:404.

70. Ibid.

71. Ibid.

9. "Two Roads"

1. V & P, 75A:6.

2. Ibid., 75B:30.

3. *N.Y. Gazette and the Weekly Mercury*, 5, 19, 26 Dec. 1774; *Pa. Gazette*, 7, 21 Dec. 1774, 11 Jan. 1775; NJA, 10:530–33.

4. The congressional petition included the usual American complaints against standing armies, parliamentary taxation, trade restrictions and the loss in America of the rights of Englishmen. It also asked for the immediate revocation of the Coercive Acts and the Quebec Act. Congress insisted that

it was asking for no new rights and had no desire to encroach upon the royal prerogative. It hoped only to return to its pre-1763 status. See *NJA*, 10:522–29.

5. WF to Lord Dartmouth, 1 Feb. 1775, *NJA*, 10:537.
6. *V & P*, 75A:5, 6.
7. Ibid.
8. Lord Dartmouth to WF, 7 Sept. 1774, *NJA*, 10:497; *V & P*, 75A:6, 7.
9. *V & P*, 75A:13, 58–62; *NJA*, 6:487, 488; [WF to JC], 12 March 1775, ibid., 10:576, 577.
10. WF to Lord Dartmouth, 1 Feb. 1775, [WF to JG], 12 March 1775, *NJA*, 10:537, 575, 576; *V & P*, 75B:15, 16; *V & P*, 75A:16. The delegates were James Kinsey, William Livingston, John de Hart, Stephen Crane, and Samuel Smith.
11. *V & P*, 75A:30, 31. See Gordon Wood, *Creation of the American Republic 1776–1787* (New York, 1969).
12. *V & P*, 75A:31, 32.
13. *NJA*, 10:534; WF to Lord Dartmouth, 18 Feb., 3 April 1775; Lord Dartmouth to WF, 19 Oct. 1774, ibid., 548, 571; 497, 498. See also *N.Y. Journal or General Advertiser*, 23 March, 6 April 1777.
14. Even BF had no idea that his son was forwarding news to the ministry, and he would certainly have taken a dim view of his actions. BF to JG, 25 Feb. 1775, *PBF*, 21:508.
15. See WF to Lord Dartmouth, 3 April, 6 May, 5 June, 4 July 1775. *NJA*, 10:570–86, 590–97, 606–19, 639–42, 644–45.
16. See William H. Nelson, *The American Tory* (New York, 1961) for an analysis of the passive nature of loyalist leaders.
17. *NJA*, 10:553–57. Dartmouth cautioned all governors to avoid showing his exact explanation of the North offer to their respective assemblies, but instead to explicate its general import. Ibid., 555.
18. WF to Lord Dartmouth, 6 May 1775, ibid., 591.
19. Ibid., p. 587; WF to General Gage, 1 June 1774, Gage Papers, American, Clements.
20. Shy, *Toward Lexington*, 418; WF to Lord Dartmouth, 6 May 1775, *NJA*, 10:592, 593.
21. See, for example, Rosenberg, "William Paterson," 19; Cohen and Gerlach, "Princeton," 82; *Pa. Packet*, 13, 17 May 1775.
22. WF to Lord Dartmouth, 6 May 1775, *NJA*, 10:591, 592; Gerlach, *Prologue*, 258–60; WF to General Gage, 20 June 1775, Gage Papers, American, Clements.
23. Gerlach, *Prologue*, 260, 261; WF to Lord Dartmouth, 6 May 1775, *NJA*, 10:592. The experience of James Allen in neighboring Pennsylvania provides some indication that WF's view was not totally incorrect, at least in the more conservative middle colonies. Allen signed the Association and joined the militia, not only to avoid recriminations but because he thought that "discreet people mixing with them, may keep them in Order." Allen, *Diary*, *PMHB* 9 (1885):186.
24. WF to Lord Dartmouth, 6 May 1775, *NJA*, 10:593, 594.
25. See Silas Deane to Elizabeth Deane, 12 May [1775], Smith, *Letters*, 1:345, 346; *NJA*, 6:533, 534.
26. WF to Lord Dartmouth, 6 May 1775, *NJA*, 10:594.

27. V & P, 75B:5.
28. WF to Lord Dartmouth, 5 June 1775, NJA, 10:602.
29. V & P, 75B:5.
30. Ibid., 6, 10, 11.
31. Ibid., 7–12. In fact, by now sovereignty, not taxation, was the real issue. North's concessions were genuine, and they may have revealed a sincere desire not to burden the colonies unfairly. But they always implied the threat of power, and consequently were unacceptable to American hard-liners. See Tucker and Hendrickson, *The Fall of the First British Empire*, 367, 368, 373–78.
32. V & P, 75B:6, 11, 12.
33. Ibid., 9–11.
34. Ibid., 7, 10, 11.
35. See WF to Lord Dartmouth, 6 May 1775, NJA, 10:593, 594.
36. V & P, 75B:12, 13, 15, 16.
37. Ibid., 24–26. Speaker Cortlandt Skinner publicly dissented from the as-sembly's response, complaining that he had not been allowed to express his disapproval in the Assembly Minutes. WF to Lord Dartmouth, 5 June 1775, NJA, 10:603.
38. V & P, 75B:27.
39. Ibid., 28, 29.
40. He privately admitted that the "mistakes" he referred to were not the products of his own hand, but rather the result of printing errors. WF to Lord Dartmouth, 5 June 1775, NJA, 10:605.
41. V & P, 75B:30.
42. BF to Peter Collinson, 25 Aug. 1755, PBF, 6:168.

10. An "Appearance of Government"

1. WF to Lord Dartmouth, 5 Sept. 1775, NJA 10:658.
2. WF to Lord Dartmouth, 5 Jan. 1775, NJA, 10:679.
3. WF to WS, 7 May 1775, Hart, "Letters," 454.
4. BF to JG, 8 May 1775, PBF, 22:33.
5. Silas Deane to Mrs. Deane, 12 May [1775], 2 June 1775, Joseph Hewes to Samuel Johnston, 11 May 1775, John Adams to James Warren, 21 May 1775, Stephen Hopkins to Ruth Hopkins, 25 May 1775, Smith, *Letters*, 1:347, 433, 347, 364, 407.
6. Silas Deane, *Diary* [23 May 1775], Smith, *Letters*, 1:371. Deane and a Mr. Moore were present at the dinner. Randall suggests that the dinner party "may well have included" both John Dickinson and Gov. John Penn, arguing that his decision to meet with such dignitaries indicates that WF had rejected any effort to use his father's influence. Randall, *Revenge*, 326. The record, however, neither confirms nor denies that WF dined with those gentlemen that night.
7. BF to JG, 8 May 1775, PBF, 22:33; Pa. Ledger, 20 May 1775; WF to Lord Dartmouth, 5 June 1775, NJA, 10:602, 603.
8. WF was not alone in his hopes. WS, who had seen BF recently, also thought that he might help reconcile the differences between England and America. WS to David Hall, 5 July 1775, Hart, "Correspondence," 250.

9. BF to WF, 22 March, 1775, *PBF*, 21:545–99.

10. John Adams to Abigail Adams, 23 July 1775, Smith, *Letters*, 1:649; *PBF*, 22:33n; BF to JG, 25 Feb. 1775, to Humphrey Marshall, 23 May 1775, ibid., 21:509, 22:50, 51.

11. Peter Orlando Hutchinson, *The Diary and Letters of His Excellency Thomas Hutchinson Esq.* (Boston, 1886), 2:237.

12. BF to WF, 22 March 1775, *PBF*, 21:546, 596; see also 567, 579.

13. *PBF*, 21:545, 551, 567, 575–78. BF did not know who was involved in the delicate negotiations. Thomas Viliers, Lord Hyde, one of the King's ministers was surely involved. Dartmouth also knew something about the negotiations and he even had reason to suspect that Lord North knew what was happening. He dealt directly with David Barclay, a British banker, merchant, and former colonial agent, and his old friend Dr. John Fothergill, Dartmouth's physician and adviser. He also conducted parallel, but intertwined discussions with Viscount Richard Howe. And he had a brief but fruitless meeting with former Governor Pownall. Ibid., 550, 551, 565, 566, 568.

14. Ibid., 554–62, 572. The "Hints" can be found on, pp. 365–68.

15. BF to WF, 7 Sept. [1774], 22 March 1775, *PBF*, 21:287, 589, 596.

16. Ibid., 595.

17. Ibid., 581–83.

18. [JG to WF], 26 March 1775, *NJA*, 10:581–84; Joseph Hewes to Samuel Johnston, 11 May 1775, Smith, *Letters*, 1:342.

19. Hutchinson, *Diary*, 2:237.

20. Ibid., 237, 238; Joseph Galloway, *Letters from Cicero and Catilene the Second* (London, 1781), 47, 48.

21. WF to General Gage, 20 June 1775, Gage Papers, American, Clements; *NJPCS*, 181–83. It had also called for annual elections so that taxpayers would be represented in the provincial assembly. Ibid., 187.

22. WF to Lord Dartmouth, 5 June 1775, *NJA*, 10:604.

23. Hills, *History of the Church at Burlington*, 511n; WF to General Gage, 20 June 1775, Gage Papers, American, Clements; Lord Dartmouth to WF, 7 June, 12 July 1775, *NJA*, 10:643, 651; BF to WF, 22 March 1775, *PBF*, 21:582.

24. Lord Dartmouth to WF, 7 June, 5 July 1775, *NJA*, 10:643, 645–47.

25. BF to Jonathan Shipley, 7 July 1775, WF to BF, 14 Aug. 1775, *PBF*, 22:98, 170.

26. WF to BF, 6 Sept. 1775, *PBF*, 22:191; Whitehead, "Biographical Sketch," 144; *PBF*, 22:xliv.

27. Mrs. D. Woolford to WTF, 29 July 1775, Franklin Papers, 101:2, APS.

28. Ibid.; WF to BF, 14 Aug., 6 Sept. 1775, *PBF*, 22:171, 191.

29. WF to WTF, 14 Sept., 9 Oct., 26 Oct. 1775, Franklin Papers, 101:4, 6, 7, APS.

30. WTF to WF, 18 Oct. 1775; WF to WTF, 26, 30 Oct. 1775, Franklin Papers, 48:145, 101:7, 8, APS.

31. WF to WTF, 9 Oct. 1775, Franklin Papers, 101:6, APS.

32. WF to WTF, 14 Sept. 1775, 5 Feb. 1776, Franklin Papers, 101:4, 11, APS.

33. WF to Lord Dartmouth, 2 Aug. 1775, *NJA*, 10:653.

34. WF to Lord Dartmouth, 5 Sept. 1775, ibid., 658.

35. Ibid., 656–59.
36. Ibid., 659.
37. Charles Pettit to Lord Stirling, 7 Sept. 1775, William Alexander Papers, 4, NYHS.
38. Lord Stirling to WF, 14 Sept. 1775, William Alexander Papers, 4, NYHS.
39. WF to Lord Stirling, 15 Sept. 1775, William Alexander Papers, 4, NYHS.
40. Even Stephen Skinner had agreed to serve on a local committee at the beginning of the summer. And by Christmas, three councilors actually threw their support to the Provincial Congress. WF to Lord Dartmouth, 5 June 1775, 5 Jan. 1776, NJA, 10:604, 678.
41. WF to WTF, 30 Oct. 1775, Franklin Papers, 101:8, APS; WF to Lord Dartmouth, 3 Oct. 1775; NJA, 10:663, 665.
42. Ibid., 622, 663.
43. Gerlach, Prologue, 287–90.
44. WF to Lord Dartmouth, 3 Oct. 1775, NJA, 10:665. Thirteen of the delegates were members of the Provincial Congress, and one was a member of the Continental Congress.
45. V & P, 75C:4.
46. Ibid., 5. He did know, of course, that on October 6, the Continental Congress had passed a resolution telling the provincial assemblies to arrest anyone threatening the "safety of the colony, or the liberties of America." While this resolution was composed with Virginia's Lord Dunmore, not WF, in mind, it did nothing to assuage his growing anxieties. Smith, Letters, 2:124–26, 127n.
47. V & P, 75C:5, 6.
48. Ibid., 9. The house approved the bill by a wide margin on the 29th. V & P, 75C:22–25.
49. Ibid., 11, 12.
50. Ibid., 6, 10, 13, 15–17; John de Hart to the Assembly, 13 Nov. 1775, William Franklin Papers, 1775–1776, Force Papers, 7E, LC; WF to Lord Dartmouth, 5 Jan. 1776, NJA, 10:680, 681.
51. V & P, 75C:19, 20, 27; WF to Lord Dartmouth, 5 Jan. 1776, NJA, 10: 681.
52. V & P, 75C:28.
53. Ibid., 28, 29.
54. The motion to dissolve was defeated when speaker Cortlandt Skinner broke a 12–12 tie and cast a negative vote. Ibid., 29, 30.
55. William Franklin Papers, Reel, 72, Force Collection, LC; WF to Lord Dartmouth, 5 Jan. 1776, NJA 10:678.
56. Smith, Letters, 2:320n; V & P, 75C:36.
57. NJA, 10:689–91.
58. V & P, 75C:36. In fact Jonathan Williams had delivered the earlier petition to Dartmouth, who in turn conveyed it to the King. But George III never "condescended" to respond to New Jersey's missive. Jonathan Williams, Jr., to BF, 19 July 1775, PBF, 22:111.
59. V & P, 75C:36, 37.
60. Pa. Gazette, 6 Dec. 1775; WF to Lord Dartmouth, 5 Jan. 1776, NJA, 10:678, 679.
61. Ibid., 676–78.

11. "An Enemy to the Liberties . . ."

1. WF to the New Jersey Assembly, 17 June 1776, NJA, 10:727, 728.
2. NJPCS, 456.
3. Just that spring, WF had invited Jane Mecom to stay with him and Elizabeth (EF) at Perth Amboy, but the offer had ultimately been rejected. BF to Jane Mecom, 17 June 1775, PBF, 22:67.
4. Jane Mecom to Catherine Greene, 24 Nov. 1775, Van Doren, Mecom, 165; EF to WTF, 9 Nov. 1775, APS; Willard Randall, The Proprietary House in Amboy (Trenton, N.J., 1975), 20.
5. Joseph Reed to Charles Pettit, n.d., Reed Papers 4, NYHS; WF to Lord Dartmouth, 5 Jan. 1776, NJA, 10:679; Valentine, Lord Stirling, 160; Richard Smith, "Diary," Smith, Letters, 3:71, 72.
6. NJPCS, 336, 337; Ford, Continental Congress, 4:18–21; Lord Stirling to President of Congress, 6 Jan. 1776; Duer, Stirling, 119; Richard Smith, "Diary," Smith, Letters, 3:71, 72.
7. Valentine, Lord Stirling, 118, 119; WF to Lord Dartmouth, 8 Jan. 1776, NJA, 10:699, 700. Winds was Morris County's representative in the colonial assembly and a deputy to the Provincial Congress in the summer and fall of 1775. NJPCS, 68, 117, 169, 197. See also Ford, Continental Congress, 4:42.
8. WF to Lord Dartmouth, 5 Sept. 1775, 8 Jan. 1776, NJA, 10:658, 699.
9. WF to Lord Dartmouth, 8 Jan. 1776, ibid., 699, 700.
10. Ibid., 700.
11. Ibid., 700, 701; WF to Lord Germain, 28 March 1776, NJA, 10:702, 703.
12. WF to William Winds, 9 Jan. 1776, Duer, Stirling, 120, 121.
13. Ford, Journals of the Continental Congress, 4:41. It was easy to order Skinner's arrest. But incarcerating the King's governor was a different matter. For the moment, "Nothing was done respecting Gov. Franklin." Richard Smith, "Diary," Smith, Letters, 3:72.
14. Lord Stirling to President of Continental Congress, 10 Jan. 1776, Col. Winds to WF, 8 Jan. 1776, Duer, Stirling, 119, 121. The lodgings were at the home of Elias Boudinot.
15. Lord Stirling to President of Continental Congress, 11 Jan. 1776, ibid., 121, 122; WF to Lord Germain, 28 March 1776, NJA, 10:703.
16. Ibid., 703, 704.
17. Ibid.
18. Ibid.
19. Ibid., 704, 705; Lord Stirling to president of Continental Congress, 11 Jan. 1776, Duer, Stirling, 122. In fact, Congress rebuffed Stirling for his precipitous behavior, which no doubt put a damper on his enthusiasm. Ibid.
20. WF to Lord Germain, 28 March 1776, NJA, 10:705, 706.
21. WF to Lord Germain, 28 March 1776, NJA, 10:706, 707, 709, 710.
22. Ibid., 707–9. In fact, after January the "tory" threat in New Jersey was minimal. A full-fledged apparatus of extra-legal governments had emerged at the town, county, and colony levels, and most New Jersey inhabitants accepted its leadership, even if they were not ready to take the final step toward independence. See Gerlach, Prologue, 302–4; 313, 314.
23. WF to Lord Germain, 28 March 1776, NJA, 10:708, 709.
24. WF to WTF, 22 Jan., 14 March 1776, Franklin Papers, 101:10, 12, APS;

EF to Sally Bache, 5 Feb. 1776, N.J. Hist. Soc., *Proc.* 2nd ser., 5 (1877):
127, 128.

25. WF to WTF, 5 Feb. 1776, Franklin Papers, 101:11, APS.
26. WF to WTF, 14 March 1776, Franklin Papers, 101:12, APS.
27. WF to WTF, 22 May, 3 June 1776, Franklin Papers, 101:15, 16, APS.
28. WF to WTF, 8 May 1776, Franklin Papers, 101:14, APS.
29. WF to WTF, 3, 13 June 1776, Franklin Papers, 101:16, 17.
30. EF to Sarah Bache, 5 Feb. 1776, N.J. Hist. Soc., *Proc.*, 2nd ser., 5 (1877),
    128.
31. WF to WTF, 5 Feb., 14 March, 8 May 1776, Franklin Papers, 101:11,
    12, 14, APS.
32. WF to WTF, 14 March 1776, Franklin Papers, 101:12, APS.
33. WF to Lord Germain, 28 March 1776, *NJA*, 10:710, WF to WTF, 3 June
    1776, Franklin Papers, 101:16, APS.
34. *NJPCS*, 325ff; Elias Boudinot, *Journal or Historical Recollections of Amer-
    ican Events During the Revolutionary War* (Philadelphia, 1894), 4–8;
    Ford, *Journals of the Continental Congress*, 4:342, 357, 358; *N.Y. Gazette*
    (Mercury), 3 June 1776.
35. WF to Lord Germain, 10 Nov. 1778, PRO 654, CO5/1002, pp. 11, 12,
    LC.
36. WF argued that this "almost self-created Body" was supported by less than
    20 percent of the electorate. Ibid., 12. Gerlach agrees that the turn-out
    was light, but attributes this, not to the unpopularity of the Provincial
    Congress, but to the fact that there was little opposition to the patriot
    leaders. Gerlach, *Prologue*, 330.
37. *NJPCS*, 454–57; WF to Lord Germain, 10 Nov. 1778, PRO 654, CO5/
    1002, p. 12, LC.
38. Ibid., 12, 13. Whether or not BF actually approved of the plans to im-
    prison his son is uncertain. It is clear, however, that he knew of Congress's
    decision, and at least publicly did nothing to stop it.
39. Jonathan Dickinson Sergeant to John Adams, 15 June 1776, Smith, *Let-
    ters*, 4:224; *NJPCS*, 457, 458.
40. Col. Heard to Samuel Tucker, 17 June 1776, ibid., 461; WF to Legislature
    of N.J., 17 June 1776, *NJA*, 10:721.
41. WF to NJ Assembly, 23 June 1776, Revolutionary Era MSS, NJHS;
    NJPCS, 461.
42. This analysis is based on his letter to the assembly, 17 June 1776, found
    in *NJA*, 10:719–32.
43. WF to NJ Assembly, 23 June 1776, Revolutionary Era MSS, NJHS.
44. Ibid.
45. Provincial Congress to John Hancock, 17 June 1776, *NJPCS*, 461, 462;
    Ford, *Journal of the Continental Congress*, 5:465.
46. WF to N.J. Assembly, 23 June 1776, Revolutionary Era MSS.
47. Ibid., WF to Lord Germain, 10 Nov. 1778, PRO 654, CO5/1002, p. 12,
    LC.

12. "Like a Bear Through the Country"

1. WF to WTF, 25 June 1776, Franklin Papers, 101:18, APS.
2. WF to N.J. Assembly, 23 June 1776, Rev. Era Mss., NJHS.
3. Ibid.

4. Ibid., *NJPCS*, 482, 483.
5. WF to N.J. Assembly, 23 June 1776, Rev. Era Mss., NJHS.
6. Joseph Folsom, "Governor Franklin in Litchfield Jail., N.J. Hist. Soc., *Proc.* 3 (Jan. 1918): 46; John Adams, "Diary," Smith, *Letters*, 1:8.
7. WF to N.J. Assembly, 23 June 1776, Rev. Era Mss., NJHS; NJ. Misc. Mss., Papers Relating to WF, LC.
8. Ibid.; *NJPCS*, 470.
9. WF to N.J. Assembly, 23 June 1776, Rev. Era Mss. NJHS.
10. Callahan, *Royal Raiders*, 103; Read, *Correspondence of George Read*, 433. Ironically, rumor had it that Witherspoon had an illegitimate son. If WF knew this—and he surely did—the Doctor's supercilious tones must have rankled even more. Ibid.
11. WF to N.J. Assembly, 23 June 1776, Rev. Era Mss, NJHS.
12. *NJPCS*, 470.
13. WF to N.J. Assembly, 22 June 1776, NJA, 10:731.
14. Ibid., 728–32.
15. WF to N.J. Assembly, 23 June 1776, Rev. Era Mss., NJHS.
16. Ibid.
17. Smith, *Letters*, 4:308; John Hancock to Jonathan Trumbull, Sr., 24 June 1776, to N.J. Prov. Convention, 24 June 1776, ibid., 309, 308. Randall suggests that BF himself made this resolution to relieve his fellow delegates from any embarrassment they may have felt as a result of this delicate task. At the end of the war, WF revealed his belief that this was the case. In fact, we do not even know that BF was present on the day of the debate. Randall, *Revenge*, 422; Thomas Jones, *History of New York During the Revolutionary Wars*, Edward F. De Lancey, ed. (New York, 1879), 1:135.
18. WF to WTF, 25 June 1776, Franklin Papers, 101:18, APS.
19. Folson, "Litchfield Jail," 46; Anna Zabriskie to Richard Varick, 30 June 1776, Varick Papers, Misc. Mss., NYPL; John Witherspoon to N.J. Prov. Cong., 3 July 1776, Smith, *Letters*, 4:377.
20. George Washington (GW) to Committee of Essex County, 30 June 1776, John C. Fitzpatrick, *The Writings of George Washington* (Washington, D.C., 1932—), 5:204, 205 (hereafter, *GW Writings*).
21. WF to Lord Germain, 10 Nov. 1778, PRO 654, CO5/1002 LC, 13; Randall, *Revenge*, 425; Charles J. Hoadley, ed., *The Public Records of the Colony of Connecticut* (Hartford, 1890), 15:467.
22. WF to Lord Germain, 10 Nov. 1778, PRO 654, CO5/1002, LC, p. 13.
23. Ibid.
24. Ibid., GW to Governor Trumbull, 11 Aug. 1776, *GW Writings*, 5:412, 413; Hoadley, *Connecticut Public Records*, 15:482.
25. Serle, *American Journal*, 49. See also William Smith, *Historical Memoirs from 12 July 1776 to 25 July 1778*, W. H. W. Sabine, ed. (New York, 1958), 113.
26. EF to Sarah Bache, 12 July 1776, Gratz Coll., *Notable American Women*, HSP; EF to WFT, 16 July 1776, Franklin Papers, Bache Coll., APS; EF to WTF, 11 Oct. 1776, Franklin Papers, 102:22, APS.
27. EF to BF, 6 Aug. 1776, *PBF*, 22:552.
28. BF to WTF, 27 Aug., 10 Sept. 1776, *PBF*, 22:581, 582, 596, 597.
29. WTF to BF, 17 Aug. 1776, ibid., 566; see also, 556n.
30. BF to WTF, 19 Sept. 1776, ibid., 612, 613.

31. WTF to BF, 21 Sept. 1776, ibid., 620, 621.
32. BF to WTF, 22 Sept. 1776, ibid., 622.
33. So precipitous was WTF's departure that he failed to post one of EF's letters to her husband at Woodbridge, as he had faithfully promised to do. EF was furious. EF to WTF, 11 Oct. 1776, Franklin Papers, 102:22, APS.
34. BF to WTF, 28 Sept. 1776, *PBF*, 22:634; BF to Richard Bache, 2 June 1779, Smyth, *Writings*, 7:344, 345.
35. WF to WTF, 6 Oct. 1776, to EF, 25 Nov. 1776, Franklin Papers, MSS., APS.
36. WF to Lord Germain, 10 Nov. 1778, PRO 654, CO5/1002, p. 814, LC; BF to Jan Ingenhousz, [6 March] 1777, *PBF*, 23:314. See Robert Oaks, "Philadelphians in Exile: The Problem of Loyalty During the American Revolution," *PMHB* 96 (1972): 309.
37. Wharton Letterbook, 1773–1784, HSP; George O. Trevelyan, *The American Revolution* (New York, 1903), 4:47–49; Randall, *Revenge*, 436, 437.
38. Serle, *American Journal*, 49; Ford, *Continental Congress* 6:977, 1004; GW to John Hancock, 27 Nov., 1 Dec. 1776, GW *Writings*, 6:309, 310, 322; John Hancock to GW, 4 Dec. 1776, Ford, *Continental Congress*, 6:1004n.
39. Moreover, a string of British victories encouraged him to believe that the move for American independence had nearly been crushed. He would obviously be rewarded handsomely for any contributions he made to restoring English hegemony in the colonies.
40. WF to Lord Germain, 10 Nov. 1778, PRO 654, CO5/1002, p. 17, LC.
41. Resolution of the Connecticut Assembly, [10 Oct. 1776], C. E. Prince, ed. *William Livingston Papers* (Trenton, 1979), 1:164, 165.
42. Smith, *Historical Memoirs*, 106; GW to Governor Trumbull, 23 March 1777; GW to Gov. William Livingston, 1 April 1777, GW *Writings*, 7:317, 344; Roger Sherman to Jonathan Trumbull, 9 April 1777, Smith, *Letters*, 6:560, 561. In fact, even before his arrest, Lord William Howe had asked WF to grant pardons to any American who would lay down his arms and swear allegiance to the King. GW to John Hancock, 15 July 1776, GW *Writings*, 5:279; Ford, *Continental Congress*, 5:574, 592, 593; *Pa. Gazette*, 24 July 1776.
43. GW to Gov. Trumbull, 21 April 1777, GW *Writings*, 7:449, 450; Smith, *Historical Memoirs*, 151; GW to John Hancock, 26 April 1777, GW *Writings*, 7:476.
44. Ford, *Continental Congress*, 7:291. See also, Smith, *Letters*, 7:82n; John Hancock to Gov. Trumbull, 23 April, 1777, ibid., 6:639. Trumbull protested that no one "in Power" in Connecticut had any knowledge of WF's activities, but William Duer, who was Congress's informant, vigorously denied the governor's claims of ignorance.
45. WF to Lord Germain, 10 Nov. 1778, PRO 654, CO5/1002, p. 14, LC.
46. Smith, *Historical Memoirs*, 151; WF to Lord Germain, 10 Nov. 1778, PRO 654, CO5/1002, pp. 14, 15, 17, LC; WF to Gov. Trumbull, 15 Sept. 1777, William Franklin MSS. NJHS.
47. WF to Lord Germain, 10 Nov. 1778, PRO 654, CO5/1002, p. 15, LC.
48. EF to WTF, 11 Oct. 1776, Franklin Papers, 10:22, APS; WF to Lord Germain, 10 Nov. 1778, PRO 654, CO5/1002, p. 16, LC.

49. GW to WF, 25 July 1777, to John Hancock, 25 July 1777, *GW Writings,* 8:476, 474.

50. GW to WF, 29 July 1777, ibid., 497, 498; John Hancock to GW, 28 July 1777, Ford, *Continental Congress,* 8:583, 584.

51. WF to Lord Germain, 10 Nov. 1778, PRO 654, CO5/1002, p. 16, LC; JM to BF, 18 Aug. 1777, Van Doren, *Jane Mecom,* 170; WF to Gov. Trumbull, 15 Sept. 1777, William Franklin MSS., NJHS. His depression was not unusual. Imprisonment, even under optimal conditions, often brought illness, even death, to those who were confined for protracted periods of time. See Oaks, "Exile," 318–25.

52. WF to Gov. Trumbull, 15 Sept. 1777, William Franklin MSS., NJHS.

53. Robert Morris to Eldridge Gerry, 22 Jan. 1778, Ely Papers, NJHS; Richard Bache to BF, 14 July 1778, William Duane, *Letters to BF from His Family* (Freeport, New York: 1970), 79; Smith, *Historical Memoirs,* 293; WF to Lord Germain, 10 Nov. 1778, PRO 654, CO5/1002, pp. 15, 16, LC.

54. John Langdon to Robert Morris, 20 Dec. 1777, Franklin Papers, Bache Coll., APS; Robert Morris to Eldridge Gerry, 22 Jan. 1778, Ely Papers, NJHS; James Kinsey to James Duane, 11 Feb. 1778, Duane Misc., MSS., NYHS; WS to BF, 14 July 1778, Franklin Papers, 10:119, APS. Part of the problem was that GW saw WF, not as an ordinary prisoner of war, but as a prisoner of state. Thus GW would not entertain any requests for WF's exchange emanating from the opposing army, referring all such proposals to the civilian authorities. Gov. Livingston to N.J. Assembly, 6 June 1778, Prince, *Livingston Papers,* 2:361.

55. Thomas McKean to George Read, 12 Feb. 1778, Henry Laurens to Rawlin Lowndes, 5 Aug. [1778], Smith, *Letters,* 9:86, 10:392; WS to BF, 14 July 1778, Franklin Papers, 10:19, APS. Ben had good reason to hold WF at arm's length. His enemies used WTF's position as private secretary against him, calling the appointment unfit "because of his father's principles." And they even tried to secure a congressional resolution condemning WTF's assignment to so sensitive a position. Richard Bache to BF, 22 Oct. 1778, Franklin Papers, APS.

56. William Livingston to John Witherspoon and Jonathan Elmer, 21 June 1778, Prince, *Livingston Papers,* 2:371; Thomas McKean to George Read, 3 April 1778, Read, *George Read Correspondence,* 309; Richard Bache to BF, 22 Oct. 1778; APS; Ford, *Continental Congress,* 11:769; Henry Laurens to Rowlin Lowndes, [18 Aug. 1778], Smith, *Letters,* 10:447. The situation was complicated by the internal politics of Delaware. Many suspected McKinly of loyalist sympathies, and a faction led by Thomas McKean did what it could to sabotage, or at least slow down, McKinly's release. See G. S. Rowe, "The Travail of John McKinly, First President of Delaware," *Delaware History* 17 (1976): 21–36.

57. Ford, *Continental Congress,* 12:909, 911, 912; WF to Lord Germain, 10 Nov. 1778, PRO 654, CO5/1002, p. 20, LC.

13. "An Unwillingness to Quit . . ."

1. WF to JG, 16 Nov. 1778, "Letters to Joseph Galloway," *Historical Magazine* 5 (Oct. 1861): 271.

2. David Sproat to JG, 11 Jan. 1779, Balch Papers, NYPL.

3. There were 5000 civilians in New York in Sept. of 1776; that population doubled by 1777; and in 1783 there were 33,000 in addition to the 10,000 soldiers living there. Oscar T. Barck, *New York During the War for Independence* (New York, 1931), 74–79; Carl Van Doren, *Secret History of the American Revolution* (New York: 1941), 119; Norton, *British Americans*, 32.

4. Barck, *New York*, 82. Another accidental fire in August of 1778 destroyed an additional 64 homes in the south of town. Ibid.

5. Ibid., 85, 88; Ewald G. Schaukirk, "Occupation of New York City by the British," *Pennsylvania Magazine* 10 (1886): 422, 423, 428; T. J. Wertenbaker, *Father Knickerbocker Rebels: New York City During the Revolution* (New York, 1948), 197, 198; Calhoon, *Loyalists*, 373.

6. Some authorities say it rose 300 percent by war's end. Barck, *New York*, 99; James Robertson to John Robinson, 4 Aug. 1780, Milton M. Klein & Ronald W. Howard, eds. *The Twilight of British Rule in Revolutionary America: The New York Letterbook of General James Robertson, 1780–1783* (Cooperstown, N.Y., 1983), 143. See also *Rivington's Royal Gazette*, 2, 12 Dec. 1778, 16 Jan., 17 April 1779, for examples of Clinton's unsuccessful efforts to fix prices.

7. Barck, *New York*, 58, 98, 112, 117, 118; Calhoon, *Loyalists*, 374, 375; Smith, *Historical Memoirs of William Smith, 1778–1783*, W. H. W. Sabine, ed. (New York, 1971), 55, 59, 212; *Rivington's Royal Gazette*, 17 June 1780; Schaukirk, "Occupation," 137, 250, 427, 435; Deposition of Mary Thompson, 23 Feb. 1782, Guy Carleton Papers, British Head Quarters Papers, Reel 12 (hereafter BHQP). See ibid., passim for other, often heart-rending accounts of the abject state of most New York refugees.

8. Norton, *British Americans*, 33; Van Doren, *Secret History*, 119.

9. Larry G. Bowman, *Captive Americans: Prisoners During the American Revolution* (Athens, Ohio, 1976), 11–14; Boudinot, *Journal*, 9–19; John Marshal et al. to Gen. Clinton, 17 Jan. 1782, BHQP Reel 12; Wertenbaker, *Father Knickerbocker*, 164, 165. There were, of course, notoriously severe and corrupt guardians of American captives like the Provost's William Cunningham who admitted to starving to death 2000 prisoners and selling their rations for personal profit. Wertenbaker, *Father Knickerbocker*, 163; Charles H. Metzger, *The Prisoner in the American Revolution* (Chicago, 1971), 181.

10. He must have envied Andrew Elliot, whose appointment as lt. gov. of New York in 1780 was obtained through his family's intercession. For him, this route was obviously closed. Robert Ernst, "Andrew Elliot, Forgotten Loyalist of Occupied New York," *New York History* 57 (1976): 310.

11. Charles Ingliss to JG, 12 Dec. 1778, "Joseph Galloway Letters," *Hist. Mag.* 5 (Oct. 1861): 301; WF to JG, 16 Nov. 1778, ibid. 5 (Sept. 1861): 271; Daniel Coxe to JG, 17 Dec. 1778, ibid. 5 (Dec. 1861): 359; Daniel Coxe to JG, 16 Dec. 1778, Balch Papers, NYPL; Richard Bache to BF, 22 Oct. 1778, Franklin Papers, APS.

12. [?] to JG, 22 Nov., 16 Dec. 1778, Galloway Letters, 1778, 1789, Force Transcripts, LC; Smith, *Historical Memoirs*, 1778–83, 39, 40.

13. See Wertenbaker, *Father Knickerbocker*, 223, 224; William B. Willcox,

ed., *The American Rebellion: Sir Henry Clinton's Narrative of His Cam-*
paigns, 1775–1782 (New Haven, 1954), 110, 127, 128; Callahan, *Royal*
Raiders, 159, 163; W. O. Raymond, "Loyalists in Arms," New Brunswick
Hist. Soc., *Coll.* 4 (1904): 190; Smith, *Historical Memoirs*, 1778–83, 398.

14. Van Doren, *Secret History*, 93; Alexander C. Flick, *Loyalism in New York*
During the American Revolution (New York, 1969), 184, 185; Serle,
American Journal, 164.
15. WF to [?], 15 Jan. 1782, Clinton Papers, Clements.
16. See George M. Kyte, "Some Plans for a Loyalist Strong-hold in the Middle
Colonies," *Pennsylvania History* 16 (1949): 179–89; Allen, *Diary*, 288,
438; Daniel Coxe to JG, 16 Dec. 1778, Balch Papers, NYPL; David
Sproat to JG, 11 Jan. 1779, "Letters to Joseph Galloway," *Hist. Mag.* 5
(Dec. 1861): 363.
17. Jonathan Potts to JG, 17 Dec. 1778, ibid., 359; Schaukirk, "Occupation,"
424, 427, 429; Smith, *Historical Memoirs*, 1778–83, 78, 79, 152.
18. Van Doren, *Secret History*, 124; Willcox, *American Rebellion*, 83, 106,
107, 109, 110, 192, 493, 516.
19. WF to [?], 15 Jan. 1782, Clinton Papers, Clements; Smith, *Historical*
Memoirs, 1778–83, 93, 177. Even moderates bemoaned Clinton's timidity,
and as the war dragged on the criticism, became louder and more pointed.
See ibid., 9, 10, 162, 350, for a few examples of the wholesale attack on
the general's character and competence.
20. Klein and Howard, *Robertson*, 32, 40, 43, 53–55; James Robertson to William Knox, 26 March 1780, to Lord Germain, 1 Sept. 1780, to Gen. Amherst, 24 Jan. 1781, ibid., 83, 147, 171; Smith, *Historical Memoirs*, 1778–
83, 285–87, passim; L. F. S. Upton, "William Smith of New York and
Quebec," Ph.D Diss., University of Minnesota, June 1957, 236–38;
Eugene Devereux, "Andrew Elliot: Lt. Governor of the Province of New
York," *PMHB* 11 (1887): 129–50; Shy, *A People Numerous and Armed*
(New York, 1976), 187–89. Smith was so moderate that some even accused him of being a "spy for the rebels," Jones, *History*, 1:315.
21. Klein and Howard, *Robertson*, 4; James Robertson to Lord Germain, 26
March 1780, ibid., 81; Shy, *A People*, 186, 187; Smith, *Historical Mem-*
oirs, 1778–1783, 73, 93, 94. And from the beginning the moderate loyalists
distrusted WF. Ibid., 40, 134.
22. WF to Lord Germain, 10 Nov. 1778, PRO 654 CO5/1002, pp. 17, 18, 20,
LC; WF to His Majesty's Commissioners, 16 Nov. 1778, Carleton Papers
MSS., 1:160, 161, Sparks MSS, 45, Houghton Library, Harvard University,
Cambridge, Massachusetts (hereafter Houghton).
23. Ibid.
24. Mariboe, "William Franklin," 486; Lord Germain to Lord of Treasury, 6,
16 Jan. 1779, PRO AO 13 109, NJHS; Jonathan Odell and Samuel Seabury to Gen. Clinton, 21 Dec. 1778, Clinton Papers, Clements.
25. Isaac Ogden to JG, 22 Nov. 1778, 6 Feb. 1779, Balch Papers, NYPL;
Smith, *Historical Memoirs*, 1778–83, 40.
26. WF to Lord Germain, 12 Nov. 1778, PRO 654 CO5/1002, pp. 20, 22, 23;
WF to Lord Germain, 20 Dec. 1778, PRO 654 CO5/1002, pp. 29–31, LC.
27. WF to Lord Germain, 12 Nov. 1778, PRO 654 CO5/1002, pp. 21, 22, 24,
25, LC.
28. Ibid., 26, 27; WF to Lord Germain, 20 Dec. 1778, PRO 654 CO5/1002,

pp. 29–31, LC. This was, of course, precisely the advice Germain wanted to hear, for it promised a sure and inexpensive solution to the American part of a war that had assumed world-wide proportions by 1778. Klein and Howard, *Robertson*, 8; Gerald S. Brown, *The American Secretary: The Colonial Policy of Lord Germain, 1775–1778* (Ann Arbor, 1963), 177.

29. Mariboe, "William Franklin," 487.

30. Isaac Ogden to JG, 15 Dec. 1778; David Sproat to JG, 11 Jan. 1779, Charles Ingliss to JG, 25 Feb. 1779, "Letters to Joseph Galloway," *Hist. Mag.* 5 (Dec. 1861), 356, 363, ibid., 6 (Aug. 1862), 239; PRO CO5 82, pp. 53, 56, LC. Interestingly, he never considered forming his own company to serve in the provincial line, although in New York, especially, this was often the route taken by active members of the loyal upper class. Raymond, "Loyalists in Arms," 194ff. Whether this was because of his age or his more lofty ambition is impossible to determine.

31. WF to JG, 6 Feb. 1779, "Letters, to Joseph Galloway, "*Hist. Mag* 6 (June 1862): 178; Smith, *Historical Memoirs, 1778–83*, 121, 134, 366; Van Doren, *Secret History*, 139.

32. *Rivington's Royal Gazette*, 17 Oct., 25 Nov. 1778; 6, 23 Jan. 1779; Schaukirk, "Occupation," 429; Barck, *New York*, 173–87; Van Doren, *Secret History*, 139, 140; Smith, *Historical Memoirs, 1778–83*, 96. Evidence of the type of activity with which WF was at least tangentially involved can be seen in Mason, "A Warning to Rebels, March 1779," Clinton Papers, Clements. See also Smith, *Historical Memoirs, 1778–83*, 93, 94, 111.

33. André was Clinton's closest confidant. He also controlled all the information funneled into the general's office by the loyalists. His support was essential for anyone hoping to get Clinton's ear. Van Doren, *Secret History*, 125.

34. WF to Major André, 29 May 1779, Clinton Papers, Clements. Moreover, he was too preoccupied with his ultimately unsuccessful Long Island campaign to devote much attention to WF's proposal.

35. William Tryon to Gen. Clinton, 20 July 1779, Willcox, *American Rebellion*, 414. A copy of this plan of 28 June 1779 is in PRO CO5 82, pp. 46–48, LC.

36. When Tryon showed William Smith the plan, he was appalled and wanted to have nothing to do with it although he did consent to propose alterations to the proposal. Clinton himself objected to the plan's cost—some £50,000 according to Tryon, as well as to the "Nature of such a Service." Still Tryon persisted. Smith, *Historical Memoirs, 1778–83*, pp. 120–22.

37. See PRO CO5 82, pp. 49, 50, LC, for a copy of the plan.

38. Smith, *Historical Memoirs, 1778–83*, 131, 134, 150; *Rivington's Royal Gazette*, 17 July 1779.

39. WF to WS, 9 Oct. 1779, Hart, "Letters," 454–56; WF to Lord Germain, 12 May 1779, PRO 654, CO5/1002, LC. In October, for instance, a new letter of marque was named "The Governor Franklin." *Rivington's Royal Gazette*, 30 Oct. 1779; WF to Major André, 6, 10, 11 June, 25 July, 4, 5 Sept. 1779, Clinton Papers, Clements.

40. WF to Lord Germain, 5 July 1779, PRO 654, CO5/1002, LC.

41. Moderates like Smith and Elliot opposed WF's inclusion, but they could do

nothing to countermand Germain's specific orders. Smith, *Historical Memoirs, 1778–83*, 195, 196.

42. WF to [?], 15 Jan. 1782, Clinton Papers, Clements; Smith *Historical Memoirs, 1778–83*, 96; Van Doren, *Secret History*, 234, 235; Willcox, *American Rebellion*, 192.

43. Smith, *Historical Memoirs, 1778–83*, 164; WF to Major André, 10 Nov. 1779, Clinton Papers, Clements.

44. André's Plan, Oct. 1779, Clinton Papers, Clements; WF to Major André, 10 Nov. 1779, Clinton Papers, Clements. In November, Tryon thought Clinton was ready to consider forming a loyalist organization but he was clearly mistaken. Smith, *Historical Memoirs, 1778–83*, 183.

45. See Sparks MSS. 53 Chalmers Papers, Houghton; *New Royal Gazette*, 3 July 1779. Leonard's plan was remarkably similar to WF's original suggestions to Tryon. The only significant difference was the substitution of a five-man board of directors for the single director WF envisioned.

46. See PRO CO5 82, pp. 56, 57, LC.

47. Smith, *Historical Memoirs, 1778–83*, 265–69; David Sproat to JG, 11 Jan. 1779, "Letters to Galloway," *Hist. Mag.* 5 (Dec. 1861): 363; Clinton Papers, passim, Clements; Van Doren, *Secret History*, 224; Klein and Howard, *Robertson*, 128n; Willcox, *American Rebellion*, 192.

48. Van Doren, *Secret History*, 364; WF to WS, 12 Nov. 1780, William Franklin MSS, Stirling; Smith, *Historical Memoirs, 1778–83*, 159, 242, 243, 250, 279, 336–38; Klein and Howard, *Robertson*, 47, 56.

49. George Leonard to WF, 3 May 1780, in Minutes of the Proceedings, PRO CO5 82, p. 150, LC (hereafter, Minutes, LC). Some of the minutes—4 Jan. 1781–Aug. 1781, and Nov. 1781—are in the Clements Library (hereafter cited as Minutes, Clements).

50. *Rivington's Royal Gazette*, 3, 10 June, 29 July, 9, 13, 30 Sept. 1780.

51. Minutes, 149, LC; Lord Germain to Gen. Clinton, 21 April 1780, Clinton Papers, Clements.

52. Minutes, 149, 150, LC.

53. Ibid., 149–151.

54. Ibid., 151, 152; Instructions & Regulations, 28 Oct. 1780; Clinton Papers, Clements.

55. Ernst, "Elliot," 312; Smith, *Historical Memoirs, 1778–83*, 343–47; WF to WS, 12 Nov. 1780, Franklin Papers, Stirling; Minutes, 152, LC.

56. WF to Major DeLancey, 17 Nov. 1780; Major DeLancey to WF, 21 Nov. 1780, PRO CO5 82, pp. 125, 126, 130, LC.

57. Major DeLancey to WF, 16, 18 Nov. 1780, WF to Captain Ward, 16 Nov. 1780, to Major DeLancey, 17, 19 Nov. 1780, ibid., 125–27.

58. For a complete copy of Clinton's nine-page proposal see Clinton Papers, Clements.

59. Ironically, despite his efforts to contain the Board's power, Clinton also washed his hands of all responsibility for its actions. Willcox, *American Rebellion*, 238.

60. Smith claimed most Board members preferred his and Elliot's plan to WF's, but this self-serving assertion does not appear to square with the facts. Smith, *Historical Memoirs, 1778–83*, 350.

61. Ibid., 349; WF to JG, 28 Jan. 1781, PRO 5 83, LC; Associated Loyalists

to Gen. Clinton, 1 Dec. 1780, Clinton Papers, Clements. The protest was
written in WF's hand and bore his signature. It was no doubt largely his
product as well.

62. This discussion is based on the Associated Loyalist protest as well as on
Clinton's Instructions and Commission of 20 Nov. 1780 in Clinton Papers, Clements.

63. David Dobson's Memorial, 15 Feb. 1782, BHQP, Reel 12; WF to Major
DeLancey, 1 Jan. 1781; WF to General Clinton, 6 Jan. 1781, PRO CO5
82, pp. 60, 61, 63, 64, LC: Captain Hubbel to WF, 30 April 1781, PRO
CO 82, LC; Smith Historical Memoirs, 1778–83, 67, Rivington's Royal
Gazette, 13 Feb. 1779. Little work has been done on the treatment of
loyalist prisoners. However, the available information indicates that loyalist
complaints, while exaggerated, were not unfounded. See Claude H. Van
Tyne, The Loyalists in the American Revolution (New York, 1929), 231,
235, 268, 269, W. S. MacNutt, "The Loyalists: A Sympathetic View,"
Acadiensis 6 (1976), 3–20, Wallace Brown, "The Loyal American Tories
in the Revolution," American History Illustrated 7 (1972): 36–43. Part of
the problem can be explained merely by American inexperience, the weakness of the central government, and the necessary dispersion of prisoners
over a vast area. Moreover, many loyalists had been influential members of
their own communities and they represented a real threat to independence.
Still, it remains true that Americans could expect significantly worse treatment than Britons. Metzger, Prisoner, 31; Van Tyne, Loyalists, 213ff,
Isaac Alyray's Deposition, July 1777, BHQP, Reel 13.

64. Olive Anderson, "The Treatment of Prisoners of War in Britain During
the American War of Independence," U. of London Institute of Historical
Research Bulletin 28 (May 1955): 63–83; John K. Alexander, "Forton
Prison During the American Revolution: A Case Study of British Prisoner
of War Policy and the American Prisoner Response to that Policy," Essex
Institute Historical Colls. 103 (1967): 365–89. In complaining of England's leniency, the loyalists conveniently failed to mention men like
William Cunningham, Marshal of the Provost, who says one historian,
"rivaled modern Nazis or Communists in humanity." Metzger, Prisoner,
62; Bowman, Captive Americans, 11.

65. Bowman, Captive Americans, 81–84; Calhoon, Loyalists, 368; Metzger,
Prisoner, 152, 153. WF must have been furious when Clinton toyed with
the idea of threatening retaliation for the execution of his close friend
John André, which surely seemed hypocritical under the circumstances.
Smith, Historical Memoirs, 1778–83, 338.

66. Thus they were pleased with Clinton's ultimate acquiescence to their request to house their own prisoners separately, and with Walter Chaloner's
commission to act as the Commissary of Prisoners for the Board. Minutes,
361, LC; Minutes, 12, 14 April 1781, Clements. Still, even this did not
satisfy WF's desire for complete autonomy.

67. Associated Loyalists to Gen. Clinton, 1 Dec. 1780, Clinton Papers, Clements. See Minutes, 373, 377, 382, 404, 405, LC, for typical examples of
the Board's attempt to use its own prisoners to alter rebel treatment of
loyalist captives.

68. He was not alone in his fears. Moderates like Smith, Elliot, and Robertson
shared the same concerns. Smith, Historical Memoirs, 1778–83, 350–53.

69. Ibid., 353–57; Gen. Clinton to Associated Loyalists, 10 Dec. 1780, Clinton Papers, Clements. William Smith dared to hope that the directors would abandon their project when they realized how useless they would be, but this was never likely. Something, it seemed, was better than nothing. Smith, *Historical Memoirs, 1778–83*, 353. See also Associated Loyalists to Gen. Clinton, 18 Dec. 1780, Clinton Papers, Clements; WF to Gov. Martin, 9 Jan. 1781, PRO CO82, LC.
70. *Rivington's Royal Gazette*, 30 Dec. 1780–3 Feb. 1781.
71. WF to Sarah Bache, 16 Sept. 1779, Franklin Papers, 101:128, APS.

14. "Deprived of Their All"

1. Proceedings of a General Court-Martial held at New York in the Province of New York from Friday the 3rd of May to Saturday the 22nd of June 1782, p. 32, Clements (hereafter cited as Court-Martial).
2. WF to WS, 12 May 1782, Hart "Letters," 462.
3. Its members resided at number four Nassau Street after the end of April 1781. Minutes, 27 March, 24 April 1781, Clements.
4. Ibid., 3, 7 April 1781.
5. Many historians agree with Clinton's perception. See, for instance, Wertenbaker, *Father Knickerbocker*, 230, 231, Jones, *History of New York*, 1:302, Sabine, *Biographical Sketches of Loyalists of the American Revolution* (Port Washington, N.Y., 1966), 2:21, Barck, *New York*, 203–6, William A. Benton, *Whig-Loyalism: An Aspect of Political Ideology in the American Revolutionary Era* (Rutherford, N.J., 1969), 196, 197. Others simply view it as a "minor organization" that contributed virtually nothing to the war effort. See Callahan, *Royal Raiders*, 244, Raymond, "Loyalists in Arms," 190. For a more sympathetic perspective, see Flick, *Loyalism in New York*, 155, Mariboe, "William Franklin," 524.
6. WF to JG, 28 Jan. 1781, PRO 5 83, p. 44, LC.
7. In fact, by the end of the first month, there were no more than 400–500 members. Ibid.
8. Ibid.; WF to Lord Germain, 20 Feb. 1781, PRO CO 175, LC; Minutes, 5, 26 July 1781, Clements; Lord Germain to WF, 2 May 1781, PRO CO 175, LC.
9. WF to Major DeLancey, 16 Jan. 1781, PRO CO5 101, pp. 173–75, LC; Major DeLancey to WF, 22 Jan. 1781, PRO CO5 101, pp. 177, 178, LC; Minutes, 19 Feb., 23 March, 2 April 1781, Clements.
10. Minutes, 157, 158, LC.
11. Ibid., 158, 159.
12. Ibid., 160.
13. See WF to Admiral Arbuthnot, 19 Jan. 1781, PRO CO5 82, pp. 75, 76, LC; Admiral Arbuthnot to WF, 20 Jan. 1781, PRO CO5 82, p. 77, LC; General Clinton to WF, 22 Jan. 1781, PRO CO5 82, p. 87, LC; Frederick Mackenzie to WF, 25 Jan. 1781, PRO CO5 82, p. 93; WF to JG, 28 Jan. 1781 PRO 5 83 LC; Minutes, 25–27 Jan., 12, 22 Feb., 13 March 1781, Clements.
14. See ibid., 13 March, 17, 21, 24 April.
15. WF to Major DeLancey, 1 Jan. 1781; WF to Henry Clinton, 6 Jan. 1781, pp. 59, 63, PRO CO 5 82, LC.

16. Major DeLancey to WF, 22 Jan. 1781, Clinton Papers. The Provost was a three-story building whose top floors had been converted into cells to house a heterogenous group of American prisoners. Some of the army's highest ranking captives stayed in "Congress Hall" located in the northeast corner of the second floor. Even there, the conditions were hardly palatial. Bowman, *Captive Americans*, 11, Minutes, 361, LC; Minutes 12, 14 April 1781, Clements.

17. WF to Joseph Reed, 11 May 1781, PRO CO 5 82, pp. 403, 404, LC. See Minutes, pp. 373, 377, 382, 404, LC for typical examples of the Board's attempt to use its prisoners to alter rebel treatment of American prisoners.

18. See Captain Hubbel to WF, 21 April 1781, PRO CO 5 82, p. 399; Smith, *Historical Memoirs, 1778–83*, 427; *Rivington's Royal Gazette*, 14 March, 9 May, 27 June 1781, for examples of the kind of raids normally conducted by the Associated Loyalists.

19. Minutes, 29 June, 14 July 1781, Clinton Papers.

20. Smith, *Historical Memoirs*, 1778–83, 437, 451–54, 461, 462; Schaukirk, "Occupation," 438, 439.

21. WF to [?], 15 Jan 1782, Clinton Papers.

22. Ibid.

23. Ibid.

24. Ibid.

25. Few historians have noted the effect of Article Ten on the loyalists. Some mention it in passing. Most are filled with praises for GW and his "honorable" and "generous" peace. The American loyalists were not so easily deceived. See Franklin and Mary Wickwire, *Cornwallis: The American Adventure* (Boston, 1970), 386; Van Tyne, *The Loyalists in the American Revolution*, 189, Norton, *British Americans*, 171.

26. Henry P. Johnston, *The Yorktown Campaign and the Surrender of Cornwallis, 1781* (New York, 1971), 152, 189. This was the only request GW completely rejected.

27. WF to Henry Clinton, 14 Nov. 1781, Clinton Papers. The issue went beyond mere degradation, for loyalist prisoners faced severe punishment when they were returned to their former governments. Moreover, GW's decision served as a dangerous precedent.

28. Willcox, *American Rebellion*, 352; Pelham Winslow to Elisha Hutchinson, 1 Dec. 1781, Hutchinson, *Diary and Letters*, 2:372, 373. See also Thomas Hutchinson, Jr., to Elisha Hutchinson, 8 Dec. 1781, ibid., 373, 374, James Robertson to Lord Amherst, 7 Nov. 1781, Klein and Howard, *James Robertson*, 225, Lord Germain to King George, 16 Dec. 1781, Sir John Fortescue, ed., *Correspondence of King George III from 1760 to Dec. 1783*, 6 vols. (London, 1928), 5:315.

29. Smith, *Historical Memoirs, 1778–83*, 465, 478, 486; Willcox, *American Rebellion*, 333–50, 463, 466, 467.

30. Ibid., 352, 353, 464; Smith, *Historical Memoirs, 1778–83*, p. 463.

31. WF to Lord Germain, 6 Nov. 1781, 25 March 1782, PRO CO 175, pp. 462, 465, 483; LC; Minutes, 13, 14 Nov. 1781, Clements; Willcox, *American Rebellion*, 352, 353.

32. WF to Henry Clinton, 14 Nov. 1781, Clinton Papers, Clements; Minutes, 8 Nov. 1781, Clements; Willcox, *American Rebellion*, 352n.

33. WF to Henry Clinton, 14 Nov. 1781, Clinton Papers, Clements.
34. Willcox, *American Rebellion*, 353, 592–94; Minutes of the Board of Advisors, 23 Jan. 1782, BHQP, Reel 12; Smith, *Historical Memoirs, 1778–83*, 477, 479, 486–91; Klein and Howard, *James Robertson*, 238–47; Henry Clinton to Lord Germain, 24 Jan. 1782; WF to Henry Clinton, 29 Jan. 1782; Henry Clinton to WF, 6 March 1782, BHQP, Reel 12.
35. Smith, *Historical Memoirs, 1778–83*, 483; WF to [?], 15 Jan. 1782, Clinton Papers, Clements; WF to Col. DeLancey, 4 May 1782, Franklin Papers, Misc. MSS. Coll., Box 69, LC.
36. WF to WS, 12 May 1782, Hart, "Letters," 462.
37. Smith, *Historical Memoirs, 1778–83*, 484.
38. It was, claims one historian in an obvious overstatement, the "most blatant act of premeditated cruelty on record during the Revolution." Bowman, *Captive Americans*, 86. Many contemporaries agreed. A group of nearly 400 residents of Monmouth County, N.J., described the execution as an "almost unparalleled murder." Committee of Monmouth to George Washington, 14 April 1782, BHQP, Reel 12. Clinton himself expressed his outrage at the "act of barbarity," calling it an "audacious breach of humanity" and an "insult to the dignity of the British arms." Willcox, *American Rebellion*, 360–71.
39. GW to Henry Clinton, 26 Feb. 1782; Henry Clinton to GW, 18 March 1782; Peace Commissioners to Henry Clinton, 1 April 1782, BHQP, Reel 12.
40. As Clinton later explained, "I Accounted for the Conduct of the Board as proceeding from resentment and perhaps from a fear that the same Spirit operated in British Councils as had done on the 10th Article of York Convention & that My Commissioners & theirs were treating on Terms from which they the Provincials as above were to be excluded and they therefore wished to make things desperate by throwing away the Scabbard." Clinton, Testimony before the Commissioners (1784), Clinton Papers, Clements.
41. Court-Martial, 23–25; Lippincott, Report to the Associated Board of Loyalists, BHQP, Reel 12.
42. BHQP, Reel 12.
43. Court-Martial, 44, 45; R. J. Koke, "War, Profit and Privateers Along the New Jersey Coast," *New York Historical Society Quarterly*, 41 (1957): 317n, 318n.
44. Court-Martial, 38–41. Reportedly, he had also assisted at other executions.
45. Calhoon, *Loyalists*, 368. See also Callahan, *Royal Raiders*, 99, 100; Lundlin, *Cockpit*, 218, 219; Koke, "Jersey Coast," 279–337; Allen, *Diary*, 280. The rebels claimed White had been shot while trying to escape. His fellow prisoners insisted he had been murdered. See Aaron White's Deposition, 30 March 1782, John North's Deposition, 15 April 1782, BHQP, Reel 13, Clayton Tilton's Deposition, William Abbatt, *Memoirs of Major-General William Heath* (New York, 1968), 309.
46. Court-Martial, 29, 30, 45; Minutes, 16 Feb. 1781, Clements.
47. Court-Martial, 19, 20, 45.
48. Ibid., 35. Lippincott implied at his trial that the paper was the one he later pinned on Huddys shirt (p. 63).

49. Daniel Coxe to Colonel DeLancey, 9 April 1782, BHQP, Reel 12; Court-Martial, 63. Indeed, Lippincott assured judge and jury that Coxe knew nothing about his plans (p. 70).

50. Ibid., 17, 18.

51. Ibid., 22, 23; Clinton, Testimony; Willcox, *American Rebellion*, 371.

52. Monmouth Inhabitants to GW, 14 April 1782, BHQP, Reel 12; Abbatt, *Heath*, 309–11; Clinton, Testimony; GW to Henry Clinton, 21 April 1782, *GW Writings*, 24:146, 147; Henry Clinton to GW, 25 April 1782, BHQP, Reel 13.

53. GW to Brigadier General Moses Hagen, 3 May 1782, *GW Writings*, 24:218; Clinton, Testimony; Minutes, 25 April 1782, BHQP, Reel 13.

54. WF to Henry Cilnton, 25 April 1782, BHQP, Reel 13. The "Statement" was intended to be incorporated as a part of Lippincott's own explanation, which he had only partially completed by the 25th.

55. Minutes, 27 April 1781, BHQP, Reel 13; Court-Martial, 48; Smith, *Historical Memoirs, 1778–83*, 501; WF to JG, 11 May 1782, PRO 5 83, p. 662, LC; WF to Lord Shelburne, 10 May 1782, PRO CO 175, p. 509, LC.

56. Court-Martial, 9, 41–43; Smith, *Historical Memoirs, 1778–83*, 501. The statement is in Appendix 5 of the Court-Martial proceedings.

57. Robertson wanted Lippincott hanged as a murderer and even WF's old friend Cortlandt Skinner supported a court-martial. Smith *Historical Memoirs, 1778–83*, 500–502.

58. Ibid., 500, 501.

59. Henry Clinton to James Robertson, 25 April 1782, Council Minutes, 26 April 1782, BHQP, Reel 13; Clinton, Testimony.

60. Council Minutes, 26 April 1782, Henry Clinton to WF, 26 April 1782, WF to Henry Clinton, 27 April 1782, BHQP, Reel 13.

61. Smith, *Historical Memoirs, 1778–83*, 502. Plans to relieve Clinton had commenced as early as December 1781, but Germain's antipathy to Carleton had impeded the proceedings. Only with North's resignation in March, and the subsequent change in the ministry, could Carleton be dispatched to America. Fortescue, *Correspondence*, 5:313–440, passim.

62. Smith, *Historical Memoirs, 1778–83*, 503; W. H. Nelson, "The Last Hopes of the American Loyalists," *Canadian History* 32 (1951): 24; Paul H. Smith, "Sir Guy Carleton, Peace Negotiations and the Evacuation of New York," *Canadian Historical Review* 50 (1969): 249, 250.

63. No doubt he was preparing the way for renewing his request for New York's return to civil government.

64. Smith, *Historical Memoirs, 1778–83*, 503, 507, 509; WF to Guy Carleton, 6 May 1782, BHQP, Reel 13; WF to JG, 11 May 1782, PRO 5 83, p. 662, LC.

65. See Guy Carleton to Gov. William Livingston, 7 May, 12 June, 21 July, 1782, in Koke, "New Jersey Coast," 324, 325, 329, 334; Guy Carleton to GW, 7 May 1782, BHQP, Reel 13.

66. Court-Martial, 8; Smith, *Historical Memoirs, 1778–83*, 507–18; Upton, "William Smith," 282, 284.

67. Smith, *Historical Memoirs, 1778–83*, 516, 517.

68. Ibid., 518; Court-Martial, 28–32. Even as the trial was about to begin in earnest, WF was protesting new attrocities perpetrated by New Jersey

rebels and complaining about Clinton's repudiation of the policy of retaliation. WF to Guy Carleton, 11 June 1782, BHQP, Reel 13.

69. Even loyalist historian Thomas Jones thought WF ordered the execution, and it is difficult to deny that the governor bore considerable responsibility for the incident. Jones, *History of New York*, 2:483; Clinton, *Testimony*.

70. Court-Martial, 37, 42, 44–47, 52–54, 77, 78.

71. Bowman, *Captive Americans*, 86.

72. WF to Lord Shelburne, 10 May 1782, PRO CO 175, pp. 510, 511, LC.

73. WF to JG, 11 May 1782, PRO 583, p. 663, LC.

74. Ibid., 660, 661; WF to Lord Shelburne, 10 May 1782, PRO CO 175, p. 511, LC; WF to JG, 11 May 1782, PRO 583, p. 661, LC.

75. GW to President of Congress, 19 Aug. 1782, *GW Writings*, 25:40, 41; Boudinot, *Journal*, 61. In the end, due to considerable international pressure and because WF left America for England and was no longer under Carleton's jurisdiction, Captain Asgill escaped execution. See ibid., 241, 243, 337–38, 389; SW to George Read, 10 Nov. 1782, Read, *Life and Correspondence of George Read*, 370.

76. Smith, *Historical Memoirs*, 1778–83, 540.

77. Schaukirk, "Occupation," 442; James Robertson to Lord Shelburne, 15 Aug. 1782, Klein and Howard, *Robertson*, 257. WF had a hand in preparing the petition. He tried to get Carleton to look at it and offer his suggestions for improving it. While the general expressed his hope that the address would be "decent," he refused even to look at it. Obviously he wished to avoid all responsibility for the effort. Smith, *Historical Memoirs*, 1778–83, 544.

78. WF to WS, 11 May 1781, Hart, "Letters," 457; Smith, *Historical Memoirs*, 1778–83, 545.

79. WF to JG, 11 May 1782, PRO 583, pp. 660, 663, LC.

80. See Berkin, *British-Americans*, for the exile experience in London.

81. WF to JG, 11 May 1782, PRO 583, pp. 660, 663, LC.

Epilogue

1. Sarah Bache to WTF, Oct. 1782, Franklin Papers, 104:108, APS; Patience Wright to BF, 22 Feb., 19 March 1783, Franklin Papers, 27:139, 209, APS.

2. WF to Lord Shelburne, 12 Nov. 1782, Franklin Papers, Photostat, Stirling.

3. See Norton, *British-Americans*, 173–84, for an account of negotiations between England and America over loyalist issues. See also, Fleming, *Lightning*, 454.

4. WF, James Wright, John Wentworth, and Robert Eden to Lord Shelburne, 6, 12, Feb. 1783, Shelburne Papers, 67:495, 502, Clements; Patience Wright to BF, 22 Feb., 19 March 1783, Franklin Papers, 27:139, 209, APS.

5. Patience Wright to BF, 28 April 1783, Frankiln Papers. 28:68, APS; Norton, *British-Americans*, 193, 194.

6. See, for example, John Dudley to WF, 26 July 1783; John Weatherhead to WF, 2 Feb. 1785, Franklin Papers, 48:146, 233, APS; James Wright to William Pitt, 1 June 1784, Franklin Papers, Stirling.

7. Benjamin Vaughan to Lord Shelburne, 31 July, 15 Nov., 10 Dec. 1782, Benjamin Vaughan Papers, APS.

8. WF to Major England, 27 Dec. 1782, Franklin Papers, 104:146A, APS; WF to BF, 22 July 1784, Franklin Papers, MSS., APS.

9. WF to BF, 26 Aug. 1784, Franklin Papers, 32:91 APS; BF to WF, 16 Aug. 1784, Smyth, *BF Writings*, 9:252.

10. Ibid; WTF to BF, 2, 7 Sept., 9 Nov. 1784, Franklin Papers, 32:100, 106, 168 APS; WF to WTF, 23 Sept. 1784, Franklin Papers, 107: 88; BF to WTF, 2 Oct. 1784, Smyth, *BF Writings*, 9:274.

11. WF to WTF, 16 Dec. 1784, Franklin Papers, 106:128. WF claimed the New York land was worth £2500 and also insisted that BF would no doubt have forgiven his debts had he not taken so active a part in the war. PRO AO 12 17; PRO AO 13 109, NJHS; Indenture Between WF and WTF, 26 July 1785, Franklin Papers, MSS., APS. On the other hand, had he not been BF's son, it is likely that his property in New Jersey and New York would already have been confiscated.

12. WF to Sarah Bache, 1 Aug. 1785, Franklin Papers, Film 750, APS.

13. Fleming, *Lightning*, 472, 473. The following discussion is based on WF, Memorial to Commissioners on Losses and Services of American Loyalists; Schedule and Valuation of WF Estates, PRO AO 12 17; PRO AO 13 83, in NJHS.

14. See ibid; PRO AO 13 109; PRO AO 13 109, NJHS; Mariboe, "William Franklin," 562; Fleming, *Lightning*, 472, 473.

15. WF to Jonathan Odell, 25 Sept. 1783, Jonathan Williams Collection Film 455 APS (hereafter, JW Coll.).

16. Among others, he enlisted merchant John Taylor, Jonathan Odell, Attorney Thomas Smith, his cousin Jonathan Williams, and even his own son and sister to work on his behalf. He also combined with Major Augustine Provost in 1787, who had claims to Croghan's estate. But none of his efforts bore fruit. See Mariboe, "William Franklin," 575–81, JW Coll., passim, for a detailed rendering of WF's abortive efforts.

17. WF to John Taylor, 7 July 1785, to Major Provost, 25 June 1791, to WTF, 1 Aug. 1785, to Jonathan Williams (JW), 22 Nov. 1808; Richard Well to WTF, 9 May 1806 Memorandum of A. J. Dallas, 25 Nov. 1807, JW Coll.

18. WF to John Taylor, 25 June 1791, JW Coll.

19. WF to WS, 26 July 1783, Franklin MSS., NJHS; WF to Sarah Bache, 30 June 1792, 23 Aug. 1794, Franklin Papers, Bache Coll., APS.

20. WF to JW, 23 July 1807, JW Coll.; Lopez and Herbert, *Private*, 307; WF to Sarah Bache, 28 April 1786, Franklin Papers, Stirling.

21. BF Will, Codicil, 23 June 1789, Franklin Papers MSS., APS.

22. WF to JW, 11 May 1791, Franklin Papers, Stirling.

23. WF to JW, 24, 30 July 1807, JW Coll.

24. WF to JW, 24 July 1807, JW Coll.; Gerlach, *William Franklin*, 42. In fact, Ellen was WTF's second "indiscretion." He fathered another child before leaving for America with BF, but this first offspring died shortly after its birth.

25. WF to Sarah Bache, 30 June 1792, 23 Aug. 1794, Franklin Papers, Bache Coll., APS.

26. WF to Aaron Burr, 3 Oct. 1808, Franklin Papers, APS; WF to JW, 2 May 1809, 28 Oct. 1811, JW Coll.
27. WF to JW, 2 May 1809, 28 Oct. 1811, JW Coll.
28. WF to JW, 30 July 1807, 28 Oct. 1811, JW Coll.; JW to WF, 22 Oct. 1807, JW Coll.
29. WF to WTF, 3 July 1812, Franklin Papers, Stirling.
30. WF to JW, 18 June 1813, JW Coll.; WF, Will, APS.

Index

Abercrombie, James, 26
Abercrombie, Mrs., 37, 298n, 301n
Adams, John, 186
Adams, Samuel, 203
Albany Conference, 17, 57, 155
Alexander, Robert, 258
Alexander, William (Lord Stirling),
    83; claims to earldom, 50; friend-
    ship with WF, 50; and Stamp
    Act, 70; heads Somerset militia,
    184, 185; intercepts WF's letter
    to Lord Dartmouth, 191, 193;
    orders WF's house arrest, 193,
    194; prepares to remove WF to
    Elizabeth, 195–97; abandons
    plans to arrest WF, 197; rebuffed
    by Congress, 331n
Amherst, Sir Jeffrey, 55, 56
André, John, 238, 241, 338n; and
    Board of Intelligence, 235; forms
    compromise plan, 238; capture
    of, 239, 339n
Annand, Alexander, 8
Arbuthnot, Admiral Mariot: and
    Clinton, 231, 240; and Board of
    Associated Loyalists, 249
Asgill, Captain Charles, 260, 264,
    345n
Association, 157, 160, 164, 166, 327n

Bache, Benjamin Franklin: born, 85;
    at Southampton, 270, 271; visits
    Europe, 274; studies medicine in
    London, 274
Bache, Richard, 152; marries Sarah
    Franklin, 84, 85; oversees WTF's
    allowance, 199; visits Europe,
    274
Bache, Sarah Franklin, xiii, 25, 26,
    44, 117, 118, 246, 271, 273;
    birth of, 5; social connections of,
    311n; flees Stamp Act riots, 68;
    visits WF, 83; marries Richard

Bache, 84, 85; and WF's house
    arrest, 198, 199; visits Europe,
    274; and WF's efforts to regain
    American land, 346n
Blowers, Sampson: secretary of Board
    of Associated Loyalists, 247; and
    murder of Joshua Huddy, 258,
    259
Board of Associated Loyalists, xi, xiii,
    271; approved by King, 239; first
    meeting of directors, 240; and
    Clinton's regulations, 242–44;
    members accept Clinton's com-
    mission, 245; duties of, 245, 247;
    and control of rebel prisoners,
    250, 255, 340n, 342n; symbolic
    significance of, 250; and York-
    town, 255; and murder of Joshua
    Huddy, 258, 260–63; activities
    indefinitely suspended, 265
Board of Loyal Refugees, 234
Boston: dead-end for BF, 7, 9; WF
    visits, 15; Stamp Act riots in, 66,
    118; troops in, 96; and Hutchin-
    son, 141; and Port Act, 149;
    refusal to pay for ruined tea, 150,
    153; parliamentary treatment of,
    162
Boston Massacre, 111
Boston Tea Party, 131, 133, 135, 140,
    143–45, 148, 150, 151
Braddock, General Edward, 17, 18, 97
British Army, view of loyalists, 229,
    230, 236, 260
Bryan, George, 19
Bunker Hill, 183
Burlington, 47, 51, 147, 154; capital
    of West Jersey, xiii, 45; WF's
    inauguration at, 48; description
    of, 49, 59; WF decides to reside
    at, 49; BF visits, 62; WF invites
    Sarah to visit, 68; council meets
    at, 67, 70; celebration of Stamp

Burlington (*continued*)
Act repeal at, 76; WF builds house at, 81; Anglican Church in, 82, 83; SW and Croghan visit, 102; New Jersey assembly meets at, 108, 110, 112, 114, 144, 186, 187, 192; WF decides to leave, 131; WF leaves home in, 157; Continental Congress sends delegation to, 190; Jane Mecom and BF visit, 192; Samuel Adams travels to, 203; Provincial Congress at, 207; WF's final journey to, xi, 209; WF leaves for Connecticut prison from, 213

Bute, John Stuart, Earl of, 40, 49, 62, 300n, 302n

Campbell, the Reverend Colin, 82
Carleton, Sir Guy, 345n; replaces Clinton, 255, 261, 344n; and American loyalists, 261; and WF, 261; and Richard Lippincott, 262; and Board of Associated Loyalists, 264
Carlisle Commission, 232–34
Carlyle, Alexander, 34, 35
Chaloner, Walter: as Commissary of Prisoners, 250, 340n; and murder of Joshua Huddy, 259
Clinton, General Henry, 224, 232, 233, 252, 336n, 345n; treatment of loyalists, 228; view of loyalists, 228, 234–36, 338n, 339n; and John André, 338n; and southern strategy, 238; and Arbuthnot, 231; and WF, 237; and Board of Associated Loyalists, 239–45, 247, 248, 250, 339n, 341n; and prisoners of war, 243, 250; and Yorktown, 251, 253; and Tenth Article, 253, 255; asks WF to remain in America, 254; and murder of Joshua Huddy, 259–61, 263, 343n; replaced by Carleton, 255, 261, 344n; praises WF's loyalist record, 271; character of, 230, 231
Coercive Acts, 148–50, 153, 156, 326n
College of New Jersey, 48, 67, 82
Collinson, Peter, 12, 27, 298n
Committees of Correspondence, 149, 324n

Common Sense, 198
Continental Congress, First, 157; WF's hopes for, 150, 151; WF gathers information concerning, 154; rejects Galloway plan, 156, 178, 326n; BF's presence desired at, 159; creates Association, 160
Continental Congress, Second, 198, 330n; New Jersey delegates at, 163, 164, 327n; and Lord North's plan, 169; New Jersey assembly takes cue from, 170; BF is member of, 175; WF loses contact with, 185; sends delegation to Burlington, 190; orders disarming of "unworthy Americans," 193; and May 10 resolution, 202; orders interrogation of WF, 203, 207; orders WF's removal to Connecticut, 213
Conway, Henry, 69, 308n
Cooper, Grey, 74, 309n
Cornwallis, Lord Charles: defeat at Yorktown, 251, 253, 256, 263; and Tenth Article, 253
Coxe, Daniel, 258, 344n
Coxe, William, 309n, 310n; named stamp distributor, 64; resigns as stamp distributor, 66, 67, 69–71, 79, 308n
Crane, Stephen, 116, 327n
Craven Street, 27, 33, 117
Croghan, George: and Weiser expedition, 11, 12; as Deputy Indian Agent, 101, 102; and Illinois Company, 102, 314n, 315n; and Fort Stanwix, 104; borrows money from WF, 105, 106, 272; financial troubles, 105, 181, 346n; and SW, 134; death of, 272
Cunningham, William, 336n, 340n
Currency Act (1751), 54
Currency Act (1764), 54, 85
Cushing, Thomas, 141

Dartmouth, William Legge, 2d Earl of, 138, 145, 149, 150, 154, 166, 170, 171, 176, 180, 183, 188, 191, 193–95, 197, 329n, 330n; and WF's salary, 132, 133, 136; and Grand Ohio Company, 135, 321n; tells WF his governorship is secure, 148; praises WF, 156, 180; out of touch with American

situation, 164; and battles of
Lexington and Concord, 165;
declares colonies in "open rebel-
lion," 180; and Lord North's
plan, 166, 327n
Davenport, Josiah, 67, 136, 210
De Berdt, Dennys, 188
De Hart, John: and assembly petition
against Coercive Acts, 162; re-
signs from Second Continental
Congress, 188; congressional
delegate, 327n
De Lancey, Major Oliver, 231, 241
Deare, Major Jonathan, 203, 204, 207
D'Evelyn, Ellen Johnson, 274
Denny, Governor William, 23, 24, 32
Dick, Sir Alexander, 34
Dickinson, John, 62, 328n; and "Let-
ters from an American Farmer,"
92; speaks before New Jersey
assembly, 190
Dunmore, John Murray, 4th Earl of,
186, 322n, 330n

East Jersey, 47, 186; description of,
44, 45; court riots in, 109–11;
guerilla warfare in, 257, 258
East Jersey proprietors, 45, 109, 110,
150; view WF with suspicion,
46–49; center of influence at
Perth Amboy, 47; finance Proprietary House, 49; dominate
New Jersey council, 303n;
quarrels with settlers of Monmouth and Elizabeth, 304n; and
court riots, 109; WF's friend-
ships with, 131; repair Proprietary
House, 157
East Jersey treasury robbery, 113,
122–32, 135–37, 140, 144, 145,
319n, 320n
Ecton, 33
Eden, William, 232–34, 237
Edinburgh, 34, 35
Elizabeth, 25; distrust of East Jersey
proprietors in, 47, 304n; riots at,
89; "junto" at, 163; Stirling's
headquarters at, 193, 196
Elliot, Andrew, 231, 336n, 338n; and
Board of Associated Loyalists,
241, 242, 339n, 340n; and murder of Joshua Huddy, 260
Elphinston, James, 139, 182
Essex County: court riots in, 109–12;
protests Coercive Acts, 149

Finley, Samuel, 82
Fisher, Mary, 33
Ford, Samuel, 127, 128, 130, 320n
Forman, General David ("Black
David"), 257, 259
Fort Stanwix, 104–6
Fothergille, Dr. John, 27, 298n, 329n
Franklin, Benjamin: early education,
9; apprenticeship, 8; marriage of,
4, 25; clerk of Pennsylvania assembly, 5, 292n; Postmaster General, 5, 15; creates American
Philosophical Society, 5; retires
from printing business, 7, 13;
encourages WF's military career,
10, 11, 294n; begins political
career, 13, 14, 295n; encourages
WF's law studies, 14, 295n;
elected to assembly, 15; and kite
experiment, 16; and Albany Conference, 17, 57, 155; and Edward
Braddock, 17, 18; composes
militia bill, 18; and Quaker
party, 17, 18, 296n; helps defend
Pennsylvania's western frontier,
19–21; assembly envoy to London, 23; and Graeme family, 24,
25, 297n; travels to New Jersey,
25; excursion to Woodbridge,
26; voyage to England, 27; on
Craven Street, 27; meets Thomas
Penn, 30; and Pennsylvania charter, 31, 55, 59, 62–64, 75, 118,
119; travels with WF, 33–35,
300n; receives degree of Doctor
of Civil Law, 35; sails for home,
38; and WF's governorship, xi,
40, 44; accompanies WF to inauguration, 47; elated at WF's
New Jersey reception, 48; returns
to London, 63; and Sugar Act,
307n; and Stamp Act, 63–67, 69,
75, 118, 307n, 308n, 310n; and
American bishops, 82; and
daughter's marriage, 84, 85,
312n; as New Jersey agent, 87;
and Mutiny Act, 88; and Townshend Acts, 92, 93; and appointment of New Jersey agents, 116,
117, 120; writes *Autobiography*,
118, 318n; loses influence in London, 119, 137, 138, 146, 147;
and Lord Dartmouth, 138; and
Hutchinson-Oliver letters, 141–
45, 323n, 324n; and Tea Act,

Franklin, Benjamin (*continued*)
143, 144, 150, 323n; and Boston
Tea Party, 144, 145, 150; humiliation at the "Cockpit," 145,
148, 153, 176, 195, 211, 252,
324n; loses post-office position,
145, 146; and Coercive Acts,
150; plans for American-English
reconciliation, 329n; and Galloway's "Plan of Union," 175;
meets with WF and JG at "Trevose," 175–79; and Lord North's
plan, 177; travels to Canada, 201;
and WF's imprisonment, 216,
217, 224, 332n, 333n, 335n; and
Lord Howe's peace commission,
217; American commissioner to
France, 218, 219; and Peace of
Paris, 268; meets WF at Southampton, 270; will of, 273, 274;
death of, 273
and Deborah Franklin, 4, 25, 84,
85, 117, 158
and William Franklin, xi, xii, xiv,
4, 5, 7–10, 13–16, 28, 31–34, 38,
40, 55, 59, 62, 63, 75, 76, 82, 84,
85, 100, 101, 116–20, 129, 135–
40, 142–44, 146–48, 152–55,
158, 159, 173–83, 192, 193, 198,
199, 201, 216, 217, 246, 269,
270, 273, 294n, 295n, 322n,
325n, 327n
and William Temple Franklin,
118, 139, 152, 153, 181–83, 199,
217–19, 270, 295n, 301n
and Lord Hillsborough, 103, 115,
120, 121, 132, 136
characteristics of, xii, 3, 8, 12, 145,
146, 181, 184, 200, 252, 324n
political beliefs: attitude toward
Pennsylvania proprietors, 16, 17,
22, 23, 296n, 307n; attitude toward British Empire, xii, xiv, 17,
28, 29, 32, 100, 118, 119, 137–
40, 144, 150, 156, 176–80, 314n
and western land speculation, 12,
21, 100–105, 119–21, 133–35,
139, 272, 314n, 315n
Franklin, Deborah Reed, xiii, 5, 25,
26, 34, 118, 300n; marriage of, 4,
25; as "Belle Dame," 294n; defends home from Stamp Act
rioters, 68, 184; and Sarah's
marriage, 84, 85; suffers stroke,
117, 148; death of, 158

and Benjamin Franklin, 4, 25, 84,
85, 117, 158
and William Franklin, 4, 5, 9, 13,
38, 83–85, 117, 291n
Franklin, Elizabeth Downes, 139, 185,
266, 316n, 331n, 334n; marries
WF, 38, 39; voyage to America,
41–43; arrival in America, 43, 44;
accompanies WF to inauguration, 47; settles in Burlington,
49, 51; homesick, 59; hosts
King's birthday celebration, 65;
end of Stamp Act crisis, 76; and
Anglican Church, 82; and social
duties, 83; plans to move to
Perth Amboy, 131; moves to
Perth Amboy, 157; and WTF,
179, 182, 214, 218, 334n; and
WF's house arrest, 194, 195,
198; and virtual house arrest of,
200, 210; bids WF good-bye,
207; and WF's imprisonment,
216–18; flees to New York, 222;
death of, 223, 229
Franklin, Ellen: birth of, 274, 346n;
and WF, 275; looks like BF, 275
Franklin, Francis Folger, 5, 10
Franklin, James, 5, 8
Franklin, Josiah, 33
Franklin, Mary D'Evelyn, 273–75
Franklin, Sarah. See Bache, Sarah
Franklin
Franklin, Thomas, 33
Franklin, William: childhood, 2–8,
292n; education, 8, 9; runs away,
9, and King George's War, 10;
joins Weiser expedition, 11,
294n; returns to Philadelphia,
12; joins Annual Assembly, 13;
begins law studies, 14, 295n; visits
Boston, 15; becomes assembly
clerk, 15; becomes controller of
North American postal system,
15; and kite experiment, 16; and
Albany Conference, 17; and
Edward Braddock, 17, 18; helps
write *Tit for Tat*, 19; defends
Pennsylvania's western frontier,
19–21; prepares for trip to England, 23; and EG, 24–28; travels
to New Jersey, 25; excursion to
Woodbridge, 26; voyage to England, 27; on Craven Street, 27;
begins legal studies, 28, 29;
enjoys London sights, 28; writes

letter to *Citizen or General Advertiser*, 30, 31, 37; garners material for history of Pennsylvania, 31; and royal charter for Pennsylvania, 31, 59, 62; travels with BF, 33–35, 300n; called to the bar, 43; receives Master of Arts degree, 36; engagement broken, 36, 37, 301n; attends coronation of George III, 38; becomes father of WTF, 38, 301n; marries EF, 38, 39, 41, 301n; secures position as New Jersey governor, 39–41, 302n; prepares for return to New Jersey, 41; voyage home, 41–43; arrival in America, 43, 44

as governor, xi, xii, xiii; reaction to WF's appointment, 39–41, 46, 47, 302n; inauguration, 47, 48; decides to reside in Burlington, 49; gains friendship of William Alexander, 50; settles in Burlington, 51; supports Anglican Church, 51, 82, 83; convenes first assembly, 51, 52; contented in New Jersey, 59, 60; and Stamp Act crisis, 62–80, 307n, 310n; builds house in Burlington, 81; as New Jersey farmer, 81, 82; and social duties, 83; as absentee patriarch, 83, 84; and sister's marriage, 84, 85; and quarrel with David Hall, 85; and Townshend Acts, 92, 93, 95–97, 313n; censured by Lord Hillsborough, 93–98; writes "Reasons for Establishing a British Colony at the Illinois," 102; and New Jersey Indian policy, 103, 104; at Fort Stanwix, 104, 315n; "Dispenser of Justice," 104; lends money to George Croghan, 105, 106; and John Hatton, 106–8; and East Jersey court riots, 110–11, 316n; and troop withdrawal from New Jersey, 115; and appointment of New Jersey agent, 116, 117; and East Jersey treasury robbery, 123–31, 320n, 322n; begins plans to move to Perth Amboy, 131, 147; and Hutchinson-Oliver letters, 142, 143; and Tea Act, 143, 144; and Boston Tea Party, 144, 145, 150; and Coercive Acts, 149, 150, 153; and Committees of Correspondence, 149; and First Continental Congress, 150, 151, 153, 154; letter to WS intercepted, 151, 152, 325n; as spy for Dartmouth, 154, 156, 157, 164, 170, 180, 184, 191, 193, 195, 201, 325n–27n; and Galloway plan, 154–57; and move toward independence, xii–xiv, 157, 160–64, 166, 171, 172, 179, 180, 183–87, 191, 198, 202, 205, 327n, 332n; moves to Perth Amboy, 157; and DF's death, 158; and assembly petition against Coercive Acts, 162, 163; and Second Continental Congress, 164, 324n, 325n; and Lord North's plan, 165–70, 174, 177, 180; and battles of Lexington and Concord, 165, 166, 168; fears capture by rebel sympathizers, 166, 179, 183, 184, 187, 189, 194; and extract of *Parliamentary Register* No. Five, 170, 171, 188, 328n; meets with BF and JG at "Trevose," 175–79; and William Alexander's defection, 184, 185; and assembly petition to King (1775), 188, 190, 192, 193; censured by New Jersey council, 189–91, 197; Col. Winds places under house arrest, 194, 195; and abortive removal to Elizabeth, 195–97; virtual prisoner at Perth Amboy, 200, 201; and congressional call for new governments, 202; calls final assembly, 202; arrest of, 203, 204, 207, 208; and government salaries, xiii, 52–54, 58, 64, 82, 91, 100, 131–33, 160, 184, 190, 191, 205, 231, 232, 308n; and military appropriations, xiii, 52, 54–58, 65, 87–92, 95, 112, 113–15, 121, 124, 131, 133; and paper money, xiii, 53–55, 86, 87, 113, 114, 124, 149, 187, 188, 190, 305n, 312n, 314n

rebel prisoner, xi, xiii; defends summons of 1776 assembly, 204–7; journey to Burlington, xi, 209, 210; interrogation by Provincial Congress, 210–12; self-defense against Provincial Congress allegations, 212, 213; removed to Connecticut, 213,

Franklin, William (*continued*)
214; negotiates with Gov. Trumbull, 214, 215; at Wallingford, 215; at Middletown, 216–20, 334n; grants protections for Howe brothers, 221; at Litchfield, 221–24, 335n; and EF's death, 222, 223, 225, 229; at East Windsor, 224; exchanged for Gov. McKinly, 224, 225
  loyalist activities: arrival in New York, 227, 228; finances in New York, 231, 232, 265; view of British war effort, 229, 230, 233, 237, 251–56, 264, 265; view of American military strength, 232, 233, 236, 251, 252, 255, 256; unofficial loyalist leader, 232–34, 236–38, 240, 338n; and Henry Clinton, 233, 234, 237, 239, 250–53, 261; establishes Refugee Club, 234; and Board of Loyal Refugees, 234, 235; and Board of Intelligence, 235; and King's Militia Volunteers, 237; and Tryon's proposal, 237, 238; and André's proposal, 238; and André's capture, 239, 340n; and prisoners of war, 228, 232, 237, 242, 243, 250, 255, 344n, 345n; as president of Board of Directors for the Board of Associated Loyalists, xi, xiii, 239–45, 247–51, 256, 271, 340n; and Yorktown, 251, 253, 264; and Tenth Article, 253–55; and murder of Joshua Huddy, 256–58, 261–64, 344n, 345n; and Carleton, 261
  exile: begins London exile, xi, 265–67, 345n; and Peace of Paris, 267, 268; and loyalist compensation, 268; reestablishes contact with BF, 269; meets BF at Southampton, 270, 346n; and parliamentary commission on loyalists, 271–73; tries to reestablish land claims, 272, 273; and BF's will, 273, 274; marries Mary D'Evelyn, 273; quarrels with WTF, 274; and Ellen Franklin, 274, 275; will of, 274, 276; Bache family visits, 274; and death of Mary Franklin, 275; plans BF's biography, 275; death of, 276
  and Benjamin Franklin, xii–xiv, 3–5, 7–10, 13–16, 28, 31–34, 40, 55, 59, 61–63, 75, 76, 82, 84, 85, 96, 97, 100, 101, 116–21, 129, 132, 135–40, 142–44, 146–48, 152–55, 158, 159, 173–83, 192, 198, 199, 201, 216, 229, 234, 246, 269–75, 294n, 295n, 304n, 316n, 319n, 322n, 328n
  and Deborah Franklin, 4, 5, 9, 13, 38, 83–85, 117, 146, 291
  and William Temple Franklin, 38, 78, 83, 118, 139, 158, 173, 174, 179, 181–83, 199, 200, 219, 269, 270, 274–76, 301n
  and Lord Hillsborough, 58, 86, 87, 91–98, 101, 106, 112, 113, 116, 118, 121, 132, 133, 136, 179, 245, 321n
  characteristics, xi, xii, xiii, 5, 7, 10, 19, 54, 55, 79–81, 84, 85, 96–98, 108, 110–12, 115, 125, 130, 131, 146, 149, 162, 178, 181, 184, 200, 245, 252, 264, 298n
  illegitimacy, xi, 3, 4, 7, 38, 40, 62, 83, 211, 252, 291n, 297n
  political beliefs: and Pennsylvania proprietors, 15–17, 19, 23, 31, 36, 37, 55–62; and assembly rights, xii, 23, 31, 32, 57, 62, 94, 96, 99, 111, 112, 161, 162, 204, 205, 317n; and Crown prerogative, 58, 72, 90, 96, 111, 112, 115, 121, 125, 126, 185; attitude toward British Empire, xi–xiv, 17, 28, 29, 32, 52, 54, 58, 74, 76, 79, 80, 85, 95, 96, 99, 100, 101, 108, 109, 118–20, 129, 139, 140, 144, 150–52, 156, 157, 163, 168, 169, 171, 179, 180, 183
  and western land speculation, 12, 21, 100–106, 119–21, 133–35, 139, 151, 181, 226, 315n, 322n, 346n
Franklin, William Temple, 202; birth of, 38, 301n; education of, 139, 152, 153, 158, 181, 182, 199, 295; travels to America, 173; travels with WF to Perth Amboy, 179; monetary profligacy of, 182, 199, 200; and WF's house arrest, 198, 199; and WF's imprisonment, 213, 216, 217; asks to visit WF at Middletown, 218; accompanies BF to France, 218, 219, 334n; BF's secretary,

335n; exerts influence on WF's behalf, 269; visits WF in London, 270; meets WF in Southampton, 270; illegitimate children of, 274, 346n; and WF's efforts to gain American land, 346n; quarrels with WF, 274; overtures to WF, 275
and Benjamin Franklin, 118, 139, 181–83, 199, 214, 218, 219
and William Franklin, 38, 78, 83, 118, 139, 158, 173, 174, 179, 181–83, 270, 274–76
and Elizabeth Franklin, 179, 182, 214, 218
characteristics, 270, 274
French and Indian War, 16, 44, 53, 55

Gage, General Thomas, 56, 57, 67, 70, 88, 103, 114, 165, 184
Galloway, Joseph, 152, 265, 295n–97n; WF's law tutor, 14; helps write *Tit for Tat,* 19; loses 1764 election, 63; and Stamp Act, 69; and David Hall, 85; and western land speculation, 134, 314n; and First Continental Congress, 150, 154, 156, 158, 326n; and "Plan of Union," 154–56, 174, 175, 178; resigns from Continental Congress, 174, 185; meets with BF and WF at "Trevose," 175–79, 181; London exile, 238, 248; praises WF's services to Crown, 274; death of, 275
Germain, Lord George, 201, 232, 234, 239, 264, 271, 339n; Secretary of State for the American Department, 197; view of loyalist strength, 230, 338n; and war effort, 231; and Board of Associated Loyalists, 239, 240, 244, 248; resignation of, 263; antipathy toward Carleton, 344n
Gnadenhütten, 19, 20
Goddard, William, 148
Graeme, Ann, 24, 25, 297n
Graeme, Elizabeth, 24–28, 30, 31, 36, 38, 44, 81, 98, 146, 301n
Graeme, Dr. Thomas, 24
Graeme family, 6, 24, 294n, 297n
Grand Ohio Company, 105, 106, 119–21, 133–35, 151, 181, 199, 322n, 324n

Granville, John Carteret, 1st Earl of, 27, 29
Grenville, George, 63, 65, 141
Grew, Theopholis, 8

Halifax, George Montagu Dunk, 2d Earl of, 41, 57, 64
Hall, David: partner in BF's printing business, 12, 13; and WS, 27, 298n; and Stamp Act, 67, 68; and quarrel with WF, 85
Hamilton, Governor James, 46
Hancock, John, 220
Hardy, Governor Josiah, 40, 46, 47, 302n, 303n
Hatton, John, 106–8, 129, 316n
Hawker, Captain James, 69
Heard, Colonel Nathaniel, 203, 204, 207, 209–11
Hillsborough, Wills Hills, 1st Earl of, 96, 106, 112–15, 118, 119, 129, 132, 133, 167, 179, 245, 312n; president of Board of Trade, 58; reprimands WF, 58; Secretary of State of American Department, 86, 90, 104; and paper money, 87, 314n; and Mutiny Act, 90, 91; and Massachusetts Circular Letter, 92, 93; censures WF, 91, 93–95; and western land speculation, 100, 103–5, 121, 133, 316n, 321n; withdraws troops from New Jersey, 114; and appointment of New Jersey agent, 116, 117, 120, 136, 318n; resigns from Board of Trade, 133, 134, 137, 156
Howe, Admiral Richard, 221
Howe, General William, 220, 221, 224, 228–30, 334n
Huddy, Joshua: terrorist activities of, 257, 260; murder of, 256–59
Hughes, John, 64, 297n, 308n, 314n
Hume, David, 34
Hutchinson, Governor Thomas, 321n; and Stamp Act, 76; on Civil List, 141; and Hutchinson-Oliver letters, 141–43, 152; petition for removal of, 145

Illinois Company, 101–4
Indiana Company, 104, 105
Inns of Court, 12

Jackson, Richard, 31, 36; writes *Historical Review of the Constitution and Government of Pennsylvania*, 31; travels with the Franklins, 34, 35, 136, 300n; and Stamp Act, 307n; and Illinois Company, 103
Jay, John, 190
Johnson, Sir William: and Illinois Company, 101, 102, 315n, 321n; and Fort Stanwix Treaty, 104, 105; death of, 325n

Keith, Governor William, 24
King George's War, 9–11, 296n
King's Militia Volunteers, 237
Kinsey, James: and East Jersey treasury robbery, 124–28, 320n; and assembly petition against Coercive Acts, 162; congressional delegate, 327n; and resignation from Second Continental Congress, 188, 324n, 325n

Leonard, George: and loyalist organization, 238, 339n; obtains Crown approval of loyalist board, 239, 240; praises WF's services to the Crown, 271
Lexington and Concord, battles of, 165–68, 174
Lippincott, Richard: and Joshua Huddy, 256, 258, 259; arrest of, 260; court-martial of, 261–64, 343n, 344n
Livingston, Governor William: and assembly petition against Coercive Acts, 162; governor of New Jersey, 220; suspects that WF is violating parole, 220, 221; recommends WF's exchange, 224; congressional delegate, 327n
Locke, John, 7, 8, 10
Logtown Treaty, 11, 12
Loudoun, General John, 23, 25
Loyalists: view of British war effort, 229, 230, 236, 237, 252; and Clinton, 230, 337n; divisions among, 231; naïveté of, 235, 236; and Board of Associated Loyalists, 250, 251; sufferings of, 242, 243, 257, 258, 263, 336n, 340n; and Yorktown, 251, 255, 256; and Tenth Article, 253, 342n; in London, 266–68

Lutwycke, Edward, 258

McKinly, Governor John, 224, 225, 335n
Mecom, Jane, 9, 15, 64, 146, 192, 312n, 325n, 331n
Middle Temple, 23, 29, 77, 110, 295n
Monmouth County, 166; conflicts with East Jersey proprietors, 304n; court riots in, 109–11; protests Coercive Acts, 149; and loyalist prisoners of war, 257; and murder of Joshua Huddy, 259, 343n
Morris, Governor Robert, 15, 18, 19, 22, 24, 46
Mutiny Act, 85, 88–91, 95, 130, 312n

New Jersey Provincial Congress, 180, 185, 330n–32n; assumes control of New Jersey militia, 184; divisions in, 186; assumes de facto control of colony, 202, 329n; plans to arrest WF, 203; seeks permission to remove WF from New Jersey, 207; interrogation of WF, 210–12
New York City, 25, 45, 49, 59, 70, 83, 149, 158, 196; EF flees to, 222; during American Revolution, 227, 228, 231, 234, 239, 240, 244, 245, 251, 254, 255, 261, 262, 265, 266, 336n
Norris, Isaac, 23, 30
North, Lord Frederick, 137, 138, 145, 252, 329n; plan of reconciliation, 165–70, 174, 177, 180, 327n, 328n; resignation of, 255, 344n

Odell, Jonathan, 82, 232, 311n
Ogden, David, 110, 112, 113
Ogden, Robert, 64, 65, 70, 72, 308n, 309n
Oliver, Andrew, 141, 145

Paine, Thomas, 198
Peace of Paris, 267, 269, 345n
Penn, John, 16, 62
Penn, Thomas, 16, 30, 31
Pennsylvania Proprietary party, 16, 18, 22, 24, 32, 68
Pennsylvania proprietors, 16–18, 23, 25, 26, 28–31, 36, 39, 40, 46, 50, 62, 73, 76

Perth Amboy, 166, 173, 182, 184, 193, 197, 199, 201, 202, 209, 212, 215, 217, 331n; capital of East Jersey, xiii, 45; inauguration of WF at, 47, 48; description of, 48, 49, 59; governor's mansion at, 49, 50, 274; assembly meets at, 51, 57, 76, 90, 92, 124, 160; lawyers discuss Stamp Act at, 67; rump session of assembly meets at, 70, 73, 77, 124; council meets at, 110; assembly meets at, 51, 57, 76, 90, 92, 124, 160; treasury robbery at, 122, 123; WF plans to move to, 131, 147; Franklins move to, 157, 158; BF visits, 181, 192; WF arrested at, 194, 203; WTF visits, 216; WTF leaves, 219; British army abandons, 222

Pettit, Charles, 185, 320n

Philadelphia, 8, 9, 14, 19, 21–23, 26, 59, 64, 81, 84, 99, 131, 151, 152, 181, 182, 192, 199, 218, 219, 247; Franklin home in, 3, 7; description of, 6, 82, 274; WF searches for deserters in, 10; WF returns to, 12, 13; serves as refuge from frontier wars, 18; WF and BF leave for New York from, 25; EF and WF return to, 43, 44, 48; serves as center of culture for West Jersey, 45, 49; WF compares to Perth Amboy, 51; WF involved in politics of, 62; and Stamp Act, 68, 75; EF and WF visit, 83; Hatton's son attacked in, 107; BF still popular in, 147; and Coercive Acts, 149; Continental Congress at, xi, 154, 156, 157, 164, 167, 174, 186, 193, 194, 202, 203, 205, 212; death of DF in, 158; WF travels to, 173; BF returns to, 178; friends of government absent from, 185; WF seeks information from, 183, 200

Pitt, William, 32, 86

Pontiac's Rebellion, 54, 55, 58, 102

Pringle, Dr. John, 27, 34, 40, 298n

Proprietary House, 47, 48, 131, 157, 158, 166, 192, 196, 203, 204, 207, 216–18, 274, 304n

Provost, 228, 250, 259, 340n, 342n

Quaker party, 16, 18, 19, 296n

Refugee Club, 234

Robertson, James, 231, 340n, 344n

Rockingham, Charles, Watson-Wentworth, 2d Marquess of, 255

Seabury, Samuel, 232

Shelburne, William Petty Fitz-maurice, Earl of, 78, 86, 89, 90, 103, 264, 267

Skinner, Cortlandt, 320n, 328n; Attorney General, 64; elected Speaker of the House, 72; and Massachusetts Circular Letter, 92, 93; and John Hatton, 107; brother of Stephen Skinner, 123; and East Jersey treasury robbery, 127, 128; flees New Jersey, 193, 197; arrest ordered, 331n; works for WF's release from prison, 220; service as loyalist, 252; and murder of Joshua Huddy, 263, 344n; praises WF's services to Crown, 271

Skinner, Stephen: and East Jersey treasury robbery, 123–29, 132, 146, 160, 319n, 320n, 322n; serves on local Provincial committee, 330n; and WF's arrest, 196

Smith, Adam, 34

Smith, Samuel, 327n

Smith, Parson William, 18, 19, 24, 43, 52, 67, 85, 181, 296n

Smith, William, 231, 265, 337n, 338n; and Board of Associated Loyalists, 241, 242, 339n–41n; and murder of Joshua Huddy, 261, 262

Smyth, Chief Justice Frederick, 208; and Stamp Act, 67; and East Jersey treasury robbery, 125; and Grand Ohio Company, 135, intercedes for WF, 196, 197

Stamp Act, 62–79, 81, 85–88, 91, 96, 99, 109, 113, 117, 118, 142, 150, 151, 198, 307n, 309n, 324n

Stamp Act Congress, 65, 68, 70, 72, 77, 151, 308n, 309n

Stevenson, Margaret, 27, 38

Stevenson, Polly, 27, 38

Steward, Anthony, 238

Stirling, Lord William, Earl of. See Alexander, William

Stockton, Richard, 106
Strahan, William, 34, 38, 48, 49, 51,
    52, 59, 84, 100, 120, 121, 139,
    151, 152, 237, 255, 323n, 328n;
    sends maps and works of Polybius
    to BF, 10, 11; enters WF's name
    at Inns of Court, 14; and BF in
    London, 27; and WF in London,
    27, 31, 38, 41; and Grand Ohio
    Company, 120; and WF's im-
    prisonment, 224; and reconcilia-
    tion between WF and BF, 269;
    and David Hall, 27, 298n
"Suffering Traders," 102, 104, 135
Sugar Act, 63, 64, 307n

Tea Act, 143, 144, 150, 179, 323n
Temple, John, 26, 100, 142, 298n
Thomas (WF's slave), 219, 222
Thomson, Charles, 16, 65, 326n
Ticonderoga, Battle of, 183
Tilton, Clayton, 257, 258
Tit for Tat, or the Score Wip'd Off,
    19, 24
Townshend Acts, 85, 92, 93, 95, 96,
    99, 108, 109, 141, 179, 313n
Treat, Robert, 214
Trent, William, 11, 12, 106, 134, 135,
    294n, 314n
"Trevose," 175, 179, 181
Trumbull, Governor Jonathan, 213–
    15, 218, 221, 223, 224, 334n
Tryon, Governor William: as governor
    of New York, 186; as loyalist,
    231; and WF's plans for loyalist
    organizations, 234, 235, 338n,
    339n; proposes loyalist organiza-
    tion, 236; remarks on WF's ill-
    humor, 239
Tucker, Samuel, 169, 170, 210, 211,
    213

Vandalia. See Grand Ohio Company

Walpole, Thomas, 152, 325n
Walpole Company, 105
Washington, General George, 252,
    255, 256, 294n; visits Newark,
    191; and WF's imprisonment,

214, 220, 222, 223, 335n; and
    Continental Army, 233; advances
    on Yorktown, 251; and Tenth
    Article, 251, 253, 254, 342n; and
    murder of Joshua Huddy, 259,
    264
Wedderburn, Sir Alexander, 145, 211,
    324n
Weiser, Conrad, 11, 12, 101
West Jersey, 44, 46, 64, 186; domi-
    nated by Pennsylvania, 45; de-
    scription of, 45; distrusted by
    East Jersey proprietors, 48; and
    treasury robbery, 128; assembly
    representation of, 124; council
    representation of, 303n
West Jersey proprietors, 45, 47
Wharton, Samuel: and Stamp Act,
    68; and Illinois Company, 102,
    104; and Indiana Company, 105;
    travels to London, 105; financial
    difficulties of, 106; as lobbyist
    for Grand Ohio Company, 120,
    121, 133, 135, 319n; quarrels
    with Franklins, 134, 321n, 325n
Wharton, Thomas: defends SW, 134;
    and WF's letter to WS, 152;
    pays WF's prison expenses, 219;
    and western land speculation,
    272
Wharton family, 85, 101, 121, 134,
    135, 152, 314n
Whately, Thomas, 141
White, Philip, 256, 258, 343n
Williams, Jonathan, 274, 330n; meets
    WF at Southampton, 270; criti-
    cizes BF, 275
Winds, Colonel William, 331n;
    marches on Perth Amboy, 193;
    places WF under house arrest,
    194, 195; prepares to move WF
    to Elizabeth, 195–97
Witherspoon, John, 333n; College of
    New Jersey president, 82; advo-
    cates independence, 202; inter-
    rogates WF, 210, 211
Wright, Governor James, 186, 268
Wythe, George, 190

Yorktown, 251, 253–55